# In Performance

EDITED BY
CAROL MARTIN

**In Performance** is a book series devoted to national and global theater of the twenty-first century. Scholarly essays providing the theatrical, cultural, and political contexts for the plays and performance texts introduce each volume. The texts are written both by established and emerging writers, translated by accomplished translators and aimed at people who want to put new works on stage, read diverse dramatic and performance literature and study diverse theater practices, contexts, and histories in light of globalization.

**In Performance** has been supported by translation and editing grants from the following organizations:

The Book Institute, Krakow
TEDA Project, Istanbul
The Memorial Fund for Jewish Culture, New York
Polish Cultural Institute, New York
Zbigniew Raszewski Theatrical Institute, Warsaw

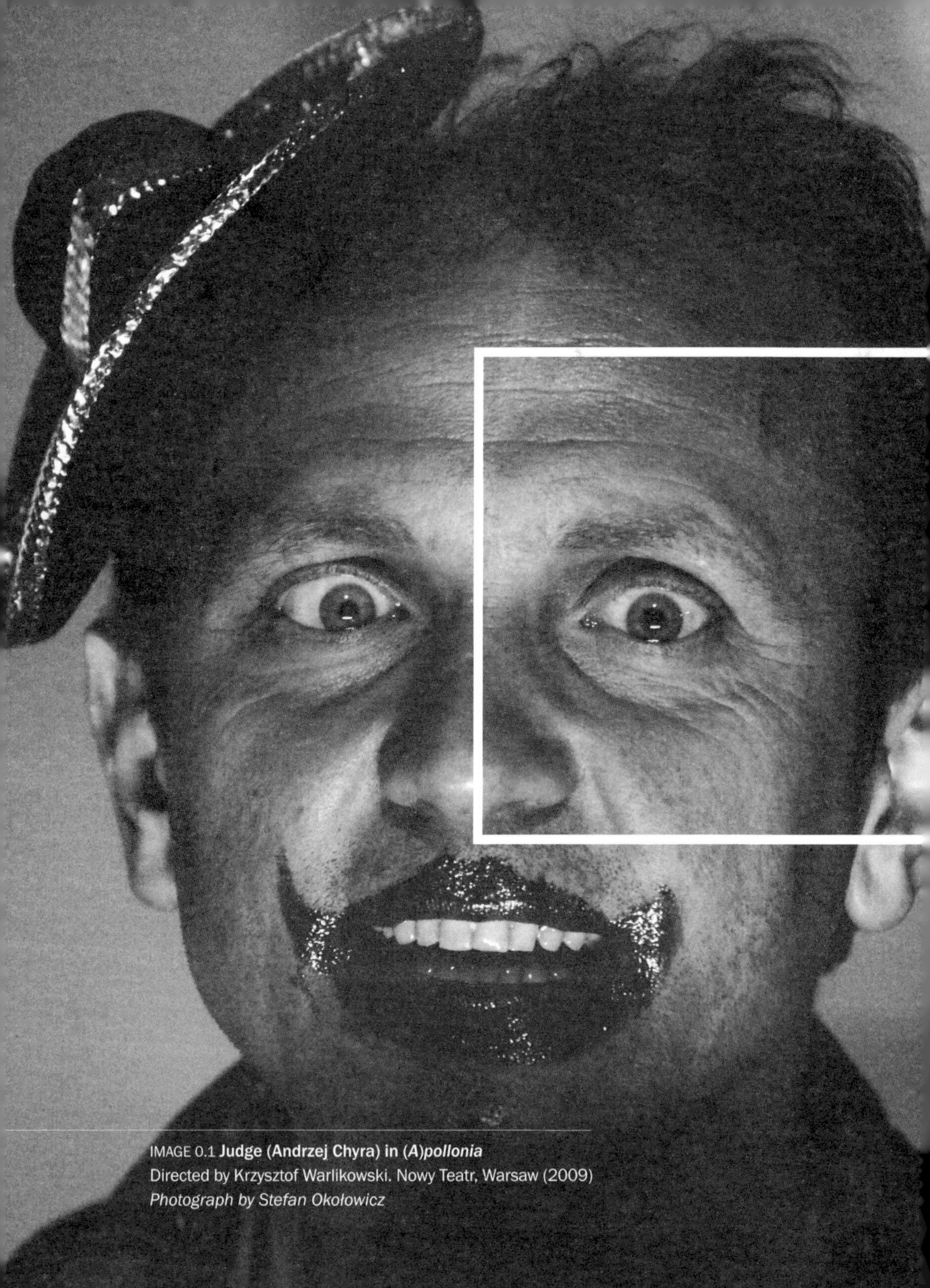

IMAGE 0.1 **Judge (Andrzej Chyra) in (*A*)*pollonia***
Directed by Krzysztof Warlikowski. Nowy Teatr, Warsaw (2009)
*Photograph by Stefan Okołowicz*

# (A)POLLONIA

## TWENTY-FIRST-CENTURY POLISH DRAMA AND TEXTS FOR THE STAGE

Edited by
Krystyna Duniec,
Joanna Klass,
and Joanna Krakowska

Translated by
Artur Zapałowski,
Benjamin Paloff,
and Wojciech Ziemilski

LONDON NEW YORK CALCUTTA

**Seagull Books, 2024**

First published by Seagull Books, 2014.

In *(A)pollonia*, the following texts were used:



ISBN 978 1 80309 534 9

**British Library Cataloging-in-Publication Data**
A catalog record for this book is available from the British Library

Designed by Bishan Samaddar and Vedika Jatia, Seagull Books, Calcutta, India
Printed and bound by Hyam Enterprises, Calcutta, India

# CONTENTS

## NOTE

The *(A)pollonia* anthology presents the latest Polish drama and texts for theater that, through new narrations, deal with the most urgent social, ethical and identity issues of our times.I am delighted that the Adam Mickiewicz Institute could contribute significantly to this edition, and I sincerely hope that, with its universal, artistic and philosophical potential, the anthology will inspire readers, researchers and artists worldwide.

Paweł Potoroczyn
Director
The Adam Mickiewicz Institute

## ACKNOWLEDGMENTS

We want to express our great appreciation to the many people, cultural institutions and institutions of higher learning that have contributed to this project, each in their own way with their own expertise.

We are deeply grateful to Carol Martin, the editor of the In Performance series. Her confidence in us, her insight, her willingness to listen and offer counsel have provided the unfailing support we so much needed along the way.

I would like to express my sincere thanks to Alan Lockwood and Dominik Skrzypkowski.

The fluid, fluent translations of Artur Zapałowski speak for themselves over the course of our anthology. We give him lasting thanks for his involvement throughout the project.

Many thanks to all the participating authors, directors and translators from the US: Erik Ehn, Velina Hasu Houston, Oliver Mayer,

Jon Rivera, Kathryn Noon, Mark Seldis, Nahal Navidar, Kevin King, Kirsa Rein, Brian Polak, Dara Weinberg, Rachel Halcyon Jendrzejewski, Theo Goodell, Benjamin Paloff, Caroline Adan and Alan Lockwood. Both Dara Weinberg and Rachel Halcyon Jendrzejewski deserve special mention as they have been deeply involved with this project from its beginning and have been our most ardent supporters and participant playwrights. Dominika Laster, Frank Hentschker, Barbara Lanciers, Linda Chapman and Jim Nicola were our steadfast, sympathetic listeners who consistently gave incisive advice as we developed the translation project, with its aims that have now come to fruition in the form of this very book. Special thanks to Philip Arnoult and John Freedman for generously sharing their experience in bringing contemporary Russian drama to the US readership.

We thank the Polish authors, translators and workshop participants whose work forms the foundation of this anthology: Wojtek Ziemilski, Artur Zapałowski, Małgorzata Sikorska-Miszczuk, Przemysław Wojcieszek, Dorota Masłowska, Piotr Gruszczyński, Jacek Poniedziałek, Krzysztof Warlikowski, Magda Fertacz, Julia Holewińska, Sebastian Majewski, Marcin Cecko, Weronika Szczawińska and Bartek Frąckowiak, as well as participants Dorota Sobstel, Adam Konowalski, Dominika Biernat, Piotr Tołłoczko, Damian Kocur and Jadwiga Thun. They all have been extraordinarily generous with their time and talents.

Laboratorium 13 facilitated the most inspiring conversations about this project, and shared their experience and expertise. Special thanks to Dorota Buchwald of Instytut Teatralny in Warsaw for research and assistance with providing images for this anthology. Many thanks to Anna R. Burzyńska and Dorota Sajewska for initial conversations concerning the selection of texts that make up this collection.

Without the Adam Mickiewicz Institute in Warsaw, with its remarkable vision for Polish theater and art, this project would not have happened. The Institute has supported all phases of this project with a substantial two-year grant. Director Paweł Potoroczyn and Deputy Director Joanna Kiliszek were visionary, supportive and had faith in our project. We are deeply grateful to Basia Krzeska who oversees statutory projects at the Institute and without whose guidance, humanity and ceaseless attention we would have not succeeded. The following staff members of the US Embassy in Warsaw have enabled bringing US playwrights to Poland for this project and embraced all the ideas that emerged from those trips: Lisa Helling, Frankie Sturm, Mark Wenig, Renata Czerw and our steadfast friend Izabella Szarek. The Trust for Mutual Understanding in New York City, with its continuous support of a steady flow of artists between the US and Eastern Europe, has been a model of innovative cultural exchange. Last but not least, our special debt of gratitude to Consul General Joanna Kozińska-Frybes and cultural attache in Los Angeles Małgorzata Cup for supporting special readings of US adaptations of Polish texts. We thank Olga Garay, director of the Department of Cultural Affairs in Los Angeles, and Kerry English for continuous and personal support of all Polish theater projects in Los Angeles.

The following theaters and educational institutions in Poland and the US have opened their doors to our project: Instytut Sztuki PAN (Art Institute of the Polish Academy of Sciences); Nowy Teatr in Warsaw; Instytut Teatralny, Warszawa (the Theater Institute in Warsaw); TR Warszawa; Teatr Dramatyczny in Wałbrzych; the Grotowski Institute, Wrocław; DCA in Los Angeles; Ghost Road Company in Los Angeles; the School of Theater at USC, Los Angeles; the Drama Department at Brown University, Providence, Rhode Island; the Drama Department at UCLA; and the Odyssey Theater Ensemble in Los Angeles.

*Joanna Klass, Joanna Krakowska and Krystyna Duniec*

# PREFACE

JOANNA KLASS

> Literature in translation is the gate to mental travels. A writer is first of all a reader and it is from reading that one becomes part of a community—the community of literature.
>
> Susan Sontag[1]

In Poland, theater has long played a role in the country's historical tectonic shifts by disseminating, filtering and transcending national debates and cultural polemics.

Although Jerzy Grotowski's "poor theatre" and Tadeusz Kantor's "theatre of memory" remain influential, it is present-day Polish performance and its dramatic texts that grapple with the new world we all live in. Globalization, wealth inequality, looming ecological disasters, the fluidity of information poured upon us by the media, the most banal historicism and nostalgia for a glorious past juxtaposed to emerging radical post-nationalism are all aspects of modernity visible in every country on this planet.

The plays collected in this anthology aim to break stereotypes about Polish people, history, culture, and expose the contradictions of the national psyche. They have been selected in cooperation with my co-editors Krystyna Duniec and Joanna Krakowska, both of whom are on the faculty of the Theater Department at the Institute of Art of the Polish Academy of Sciences in Warsaw, and both of whom are authors making valuable contributions to theater scholarship with their books.

After Carol Martin invited me to prepare an anthology of new Polish drama for this series, I thought about how a selection of plays

**1** Susan Sontag, "The World as India," in *At the Same Time: Essays and Speeches* (New York: Farrar, Straus and Giroux, 2007), pp. 156–79; here, p. 177.

from a specific place could represent the far-reaching changes in Poland today and, by extension, in the world. The goal was to create a transnational project through an open process of mutuality and exchange between artists in Poland and the US. My work as an international curator and presenter has made me acutely aware of contextual differences in how theater is created and conceived in diverse cultures, and of the fact that a collaborative project between nations creates an opportunity for a much wider local reception, and for organic development and ongoing, nuanced international dialogue.

The starting point for this project was simple: to use the process of preparing an anthology of provocative contemporary Polish plays and theatrical texts as a means to engage with theater professionals in creating playable translations for English-speaking audiences on both sides of the Atlantic.

After choosing texts that would resonate with a global readership, the task of translating these texts into English, the most international language we have now, was anything but simple. In this endeavor, I was guided by the standard that Susan Sontag set for translation: "To translate means many things, among them: to circulate, to transport, to disseminate, to explain, to make (more) accessible."[2]

Thus the book you hold in your hands is the result of a two-stage process of "translation." First, I invited Artur Zapałowski, one of the most experienced translators from Polish into English and a top specialist in translating contemporary theater work, to join us for a journey that lasted nearly two years. Zapałowski is responsible for the superb translations of most selections in this volume. In addition to Zapałowski, I invited Benjamin Paloff, a poet and professor of Polish literature at the University of Michigan, to translate

---

**2** Susan Sontag, "The Conscience of Words," in *At the Same Time: Essays and Speeches* (New York: Farrar, Straus and Giroux, 2007), pp. 145–55; here, p. 156.

Magda Fertacz's *Trash Story*, and Wojciech Ziemilski to translate *Small Narration* from his performance piece, *Mała narracja*.

The next phase was an invitation for native English-speaking playwrights to help us read, interpret and adapt our philological translations. More than a dozen US playwrights, dramaturges, teachers and students of playwriting got involved with as many Polish authors of the original texts. The translation workshops took place over the past two years, ferrying about 20 artists both ways across the Atlantic. In most cases, the US playwrights who took up the translated Polish texts were able to meet with the authors, view documentation of the Polish productions, engage in conversations or debates with the authors and/or directors, hear the texts read aloud in both English and Polish, and more often than not exchange observations with a translator.

The results of this process of exchange and collaboration were unique in each case: what mattered was that we "circulated, transported, disseminated, explained." Some playwrights made excellent suggestions about wording and phrasing and offered better English equivalents for Polish metaphors. They annotated the Polish texts with numerous questions or requests for clarification and made comments that assisted the translators and the editors in preparing footnotes. Some playwright collaborators chose not to alter the translations. What they offered instead were very competent, insightful analyses of the content, structure, and style of the texts. They suggested how the structure might be made more understandable to English readers while leaving intact the "foreignness" of the content and its lexical choices. At the same time, some fierce debates took place on such topics as racism and the ideological negotiations of postcolonial discourse, between Polish and US playwrights.

The results of these translation workshops are legible in this volume. Hopefully they also created a foundation for an afterlife to this project. In certain cases, playwright collaborators wrote new plays adapting the Polish texts, and we intend to make these available on a website and thus offer a deeply interactive, relational approach to the process of translation.

The accompanying DVD shows scenes from original staging of five texts in this volume, illustrating the leap that Polish theater has made from Grotowski's poor theatre to today. Through formal dramatic and theatrical innovation, writing about topics that have been sacrosanct or taboo until now has generated a new range of important aesthetic questions and approaches. Poland's new "poor-pop" theater, where popular icons are stripped of their authority, has made great progress in exposing and demystifying the nation's concerns and identity, and in the process has made useful universal revelations about the working order of the world in which we all now live.

*Warszawa/Warsaw*
*January 14, 2013*

# INTRODUCTION



KRYSTYNA DUNIEC
AND JOANNA KRAKOWSKA

Polonia was beautiful, proud, and unhappy. She suffered with sublime dignity. She demanded adulation and allowed her worshippers to die for her. Finally, she herself died. She couldn't handle the new circumstances in which, instead of consoling soldiers and inspiring poets, she had to take freaks, aliens and outcasts under her wing; instead of uniting everyone under her banner, she had to learn to accept diversity; instead of telling beautiful stories, she finally had to learn the ones that had been forgotten and repressed. As a result, she grew ugly, got lost, sunk into depression and went away. She returned as (A)pollonia, Transpolonia, Postpolonia, Lack-of-Polonia and in many other guises, to tackle her own uncertain identity, past, and memory, and face problems she had never even dreamed existed . . .

"Polonia" was the established historical narrative about Poland, a conceptualization of the Polish national identity that was born and nurtured in subjugation. Polonia was a myth that had to be continually retold. A romantic and *fin de siecle* myth that, denying modernity, persisted as long as it could not be made material. This myth persisted under the partitions through the nineteenth century until 1918, when Poland briefly regained its statehood, and after World War II, when nation's sovereignty was limited by communism and the Soviet Union.

Poland as Polonia was, therefore, a fantasy of national identity and, as such, she was not a woman but an illusion; her relationships were all platonic and she knew nothing of real life. Only after regaining freedom and independence in 1989 did she—as (A)pollonia, Transpolonia, Postpolonia, etc.—acquire a body, and with it, the bitterness of heartbreak, the burden of unfulfilled expectations, and the onus of settling historical accounts and identity dilemmas.

Above all, she now had to contend with the real problems of real people and social groups, with local conflicts and global politics, with the standards of political correctness, and with postmodernist uncertainty. In short, she had to face the permanent crisis typical of the liquid modernity in which Western societies live.

Consequently, the readers of this anthology of texts for theater should not assume that, as one of Dorota Masłowska's characters says, "in Poland all you get is Poland."

## 1. IN POLAND—THAT IS TO SAY, EVERYWHERE

The title of the anthology—*(A)pollonia*—has been taken from a text for the theater which attempted to challenge the founding myth of Polish identity that had been preventing it from embracing modernity. Proof that the nation has embarked on this road is found in the subject matter, conflicts, and dilemmas addressed by nearly all the plays in this volume, and prevalent in the Polish theater of the last decade. The anthology includes Polish dramas and texts for the theater written in the twenty-first century that, while retaining a uniquely Polish flavor, take up painful issues of the contemporary world and highlight ethical and political aspects of historical narratives and constructs of identity. With their universal potential and political commitment, these texts will interest readers, appeal to stage directors and theatergoers, and inspire academic discourse outside of the Polish context. In recent years, Polish literature and theater have stopped dwelling on obscure topics peculiar to the local situation, joining a broader debate on global conflicts and dialogue between cultures. These texts bring to light matters that have been repressed or neglected, creatively transforming our shared historical and cultural heritage and enhancing public debate by setting out new dimensions of interpretation.

The anthology's subject matter is directly related to the historical and political shift in Polish theater, which, at the beginning of the twenty-first century, began revisiting issues such as wartime trauma and postwar displacement, the Holocaust and anti-Semitism, the fall of communism in 1989 and the subsequent political transformation, and attempting to take stock of past complexes. The language used to discuss these topics is modern and innovative, supra-national, and politically aware of gender and of postcolonial contexts. In order for the plays to be enjoyed by readers unfamiliar with Polish culture, all specific Polish references are explained in the present introduction and the editors' notes to individual texts.

Three types of dramatic texts have been included in the anthology: stage plays utilizing more or less traditional methods, docudramas drawing on archival and documentary material, and texts for the theater that use the found-footage method to compile, adapt and dramatize many literary sources. They have been arranged not in terms of style or genre—today such distinctions seem anachronistic, if not invalid, given that contemporary aesthetic development in the performing arts typically combines styles and genres—but in terms of content, that is, in terms of the problems they address. Consequently, the texts form a polyphonic narrative about Poland as a symbolic site that, in "mixing memory and desire," brings into focus the transnational experience of the twentieth century and the anxieties of the twenty-first.

This thematic arrangement covers the main chapters of Poland's history in the twentieth century—from World War II and the Holocaust through the fall of communism and the political transition after 1989—and reflects the main directions in which contemporary art and public debate are developing as they take up the discourses of guilt and victimization, memory and oblivion, cultural changes and economic exclusion. The plays contained in this anthology address the four major themes on which Polish narratives of identity are based today: the fate of the Jews (*(A)pollonia*; *The Mayor*); the war and its consequences (*Transfer!*; *Trash Story*; *right left with heels*); debunking national myths (*Foreign Bodies*; *In Desert and Wilderness*; *Small Narration*); and life in a free-market economy (*No Matter How Hard We Tried*; *Diamonds Are Coal That Got Down to Business*; *I Love You No Matter What*). Each of the four sections of the anthology—Polin, Transpolonia, Postpolonia, Lack-of-Polonia—refers to Poland, although in a slightly different way. Each is a metaphor that needs to be explained.

Yet before we elucidate the titles and metaphors, we need to emphasize that, in using the word "Poland" so often, and in so many prefixed and modified variants, we are by no means waving the national flag but actually trying to defuse nationalist rhetoric. The term "national" has become unwelcome today because of its exclusive, restrictive and divisive aspect that can lead to symbolic oppression, confinement and xenophobia. We want to open up the concept of national allegiance so that it becomes an invitation that includes the invitation of hope. This anthology and the texts it contains are pervaded by the possibly utopian hope that other minds will find a home in the Polish cultural imaginarium and vice versa. Our aim, on the one hand, is to undertake an ironic game with jingoism and, on the other, to shrug off the sense of uniqueness and exceptionalism, try to subvert stereotypes, and give our own mentalities and those of others a good airing.

Poland, in all its guises, is treated here not as a fetish but as a fluctuating mix of identities, experiences, and contexts. Alfred Jarry set *Ubu Roi* "in Poland—that is to say, nowhere." We are telling stories that could take place in Poland—that is to say, everywhere.

## 2. CURRICULUM VITAE

Any dialogue between cultures requires a degree of frankness. Polonia/(A)pollonia should say something about herself—a bit about what she's gone through, what she's guilty of, and what hurts her the most. What is it in her past that keeps coming back to her, causing nightmares and self-pity? Why does she have so much pride and so many complexes? Where does her prudishness and impeccably clean conscience come from? The answers to these questions are to be found in history, which is worth looking into if we are to understand certain motifs, threads, and symbols recurring in the plays contained in this anthology.

Where then does Polish megalomania come from? From recollections of the distant past when, according to estimates, she was the largest country in Europe. From the tolerance she practiced in the sixteenth century, when she was famed as "a state without stakes." From pride at one of the oldest parliamentary traditions in the world, the nobles' democracy that emerged in the fifteenth century, and the first constitution in Europe, adopted in 1791, just four years after the US Constitution.

Why the self-pity? Because of her cruel neighbors who, at the end of the eighteenth century, divided Poland up among themselves and kept her under their yoke for over 120 years. Because of the failed nineteenth-century uprisings against those partitioning powers. Because of her precarious position between Germany and Russia. Because her Western allies did not honor their treatise with Poland when Nazi Germany invaded the country starting World War II. Because of the indifference with which she was handed over to Stalin at the Yalta Conference. Because she feels that nobody in the world remembers that Poland was the first nation to overthrow communism, when the Berlin Wall was still standing.

Why does Poland feel she is special? It is due to her Romantic poetry and her vision of Poland as the Christ of nations. Due to the messianic ideals that inflamed the imagination of an enslaved nation. Due to having given birth to Nicholas Copernicus, Madame Curie, John Paul II and Lech Wałęsa . . .

Where did the unfailingly clean conscience come from? From a constant retelling of stories about the suffering she has endured and denial of the pain she has inflicted. From glorifying her heroic deeds, performed in noble causes. From the number of Polish trees planted in Yad Vashem.

Whence the prudishness and conservative mores? From Catholic fundamentalism and everyday hypocrisy. From the cult of the Virgin Mary and devotion to the icon of Our Lady of Częstochowa. From petit-bourgeois hypocrisy and peasant fanaticism.

As the above indicates, Polonia/(A)pollonia constructs her identity on dubious premises, rehashed clichés, and rote learning. This is aggravated by her complexes, the ones she acquired when living under communism—poverty and a sense of backwardness—and the ones that emerged after 1989—unemployment and social stratification.

She also has to grapple with nightmares: images of the war, the massacre of Warsaw during the 1944 uprising, postwar deportations, Stalinist terror and the torture chambers of the secret police, and life in the communist matrix. Then there is the sudden disappearance of her neighbors—the Jewish nation that had lived here for centuries—which haunts her with images of camps, but also of the pogroms and expulsions committed in her name.

If there is something that hurts Polonia/(A)pollonia, it is when foreigners refer to "Polish death camps" instead of "German death camps in occupied Poland" as Barack Obama inadvertently did in May 2012 when posthumously awarding the Presidential Medal of Freedom to Jan Karski. Karski was a courier and the emissary of the Polish Underground State who, during World War II, tried unsuccessfully to bring the attention of the West, including President Roosevelt, to the plight of the Jews. The medal was accepted on Karski's behalf by Adam Daniel Rotfeld, a Polish diplomat and Holocaust survivor whose parents were killed by the Germans in 1943. The story is a telling example of historical paradoxes that shape public life and the image of Poland in the eyes of the West.

## 3. POLIN

"Polin" means Poland in Yiddish and Hebrew. According to a Jewish legend, when Jews who were fleeing Spain, Portugal, and the German states in 1492 reached Poland, they read the country's name as "Po lin" ("stay here") and took this as a good omen. For centuries,

Jews coexisted in Poland alongside the Poles—retaining and cultivating their distinctness, and sometimes adopting the local language and customs. Whichever option they chose, the Jews were "at home" in Poland, though—as often happens among neighbors —this coexistence was not free of Polish-Jewish tensions and conflicts, often exploited by authorities pursuing a "divide and conquer" policy. The anti-Semitism of which Poles are often accused—even though their crimes against the Jews pale when compared to those of most other European nations—was not just the result of a reluctance to accept a different culture and religion, the urge to find a scapegoat in times of social unrest, nor of any psychological susceptibility to extreme ideology, but was also often motivated by political and economic factors, and was an easily exploited instrument in power struggles as well as a way of channeling social frustrations. Nonetheless, Jewish culture became an inseparable part of Polish art and material culture. The Polish imagination and mental landscape have been shaped by characters from the literary canon such as Jankiel in Adam Mickiewicz's *Pan Tadeusz* (1834), Judyta in Juliusz Słowacki's *Father Marek* (1843), Doctor Szuman in Bolesław Prus' *The Doll* (1890), Meir Ezofowicz in Eliza Orzeszkowa's novel of the same name (1878), and Rachela in Stanisław Wyspiański's *Wedding* (1901).

If Poles persisted in feeling blameless with regard to the Jews, it was owing to such literature, to the invaluable contribution Jewish intellectuals made to the scientific, cultural, and social life of the nation, to a large Yiddish-speaking Jewish population of towns and cities in Poland before 1939, to a belief in Polish tradition of tolerance for other religions, as well as to a focus on their own national suffering. These attitudes resisted even the Holocaust for decades after the war, as Jewish people were understood to have suffered the same afflictions that befell the Polish nation at the hands of the Nazis and the Soviets as of 1939. Jewish victims were initially numbered among the Polish war dead, then once it was no longer possible to deny the exceptionality of Jewish fate, the prevailing narrative focused on Poles selflessly risking their lives to save the Jews, or on the condition of being helpless witnesses of the Holocaust. All the greater was the shock that greeted the publication of Jan T. Gross' *Neighbors* (2000). Now the times of innocence were over.

To quote the eponymous Mayor from Małgorzata Sikorska-Miszczuk's play:

> That's me from the Times of Innocence. Those times are over. The other me, the same me (after all, there's only one of me), is sitting in a chair with an outstretched hand, pointing at me. He's covered in wounds, he's all in pieces, hanging on by the skin of his skin, he won't talk much. All he can do is repeat, hand pointing at me: "It's me, it's me."

In 2000, Jan T. Gross shook a hitherto-complacent public with his account of a previously little-known atrocity in Jedwabne, a small town in eastern Poland where, in June 1941, Polish residents, instigated by the German occupying forces, brutally rounded up their Jewish neighbors in a barn and burned them alive. Gross' next books, *Fear* (2008) and *Golden Harvest* (2011), also concerned Polish persecution of the Jews in wartime and the anti-Semitic outrages perpetrated just after the war. In the context of Polish Holocaust studies and numerous historical works on the subject, these books were not the only accounts of atrocities, but owing to their sometimes controversial rhetorical edge and the author's talent for publicity, they reached a wide audience and shook public opinion. The atrocity in Jedwabne—emblematic of all other acts of Polish aggression against the Jews—posed a challenge to the nation's "clear conscience" and forced a reckoning with the question of blame at all levels of public debate.

Sikorska-Miszczuk has taken coping with this blame—its admission and denial—as the subject of her two-part play, *The Mayor* (2008–11), inspired by the atrocity in Jedwabne, its being brought to light, and the reactions of the town's present-day authorities and residents. The protagonist is based on the real-life mayor of Jedwabne, Krzysztof Godlewski, who valiantly faced up to the historical truth and, in opposition to the wishes of his fellow townspeople, decided to speak of and commemorate the martyrdom of the Jews of Jedwabne. Sikorska-Miszczuk places the conflict stirred up by memories of a Polish crime against Jews in the context of Polish mental clichés, such as the figure of the Penitent German —seen until then by Poles (and by himself) as being uniquely responsible for atrocities during the war—and by the Monument, an icon of Polish national megalomania:

> The whole Radiant Figure glistens with gold, platinum and pearls. Such is the purest stuff the Monument is cast of, as indestructible as our pride.

In *(A)pollonia* (2009), director Krzysztof Warlikowski undertook the deconstruction of historical and mental clichés from another perspective: that of sacrifice. By questioning the meaning of sacrifice as an ethical imperative, he struck a blow at Polish identity and provided a critical insight into the Christian and Mediterranean mythology in which it is rooted.

In *(A)pollonia*, setting the sacrifice of Iphigenia and Alcestis against the sacrifice of a Polish woman sheltering Jewish children at the cost of her life reveals its morally ambiguous nature by making it relative instead of absolute. Ryfka was spared death thanks to Apollonia Machczyńska. Admetus was to be spared from death as long as he could find someone who would die in his place:

> It's hard to be someone's saviour. / He asked everyone. They all refused / All but one. / One silently said yes. Just that: Yes / His beloved wife said that, Alcestis . . .

Iphigenia says: "It's a great honour for me to be able to save my homeland." Yet her death leads to others: her mother kills her father, to be killed in turn by her son. Just before his death, Agamemnon will quote the war-criminal narrator of Jonathan Littell's *Kindly Ones*:

> The only difference between the Jewish child gassed or shot and the German child burned alive in an air raid is one of method; both deaths were equally vain, neither of them shortened the war by so much as a second; but in both cases those who killed them

> believed it was just and necessary. Like most people I never asked to become a murderer . . . You can never say: I shall never kill. The most you can say is: I hope I shall never kill.

Violence blurs the outlines of intentions, motives, and attitudes: There is little difference between vengeance killing, offering a sacrifice, and plain murder, Warlikowski seems to be saying, when he invokes Apollo and Hercules, Greek heroes affected by or accused of the death of their loved ones. What's worse, killing oneself is also murder, and laying down one's life means acquiescing to violence and death. As the son of Machczyńska, murdered by the Germans for sheltering Jews, frantically asks: "Doesn't a man have a right to save his own life?" Admetus, for whom his wife, Alcestis, laid down her life, addresses the audience: "You would not have agreed to such a sacrifice. / Someone sacrificing their life. Never. / You'd rather die. Would someone here prefer to die? You, sir? Madam? You wouldn't, sir? So that makes two of us: That's a relief. / Because all the rest love the lives of others more than their own. / We love our own life. And that's a sin!"

Such risky juxtapositions and provocative questions serve to challenge the uncritically accepted dogma about the absolute value of laying down one's life for another. This demystifies the myth of sacrifice and, above all, exposes the symbolic violence that underpins it. The revision of history accomplished in *(A)pollonia* is not just about the collateral suffering that sacrificing oneself for someone causes. Desacralizing sacrifice involves a revision of the paradigm on which Western culture—and, incidentally, Polish messianism—are founded.

The discourse of guilt in *The Mayor* and the discourse of the victim in *(A)pollonia* are two ways of addressing the immense sense of loss prevailing ever since the Holocaust, specifically in a nation that witnessed it first hand. Historically conditioned, rooted in myth and the collective unconscious, these two orders reflect the key tensions inherent in Western culture.

## 4. TRANSPOLONIA

In taking up the subject of relations with Germany, new Polish drama comes face to face with some of the most painful chapters of the nation's history: the long-term consequences of the German invasion of Poland on September 1, 1939, which began World War II. The course of the war and its consequences determined the history of Europe until 1989 and to the present day. For Poland, the war was a pivotal event that turned it from a multinational state into an ethnically homogenous one, moved its population and its borders to the west, deprived it of independence by placing it in the Soviet sphere of influence. It continued to affect the national mentality for decades as the new authorities perpetuated wartime psychosis, stirred up anti-German sentiment, and dwelt on the nation's martyrology while disregarding the sufferings of others. It was only after 1989 that it became possible to carry out a revision of entrenched narratives about the war, restore knowledge of facts that had been blotted out or corrupted by censorship, exercise independence in the assessment of political processes set in motion by the war, and show empathy toward its victims, regardless of their nationality. The spotlight was no longer on the strategies of generals but on the fate of the civilian population; not on heroic deeds but on acts of rape; not on military victories but on postwar displacement. One could say that what occurred was a shift of focus in historical narrative from commemorating a collective tragedy to the recollection of individual ordeals—a shift from the national perspective to the human one.

Poland lost its eastern provinces to the USSR in the wake of the Yalta Conference, while gaining land in the west that had previously belonged to Germany. This launched a new age of migrations. Poles from Vilnius and Lviv were resettled in and around the cities of Wrocław and Szczecin, cities that had been abandoned by their previous German residents, who had been themselves forced to resettle. It was only recently—in a Poland liberated from political constraints and artificially fuelled social anxieties—that one could take an interest in these former residents and ask: Who were the people who built these houses?

In that sense, Jan Klata's 2005 production, *Transfer!*, based on a script by Dunja Funke and Sebastian Majewski, was a turning point in Polish theater. It achieved a shift that was both historic and historical, bringing to the stage a vivid historical subject after a long period of unwillingness to address history in general, giving voice to witnesses who had until then been excluded from the historical narrative, and providing a vehicle for stories repressed by the Polish collective memory. The cast consisted mostly of non-professional actors: real-life eyewitnesses to and participants in historical events. The contribution of the dramaturges was to take down their stories, edit and arrange them, and hand them back to their owners, the cast of *Transfer!*

German men and women born before the war in what Polish authorities would later call the Regained Territories spoke about their experiences during and after the war, which led to them becoming Expellees, to use a term later adopted in Germany. Old people told their life stories on stage: "[E]verybody had a copy of *Mein Kampf* but nobody ever read it," recalled Hanne-Lore Pretzsch. Ilse Bode said, "[W]e had a really loving father. But, unfortunately, he had to go off to the war. That's when all good things came to an end." Pretzsch described the fate of German women at the hands of the victorious Red Army: "The women tried smearing soot on their faces, and putting on dirty long dresses, but it was no use. It was all the same to the Russians."

Parallel stories were told by Poles from the same generation who were relocated from the east. "When the Germans came / the Ukrainians started killing people / I don't know why / it was horrible," reminisced Karolina Kozak. "I don't know whether I saw any Germans / well, maybe one because I remember that he was nicely dressed / a belt saying: God Is with Us and he had elegant boots." Zygmunt Sobolewski recalled that "When they were coming back from the Eastern Front / the Germans weren't that elegant anymore / they would come to our house / grab some hay / pull off their shoes / then you could see the wounds, the blisters, the calluses, the frostbite." The Poles also recollected how, after being resettled to Wrocław from the east after 1945, they moved in to houses and apartments from which their German owners were being evicted: "[A] militiaman took me / to a three-room place on Grunwaldzka Street / but there were Germans still living there—/ a woman with her daughter / of twenty / the militiaman says I'll be taking the apartment / and they will be resettled / I moved in."

A backdrop to these parallel and intertwining accounts of displacement was provided by the grotesque dialogue of actors playing the Big Three: Stalin, Churchill, and Roosevelt, who, at the Yalta Conference, made decisions about moving borders and nations on the map of Europe. This blending of the macro and micro perspective—the imperial and the individual, history and memory—helped to realign established thinking about right and wrong, and to reconsider the distinction between allies and enemies.

*Transfer!* transformed Polish collective memory by forcing Poles to realize that others shared a similar fate, and that historical enemies were victims of the same upheavals. It shook up accepted historical thinking by replacing traditional Polish-German enmity with a Polish-German community of displacement. Without reapportioning the guilt, it introduced an element of empathy that undermined the discourse of authority. Empathy disarmed militaristic doctrine and ideological prerogatives of the rulers by focusing on human tribulations instead of the *raison d'état*.

*Transfer!* gave rise to a unique theatrical event, combining storytelling with stagecraft—the text has unquestionable literary merits—and successfully transferring documentary material onto a universal tale about existential entanglement in history.

This universality is even more apparent in Magda Fertacz's *Trash Story* (2008), which presents male stories from the war's front lines through the prism of women's experience. The women in question are the ghost of Ursula, a German girl, whose father was killed on the Eastern Front, who was hanged by her mother so she wouldn't be raped by Red Army troops, and the daughter of a concentration-camp inmate, who spent her childhood in the shadow of his wartime trauma, and the widow of a veteran of the Iraq war. They all live in the house that once belonged to Ursula's family, who didn't manage to flee before the advancing Red Army.

The women's stories have a common denominator: They all testify to a life marked by male violence, and a loyalty towards the male narrative. All of them carry letters written by men in their hearts. A letter from Auschwitz: "My having survived is an act of terrible arrogance . . . I can't write anymore. I no longer have an internal 'no' . . . It's dead. I'm consumed with dread at the thought of the reality awaiting me just past the gate. There's no desire in me to face up to it . . ." A letter from Stalingrad: "We lie among corpses. The ground is too hard to dig graves . . . I am unmoved by anything; I kill on my left, I kill on my right—the more I kill, the faster this will end." A letter from Iraq: "The bomb that was supposed to blow our car apart went off a few seconds too early. A few seconds. My friends from another patrol weren't so lucky. Bodies torn to shreds . . . If I come back without my legs, with scars all over my body, promise me that you'll finish me off."

In *Trash Story*, the distant past provides a context for the suicide of the traumatized veteran of the Iraq war. The play reveals how World War II is no longer just a point of reference for a peculiarly Polish narrative but part of a broader reflection on violence as the driving force of history, where bearing witness to individual suffering is more important than settling scores.

Micro-history is also at the center of pilgrim/majewski's *right left with heels* (2008), which undertakes an ironic game with German guilt as the founding myth of what Tony Judt called "the postwar." The symbol of German guilt here are the shoes of Magda Goebbels, sentenced in 1946 by the "special section for degenerate objects" in Nuremberg to deportation to the East. As they change owners, they witness snippets of individual biography, changing mores, and the by-products of political conflicts. It is from such episodes that the historical narrative of postwar Polish history, marked as it is by the war and its consequences, is woven. In this narrative, the punishment of the shoes of Magda Goebbels has just come to an end, so it would seem that this stage in the settling of historical accounts is a thing of the past.

## 5. POSTPOLONIA

The events of 1989 definitively overturned the postwar order established in Yalta. A turning point in the history of Poland and Europe alike, they sealed the fate of communism, and ushered in political and economic transformations that led to profound changes in the collective and individual consciousness. Consequently, a need arose to take stock of the former system and settle accounts with the communist authorities and their adherents. There was a concurrent need to validate existing constructs of identity: the hierarchy of values, cultural models and attitudes in the face of the changes affecting the postmodern world, and the new challenges related to liberalism, postcolonialism, and issues of gender.

The new situation called for reflection on the validity of a community founded on dreams of independence and the autonomy of the individual within that community, analyzing the national mentality in terms of postcolonial and gender theory and, finally, coping with actual and metaphysical guilt with respect to the past. The point of reference for such a perspective were no longer specific historical events but, rather, a critical outlook on those events, transcending the mental legacy of the former era, and opening up to new possibilities, new values and new contexts. Even though, in the spirit of Romantic myths, Polonia still occasionally celebrated herself as heroine and martyr, she was far more inclined to challenge this image by (post)modernizing her narratives of history and identity. And since, as remarked previously, Polonia gained a body after 1989, it is through the prism of the body that her metamorphosis needs to be presented.

By inscribing political transformation into the story of the sex change undergone by its hero/ine, Julia Holewińska's *Foreign Bodies* (2010) takes a look at the Polish revolution of 1989 in the context of a struggle between the individual and the collective, and sees transformation as a painful process of regaining one's self outside of a disintegrating community. The play is based on the true story of a political dissident active in the underground movement after the imposition of martial law in 1981, jailed for his beliefs, who decided to undergo sex-reassignment surgery after the country regained its independence in order to assert his/her true identity that had been hidden until then. The heroine, who appears as the characters of Adam and Ewa, pays an enormous price for her decision: She is shunned by her nearest and dearest, humiliated in social situations, and cannot enjoy privileges she would have almost certainly been entitled to in the new system if she had gone into politics as a man. In this situation, gender change becomes a metaphor of social transformation, by clashing the public with the private, collective versus individual freedom, and by confronting paradigms of masculinity and femininity. It turns out that, even in a free country, subjectivity, freedom and emancipation must still be fought for and continually negotiated. In the context of individual freedom, Julia Holewińska's play asks fundamental questions about community. The hero, Adam, after becoming Ewa, asks:

> Where are you now, friends of mine? Communism's dead, Adam's dying. Celebrate with me. Is that so hard? Do I sicken you? I won't change. Maybe just a bit, but you'll get used to it soon enough. Where are you? Why aren't you here? This is what we were fighting for. For freedom, tolerance and the truth. This is my truth. Here I am. Give me your hand, I'm a little scared. I really need you now. A lot! Where are you? You're not here? That can't be. We swore before God and the crowned eagle banner that we'd always be together. For better or worse. Now you're not here. And me? Now I can finally be me.

Perhaps Adam/Ewa is really asking: What good is a self without a community? If *Foreign Bodies* is about negotiating one's place within a collective, then *In Desert and Wilderness. After Sienkiewicz and Others* (2011) tries to deconstruct and question that community, and undermine the foundations of collective awareness.

The starting point of Weronika Szczawińska and Bartosz Frąckowiak's text for the theater is Poland's most popular young-adult novel, Henryk Sienkiewicz's *In Desert and Wilderness* (1912), which traces the adventures of two children, a Polish boy and an English girl, in Africa. By altering the story, adding new lines, and above all by encrusting the text with fragments of many other works of literature, philosophy and journalism, and entries from encyclopedias and reportage, the authors carry out a postcolonial critique of the colonial discourse underpinning classic adventure stories—present not only in Sienkiewicz's novel but also in all dreams of "the Polish empire, come alive" and in aspirations to "territory being taken for the glory of the fatherland." This critique employs such key categories as hybridity, orientalism, epistemic violence, mimicry and the distinction into the center and peripheral territories. Its end product is a found-footage text—an open dramatic structure, full of distortions and all sorts of interference, which radically deconstructs the colonial mentality of a nation that, though itself colonized, never renounced its imperial cravings and sense of supremacy over the Other:

> Our forefathers told us that the Polish mind contains, and every now and then manifests, a dream of imperial existence. Perhaps now is the time to discuss whether we want to be an empire or not. And if we don't, what do we want to be?

"And if we don't, what do we want to be?" is the key question after 1989. In its colonial aspirations and dreams of glory, Polonia compensated for its subjugation and historical humiliation. Postpolonia renounces dreams of grandeur in its quest for modernity but, in the process of constructing its identity, challenges other hitherto indispensable components of that identity. "Not wanting" can therefore also apply to history, which had until now defined the collective awareness. In *Small Narration* (2010), Wojciech Ziemilski makes such an attempt to cut himself free from history:

> It began when while telling the story you realized you don't want this history. You don't want World War II, or WWI, or communism, or the fall of communism, you don't want September 1, September 17, May 8, July 11, May 3, April 19, August 1, December 13, June 4. You don't want the Holocaust, you don't want the Ribentropp-Molotov treatise, you don't want Solidarność, you don't.

The attempt fails. There is no escaping history. In *Small Narration*, the author has to grapple with the personal and family trauma caused by the discovery that his grandfather, Wojciech Dzieduszycki, had been an informer for the secret police. To understand, overcome, and recount that past, Ziemilski had to deal with his own distance towards history, confront it with family feelings, childhood memories, images inscribed in his memory. He juxtaposed these feelings and memories with press clippings and snippets of documents. The vetting of the past, in its familial, moral, political, administrative, and historical dimensions became a source of individual self-knowledge. Ziemilski was forced to ask what happened to his private history once it became public, and once the public turned out to be private.

## 6. LACK-OF-POLONIA

Economic transformation, the transition from a centrally planned to a free-market economy, entailed painful social consequences: unemployment and destitution, as well as the emergence of profound differences in standard of living between those who found a place for themselves in the new realities and those who proved helpless in the face of it. This gave rise to frustration at the inability to satisfy newly awakened consumer desires and to complexes at not fitting in with the lifestyle promoted in the media. The vision of success, of becoming true Europeans, targets of advertising campaigns, clients of mutual funds and "consuming consumers" proved unattainable for many.

The "victims of transformation" are people who were told they were "not up to it," who have a "psychiatrist treat [them] for lack of social opportunities," read advertising brochures pulled out of a recycling bin, and shop at discount supermarkets for "Ye Olde Poultry Loin" made out of pork rinds and dishwashing liquid. They are the subjects of plays by Dorota Masłowska and Paweł Demirski, who see the changes after 1989 in terms of not historical success but the failings in everyday existence.

In Masłowska's *No Matter How Hard We Tried* (2008), these failings are manifest in the crisis of identity (caused to an equal degree by the ghosts of the past and by the tackiness of everyday life) and the commercializing of the public sphere. Free-market mechanisms prove an insufficient remedy for traumatized memory: supermarket price wars have not displaced the recollections of World War II. The deadlock caused by poverty, complexes, and history can be broken only by denial: "We're no Poles, just normal folks!" Lack-of-Polonia therefore describes a state of mind marked equally by a longing for "normality," or some vision thereof, and by the stigma of the past.

In Demirski's *Diamonds Are Coal That Got Down to Business* (2008), the failure is related to the economic shock treatment, or austerity program, that boosted the Polish economy in the early 1990s without paying heed to the social costs:

> This house was no longer able to pay for itself
> So my father did the math
> And the neoliberal calculator
> which was the only calculator he had told him
> the house should be sold and that was that
> and that the only therapy that would keep us alive
> was shock therapy and mass layoffs too

The play, a paraphrase of Anton Chekhov's *Uncle Vanya*, shows the incompatibility of neoliberal rhetoric, which encouraged people to take matters into their own hands ("cultivating diamonds") and embrace the spirit of free enterprise, with the material and social condition of people regarded as the victims of transformation. On the one hand, we have Chekhov's characters cast into present-day capitalist Poland, who feel that "there's nothing anyone can do about poverty and social exclusion which is the cost you have to pay for transformation and our neoliberal economy," and see the charater of Uncle Vanya as having "precisely this educational tenor." On the other hand, in *No Matter How Hard We Tried*, we have the tenants of a cramped apartment in a prewar Warsaw tenement, with its "ongoing failure to renovate the premises since the war ended, or thereabouts," and which "still lacks the tidiness, dryness and spaciousness so fashionable of late." All of them live "teetering between panic and boredom," feckless, damaged, and bereft of hope.

If this sense is absent in Przemysław Wojcieszek's *I Love You No Matter What* (2005), it is because he does not approach the present as a vehicle for social satire, but in order to tell a sentimental story. The focal point here is not capitalist exploitation and lack of prospects for the future, not the working conditions of dishwashers in a fried-chicken joint, but the hope that love offers. Seeing as that love is between two lesbians, it shatters social conventions, becoming an instrument of social criticism that strikes at patriarchal habits, actively opposes violence, and overthrows the established system of values. "We'll start a little lesbian family. A tiny, subversive cell that will blow this fucked-up society to smithereens," states one of the main characters.

When her macho brother comes back from tour of duty in Iraq and finds out his sister has a girlfriend, he bursts out: "You know, I spent the last six months of my life in a place where things were for real. Death was for real and life was for real. And now I come home and everything's make-believe! Two chicks planning a wedding and a wonderful life together. It's ridiculous, man! Would you die for her?" "Yes," Magda replies.

The whole subversive potential of love is brought out in Magda's closing monologue:

> we are
> lovers
> let's do it on the tombs of kings, commanders of uprisings lost
> the day they began
> let's do it on monuments to patriotic youth
> who without hesitation laid down their lives at the command
> of a bunch of old men
> while you and me were kissing in some corner
> and we're alive and well today while they're dead, and our
> conscience
> is clear because we came to know the taste of love instead of
> waving the flag

This opting for life over the ghosts of the past, personal happiness over patriotic sentiment, and the individual present over collective memory gives rise to the hope of overcoming the crisis of identity: of no longer being torn between shame and pride at being Polish.

Lack-of-Polonia is a state of mind where real problems are not hidden and replaced by the tombs of kings and monuments to patriotic youth. The legacy of Polonia has been overcome—but there is no reason to be proud that what absorbs us now is mostly shopping and fucking, aroused appetites, social inequity, economic exclusion, collective egoism, the compulsion to consume and the vulgarity of pop culture.

*Translated by Artur Zapałowski*

## CHARACTERS

AMAL
MADHAB DATTA
IPHIGENIA
CLYTAEMNESTRA
AGAMEMNON
ALCESTIS
ADMETUS
ORESTES
APOLLO
THANATOS
DOCTOR
MOTHER
HERCULES
ATHENA
FERES
APOLONIA
OFFICER
ELIZABETH COSTELLO
JUSTICE
SŁAWEK
GRANDSON
RYFKA
JUDGE

KRZYSZTOF WARLIKOWSKI,
PIOTR GRUSZCZYŃSKI, AND
JACEK PONIEDZIAŁEK

Translated by Artur Zapałowski

# (A)POLLONIA

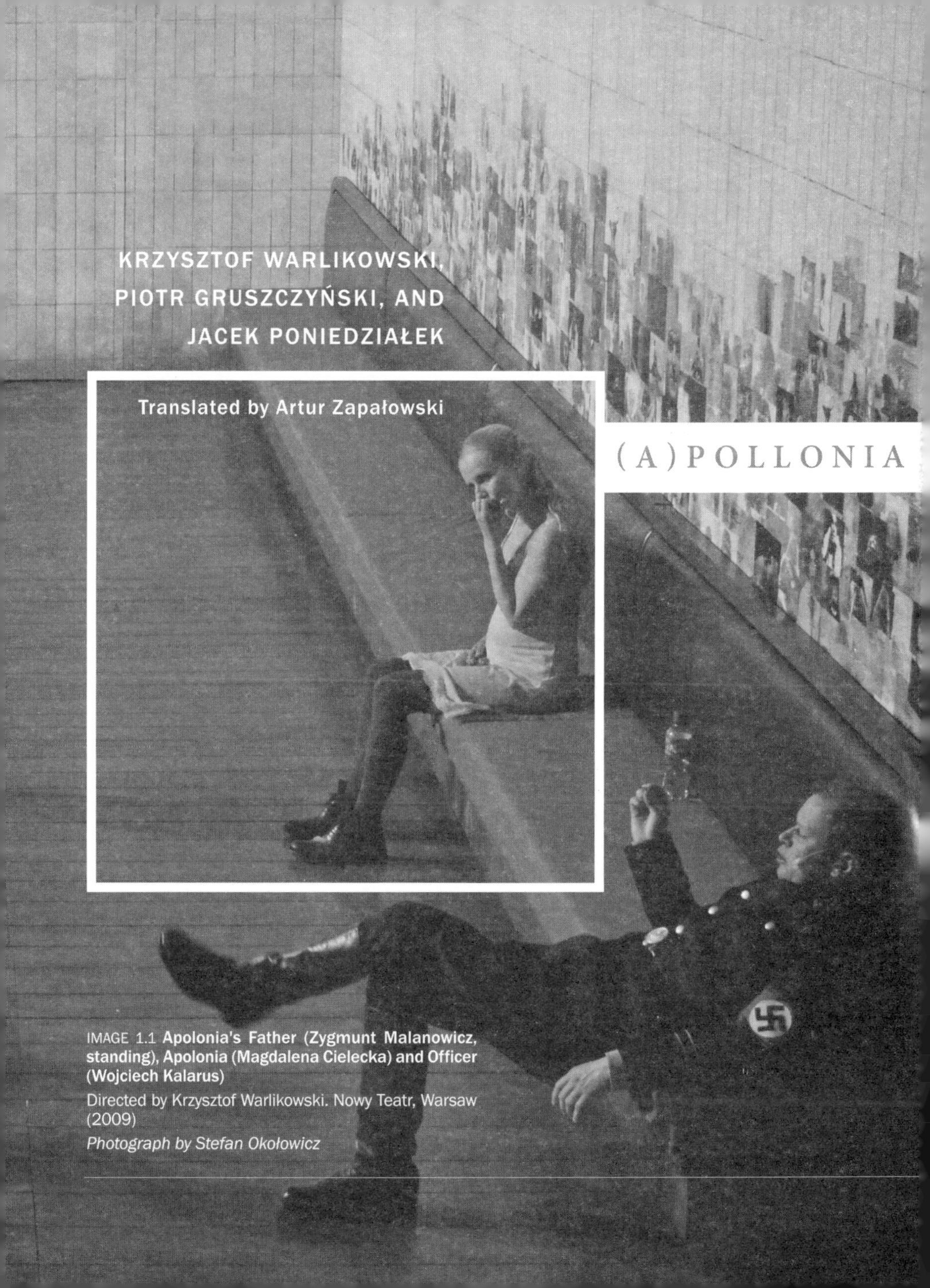

IMAGE 1.1 **Apolonia's Father (Zygmunt Malanowicz, standing), Apolonia (Magdalena Cielecka) and Officer (Wojciech Kalarus)**
Directed by Krzysztof Warlikowski. Nowy Teatr, Warsaw (2009)
*Photograph by Stefan Okołowicz*

## NOTE

*(A)pollonia* is a text for theatre that uses drama, poetry and prose from various periods to examine the subject of sacrifice and responsibility, and to show the story of mankind as a killing machine where every act of violence inexorably leads to more violence.

*(A)pollonia* is based on the following texts:

Aeschylus, *The Oresteia* (English translation: E. D. A. Morshead)

Hans Christian Andersen, *The Story of a Mother* (English translation: Susannah Mary Paull)

J. M. Coetzee, *Elizabeth Costello*

Andrzej Czajkowski, *Mother, Where Are You*?

Euripides, *Iphigenia at Aulis* (English translation: Edward P. Coleridge), *Heracles* (English translation: Edward P. Coleridge), *Alcestis* (English translation: Richard Aldington)

Hanna Krall, *Pola* from *Tam już nie ma żadnej rzeki* and *Narożny dom z wieżyczką* from *Żal*

Jonathan Littell, *The Kindly Ones* (English translation: Charlotte Mandell)

Marcin Świetlicki, *Pobojowisko* from *Zimne kraje. Wiersze 1980–1990*;

Rabindranath Tagore, *The Post Office* (English translation: Devabrata Mukherjee)

*(A)pollonia*, directed by Krzysztof Warlikowski, with a set design by Małgorzata Szczęśniak, had its premiere on May 16, 2009, in Warsaw. The production makes use of classical and contemporary music and songs written and performed live by Renate Jett. The action, which takes place on several planes at once in a vast performance space, was augmented by video projections. Equally diverse as the space and the literary and musical components of the production were its acting styles: rhetorical flourishes, brutal caricature and heightened physical expression, psychological realism, and grotesque lampooning.

*(A)pollonia* was produced by Nowy Teatr in Warsaw in association with Festival d'Avignon, Théatre National de Chaillot (Paris), Théatre de la Place de Liege, Comédie de Genève-Centre Dramatique, Théatre Royal de la Monnaie de Bruxelles, and Narodowy Stary Teatr (Kraków).

# (A)POLLONIA



## PROLOGUE

"We are not quick to promise as we have no certainty.

We are certain, however, that this hour spent with a beautiful tale by a philosopher and poet will stir emotion of the highest level of feeling.

Therefore we invite you on Saturday, July 18, 1942, at 4:30 p.m.

Admission is free."

The invitation to a performance of Rabindranath Tagore's *Post Office* was from Janusz Korczak, director of the Orphans' Home.

The Home was located in the Warsaw ghetto.

**AMAL.** Auntie!

**MADHAB DATTA.** Yes, Amal.

**AMAL.** Can I go out?

**MADHAB DATTA.** No, my son.

**AMAL.** A squirrel is holding broken grains in her paws and crunching them while supporting itself with its tail. Can I go and watch?

**MADHAB DATTA.** No, son.

**AMAL.** I wish I was a squirrel. Auntie, why can't I go out?

**MADHAB DATTA.** The doctor said it would make you worse.

**AMAL.** And how does he know?

**MADHAB DATTA.** The doctor wouldn't know? Think of all those thick books he's read.

**AMAL.** I haven't read even a single book so I don't know.

**MADHAB DATTA.** You Amal, you will become a great scholar when you grow up, too.

AMAL. No! I beg you, I don't want to be a scholar!

MADHAB DATTA. What are you saying, Amal! I would be so happy if you were to be a scholar.

AMAL. But I want to see the world! I want to travel!

MADHAB DATTA. What is there worth seeing?

AMAL. I'd like to go far, behind this mountain you can see from our window.

MADHAB DATTA. Don't you understand that mountain stands as high as a barricade, so that you can't go behind it? What would be the sense in heaping such a huge amount of stones in one place otherwise?

AMAL. Do you think it is not allowed? It seems to me that, since the Earth can't speak, it calls to the blue sky by reaching out its hand. This calling is heard by those who can't leave home and sit lonely by the window at noon.

MADHAB DATTA. They do very well. First you must get better, and then . . .

AMAL. Just don't tell me to become a scholar!

MADHAB DATTA. And who would you like to become?

AMAL. Nothing comes to my mind yet. I'll think about it and tell you later.

MADHAB DATTA. Supposedly you told the milkman that you would sell yogurt when you grow up.

AMAL. Auntie, don't tell the doctor, please. I'll lie here quietly, I promise. But when I get healthy I'll say the fakir's spell, and no mountains, no woods, no oceans will be able to stop me then.

MADHAB DATTA. Why do you keep talking about this travel? My heart aches when I listen to it. Very well then. Just remember not to talk to strangers.

AMAL. But I like strangers.

MADHAB DATTA. And what if they take you with them?

AMAL. That would be marvelous!

**MADHAB DATTA.** I have to go back to work. Just remember you can't go out.

**AMAL.** Fine, Auntie but I'll be sitting at the street window.

Milkman, hey milkman . . .

*

The following day, a review came out in the press: "Amal, for whom death is a godsend and the life he had dreamed of, performed his part with understanding and artistry."

Four days later, the reviewer and the audience would be shipped off to the gas chambers of Treblinka.

A fortnight later, Amal and the rest of the orphans from the Home would march off to the boxcars. Korczak would help the children climb to that "highest level of feeling," up the boxcar steps.

## PART ONE

### SCENE I

**IPHIGENIA.** Why are you so silent, Mother?

**CLYTAEMNESTRA.** I have reason to be!

**IPHIGENIA.** Do not make me lose heart! Listen!

**CLYTAEMNESTRA.** Speak my child, I will surely not harm you.

**IPHIGENIA.** Do not wear mourning clothes!

**CLYTAEMNESTRA.** But I'm about to lose you!

**IPHIGENIA.** I shall bring you glory!

**CLYTAEMNESTRA.** Am I not to wear mourning clothes?

**IPHIGENIA.** No, since I won't have a tomb.

**CLYTAEMNESTRA.** Death is what counts, not a tomb!

**IPHIGENIA.** The altar will be my tomb!

**CLYTAEMNESTRA.** So I shall obey your request, my child.

**IPHIGENIA.** It's a great honour for me to be able to save my homeland.

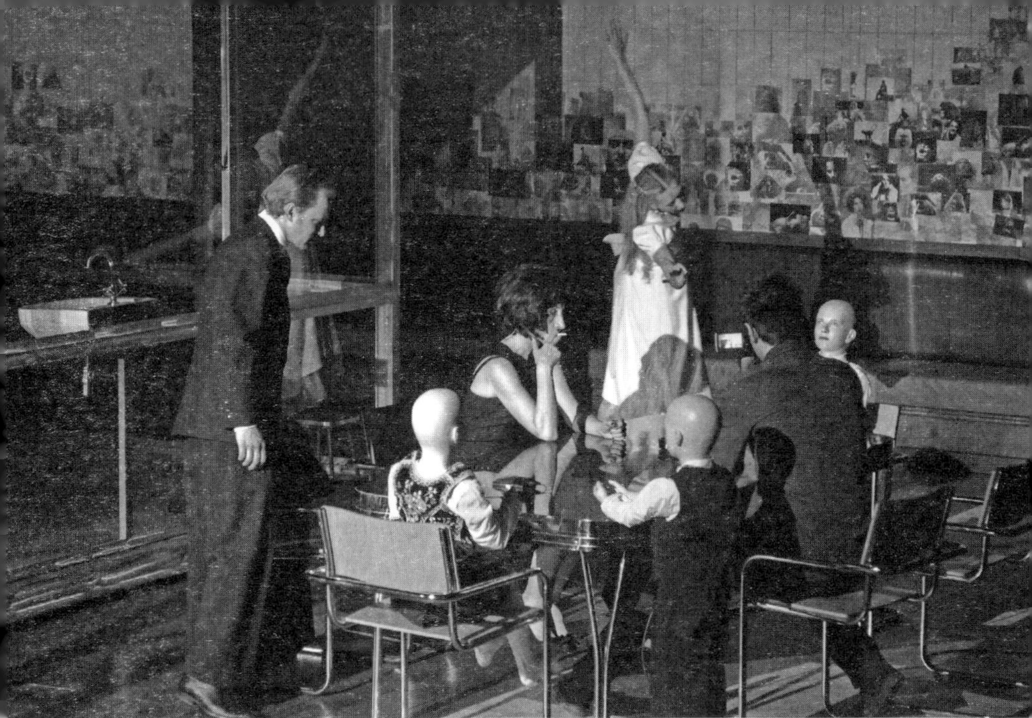

IMAGE 1.2 **Agamemnon (Maciej Stuhr), Clytaemnestra (Małgorzata Hajewska-Krzysztofik) and Iphigenia (Magdalena Popławska)**
Directed by Krzysztof Warlikowski. Nowy Teatr, Warsaw (2009)
*Photograph by Stefan Okołowicz*

---

CLYTAEMNESTRA. And what message shall I carry to your sisters?

IPHIGENIA. Bid them good speed! And raise Orestes to manhood!

CLYTAEMNESTRA. It's the last time you see him so kiss him!

IPHIGENIA. You've helped me as much as you could, my dear!

CLYTAEMNESTRA. Is there anything else?

IPHIGENIA. Do not loathe my father.

CLYTAEMNESTRA. He will go through severe trials because of you.

IPHIGENIA. He is ruining me against his will—for the sake of our homeland.

Who shall escort me? I don't want to be dragged by the hair . . .

CLYTAEMNESTRA. I shall go with you . . .

IPHIGENIA. Not you! It wouldn't be right!

CLYTAEMNESTRA. I'm clinging to your robe.

IPHIGENIA. Father shall conduct me to a meadow where I'll be sacrificed.

CLYTAEMNESTRA. Are you leaving, my child?

IPHIGENIA. And shall not return again.

CLYTAEMNESTRA. Will you abandon your mother?

IPHIGENIA. One ought to!

CLYTAEMNESTRA. Hold, don't leave!

AGAMEMNON. I know what should move my pity and what should not; I love my children. I am not mad. 'Tis terrible for me to bring myself to this, nor less terrible is it to refuse, wife; but I must do this.

This is no time for making excuses—it's time to face the truth: that somebody better and richer has stolen you, and my happiness, too. I don't ask for much, but I'll ask you, this once, one (last) favor before we part—

let me have just this Sunday, this one final Sunday, and then let the world fall apart.

This is our last Sunday— darling, please don't deceive me—today, you're going to leave me forevermore. This is our last Sunday—one last time, don't begrudge me—look at me like you love me—as you did before. You'll have all the Sundays you could wish for. As for me, who knows? Best not to ask . . . This is our last Sunday—all the dreams you inspired, all the joys I desired—over at last.

You look at me and ask what I'm planning. I'm heading to . . . who knows where? There's only one cure for such heartbreak as this, and that cure is—(well,) let's not go there. All that I care about is that you're happy. Don't mind me. I'll be fine. But before the Fates send us separate ways—For (this) one last Sunday—be mine.

This is our last Sunday—darling, please don't deceive me—today, you're going to leave me forevermore. This is our last

Sunday—one last time, don't begrudge me—look at me like you love me—as you did before.

You'll have all the Sundays you could wish for. As for me, who knows? Best not to ask . . . This is our last Sunday—all the dreams you inspired, all the joys I desired—over at last.

## SCENE II

**AGAMEMNON.** The war is over!

We've learned our lesson, it won't happen again. But are you sure we've learned our lesson? Are you certain it won't happen again? Are you even certain the war is over? In a manner of speaking, the war is never over, or else it will be over only when the last child born on the last day of the war is safely dead and buried. But even then the war lives on in his or her children and then in theirs.

In wartime, the male citizen loses one of his most basic rights, his right to life. But the citizen in question also loses another right, one just as basic: the right not to kill. No one asks you for your opinion.

Let's do the math.

Killed on the Eastern Front: 21.5 million

Final Solution: 5.1 million.

Total: 26.6 million.

The conflict with the USSR lasted from June 22, 1941, at 3:00, until May 8, 1945, at 23:01, which adds up to 3 years, 10 months, 16 days, 20 hours and 1 minute, or 46.5 months, or 202 weeks, or 1,417 days, or 34,004 hours, or 2,040,241 minutes. For the program known as the Final Solution, we'll use the same dates. That results in 572,043 people killed per month, 131,410 people killed per week, 18,772 people killed per day, 782 people killed per hour and 13.04 people killed per minute. Silence! You could also calculate the intervals between each death: this gives a new dead body on average every 4.6 seconds. Stopwatch in hand, count off 1 death, 2 deaths, 3 deaths, etc., every 4.6 seconds and try to picture them in front of you. It's a good meditation exercise.

I am not trying to say I am not guilty of this or that. I am guilty, you're not, fine. But you should be able to admit to yourselves that you might also have done what I did. With less zeal, perhaps, but perhaps also with less despair. In any case one way or another. If you were born in a country or at a time not only when nobody comes to kill your wife and children, but also nobody comes to ask you to kill the wives and children of others, render thanks to God and go in peace. But always keep this thought in mind: you might be luckier than I, but you're not a better person.

What I did, I did with my eyes open, believing that it was my duty and that it had to be done, disagreeable or unpleasant as it may have been. For that is what total war means: there is no such thing as a civilian. The only difference between the Jewish child gassed or shot and the German child burned alive in an air raid is one of method; both deaths were equally vain, neither of them shortened the war by so much as a second; but in both cases those who killed them believed it was just and necessary. Like most people I never asked to become a murderer. I would have liked to play the piano.

There were always reasons for what I did. Good reasons or bad, I don't know, in any case human reasons. Those who kill are humans, just like those who are killed, that's what's terrible. You can never say: I shall never kill. The most you can say is: I hope I shall never kill. I too hoped so. But unfortunately my sincerity was placed at the service of an ultimately evil and corrupt work. I crossed over the bounds of evil, and all this evil entered my own life, and none of all this can be made whole, ever. Words are of no use either, they disappear like water in the sand, this wet sand that fills my mouth. I live, I do what can be done, it's the same for everyone, I am a man like other men, I am a man like you.

The fact of the matter, I'm not ashamed to say, is that I probably would rather have been a woman. Not necessarily a woman living and functioning in this world as a wife or a mother; no, a woman naked, on her back, her legs spread wide open, crushed beneath the weight of a man, clinging to him and pierced by him, drowning in him as she becomes the limitless sea in which he himself is drowned, pleasure that's endless, and beginningless too. But things did not turn out that way. How to describe these sensations to one who has never experienced them? In the beginning, when it enters, it can be difficult, especially if it's a little dry. But once inside, oh how nice it is, you can't imagine. Your back arches and it's like a blue, luminous stream of molten lead filling your pelvis and rising slowly up your spine to seize your head and erase it. This remarkable effect might be due to the contact of the penetrating organ with the prostate, the poor man's clitoris, which, in the one penetrated, sits just against the rectum, whereas in the woman, if my notions of anatomy are correct, it's separated from it by a part of the reproductive apparatus, which would explain why women, in general, seem to have so little taste for sodomy, or else just as an intellectual pleasure. For men, it's different; and I've often told myself that the prostate and war are God's two gifts to man to compensate him for not being a woman.

Let us begin, since I tell you I am just like you!
Now I'll go inside my home, to greet the god of the hearth
who sent me off across the sea and today brings me back.

CLYTAEMNESTRA. Enter your home, but, my king,
don't place upon the common ground the foot
which stamped out Troy!
Let his path be covered all in red, so Truth
can lead him back into his home!

AGAMEMNON. Honour me as a man, not as a god.

CLYTAEMNESTRA. Don't say that just to flout what I've arranged.

AGAMEMNON. You should know I'll not go back on what I've said.

IMAGE 1.3 **Clytaemnestra (Małgorzata Hajewska-Krzysztofik) and Agamemnon (Maciej Stuhr)**
Directed by Krzysztof Warlikowski. Nowy Teatr, Warsaw (2009)
*Photograph by Stefan Okołowicz*

---

CLYTAEMNESTRA. You must fear something.
You've made some promise to the gods?

AGAMEMNON. I fully understand,
as well as any man, just what I'm doing.

CLYTAEMNESTRA. So do not be ashamed by what men say. The man whom people do not envy is not worth their envy.

AGAMEMNON. Do you want to fight?

CLYTAEMNESTRA. It's fitting that the happy conqueror
should let himself be overcome.

AGAMEMNON. And in this contest that's the sort of victory you value?

CLYTAEMNESTRA. You are the victor. Yield to me of your own consent.

**AGAMEMNON.** Well, if it's what you want . . .
Quick, someone get these sandals off. As I now walk on these red tapestries.

**CLYTAEMNESTRA.** Your return to your father's hearth and home
brings us the summer's heat in wintertime.

## SCENE III

**CLYTAEMNESTRA.** Before this moment I said many things
to suit my purposes. I'm not ashamed
to contradict them now. How else could I
act on my hate for a man,
who feigned his love, how else prepare my nets
of agony so high no one could jump them?
I've brooded on this struggle many years,
the old blood feud. My moment's come at last,
though long delayed. I stand now where I struck,
where I achieved what I set out to do.
I shall say now how. I won't deny the fact.
Round this man I cast my all-embracing net,
rich robes of evil—he had no way out, no chance to fight back.
I stabbed him twice. He gave out two groans.
Then as his limbs went limp, I hit again,
a third blow, my prayerful dedication
to Zeus, underground protector of the dead.
He collapsed, snorting his life away,
spitting great gobs of blood all over me,
drenching me in showers of his dark blood.
And I rejoiced—just as the fecund earth
rejoices when the heavens send Zeus spring rains.
That's how things stand,
Be joyful, if that's how you feel. For me,
this is my triumph.
You're testing me, as if I were some silly woman.
But my heart is fearless. Let me tell you

what you already know—then you can praise
or criticize me as you like. I don't care.
This man is Agamemnon, my husband.
He's a corpse, the work of this right hand,
a work of justice. That's how matters stand . . .
Do you hear?
Silence! Hush! Do you hear?
Here he lies the man who abused his wife!
So tormenting is this view that you're invoking death for yourself?
Are you saying this work is mine? That's not so.
A daemon: by his will does the man
pay in blood for two butchered children.
At my hands he collapsed in death.
I'll bury him. But you will not weep.
No. The daughter greets her father
happily by that swift stream of sorrow.
Then she'll embrace the man with love.

SCENE IV

**VOICE.** Hi.

**ALCESTIS/ADMETUS.** Hi.

**VOICE.** What's your name?

**ALCESTIS.** Alcestis.

**ADMETUS.** Admetus.

**VOICE.** What is to happen in May of this year?

**ALCESTIS.** A big bang.

**ADMETUS.** I will be reborn.

**VOICE.** What do you call each other when you're alone?

**ALCESTIS.** Honey-bunny.

**ADMETUS.** Sweetheart.

**VOICE.** Does he/she love you?

ALCESTIS. Madly.

ADMETUS. I hope so.

VOICE. What about you?

ADMETUS. Very much.

ALCESTIS. Yes.

VOICE. Think about him/her.

ADMETUS. I do all the time.

ALCESTIS. I have already.

VOICE. Your dream vacation?

ADMETUS. With her, on a desert island.

ALCESTIS. With a book, in a hammock, with him.

VOICE. Do you like your mother-in-law?

ADMETUS. She's dead.

ALCESTIS. She's okay.

VOICE. Do you like your father-in-law?

ALCESTIS. Yes, I do.

ADMETUS. He's dead.

VOICE. Do you like jellied carp?

ADMETUS. I do, but I prefer . . .

ALCESTIS. I prefer sushi.

ADMETUS. . . . pork in aspic.

VOICE. The three most important things in life?

ALCESTIS/ADMETUS. Love, friendship . . .

ADMETUS. Respect.

ALCESTIS. . . . a sense of security.

VOICE. What were you thinking on your first date?

ADMETUS. That she smells nice.

ALCESTIS. That he looks like some actor.

VOICE. Where did you first kiss?

ADMETUS. In my car.

ALCESTIS. In the car.

**VOICE.** Who made the first move?

**ADMETUS.** I did.

**ALCESTIS.** He did.

**VOICE.** What do you like most about him?

**ALCESTIS.** He's shy.

**ADMETUS.** She's wise.

**VOICE.** What do you like least about him?

**ALCESTIS.** His shyness.

**VOICE.** Which of you first said: "I love you"?

**ALCESTIS.** He did.

**ADMETUS.** I did.

**VOICE.** Rubens, or Picasso?
Paul Newman, or Robert Redford?
Catherine Deneuve, or Brigitte Bardot?
Do you believe in God?

**ADMETUS/ALCESTIS.** No.

**VOICE.** And in love?

**ALCESTIS/ADMETUS.** Yes.

**VOICE.** In plastic surgery?

**ALCESTIS.** Yes.

**VOICE.** In UFOs?

**ALCESTIS/ADMETUS.** No.

**VOICE.** In sharing the load?

**ALCESTIS/ADMETUS.** Yes.

**VOICE.** On a scale of 1 to 10, how much does the following mean to you:
Love?

**ALCESTIS/ADMETUS.** 10.

**VOICE.** Partnership?

**ALCESTIS/ADMETUS.** 9/7.

**VOICE.** Sex?

ALCESTIS/ADMETUS. 15/10.

VOICE. Bank account?

ALCESTIS/ADMETUS. 7/9.

VOICE. Sense of humor?

ALCESTIS/ADMETUS. 15/10.

VOICE. Principles?

ALCESTIS/ADMETUS. 10.

VOICE. What does marriage mean to you?

ALCESTIS. Beautiful responsibility.

ADMETUS. The government interfering with a relationship between two people.

VOICE. Three adjectives that best describe your partner?

ADMETUS. Smart . . .

ALCESTIS. Shy . . .

ADMETUS. . . . witty, beautiful.

ALCESTIS. . . . a bit chaotic, sweet.

VOICE. The most beautiful city in the world?

ADMETUS. London.

ALCESTIS. Paris.

VOICE. What are you ashamed of?

ALCESTIS. I can't say!

ADMETUS. Crooked legs.

VOICE. Criticize each other.

ALCESTIS. Not bold enough

ADMETUS. Uses too much cold cream.

VOICE. Now say "I love you" as if you were:
in a soap opera.

ADMETUS. Do I have to?

VOICE. In a Western,
in a porno movie.
Would you die for each other?

**ORESTES.** Sorry, I needed to freshen up a bit.
They sent me from the family counseling center.
I'm here to help you.
Do you believe in the next world?

**CLYTAEMNESTRA.** Do you?

**ORESTES.** I believe in my world, but I don't know if you could go there.

**CLYTAEMNESTRA.** But don't we all have the same heaven?

**ORESTES.** I don't know, I can only speak for myself. Did you ever have a dream or another experience indicating that a next world exists?

**CLYTAEMNESTRA.** No.

**ORESTES.** Then you have to live as if it didn't exist.
This was found on his person. Library property. It'll have to be returned.

**ORESTES.** "Dear Mom, regards from Venice. I love you and I miss you."
Jesus, I'm sorry. I'll be brief: your son, Orestes, is dead.

**CLYTAEMNESTRA.** H. C. Andersen. *The Mother*:

"Both fates are the will of God," said Death.

"Which is the unhappy flower, and which is the blessed one?" the mother said.

"That I may not tell you," said Death; "but thus far you may learn, that one of the two flowers represents your own child. It was the fate of your child that you saw—the future of your own child." Then the mother screamed aloud with terror.

"Which of them belongs to my child? Tell me that. Deliver the unhappy child. Release it from so much misery. Rather take it away. Take it to the kingdom of God. Forget my tears and my entreaties; forget all that I have said or done!"

"I do not understand you," said Death. "Will you have your child back? or shall I carry him away to a place that you do not know?"

Then the mother wrung her hands, fell on her knees, and prayed to God, "Grant not my prayers, when they are contrary to Thy will, which at all times must be the best. Oh, hear them not;" and her head sank on her bosom.

Then Death carried away her child to the unknown land.

Is that all?

**ORESTES.** May I not kill?

**CLYTAEMNESTRA.** I nursed you, and would spend my old age with you.

**ORESTES.** My mother cast me homeless from my father's house.

**CLYTAEMNESTRA.** Not cast thee out, but to a friendly home.

**ORESTES.** You sold me.

---

IMAGE 1.4 **Orestes (Maciej Stuhr) and Clytaemnestra (Małgorzata Hajewska-Krzysztofik)**
Directed by Krzysztof Warlikowski. Nowy Teatr, Warsaw (2009)
*Photograph by Stefan Okołowicz*

**CLYTAEMNESTRA.** Where then the price that I received for thee?

**ORESTES.** I'm ashamed to say it to your face.

**CLYTAEMNESTRA.** It is hard for wives to live as widows, child.

**ORESTES.** You killed my father.

**CLYTAEMNESTRA.** Not I alone. Fate bears the onus for me.

**ORESTES.** Yes, and fate has ordained you die today.

**CLYTAEMNESTRA.** So you would kill your mother, Son?

**ORESTES.** I kill thee not. Thyself dost kill thyself.
But she who plotted this accursed thing to slay her lord,
by whom she bare beneath her girdle once the burden of her babes—What deem ye of her?
Lodge no such mate with me!
Sooner may I
Live by high Heaven accursed, and childless die.
Did she the deed or not?
I conquered!
Most foul!
Hark ye and learn, friends, ere my reason goes!
I say that rightfully I slew my mother . . .

## SCENE VI

**APOLLO.** Dad! Father! You struck down my son, Asclepios, piercing his young heart with your famed bolt;
I owe you gratitude
For giving my child such a celebrated death.
Not everyone deserves such a death
I thanked your smiths for it
I quashed their miserable lives
And you cast me forth to bear the yoke
Of service to a mortal.
Here I am.
Working for Admetus.
I clean. I do the dishes. I do the laundry.

I'm up to my elbows in shit.
But I find the time to protect Admetus.
The best a god can protect a man.
I saved his life.
Admetus shall not die if he finds one who will die in his stead.
If he finds a saviour, he will live.
So he went searching.
He went to his nearest and dearest.
Asking.
Begging.
All of them.
Will you be my saviour?
Will you die for me?
Please . . .
First he went to his father
On his knees
Begging.
Then his mother
Silence.
Nothing.
Will you be my saviour?
Will you die for me?
It's hard to be someone's saviour.
He asked everyone
He begged.
All of them
They all refused
All but one
One
Silently said yes
Just that
Yes
His beloved wife said that
Alcestis
Truly you are a great god!
How unsearchable are your judgements.

Today is the day
The day ordained for Admetus to die
Alcestis is waiting obediently,
For her soul to slowly depart.
Today is also the end of my punishment
Farewell Alcestis
Farewell palace I have come to love
I shall miss you.
I'll miss your way of life,
the civilization that made me.
Glenn Gould playing the Goldberg Variations, Rimbaud's poetry . . .
I liked your movies a lot, especially Westerns.
I can't stand French New Wave cinema. Truffaut and all that.
John Wayne, now that was a character!
The world of gods is boring.
Apollo-fucking-Belvedere.
Right, I'm out of here.
Yet I won't bear the stench of death again
However celebrated.
I feel him, I see him coming
The joyful priest death, Thanatos
He's here already
Always on time
To attentively see to the execution
And bask in the applause.
Whatever . . .

SCENE VII

**THANATOS.** The door!
Apollo! Lord, what a surprise!
What are you doing here?
Are you scheming against fate again?
This is no place for conceited gods, who walk this world making life difficult for others.

Go away, it's easy to get your hands dirty where death does its hard, thankless job.

**APOLLO.** Don't overdo it, girlfriend.

**THANATOS.** Why the heavy artillery then?

**APOLLO.** Are you afraid of my bow? I like wearing it. It's a very handsome bow.

**THANATOS.** Are you threatening me? Have you grown so fond of Admetus that you would risk ridicule in order to postpone the misfortune about to strike your master?

**APOLLO.** My friends' misfortunes are my passion.

**THANATOS.** Do you intend to steal another body from me?

**APOLLO.** I never stole the first one.

**THANATOS.** Why then is Admetus still walking the Earth instead of joining his friends in the netherworld?

**APOLLO.** He struck a bargain. You will take his wife instead of him.

**THANATOS.** He struck a bargain and I will strike her.

**APOLLO.** What are you waiting for? Nobody is going to beg you for mercy, though you like listening to the whines of the dying and their families.

Well, I'm sorry. You're wasting your time.

**THANATOS.** A job well done is all I need to be happy.
The doomed will not escape her fate.
You can't stop death.

**APOLLO.** Stop—no. But postpone . . .

**THANATOS.** What do you want from me? I'm here because I was called. Besides I like my job. It's a good job,

As good as any other.

**APOLLO.** One body's all you're getting.

**THANATOS.** Younger bodies are more beautiful.

**APOLLO.** Old men arrange more lavish funerals.

**THANATOS.** Since when have you been serving rich old men?

**APOLLO.** Since when does death have a sense of humor?

**THANATOS.** Ever since old men have been bribing gods so they can die at an advanced age.

**APOLLO.** I'm asking you for the last time. Let her live a few short years longer.
Do it for me. Please.

**THANATOS.** Wait.
Baby, you know how terribly conscientious I am.
I'm only doing my duty.
You've known me for a long time.

**APOLLO.** I know the contempt gods and mortals feel for you.

**THANATOS.** Yes, that's regrettable. Unfortunately you can't have everything.
Guess it must be my fate.

**APOLLO.** Nobody knows their fate, not even you. Know then:
As we're talking, a man is heading for Admetus' house,
The man who will, with my blessing, take Alcestis from you,
In the name of the sincere repulsion I feel for you.

**THANATOS.** I'm trembling with fear at the sound of your prophecy.
Enough talk.
Let the ceremony begin.

## SCENE VIII

**DOCTOR.** Alcestis! You look lovely!
No thanks, I ate on the plane . . .

**ALCESTIS.** I couldn't sleep. I turned on the TV and there was a film about a man who has sex with dolphins. God! At first I couldn't believe it. And then I found myself being moved by that tale of a love fulfilled. The guy has a relationship with a she-dolphin, or a cow, I think they call them. He has sex with her. They meet in shallow water. He goes out to meet her at night in just his Speedos. He waits for her on the shore. Then a nose comes out of the water, sleek and wet. Sometimes they just cuddle, sometimes they have sex. Dolphins are very sexual beings, they like mating with each other and humans too. They have no inhibitions, they enjoy it. I never knew that.

When they cuddle, the she-dolphin turns her face toward him. Her belly turns pink when she is aroused. The man inserts his penis inside her, the she-dolphin draws him into her huge, muscled vagina, and starts moving back and forth. She's gentle and contented. They always climax at the same time. No one knows whether she does it on purpose or whether it's just a coincidence.

Afterwards they cuddle for a long time. Dolphins, even the males, need tenderness. In exchange they give you the big blue. They're passionate and faithful. It's all true, I looked it up online. Anal sex with dolphins is out of the question, it can even be lethal. Bad news for gays. Dolphins ejaculate with such force that it can tear you apart. The only option here is masturbation, although I don't know whether it can be mutual. But that's not so interesting. The dolphin's penis is very supple: it can wrap itself around things.

Why do we consider this passionate love to be abnormal? It's a lot more beautiful than the lukewarm emotional soup we sustain, or rather feed ourselves with. If there were a dolphin in my bed, a cool, slippery mammal, I think I'd finally feel warm.

Governments ignore calls to legalize sex with dolphins. That's not fair. I think all of us should sign a petition on the issue. Is there a foundation for mammal rights? Since there's an organisation dealing with human rights, we should defend the rights of dolphins, too. Especially as they're more intelligent than humans, that's for sure. And if they had rights they certainly wouldn't violate them. Maybe they'd start a civilization of their own, superior to ours, and we'd become their colony or mandate. I think that's what you call it.

**ADMETUS.** Alcestis, don't do this. Please.

Mom, Dad.

I take it all back, do you hear me?!

I don't need this.
I'll jump in front of a train if you want.
Don't move, Mother, or I'll fucking kill you.

MOTHER. Can you give her a shot?

DOCTOR. Can you fix me a drink?

MOTHER. So you want a drink?

DOCTOR. Yes.

MOTHER. Martini?

DOCTOR. It'll do.

MOTHER. Fix it yourself.
What about you, are you here on vacation?
Can you put an end to this?
This woman, she has to go.

ADMETUS. Stay out of this.

MOTHER. The things my son told me . . .

ADMETUS. What things?

MOTHER. That you're empty inside.

ADMETUS. Mom!

MOTHER. How you don't give him anything!

ADMETUS.Stop it!

MOTHER. Your children run around naked, dirty and hungry!

ADMETUS. I never said that.

MOTHER. That's what he told me, doctor! My son is a good boy. He never tells me anything.

ADMETUS. I've never said that.

MOTHER. This woman is sick! She's crazy!

ADMETUS. We're all suffering, Alcestis, all of us who loved you.

ALCESTIS. Do you love me?

MOTHER. She's crazy!

ADMETUS. Stay out of this.
I love you.

Would you go upstairs now?

MOTHER. I'm not going anywhere.

ADMETUS. Upstairs! Right now!
Dad, take her upstairs! Just look at yourself, look what you've done to me, look!
This is where you belong. I hate you!

ALCESTIS. I'm a good mother.

ADMETUS. Yes, you are a good mother.

ALCESTIS. I'm a good mother.

ADMETUS. You're a wonderful mother. You've made me happy. I made a mistake, I'm sorry.

ALCESTIS. Remember to look after the children.

ADMETUS. All right, my love.

ALCESTIS. Up in the morning. To bed at night. Sleep.

ADMETUS. All right, my love.

ALCESTIS. Can you see my feet in the mirror?

ADMETUS. Yes.

ALCESTIS. Do you like them?

ADMETUS. Very much.

ALCESTIS. Do you like my ankle?

ADMETUS. Very much.

ALCESTIS. Do you like my calves?

ADMETUS. Very much.

ALCESTIS. And my thighs?

ADMETUS. Very much.

ALCESTIS. Do you like my butt?

ADMETUS. Yes. Very much.

ALCESTIS. I can't hear you!
What about my knees?

ADMETUS. Yes. Very much.

ALCESTIS. Do you love my knees?

I can't hear you!
My face?

ADMETUS. Yes.

ALCESTIS. All of me? My lips? My eyes? My nose? My ears?

ADMETUS. Yes, all of you.

ALCESTIS. I can't hear you!
Do you love me completely?

ADMETUS. Yes, I love you completely, deeply and tragically.

ALCESTIS. I can't hear you . . . What are you saying?
Give me your hand, Admetus.

ADMETUS. Look, you have to look. Look.
I love you completely, deeply and tragically.

## SCENE IX

ADMETUS. The bathroom's out of order. What brings you here? Another of your labours?

HERCULES. I'm off to harness the mares of Diomedes that, bitless, feast on human flesh from mangers of carnage.

ADMETUS. Are you looking for death?

HERCULES. Well, it won't be my first meeting with that lady.

ADMETUS. And how are you managing?

HERCULES. Not bad. I've been worse.

How about you? How are you, man?

ADMETUS. I've been better.

HERCULES. Why is it so quiet here?

ADMETUS. We're having a funeral . . .

## SCENE X

ORESTES. Good evening! Welcome one, welcome all!
It's good to have you back here with us!
Welcome to our studio in the john, and that includes those of

you who didn't like my panties last night.

It's the usual lineup tonight: Mom and me. Mom's got pretty panties. I should know: I put them on myself.

We'll play you Mom's favorite song. It's called . . . well, Mom, what's it called? "Your Eyes."

And now for the second verse.

Look, Mom, we have a caller.

THE SHADE OF CLYTAEMNESTRA. No one will save you—not God,

Nor any law! You will learn what it means to be stripped of joy! You will die in misery, forgotten by everybody, a prey to demons, a shadow, a bloodless ghost!

Silence? No answer?

And yet you're mine—you were groomed for me, to become the offering!

A scapegoat—not slaughtered, yet still alive!

ORESTES. Say hello to our second caller, Mom.

ATHENA. Who are you?

ORESTES. Mother! It's God speaking.

THE SHADE OF CLYTAEMNESTRA. My anger is chasing a murderer!

ATHENA. Whither are you chasing him?

THE SHADE OF CLYTAEMNESTRA. The place where no human joy can be found.

ATHENA. Do you bay this man to such a flight?

THE SHADE OF CLYTAEMNESTRA. Yes, I do. He murdered his own mother!

ATHENA. For what reason?

ORESTES. Exactly: for what reason?

ATHENA. Perhaps someone's wrath scared him?

ORESTES. Perhaps someone's wrath scared me.

APOLLO. I made this man kill his own mother.

ATHENA. The plaintiff will speak first.

THE SHADE OF CLYTAEMNESTRA. Speak: have you killed your mother?

ORESTES. I have.

THE SHADE OF CLYTAEMNESTRA. And now, say how you killed her.

ORESTES. I stabbed her in the throat . . .

THE SHADE OF CLYTAEMNESTRA. And who talked you into it?

ORESTES. God.

THE SHADE OF CLYTAEMNESTRA. God told you to kill your mother?

ORESTES. My mother has stained herself with a double crime.

THE SHADE OF CLYTAEMNESTRA. What do you mean: "double"?

ORESTES. She killed her husband and my father.

THE SHADE OF CLYTAEMNESTRA. You're alive and she's killed—and free.

ORESTES. Why didn't anyone prosecute the guilty one when she was alive?

THE SHADE OF CLYTAEMNESTRA. She and her victim had not blood in common.

ORESTES. Am I the same blood as my mother?

THE SHADE OF CLYTAEMNESTRA. And what did I feed you in my womb, murderer?

Do you dare to disown your mother's precious blood?

APOLLO. A mother is merely the one who bears the child and stores the seed in her womb.

The parent is the one who plants the seed; she merely preserves the growing life, unless God injures it.

ORESTES. So must the fate have been fulfilled?

ATHENA. This man is free by the judgement of this court.

I've never had a mother that's why in everything but marriage the man is close to my heart; I belong to my father entirely.

Thus a woman's death who did her husband slay, the guardian of her home, cannot weigh more.

I wish Orestes free, even if the votes are equal.

ORESTES. Not guilty!

We're nearly through. And now for some good news. It's going to be a lovely day tomorrow: 30 degrees in Bangkok, 33 in Hong Kong, 44 in Caracas, Venezuela. Record temperatures in Mumbai and Reykjavik. Ground-frost possible in Africa. A low-pressure front from the Arctic will cause snow squalls and flurries. But the rest of the world will be balmy. A day to brighten your spirits.

She's lying by my side. Pretending to sleep.
Will something nice survive this devastation?
We've killed it all. Bright moths
Brushing both sides of the pane. Peace in the house.
All quiet for now.
She's made it clear she doesn't want me
Though I tried all the masculine wiles. She's here
By my side, on somebody's couch.
She lost. She won. I won. I lost.
She's lying there. I sat off a ways, dressed.
Watching and smoking. Looking.
Two glasses of tea tipped over and broken.
An ashtray with two long dog-ends.
When she opens her eyes, I will open fire.
What?

**HERCULES.** I'm breathing

**ORESTES.** What have you done? Do you remember? 9/16, 420 BCE, in Corinth.

**HERCULES.** Where am I?
I don't know this place.
Whose corpses are these?
Surely I am not come to Hades again.

**ORESTES.** What have you done? Do you remember?

**HERCULES.** Why do you weep? What sadness has befallen me?

**ORESTES.** Those are your children.

**HERCULES.** Who killed them?

**ORESTES.** You did.

**HERCULES.** My wife too?

**ORESTES.** Yes.

**HERCULES.** I want to die.

**ORESTES.** You think the gods take heed of your threats?

**HERCULES.** The deity, if he be really such, has no wants.
Children, it was your father who killed you!
It was I who killed you, wife!

**APOLLO.** But a man, if he so wants,
Need not have fear of God,
As long as he is helped by
The absence of God.

**ORESTES.** When she opens her eyes, I will open fire.

## SCENE XI

**HERCULES.** But none of your children, is it?

**ADMETUS.** No.

**HERCULES.** Your father?

**ADMETUS.** No.

**HERCULES.** You're not saying it's Alcestis . . .

**ADMETUS.** Do you think one can be alive, even though he's died?

**HERCULES.** Is that a riddle?

**ADMETUS.** You know what she's promised?

**HERCULES.** What?

**ADMETUS.** To sacrifice her life for me.
So how can she be alive if she has sacrificed her life for me?

**HERCULES.** You'll cry when she's really dead.

**ADMETUS.** He is dead who waits for death.

**HERCULES.** No my friend. Life and death are very different matters.

**ADMETUS.** You don't understand.

**HERCULES.** I will if you tell me whose funeral this is.

**ADMETUS.** I have to bury a woman.

**HERCULES.** A relative?

**ADMETUS.** Yes. No, a stranger . . .

**HERCULES.** A stranger who died in your house?
I'll leave you to it . . .

**ADMETUS.** Leave the dead to the dead and let the living look after the living.

**HERCULES.** Now you're talking.
Prayer achieves more than people ever dreamed.

**ADMETUS.** You don't have to come to the funeral.
Make yourself at home, take a shower, have a shave.
I'll be back soon

**HERCULES.** More things are achieved through prayer than people dream possible.

## SCENE XII

**FERES.** I sincerely feel for your loss, my son!
She was a sensible and decent wife.
It's a great loss but you have to face it like a man. She has taught both of us to love life again.

**ADMETUS.** How could you have allowed her to take your place?

**FERES.** Show me the law that says a father must die for his son.
There is no article you could invoke.
You have unleashed the hysteria that killed your wife.
What else will you do? Will you take another wife, and another, so you can live forever at someone else's cost?

**ADMETUS.** How long will I see fathers who want to live as long as their sons?

**FERES.** I would have died for you if I had two lives instead of one.

**ADMETUS.** I wonder whether you'll live to see the end of the world.

**FERES.** Go and find another idiot who'll die for you!
Don't interrupt me when I'm talking to my son!

**ADMETUS.** When are you going to finally die, Dad?

**FERES.** I know how to enjoy every single day, even one like today.

**ADMETUS.** God, you're so old. Death would serve you well.

**FERES.** At least you will be able to spit on my grave.

**ADMETUS.** True. I wouldn't count on an eulogy if I were you.

**FERES.** You can even dance on my grave.

**ADMETUS.** So I will!

**ALCESTIS.** It's, it's today. Not tomorrow, not on Monday. Today I die for you.
There's nothing I can do. I no longer belong to you. Don't you see?
I could have refused. I haven't given a thought to myself ever since I met you.
But I didn't want to live any longer. Nor sleep in this bed.
You can't imagine how many dreams I had. How much more may have been in store for me.

IMAGE 1.5 **Feres (Zygmunt Malanowicz) and, on the screen, Grandson (Tomasz Tyndyk)**
Directed by Krzysztof Warlikowski. Nowy Teatr, Warsaw (2009)
*Photograph by Stefan Okołowicz*

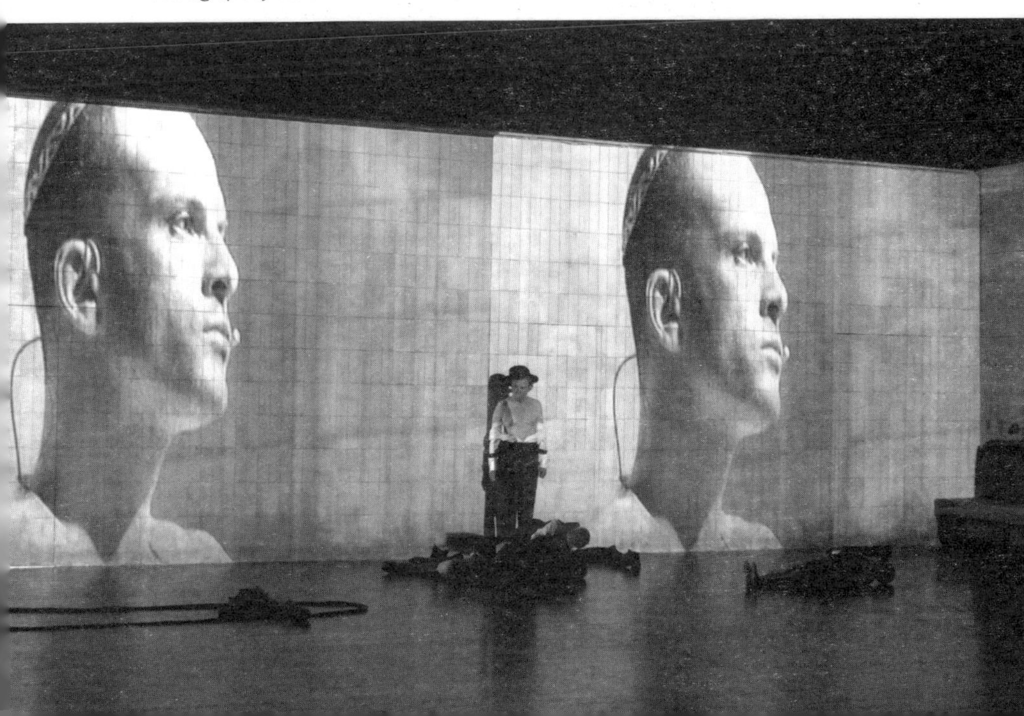

IMAGE 1.6 **Admetus (Jacek Poniedziałek), Alcestis (Magdalena Cielecka), and Hercules (Andrzej Chyra)**
Directed by Krzysztof Warlikowski. Nowy Teatr, Warsaw (2009)
*Photograph by Stefan Okołowicz*

I could have refused. Married whomever I wanted, and lived.
But no. Hades awaits. I no longer belong to you.
Don't you understand?
There's nothing I can do. I belong to another now.
Your parents have forsaken you,
even though they will be dead soon.
I will make a widower of you.
As for me . . . Enough

**HERCULES.** Pray, for Hercules has another task to do before leaving this house.
I'll find you, Death, I'll recognize you by your black robe and the fresh blood on your lips.

I'll grab you and squeeze you and force to make an arrangement: either you'll give back Alcestis,
Or I'll break your neck and rip your back in half.
Alcestis will come back here sooner than you think . . .

SCENE XIII

**ADMETUS.** I am standing here before you. Look at me. Are you looking? With contempt, right? Contempt and disgust. And superiority.

You would not have agreed to such a sacrifice.
Someone sacrificing their life. Never.
You'd rather die. Would someone here prefer to die? You, sir? Madam? You wouldn't, sir?
So that makes two of us: that's a relief.
Because all the rest love the life of others more than their own.
We love our own life. And that's a sin!
Some Jew once said it was a sin to survive if you took a slice of bread away from someone.
A slice of bread! What if you took someone's life away?
Excuse me for wanting to live.
But I'm not asking for your pity, I'm not asking you for anything.
You can stick your pity up your righteous asses!
Why am I even saying all this?

Words are of no use either, they disappear like water in the sand, this wet sand that fills my mouth. I can feel the sand, so I'm alive. I'm alive.

**HERCULES.** Do me a favour, man!
I have this lady here with me—and I'd like you to look after her until I return,
Until I steal those stupid horses.
How did I get her? In a fight, like all the others!
I went to this gig,
It was a competition actually, you know, the place was packed,
First prize was supposed to be a horse but it turned out they

only had a herd of cows for the strongest;
boxing and wrestling, you know.
The lady was the audience prize,
So I decided to try my luck and won!
Keep an eye on this woman, will you?
I worked hard to get her
I went through hell.

**ADMETUS.** I shall get the most highly paid sculptor to carve her statue. I'll put it in my bed, so I can lie with it every night whispering her name. Pretending I'm with her, though I'm not.

**HERCULES.** Do you think you know what sorrow is?
Do you think you know what despair is?

**ADMETUS.** I wish you'd never won that fight!

**HERCULES.** You'd rather have me dead?

**ADMETUS.** No, but take her away, please . . .

**HERCULES.** Don't be a coward.

**ADMETUS.** God, woman, you look just like her.

**HERCULES.** So take her!

**ADMETUS.** I can't touch her.

**HERCULES.** As you wish. I won't force you.

**ADMETUS.** Wait.

**HERCULES.** Pray that the gods don't burst with envy!

**ADMETUS.** Wait, don't leave me alone! Not now!
Is that you? Is that you, my love?
Why won't you say anything?

**OFFICER.** Who hid the Jews?

**APOLONIA.** I did.

**ADMETUS.** Yes. It was you.

## SCENE XIV

**OFFICER.** We know that. Who else?

**APOLONIA.** Nobody. I did it alone.

**ADMETUS.** I'm going to sleep. Are you coming? I'll make the bed.

**OFFICER.** Perhaps you will tell us?

**APOLONIA.** I assure you . . .

**OFFICER.** I'm asking him! Well?

**APOLONIA.** I've told you. No one else knew.
No one!

**OFFICER.** You didn't know anything either, did you?
Only the person who hid the Jews is going to be punished.
If it was you—your daughter will live.
If it was your daughter—you will live.
All you need to do is say: I hid them, my daughter didn't know about anything.
Well . . .?

## PART TWO

### SCENE I

**ELIZABETH COSTELLO.** Good evening, ladies and gentlemen. It is two years since I last spoke in the United States. In the lecture I then gave, I had reason to refer to the great fabulist Franz Kafka, and in particular to his story "Report to an Academy", about an educated ape, Red Peter, who stands before the members of a learned society telling the story of his life—of his ascent from beast to something approaching man. On that occasion I felt a little like Red Peter myself and said so. Today that feeling is even stronger, for reasons that I hope will become clearer to you.

Lectures often begin with lighthearted remarks whose purpose is to set the audience at ease. The comparison I have just drawn between myself and Kafka's ape might be taken as such a lighthearted remark, meant to set you at ease, meant to say I am just an ordinary person, neither a god nor a beast. Even those among you who read Kafka's story of the ape who performs before human beings as an allegory of Kafka the Jew performing for Gentiles may nevertheless—in view of the fact that I am not a Jew—have found the comparison to be ironic.

I want to say at the outset that that was not how my remark—the remark that I feel like Red Peter—was intended. I did not intend it ironically. It means what it says. I say what I mean. I do not have the time any longer to say things I do not mean.

In addressing you on the subject of animals, I will pay you the honour of skipping a recital of the horrors of their lives and deaths. Though I have no reason to believe that you have at the forefront of your minds what is being done to animals at this moment in production facilities (I hesitate to call them farms any longer), in abattoirs, in trawlers, in laboratories, all over the world, I will take it that you concede me the rhetorical power to evoke these horrors and bring them home to you with adequate force, and leave it at that, reminding you only that the horrors I here omit are nevertheless at the centre of this lecture.

Between 1942 and 1945 several million people were put to death in the concentration camps of the Third Reich: at Treblinka alone more than a million and a half, perhaps as many as three million. These are numbers that numb the mind. We have only one death of our own; we can comprehend the deaths of others only one at a time. In the abstract we may be able to count to a million, but we cannot count to a million deaths.

The people who lived in the countryside around Treblinka—Poles, for the most part—said that they did not know what was going on in the camp; said that, while in a general way they might have guessed what was going on, they did not know for sure; said that, while in a sense they might have known, in another sense they did not know, could not afford to know, for their own sake.

It is not because they waged an expansionist war, and lost it, that Germans of a particular generation are still regarded as standing a little outside humanity, as having to do or be something special before they can be readmitted to the human fold. They lost their humanity, in our eyes, because of a certain willed ignorance on their part. Under the circumstances of Hitler's kind of war, ignorance may have been a useful survival mechanism, but that is an excuse which, with admirable moral rigour, we refuse to accept. In Germany, we say, a certain line was crossed which took people beyond the ordinary murderousness and cruelty of warfare into a state that we can only call sin. The signing of the articles of capitulation and the payment of reparations did not put an end to that state of sin. On the contrary, we said, a sickness of the soul continued to mark that generation. It marked those citizens of the Reich who had committed evil actions, but also those who, for whatever reason, were in ignorance of those actions. It thus marked, for practical purposes, every citizen of the Reich. Only those in the camps were innocent.

"They went like sheep to the slaughter." "They died like animals." "The Nazi butchers killed them." Denunciation of the camps reverberates so fully with the language of the stockyard and slaughterhouse that it is barely necessary for me to prepare the ground for the comparison I am about to make. The crime of the Third Reich, says the voice of accusation, was to treat people like animals.

We—even we in Australia—belong to a civilisation deeply rooted in Greek and Judaeo-Christian religious thought. We may not, all of us, believe in pollution, we may not believe in sin, but we do believe in their psychic correlates. We accept without question that the psyche (or soul) touched with guilty knowledge cannot be well. We do not accept that people with crimes on their conscience can be healthy and happy.

We look (or used to look) askance at Germans of a certain generation because they are, in a sense, polluted; in the very signs of their normality (their healthy appetites, their hearty laughter) we see proof of how deeply seated pollution is in them.

It was and is inconceivable that people who did not know (in that special sense) about the camps can be fully human.

I was taken on a drive around Berlin this morning. It seems a pleasant enough town. I saw no horrors, no drug-testing laboratories, no factory farms, no abattoirs. Yet I am sure they are here. They are all around us as I speak, only we do not, in a certain sense, know about them.

Let me say it openly: we are surrounded by an enterprise of degradation, cruelty and killing which rivals anything that the Third Reich was capable of, indeed dwarfs it, in that ours is an enterprise without end, self-regenerating, bringing rabbits, rats, poultry, livestock ceaselessly into the world for the purpose of killing them.

And to split hairs, to claim that there is no comparison, that Treblinka was so to speak a metaphysical enterprise dedicated to nothing but death and annihilation while the meat industry is ultimately devoted to life (once its victims are dead, after all, it does not burn them to ash or bury them but on the contrary cuts them up and refrigerates and packs them so that they can be consumed in the comfort of our homes) is as little consolation to those victims as it would have been—pardon the tastelessness of the following - to ask the dead of Treblinka to excuse their killers because their body fat was needed to make soap and their hair to stuff mattresses with.

Pardon me, I repeat. That is the last cheap point I will be scoring. I know how talk of this kind polarises people, and cheap point-scoring only makes it worse. I want to find a way of speaking to fellow human beings that will be cool rather than heated, philosophical rather than polemical, that will bring enlightenment rather than seeking to divide us into the righteous and the sinners, the saved and the damned, the sheep and the goats.

Now that I am here, says Red Peter, in my tuxedo and bow tie and my black pants with a hole cut in the seat for my tail to poke through (I keep it turned away from you, you do not see it), now that I am here, what is there for me to do? Do I in fact have a choice? If I do not subject my discourse to reason, whatever that is, what is left for me but to gibber and emote and generally make a monkey of myself?

Red Peter was not an investigator of primate behaviour but a branded, marked, wounded animal presenting himself as speaking testimony to a gathering of scholars. I am not a philosopher of mind but an animal exhibiting, yet not exhibiting, to a gathering of scholars, a wound, which I cover up under my clothes but touch on in every word I speak.

In 1912 the Prussian Academy of Sciences established on the island of Tenerife a station devoted to experimentation into the mental capacities of apes, particularly chimpanzees.

Let me recount to you some of what the apes on Tenerife learned from their master Wolfgang Köhler, in particular Sultan, the best of his pupils, in a certain sense the prototype of Red Peter.

Sultan is alone in his pen. He is hungry: the food that used to arrive regularly has unaccountably ceased coming.

The man who used to feed him and has now stopped feeding him stretches a wire over the pen three metres above ground level, and hangs a bunch of bananas from it. Into the pen he drags three wooden crates. Then he disappears, closing the gate behind him, though he is still somewhere in the vicinity, since one can smell him.

Sultan knows: Now one is supposed to think. That is what the bananas up there are about. The bananas are there to make one think, to spur one to the limits of one's thinking. But what must one think? One thinks: Why is he starving me? One thinks: What have I done? Why has he stopped liking me? One thinks: Why does he not want these crates any more? But none of these is the right thought. Even a more complicated thought—for instance: What is wrong with him, what misconception does he have of me, that leads him to believe it is easier for me to reach a banana hanging from a wire than to pick up a banana from the floor?—is wrong. The right thought to think is: How does one use the crates to reach the bananas?

Sultan drags the crates under the bananas, piles them one on top of the other, climbs the tower he has built, and pulls down the bananas. He thinks: Now will he stop punishing me?

The answer is: No. The next day the man hangs a fresh bunch of bananas from the wire but also fills the crates with stones so that they are too heavy to be dragged. As long as Sultan continues to think wrong thoughts, he is starved. The pangs of hunger are so intense, so overriding, that he is forced to think the right thought, namely, how to go about getting the bananas.

The man drops a bunch of bananas a metre outside the wire pen. Into the pen he tosses a stick. The wrong thought is: Why has he stopped hanging the bananas on the wire? The wrong thought (the right wrong thought, however) is: How does one use the three crates to reach the bananas? The right thought is: How does one use the stick to reach the bananas?

At every turn Sultan is driven to think the less interesting thought. From the purity of speculation (Why do men behave like this?) he is relentlessly propelled toward lower, practical, instrumental reason (How does one use this to get that?) and thus towards acceptance of himself as primarily an organism with an appetite that needs to be satisfied. Although his entire history, from the time his mother was shot and he was captured, through his voyage in a cage to imprisonment on this island prison camp and the sadistic games that are played around food here, leads him to ask questions about the justice of the universe and the place of this penal colony in it, a carefully plotted psychological regimen conducts him *away* from ethics and metaphysics towards the humbler reaches of practical reason. And somehow, as he inches through this labyrinth of constraint, manipulation and duplicity, he must realise that on no account dare he give up, for on his shoulders rests the responsibility of representing apedom. The fate of his brothers and sisters may be determined by how well he performs.

In his deepest being Sultan is not interested in the banana problem. Only the experimenter's single-minded regimentation forces him to concentrate on it. The question that truly occupies him, as it occupies the rat and the cat and every other animal trapped in the hell of the laboratory or the zoo, is: Where is home, and how do I get there?

Measure the distance back from Kafka's ape, with his bow tie and dinner jacket and wad of lecture notes, to that sad train of captives trailing around the compound in Tenerife. How far Red Peter has traveled! Yet we are entitled to ask: In return for the prodigious overdevelopment of the intellect he has achieved, in return for his command of lecture-hall etiquette and academic rhetoric, what has he had to give up? The answer is: Much, including progeny, succession. If Red Peter had any sense, he would not have any children. For upon the desperate, half-mad female ape with whom his captors, in Kafka's story, try to mate him, he would father only a monster. It is as hard to imagine the child of Red Peter as to imagine the child of Franz Kafka himself. Hybrids are, or ought to be, sterile; and Kafka saw both himself and Red Peter as hybrids, as monstrous thinking devices mounted inexplicably on suffering animal bodies. The stare that we meet in all the surviving photographs of Kafka is a stare of pure surprise: surprise, astonishment, alarm. Of all men Kafka is the most insecure in his humanity. This, he seems to say: this is the image of God?

I return to the death camps. The particular horror of the camps, the horror that convinces us that what went on there was a crime against humanity, is not that despite a humanity shared with their victims, the killers treated them like lice. That is too abstract. The horror is that the killers refused to think themselves into the place of their victims, as did everyone else. They said, "It is *they* in those cattle cars rattling past." They did not say, "How would it be if it were I in that cattle car?"

They did not say, "It is I who am in that cattle car." They said, "It must be the dead who are being burned today, making the air stink and falling in ash on my cabbages." They did not say, "How would it be if I were burning?" They did not say, "I am burning, I am falling in ash."

In other words, they closed their hearts. The heart is the seat of a faculty, s y m p a t h y , that allows us to share at times the being of another. Sympathy has everything to do with the subject and little to do with the object, the "another", as we see at once when we think of the object not as a bat ("Can I share the being of a bat?") but as another human being. There are people who have the capacity to imagine themselves as someone else, there are people who have no such capacity (when the lack is extreme, we call them psychopaths), and there are people who have the capacity but choose not to exercise it.

I return one last time to the places of death all around us, the places of slaughter to which, in a huge communal effort, we close our hearts. Each day a fresh holocaust, yet, as far as I can see, our moral being is untouched. We do not feel tainted. We point to the Germans and Poles and Ukrainians who did and did not know of the atrocities around them. We like to think they woke up haggard in the mornings and died of gnawing cancers. But probably it was not so. The evidence points in the opposite direction: that we can do anything and get away with it; that there is no punishment.

**HERCULES.** Look, ma'am. Man is made in the likeness of God but God does not have the likeness of man. If Jews were treated like cattle, it does not follow that cattle are treated like Jews.

SCENE II

**HERCULES.** And now, the impossible will finally happen.
Things beyond imagining.
Magic.

But when you practice magic there are many things you cannot explain.
There are ancient fossils of amphibians and fossils of birds.
But there is no paleontological evidence for the existence of an intermediary species.
This implies a quantum leap of the imagination.
Amphibians wanted to take flight, and birds appeared as the outcome of that intent.
And what came between the two? Nothing!
The lack of a missing link in the process of evolution is ultimately reassuring. It gives hope that another quantum leap of the imagination will soon take place, one made by ourselves.
Even if you don't want it to!

SCENE III

**JUSTICE.** "Whosoever saves a single life, saves an entire world," it is written in the Talmud. We engraved those words on a medal. We bestow the medal upon Apolonia Machczyńska, who has saved a single life.

And did she save an entire world? Can this world still be saved?

**OFFICER.** Perhaps you can tell us.

**SŁAWEK.** We buried Mom in January.
And Grandpa in the Spring. He wasn't sick: He stopped talking and eating.
Our mom's dog, Fifrek, stopped eating after Mom died, and died two weeks later.
The other Spitz in the family was called Dryf.
My brother and Dryf went for a walk and the dog ran away.
My brother was looking for him.
He saw this abandoned well, somebody had stolen the top cover.
My brother leaned over . . .
Our neighbours pulled out both the corpses.
Father was in the Resistance and only came to the funerals.
He got married right after the war.

**RYFKA.** It's a pity I didn't think of inviting you to Tel Aviv.

**SŁAWEK.** What for?

**RYFKA.** I'd have shown you my cafe on Ben Yehuda.
Fifteen tables inside, eight outside, you could have had a Viennese cake, the clientele were classy.
Only German Jews. They liked two things: Viennese cake and intelligent conversation.
One of them had a friend . . .

**GRANDSON.** Franz Kafka.

**RYFKA.** That's right, Chaim: Kafka. He gave him a suitcase full of papers before he died and asked him to destroy it, preferably on the day of his funeral.

But Herr Doktor Max Brod didn't burn it and wasn't sure whether to be happy or feel stings of remorse.

I cut in. I said: if somebody wants to destroy his papers, he ought to do it by himself, like the tzadik, Mendel from Kotzk . . .

The tzadik was always writing down his thoughts, but he didn't want people to read them, so every year he would destroy his notes.

What tzadik? What Kotzk?
Oh, Frau Ryfka comes from there . . .

I was an Easterner to them: I was Ost-Judin, not one of them with their highbrow German culture. So I never cut in again . . . Just: would you like yours with poppy-seed or nuts, Herr Doktor?

**JUSTICE.** Did you write the letter?

**RYFKA.** No.

**GRANDSON.** I did. I drove her around, I took notes, I wrote to Yad Vashem. I have no idea what went on back then, but it's thanks to people like you that we survived. I'm alive thanks to your mother.

**RYFKA.** This is Chaim. My eyes have gone bad after the stroke. I don't really see much—only darkness and light.

But I still have my memory.
I told him and he wrote it down.
Tell the man who you are. He's a lawyer.
Excuse me, can I touch your face?
I'm so happy I lived to see the day when I can give you a kiss.
How was I supposed to send you oranges?

JUDGE. I am a Supreme Court justice of the State of Israel, we need to make sure that the events described in this letter really took place.

RYFKA. Your honour doesn't believe me?

JUDGE. I'm just going to ask you a few questions.
How did you know Apolonia?

RYFKA. My father knew her.

JUDGE. And he asked her . . .

RYFKA. No. She came on her own. She said: You don't look like a Jew at all, child. Because my sisters—Sara, Lea, Bluma, Chava and Cesia—they did, they looked Jewish.

She said: You shouldn't die, looking the way you do. And she gave me a baptism certificate. And an address in Warsaw—18, Chłopickiego Street.

JUDGE. What did that mean—"you shouldn't die"?

RYFKA. I had blue eyes, a short nose—that's what she meant. She didn't want to waste this great, Aryan face! Do you understand now?

JUDGE. And with the baptism certificate you went . . .

RYFKA. First I asked my father: Father, should I go?
Gey, Ryfke, du vest in fayer nisht verbrentvern.

GRANDSON. What does that mean?

RYFKA. Go, Ryfka, you can't die in the fire.
And I always obeyed Daddy.

JUDGE. Did she say how much it would cost?

RYFKA. Daddy asked. She said she hadn't come to talk about money.

JUDGE. And she didn't want anything in return?

RYFKA. From a Jewish carpenter in 1942? What could she possibly want?

JUDGE. This is very important, Mrs. Goldfinger. The Righteous don't want anything . . . They shouldn't want anything in return. That's why they are righteous . . .

So you went to Warsaw with your baptism certificate?

RYFKA. In this nice fur collar. It was winter and I sewed it on my coat.

GRANDSON. You don't have to go into details.

RYFKA. I do. The fur collar was important. Jews didn't have fur coats anymore, so I looked even more Catholic.

GRANDSON. Catholic, right.

JUDGE. Was it Apolonia's collar?

RYFKA. No. This German gave it to me. Apolonia's acquaintance. He liked her. He liked her a lot. And then he organized a cart.

JUDGE. Where did the German get this fur collar?

RYFKA. How should I know?

JUDGE. Maybe he took it from another Jewish girl?

RYFKA. What? You think so? You know, it could have been a Jewish collar. It smelled nice. I thought: this woman had nice perfume . . .

So I shouldn't have worn it then?

JUDGE. Where did he get the cart?

RYFKA. Our neighbour didn't want to take me to the train but the German took out his gun and he did. This German really liked . . .

GRANDSON. You've said that already.

RYFKA. So what? It was important that he liked her. That's why she took those other Jews in. She thought that if it came to the worst, the German would save them.

JUDGE. What other Jews?

RYFKA. Jews from Kotzk.

GRANDSON. But he didn't save them . . .

**JUDGE.** We're only concerned with saved Jewish witnesses.

**RYFKA.** You'll have to manage without witnesses then.

**JUDGE.** So you left wearing the fur collar . . .

**RYFKA.** I got on a tram. In Warsaw. I bought a ticket. The conductor smiled and said: A Jew-girl always looks Jewish, no matter what she's wearing.

**GRANDSON.** A Jew-girl, he said.

**RYFKA.** Then he asked: Is the Jew-girl hungry? I can give you a sandwich.
I thanked him and asked how to get to Chłopickiego.

**GRANDSON.** "All human beings are born free and equal in dignity and rights."
Universal Declaration of Human Rights, Article 1.
Right?

**JUDGE.** Right. And what about Apolonia's death?

**RYFKA.** A telegram came, saying, "Pola is dead."

My landlords got scared and asked me to leave. I took my papers and volunteered for public works. I went to Germany. I survived the war. Without my parents. Without sisters.

**JUDGE.** Didn't Apolonia want to help them?

**RYFKA.** Apolonia was gone.
They hid under the floor of our woodworking shop: Sara, Lea . . . Bluma, Chava and Chava's baby . . .
And the baby began to cry.
Shame to smother her.
She was six, maybe eight months old . . .

**GRANDSON.** Smother?

**RYFKA.** What do you mean: smother?

**GRANDSON.** You just said they smothered . . .

**RYFKA.** I did? They took her out. Into the street.

**GRANDSON.** They smothered her!

**RYFKA.** She was crying!
They could have been killed!

They had to sacrifice . . .
Will you always need an explanation for everything?

**GRANDSON.** Yes.

**JUDGE.** And so they took her out.

**GRANDSON.** They smothered her.

**RYFKA.** Daddy felt sorry his granddaughter was lying there all alone, so he sat down beside her.

A German was passing by. He began to search and found all of them—Sara, Lea, Bluma, Chava . . .

**GRANDSON.** See? They didn't have to . . .

**RYFKA.** But they would have been killed!

**GRANDSON.** They were anyway.

**JUDGE.** You can explain it to your grandson later.

He is an educated man, he'll understand.

**RYFKA.** They should have known that if someone finds a baby, he'll look for the adults, but they weren't able to think straight anymore.

And perhaps they were able, but felt sorry about the little one . . .

**JUDGE.** Is that all?

**RYFKA.** All, Your Honour?
Only God knows all.
And maybe our tzadik from Kotzk.

## SCENE IV

**JUDGE.** "Whosoever saves a single life, saves an entire world," it is written in the Talmud. We engraved those words on a medal. We bestow the medal upon Apolonia Machczyńska, who has saved a single life.

We thank the Survivor, Ryfka Goldberg, for joining us today.

The Righteous Among Nations medal is presented to Apolonia's son, Mr. Sławomir Świątek.

Let's welcome him on the stage.

**SŁAWEK.** On behalf of my mother, Apolonia Machczyńska, I'd like to thank you for this honor. I'll read a poem by the late Jewish composer, Andrzej Czajkowski. I dedicate it to my mother.

Mother, where are you?
Why aren't you here?
Exactly, why?
Should I tell you why?
You liked Albert more, didn't you?
You called him a pig, I remember.
But you preferred dying with him to living with me.
I needed you.
I had the same right to die as you did.
You deprived yourself of life and you deprived me of a place next to you wherever you went.
And, like a whore, you deceived me, remember?
You said: "Mom will be back in a few days."
I knew right away that you were lying.
I saw right through you.
You know it's true so don't be so damn angelic..
You're probably a bar of soap by now.
Darling stop, please.
You really shouldn't miss me so much.
It hurts you and doesn't help me either.
Miss you! I haven't thought about you since that day,
That day you didn't have enough courage to say goodbye.
Miss you?
You stupid, sentimental cunt.
You probably went through a lot of trouble to make that pig, Albert, not miss you.
They let him into Treblinka, I wasn't.
How was your honeymoon?
It had to be a pretty picture, when you were dying holding each other in your arms.
And what do you know about Treblinka?
Men and women died in separate gas chambers.
Do you feel a bit better now?

Mother, is it true that sometimes the gas didn't flow right and people were dying for a few days?
You were not among those, were you?
I am sorry for everything I said, just tell me that.
Thank you on behalf of my mother . . .

**JUDGE.** Whose poem did you say that was?

**SŁAWEK.** I told you: a dead Jewish composer named Andrzej Czajkowski. His mother chose to die rather than live with her son. He was eleven when he wrote that poem.

We were the same age . . .

**JUDGE.** And? Is he a dybbuk inside you?

**SŁAWEK.** What do you mean?

**JUDGE.** The souls of the departed can inhabit our persons.

**SŁAWEK.** I'm not familiar with your superstitions.

**RYFKA.** Our superstitions have helped us survive for 5,000 years.

**SŁAWEK.** You survived thanks to people like my mother. Do you understand?

**RYFKA.** I do.

**SŁAWEK.** Thanks to people like my mother!

Thank you . . . on behalf of my mother who died because she wanted more . . . No, not the world . . . She wanted to save twenty-five Jews.

**JUDGE.** And the Survivor is one of them.

**SŁAWEK.** No, they all died.

**JUDGE.** Twenty-five? Did you see them?

**SŁAWEK.** Yes. They were sitting in the barn. My ball fell inside and I saw these strange people through a crack in the floor.

**RYFKA.** I knew them. They weren't strange at all.

**GRANDSON.** Maybe you're the one who's strange.

**SŁAWEK.** They were sitting on the ground and they were nodding: back and forth, back and forth.
Mom said we shouldn't be scared, that they were our guests.
What guests? They were Jews.

**RYFKA.** There were two Zakaliks, Chava and Froim, Esther Hinda.

**SŁAWEK.** One more thing.

I shouldn't be here. I'm a stand-in. There was my older brother. There was my mom's dad. They would be receiving this medal. If they were alive.

But I'm left alone . . . So here I am.

**JUDGE.** Did they die with Apolonia?

**SŁAWEK.** No. My brother was saving a dog. You could say he was saving a life too, only it was a dog's life.
And Grandpa didn't save anybody's life. Except his own.
Doesn't a man have a right to save his own life?

**RYFKA.** Exactly.

**SŁAWEK.** I'm asking whether a man should save his own life?

**JUDGE.** Why did your mother do it?

**SŁAWEK.** I don't know why.

**RYFKA.** Perhaps she thought that this German.
That he would save them, if worst came to worst.

**SŁAWEK.** Why do you keep going on about that German? Well?

**RYFKA.** He was a human being. A German, but a human being.

**SŁAWEK.** She risked her life though she had us . . .

**RYFKA.** Do you bear a grudge against her?

**SŁAWEK.** Not anymore. I've forgiven her.

**RYFKA.** My mother is gone too.

**SŁAWEK.** My mother had a choice.

**RYFKA.** Do you want me to apologise?
For having survived?

**SŁAWEK.** Go ahead and apologise if that's what you want. Go ahead.

**JUDGE.** Excuse me. How did the Germans know that your mother was hiding those people? Who denounced her?

**SŁAWEK.** A Jewish woman.

**RYFKA.** She didn't denounce her. She told them.

SŁAWEK. She denounced them all right. It was a Sunday. People were coming out of the church. There was smoke coming out of an abandoned shanty.

Children looked inside and shouted: A Jew, come and see!

The woman came out with a girl and a boy. They were all soiled with soot.

The Jew began to wash her hands and face in the snow and then she washed the children. And the people who came out of the church were watching.

RYFKA. It was quite a sight. A Jewish woman washing her children in the snow, in the middle of the day!

SŁAWEK. Then the Germans came. They promised to spare her life if she told them where the other Jews were hidden.

She did . . .

JUDGE. How did your mother die?

SŁAWEK. On a Sunday.

There was snow everywhere.
Our guests were running across that snow. The Germans had a machine gun,
Only one of them made it to the woods.
The other Jews were left in the field . . .

RYFKA. Hersh Goldfarb . . . Handelsman . . . Little Gucia . . .

There were gunshots and dead bodies all around, and she was sitting calmly and only lifted her arms as if trying to protect herself from the noise. A German took aim at the back of her head.

She kept on sitting and only her hair flew up from the blast—like whoosh. They were lying around her, she sat there, she curled up even more and that hair, whoosh . . . Why? I don't know.

JUDGE. How did Apolonia die?

SŁAWEK. She knocked at her neighbours' doors. Nobody let her in. We went to Grandpa's.

She said the Germans would be there soon, and she took off her dress and put on the nightgown. She went to bed. She didn't try to hide. I don't know why.

My brother and I were throwing snowballs.

The Germans came. They had some man attached to their sleigh with a rope.

Probably a Jew. He was dead.

Then there was the interrogation.

Mom put her coat on.

She didn't fix her hair.

She had golden-red, curly hair.

**RYFKA.** Very pretty.

**SŁAWEK.** She didn't tie her shoes. The laces trailed behind her on the floor, and in the snow later.

The Germans cut off the rope with the man.

They ordered Mom to get on the sleigh.

Grandpa helped her to climb because she was pregnant and she hardly managed.

They took her to the next village.

They put her against a barn . . .

My brother and I went back home.

Our guests were lying in the field.

**RYFKA.** They were naked because people had taken off their clothes and shoes.

Boys from the neighbourhood came and began to put those bodies together—two or three of them. Those bodies were in various positions, depending how they fell.

They stood there like some sculptures. Rigid, naked, white sculptures in the white snow. Why—I don't know.

**SŁAWEK.** An officer ordered one of the Germans to shoot.

**RYFKA.** The one who loved her a lot.

**SŁAWEK.** The one who loved her a lot.

The German lifted his gun.

He said, Ich kann nicht.

He lifted it again.
And lowered it again.
The officer put a gun to his head: Now can you do it?

GRANDSON. Do you have a photo of your mother? I can't picture her. You don't get people like her. I keep seeing one face. She was lying there, wheezing, she kept looking at me, her pretty mouth was quivering. That gaze pierced through me. It slashed my gut. Sawdust trickled out of me. I was a puppet. I didn't feel a thing. I wanted to wipe the sweat and blood from her brow. To tell her that everything would be all right. Instead, I put a bullet through her head. It was all the same in the end. For her at least. I didn't kill her. I saw her picture in the paper. I live in Israel. I'm a soldier and I'll do it if I have to. I will kill.

## EPILOGUE

ELIZABETH COSTELLO. I was born in the city of Melbourne, but spent part of my childhood in rural Victoria, in a region of climatic extremes: of scorching droughts followed by torrential rains that swelled the rivers with the carcasses of drowned animals. That, anyhow, is how I remember it. When the waters subsided, acres of mud were left behind. At night you would hear the belling of tens of thousands of little frogs rejoicing in the largesse of the heavens. Some as small as the tip of my little finger, creatures so insignificant and so remote from your loftier concerns that you would not hear of them otherwise.

Where do they suddenly arrive from, these thousands of frogs? The answer is, they are always there. In the dry season they go underground, burrowing farther and farther from the heat of the sun until each has created a little tomb for itself. And in those tombs they die, so to speak. Their heartbeat slows, their breathing stops, they turn the colour of mud. Once again the nights are silent.

Silent until the next rains come, rapping, as it were, on thousands of tiny coffin lids. In those coffins hearts begin to beat, limbs begin to twitch that for months have been lifeless. The dead awake. As the caked mud softens, the frogs begin to dig their way out, and soon their voices resound again in joyous exultation beneath the vault of the heavens.

I believe in those little frogs.

It is because of their indifference to my belief, it is because of their indifference to me that I believe in them.

I will conceal nothing, bare all.

I will present transparently, without disguise, the vivifying flood, the chorus of joyous belling, followed by the subsiding of the waters and the retreat to the grave, then drought seemingly without end, then fresh rains and the resurrection of the dead.

# THE MAYOR

MAŁGORZATA SIKORSKA-MISZCZUK

Translated by Artur Zapałowski

NOTE

*The Mayor* is a play in two parts. The first part, written in 2009, tells the story of a mythical Town that has to face the Truth about a past atrocity. Part Two was written in 2011, as a retelling of the same story in historical terms without resorting to metaphor.

Whereas the characters in *The Mayor I* are mainly symbolic, the cast of *Mayor II* includes real-life figures such as Professor Jan T. Gross, whose book *Neighbors: The Destruction of the Jewish Community in Jedwabne, Poland* shook the nation out of its complacency with its description of the mass murder of Jews by residents of the Polish town of Jedwabne in 1941. Though not quite a docudrama, *Mayor II* does depict real-life events and contains fragments of actual statements. The Mayor of the title is based on Krzysztof Godlewski, the mayor of Jedwabne, who significantly contributed to raising awareness and commemorating the victims of the atrocity committed by Poles against their Jewish neighbors. Godlewski actively took part in the sixtieth anniversary commemoration of the atrocity together with Polish president Aleksander Kwaśniewski and Israeli ambassador Szevah Weiss (both of whom also appear in the play). The mayor's involvement was not appreciated by the people of Jedwabne, and, faced with the hostility of the local population who refused to admit historical responsibility for the crime, he ultimately chose to leave Poland.

*Mayor I* and *Mayor II* may be treated as a whole or can be staged independently. Both have been published in Poland but neither has been produced on stage. In 2009, Warsaw's Teatr na Woli organized a staged reading of *Mayor I*, and in 2011, it was produced as a radio play on Polish State Radio.

# THE MAYOR I

| CHARACTERS | THE MAYOR, BEFORE AND AFTER |
|---|---|
| | A PENITENT GERMAN |
| | A BEAUTY QUEEN |
| | THE MOTHER OF GOD |
| | THE MAYOR OF NEW YORK |
| | A TOWNSPERSON |
| | TOWNSPERSON'S TWELVE SONS-IN-LAW |
| | TOWNSPERSON'S TWELVE DAUGHTERS-IN-LAW |

## TWO MAYORS, ONE WITH AN OUTSTRETCHED HAND

*A gravestone letter is lying on the table. Being made of stone, it can't be sewn or stitched back in place. So how did it get there? Well, time's had its way with it. The inscription turned to dust, but the letter has survived. Now it's lying on the table, watching. It's a fine, respectable letter, but it's all alone. It's sad, mostly because it's passed the test of time.*

MAYOR. That's me from the Times of Innocence. Those times are over. The other me, the same me (after all, there's only one of me), is sitting in a chair with an outstretched hand, pointing at me. He's covered in wounds, he's all in pieces, hanging on by the skin of his skin, he won't talk much. All he can do is repeat, hand pointing at me: "It's me, it's me."

That's me from the Times of Innocence; that's me from the times before; that's me from back when the air stood still and never quivered, when no voices called, when the land was either clayish or parched, when it bore fruit, when it was just land, and when I was just a denizen of that land, a normal, decent human being who saw nothing unusual about it all. Those were the times that are over, and they will never return.

Who was I back then? How can I explain? One could begin by establishing a Before situation that could clearly be contrasted with the After situation. A Before situation: I'm walking, I drop my newspaper. What does that say about me, about the Mayor of this town?

I drop my paper. Somebody cries: "You dropped your paper, SquireJollyOldFellowGoodBuddy!" That says what it says about me. Or: "Mayor, begging your pardon, you've dropped your paper, sir"—and that's how this story begins, a story that will inexorably lead up to me sitting with an outstretched hand (covered in wounds, all in pieces hanging on by the skin of my skin), pointing at myself and saying: "It's me, it's me."

The After condition.

*After, after, after.*

*The After condition has inspired many fine artists who rightly, even brilliantly, intuited that the After condition has something child- or idiot-like about it. The rhyme says it all:*

*Jack fell down*
*and broke his crown*
*and Jill*
*came tumbling After*

## THE MAYOR DROPS HIS PAPER

*It is picked up, as foreshadowed, by a Townsperson.*

**TOWNSPERSON.** I'd like to say a few words about our Mayor before I pick up the paper he just dropped. This Mayor of ours is a jolly old fellow, a good buddy, a friend-in-need. I wouldn't ever say a bad word about him. He looks after our Town, does right by the people, is liked by the people, and gets their vote because he deserves to. He takes care of everything, looks after the land and the Monument, and wears a mustache as per the local fashion, and his holy namesake wishes him well, looking down from heaven and showing him the right path.

Nowadays, people don't believe in God. Why? That's their business.

(*To the patiently waiting Mayor*)

You dropped your paper, SquireJollyOldFellowGoodBuddy.

**MAYOR BEFORE.** Thank you, thank you! I don't know how I happened to drop my paper! It's as if an act of God knocked it from under my arm! The paper would have been lost if it weren't for you, but what counts most is this chance meeting of ours!

**TOWNSPERSON.** So you won't be reading that paper?

**MAYOR BEFORE.** Well, no, since we're standing here, I won't.

**TOWNSPERSON.** Then I'll sit down and read it myself.

**MAYOR BEFORE.** My pleasure! I'm very, very happy that this paper of mine can be of some use to you.

**TOWNSPERSON.** I'll let my son-in-law read it later. Shall I tell you what it says?

**MAYOR BEFORE.** I wouldn't want to interfere with your reading.

**TOWNSPERSON.** I always read out loud anyway. So this paper of yours says that, in the world outside, they've opened up a thick envelope. Sealed with wax it was. It says they weren't supposed to open it for a thousand years.

**MAYOR BEFORE.** Was that a thousand years from now or a thousand years ago?

**TOWNSPERSON.** It says . . . It doesn't say when they started counting.

**MAYOR BEFORE.** So maybe it was time?

**TOWNSPERSON.** It doesn't say. It says that secrets will come out of that envelope. They'll be holding a news conference. It says the truth will circle the world and reach the right ears.

**MAYOR BEFORE.** So it'll reach us, too.

TOWNSPERSON. No it won't. It won't reach our Town. What could it possibly say about our Town in a thick, sealed envelope? What message could there be? None, if you ask me.

MAYOR BEFORE. Let me have that paper before you let your son-in-law read it. I need to see when the conference is being held. I have important official instructions regarding conferences in the outside world.

TOWNSPERSON. Your paper's nothing but trouble. Without it, you wouldn't need to prepare for no conference.Why don't I read you what our local paper says?

(*Takes out the local paper, which deals with the issues of their Local Community, one not unlike our own*)

MAYOR BEFORE. Oh, no. They keep writing the same things. They're beautiful, but I know them by heart already.

TOWNSPERSON. That I can't believe.

MAYOR BEFORE. Let's put it to the test. There's nothing wrong with me knowing the contents of the local paper by heart.

TOWNSPERSON. Want me to give you the first letter as a hint?

MAYOR BEFORE. No need. (*Reciting from memory*) "Sunbeams shimmer since the morn upon the amethyst brow of our Monument."

TOWNSPERSON (*looking at the article in the local paper*). That's exactly what it says!

MAYOR BEFORE. "They slide off its sapphire lashes to cast light into the depths of its emerald eyes."

TOWNSPERSON. That's what it says!

MAYOR BEFORE. "The gaze the Monument casts upon us."

TOWNSPERSON. But surely there's no full stop there!

MAYOR BEFORE. I know, I was kidding.

TOWNSPERSON. God keep you from such levity!

MAYOR BEFORE. Alright-alright. "The gaze the Monument casts upon us is profound and clear. It is hard to believe it is only a statue: even the wind, convinced the Monument is alive, attempts to ruffle its golden locks. But to no avail, for gold of the highest standard will never yield to the loving caress of warm gusts of wind. Its emerald eyes are profound and clear. The figure is clad in a uniform of chrysoprase girt with an amber sash. The ruby buttons scintillate like blood in the sunlight. The silver saber in its hand shines day and night, its hilt studded with diamonds. The whole Radiant Figure glistens with gold, platinum, and pearls. Such is the purest stuff the Monument is cast of, as indestructible as our pride.

Let us ask out loud: what is it that brightens each day? It is the Monument, this Town's pride and joy, that brightens each day."

**TOWNSPERSON.** Now that's a surprise. Now that's something.

**MAYOR BEFORE.** Nothing to it. It's just such a lovely text.

**TOWNSPERSON.** I'll go tell my son-in-law.

**MAYOR BEFORE.** What about the paper?

**TOWNSPERSON.** No need, it's past his bedtime.

## DOUBTS

*The Mayor starts sobbing out of the blue.*

**MAYOR.** Something terrible will happen when I drop my paper a second time. That's why I'm clutching it for dear life. It anchors me in This Moment—and nothing's happened yet. I won't submit to any ordeal. Would any of you like to submit to an ordeal?

I want to live a normal life! That's all! So why am I crying now? I don't want to stand for anything in particular. These are normal times. These aren't "those" times. I don't feel cut out for anything like that. I'm no hero. There's nothing heroic about me. My head is far from noble, my features by no means stately—I'm allowed to make fun of them, right? Or take my chest: it's not some hero's chest, I don't have a hero's chest, I have a mediocre, so-so chest, and the rest of me's also so-so, average like. When I strip down to my undies, my briefs, it's nothing to write home about either, trust me. Can't I just have a normal life? Lead my life in peace and quiet? Do something to stop me crying like this!

## THE MAYOR'S WISH IS NOT GRANTED

*The Mayor stands, clutching his paper for dear life. The truth of the matter is he has no choice. For dear life is the only way he can clutch. Let us add that fate . . . fortune . . . destiny is intransigent. Silently, pussyfooting, it creeps up to him, ever closer, three-two-one. Bang!*

**PENITENT GERMAN.** Before I go Bang!
A word about me,
By way of an explanation:
Around my neck I wear
A ring on a string
As a punishment
A pendant
So everyone sees me
Straightaway and from afar
So I stand out
As the son of a murderer
People say I overdo it
That I wear the ring just so it jingles
And that nobody's making me
Bang!

**MAYOR BEFORE.** Sweet Mother of God!

(*drops the paper, stops crying and hiccuping*)

**PENITENT GERMAN.** Mister Mayor, begging your pardon, sir, you have dropped your paper.

**MAYOR BEFORE.** I just remembered I dreamt of Our Lady last night.

**PENITENT GERMAN.** Naked?

**MAYOR BEFORE.** No, she wasn't naked. She was gigantic, you know? There was nothing except for the sky, the universe of the sky, and all that sky, all of it, was filled by the Mother of God in a blue gown, and she was radiant. I woke up with my heart pounding.

**PENITENT GERMAN.** I never have dreams like that.

**MAYOR BEFORE.** I just remembered. When fear made me drop my paper, the dream came back to me.

**PENITENT GERMAN.** I cried "Bang" because something made me.

**MAYOR BEFORE.** It was a terrible dream, terrible. The Mother of God told me she heard a cry, and a fearful cry it was.

**MOTHER OF GOD.** I still hear that horrible cry coming from your Town, Mayor. That cry made me tremble underneath my blue gown, and my neatly combed hair stood on end; and, even though I fill the entire sky, I felt myself shrinking, so terrible was that cry. So I have dispatched myself unto the Town, and if it's true that the cry was brought about by the people of this Town, I shall destroy this Town.

**MAYOR BEFORE.** That's what she said, and, still stunned that she was talking to me, I asked: "You want to destroy the whole Town because you hear voices? Do you want the guilty to perish alongside the innocent? What if there are fifty righteous men among all the sinners . . ." I remembered there was this loophole . . . "will you destroy the Town then?"

**MOTHER OF GOD.** If there are fifty righteous men in your Town, I shall not destroy it.

**MAYOR BEFORE.** That's what she said, and I'm going: "What if there's only forty-five righteous men?"—when suddenly I get all pissed off. I get so terribly pissed off that I say: "Motherfucker," though I normally don't use such language, "what is this—a game? We're supposed to get the number down to ten as I recall, but . . ." and I'm being real mean to her here, "but what do you think you're doing!?" And suddenly I start yelling at her, the Mother of God, and shaking her—because she's gotten small, that is to say, normal-sized—and I say: "Listen to me! You're off your rocker thinking there's ten righteous men to be found in this fucking Town! There ain't! Look at me before I start shouting, because you don't seem to be listening! You'll be lucky to find just one, so you'd better not even try and lay a finger on this Town! Don't you even try!"

**MOTHER OF GOD.** Okay.

**MAYOR BEFORE.** That's what she said. "Okay."

**PENITENT GERMAN.** I would say it was a perceptive assessment of the situation, your saying there is no chance of finding ten righteous men in your Town. I also liked the way you conducted that conversation in your dream, which I'm jealous of, by the way. Remember though: the Mother of God does not exist.

**MOTHER OF GOD.** Come now, Murderer's Son. I do exist, and I love you.

## THE NIGHTS OF MAYORS

*At night, the Mayors of the world cannot sleep.*

*Cynical Mayors hatch cynical schemes. Honest Mayors wonder how many faces of Evil there are in the world, and what it's like to be a Mayor in a world with so many faces of Evil.*

*The answer to the first question is simple: the world has 365 faces of Evil, and every four years it has 366. Every night, one of those faces looms over a good and honest Mayor. Each face of Evil is entitled to one terrifying sneer.*

*The second question—what it's like to be a good Mayor in a world with so many faces of Evil—is a tougher one. Every Mayor has to deal with it on his own.*

## THE NIGHTS OF THE MURDERER'S SON

*At night, the Murderer's Son, the Penitent German, cannot sleep either.*

**PENITENT GERMAN.** Daddy's dead
I like looking at his photo

And masturbating
I'd never have hit upon the idea myself
But I once read
That such is the custom among sons
Who hate their fathers
An intimate situation
An ice-breaker:
Look, I exist, and you don't
Do you recognize the wet stain
On your nose?
That's me.
I'm searching for closeness
That is all I can do
Are you glad that I can?
You know, between us men,
We never had a chance to talk properly
Maybe you would have taught me
To use other photos
But you were too busy killing

You bastard
You shit
You're the one who begat me
I'm dying because of you
I've signed up for a lobotomy
Everything is better than knowing
Who I am
Friends say
Don't worry
What do you care
Who your father was?
Spread your arms
Start loving the world
Get a massage
Say a prayer
God loves you

You're his child
I am not a child of God
I reply
I am the son of a murderer
I reply

## IN THE MORNING

**TOWNSPERSON.** Sweet Mother of God, Mayor! We have guests!

**MAYOR BEFORE.** Who is it?

**TOWNSPERSON.** A Lady.

**MAYOR BEFORE.** Sweet Mother of God.

**TOWNSPERSON.** A lovely lady, and there's some guy with her.

**MAYOR BEFORE.** It must be Her.

**TOWNSPERSON.** Her who?

**MAYOR BEFORE.** Our Lady, come to check whether to destroy the Town or not.

**TOWNSPERSON.** Aren't you up yet? You have to go and officially ask who they are and what they require.

**MAYOR BEFORE.** Where have they come from?

**TOWNSPERSON.** Folks say they crawled out of a hole by yonder stream.

**MAYOR BEFORE.** Not out of a hole, out of the tunnel.

**TOWNSPERSON.** Whatever.

## THE MEETING

**MAYOR BEFORE.** Mayor, it's me, the Mayor of this Town. I take it you're on a tunnel visit?

**THE MAYOR OF NYC.** Yes, but I kind of thought this would be Beijing.

**MAYOR BEFORE.** It's not Beijing. But I know your face, you're the Mayor of New York.

**THE MAYOR OF NYC.** Yes, and this is my assistant, The Beauty Queen.

**MAYOR BEFORE.** After you, ma'am. Since fate has ordained it thus. Let's go.

## THE PRESENTATION AND THE EXPLANATION

*Since the Town has been graced by a random tunnel visit from the Mayor of New York, who knows nothing about the Town because he came out of the tunnel where destiny wanted him to, and not where he felt like going, a Presentation is arranged for him, with an Explanation being provided for the Townspeople.*

*Fortunately, the Townspeople don't know anything about New York either, which results in a balance of ignorance where no one can accuse anyone of imposing their culture and civilization on anyone else, and so there is no division into Colonizer and Colonized.*

**MAYOR BEFORE.** Townspeople! The Earth is a sphere. Inside that sphere there are tunnels running every which way: up and down, and side to side. Nobody knows about them, but they exist. Once a year, Mayors from all countries, not knowing when, how and why, enter those tunnels. They wander through them and come out on the other side. What do they come out for? To learn about the Town they've ended up in, and reflect upon its history. And so it has come to pass that we have been visited by the Mayor of New York and his assistant, The Beauty Queen.

*The Mayor of NYC and The Beauty Queen smile. The Mayor of NYC tries to shake off the nagging thought that this is some kind of misunderstanding.*

**TOWNSPERSON.** In our Town, we have a monument made of gold, silver and precious stones. It makes us proud. No one, near or far, has a monument quite like it.

**MAYOR BEFORE.** Besides that, we don't really stand out. Is the countryside here special in any way? Not really. I'd put it this way: meadows, trees, four seasons; in the Fall, the roads get muddy (and no wonder). No wildlife to speak of: hares and deer, the odd stray dog not even worth mentioning; nothing out of the ordinary: cats, sparrows. Run of the mill fauna and flora, the kind you can get anywhere. No mountain or lake in the vicinity, much less a sea. Nor are there any volcanoes or waterfalls, craters, caves, or jungles like the ones Sting or Bono are fighting to prevent being chopped down. Maybe we do have something for which Bono and Sting could fight, but nothing of the sort springs to mind.

Though there's nothing that sets us apart, I do like this place. It's mine. The landcape has grown on me.

TOWNSPERSON. Most extraordinary is our extraordinary Monument. I already said it was made of gold, silver and precious stones. What kind of stones? Rubies, sapphires, amethysts, emeralds, all the riches of the Sesame.

Besides our Monument, there's nothing world-class here. When you have so little, every square inch of monument is priceless.

Thank you.

MAYOR BEFORE. And I'd also like to say something about our cemetery.

*The numerous Townspeople in attendance, especially the Townsperson's Twelve Sons-in-Law, and the Townsperson's Twelve Daughters-in-Law, are not in favor. The Mayor respects the wishes of the community that elected him Mayor.*

MAYOR BEFORE. Or, then again, maybe not. It's nothing to write home about.

THE BEAUTY QUEEN. Who does the cemetery belong to?

TOWNSPERSON. These people who used to be here and aren't any more. They took their suitcases, and up and left. They left us their dead.

TWELVE DAUGHTERS-IN-LAW *(chorus)*. Just skulls and bones
Down in the ground
Beneath a mound

No crosses on top
No names on the stones
Just skulls and bones

TOWNSPERSON. Nothing but trouble.

THE BEAUTY QUEEN. Where did they go?

TOWNSPERSON. Depends. Some got killed by the Germans, the rest scattered all over the place. They're happily settled in America, mostly. That's what we heard from those of us who've been abroad.

THE MAYOR OF NYC. I know who you mean. You mean the Jooz!

TOWNSPERSON. Could be the Jooz. Have it your way. Maybe that's what they call 'em now. Whatever.

THE MAYOR OF NYC. My assistant, The Beauty Queen, she's a Joo too!

TOWNSPERSON. Whatever. Why don't she tell us how Jooz live in America? Something about herself. Getting to know each other will liven things up.

BEAUTY QUEEN. I don't know where to start. What do you want to know?

TOWNSPERSON. What you have for dinner. Do you have meat?

BEAUTY QUEEN. We do. In our family we do. My father and my mother are very different, but they eat the same things, and they both have these blue numbers on their forearms. I must have seen them a million times but I can't remember the actual digits. Isn't that funny?

TOWNSPERSON. Why don't you tell us what you eat? Cause those of us who travel say you don't eat like regular people.

BEAUTY QUEEN. We eat like regular people, at a table. When I was little, my father would slice meat and put it on my plate. He carved thick slices and waited. I put the first bite in my mouth. There was this custom in our family that you had to listen to your parents, and eat meat. I put the first bite in my mouth. Time passed, and I'd still be chewing on that first bite. My father looked at my mother. Then my mother would stop breathing.

But my father was breathing enough for two. My mother would sag, while my father puffed up and grew bigger. I don't know how he fit inside the room.

Then he spoke to me, his daughter, and it went like this:

"You pig! Stop staring at me! Eat up! You should be grateful for having meat!"

But I still wasn't eating, so he yelled:

"Pig! Back in the camp . . ."

And he grabbed the table and threw it up in the air like a ball. "You have to eat if you want to live," he said. "You have to live." Then he went to the other room and began checking our household accounts.

My mother, who was a ghost by then, would walk past me and disappear into the bathroom. I forgot to mention that we had a bathroom.

TWELVE DAUGHTERS-IN-LAW *(chorus)*. Little skulls
Little bones
Scattered here
Meat for lunch
Left untouched
Over there
Hot water's great
From the tap
In the States
And that there missy's
Sort of hissy

BEAUTY QUEEN. All was quiet in the bathroom. I sat by the door and listened to what couldn't be heard. I'd go, "Mom, Mom, say something." I was very scared. I'd go, "Mom, Mom, say something." And finally she'd say: "I'm in the bathroom." Then I knew she was still alive.

That was our after-dinner routine. Mom was in the bathroom. Dad was at the accounts. I was by the door. That's how us Jooz with blue numbers on our arms would eat meat in New York, in America.

**THE MAYOR OF NYC.** Your parents never read Doctor Spock. It says there how kids in America ought to be fed.

**BEAUTY QUEEN.** My father checked the accounts. Then he went to bed and turned his back on everyone.

**TOWNSPERSON.** Back when you Jooz dwelled here—alive, and not the way you are in the cemetery now—you'd put blood in your bread. Do you still do that?

**BEAUTY QUEEN.** I can't speak for all of us, but my mother can add blood to everything. Whenever she talks about the old days, she lights a cigarette and adds blood to the conversation. When she talks, her words flow red. Everything gets soiled. That's why father won't let mother talk about the old days.

**TOWNSPERSON.** Miss Queen, we were hoping you'd tell us something entertaining about your strange customs, do songs and dances, and wave your hands around—the way we like it. But you come back here with stories we don't want to hear. Those aren't stories for us. But fortunately we have a German here, a Penitent German, so the right person did hear you out after all.

Show yourself, Son of a Murderer.

Tell the young lady why you're here and what it is you seek in our land.

**PENITENT GERMAN.** I am here to show this Town how guilty I feel for the sins of my father. That is all I can do as regards this matter.

**TWELVE SONS-IN-LAW** (*chorus*). He settled here
The Penitent German
Ostensibly to grow cauliflowers
In our pristine region
What's he know about cauliflowers?
He grows them small
Like tiny fists
Like babies' heads
He plays them music
Those cauliflowers
But if he wants to, let him

We're not stopping anyone
Tolerance is tolerance
It's just such a hoot
When he plays music to those cauliflowers

**TOWNSPERSON.** Forget the cauliflowers. He's doing the right thing, our German. It was high time he came. Let him do his penance. The world must never forget how the German kills.

**TWELVE DAUGHTERS-IN-LAW** *(chorus)*. How the German kills
Sing, women, sing
Hey nonny nonny
How the German kills
*(song)*
German's gonna shoot you
And torture you, too
Pull your nails with pliers
Beat you black and blue
Hey nonny nonny
Hose the water down your throat
Give a pregnant girl the boot
One of them gets killed
Scores of us get hanged
Hey nonny nonny
He'll commandeer the cattle
Smugglers he'll treat badly
Break your arms and legs
Electrocute you gladly
Hey nonny nonny
Drive tanks down the street
Detonate the bombs
Set fire to the village
Set fire to the town
Hey nonny nonny
Burn our country down
Plotting with the Russkie
Way above our heads

Always dealing death
Hey nonny nonny
The German
The way of the German
A born killer, he.

**PENITENT GERMAN.** I'm so sorry.

**MAYOR BEFORE.** Enough. Time to lay flowers before the Monument.

**BEAUTY QUEEN.** I'm staying here. There's something I need to tell that man.

## LOVE

**PENITENT GERMAN.** You're not my type
Your eyes are too blue
That kerchief—
But, listening to you,
I understood: you're like
The other half of my apple,
Like a cherry hanging from my ear

**BEAUTY QUEEN.** I never met anyone like you
I don't know how you could listen to
That song
Those people
Savages
How did you feel?
How could you stand it?
You must be a saint
To be doing penance here

**PENITENT GERMAN.** I came here racked by a fever.

**BEAUTY QUEEN.** They were looking at you
Like you came from the beyond
It seemed they were going
To touch you to check

If your skin's really that white,
Your eyes really that green,
Or if they're made of stone.
That they'd tug at your hair
Or prick you with a knife
To see if you bleed.
I don't see how you could listen
To what they were singing.
How do you cope,
How can you live among them?

**PENITENT GERMAN.** I'm so sorry.
I don't really know
What you're saying right now
I'm still shaking all over
With the shaking
That started
When you told them about yourself
I came here racked by a fever.
I wrote a poem, actually I write the same one every night:
"Daddy's dead
I like looking at his photo
And masturbating."

**BEAUTY QUEEN.** That's enough.

**PENITENT GERMAN.** That's the point: that's why I'm shaking all over
It's because I know that you know, that you understand it's enough
I was listening to you closely,
Your father was a monster
Your mother added blood to everything
By what miracle you survived outside that bathroom door I don't know: by the same one I did, I guess
It must have been in spite of it all
In spite of the hateful love
Of our parents
In spite of their crime

I can't live like this
That hate oppresses me
Help me
Love me

**BEAUTY QUEEN.** I love you.

**PENITENT GERMAN.** How's that?

**BEAUTY QUEEN.** I love you.

**PENITENT GERMAN.** Already? So soon?

**BEAUTY QUEEN.** Yes.

**PENITENT GERMAN.** You love me? How . . .?

**BEAUTY QUEEN.** Any way you want me to.

**PENITENT GERMAN.** I'd like you to be with me always.

**BEAUTY QUEEN.** I'll be with you always.

**PENITENT GERMAN.** And you'll never leave me?

**BEAUTY QUEEN.** Never.

**PENITENT GERMAN.** How do you know?

**BEAUTY QUEEN.** I just know.

**PENITENT GERMAN.** Such certainty. You only just met me.

**BEAUTY QUEEN.** You're the one who's just met me.

**PENITENT GERMAN.** I'm overwhelmed. I don't know whether to believe you.

**BEAUTY QUEEN.** What would you like to believe?

**PENITENT GERMAN.** I don't know.

## LOVE: IN WHOSE FOOTSTEPS DOES THE UNICORN TREAD?

**MAYOR BEFORE.** I feel like I know you. That's silly of course. What do you think about that? Did anyone ever tell you they'd seen you in a dream?

**BEAUTY QUEEN.** Often.

**MAYOR BEFORE.** Here we are. This is it.

**BEAUTY QUEEN.** This?

**MAYOR BEFORE.** This is the cemetery.

**BEAUTY QUEEN.** This?

**MAYOR BEFORE.** Yes. The cemetery.

**BEAUTY QUEEN.** Where?

**MAYOR BEFORE.** Everywhere.

**BEAUTY QUEEN.** I don't see it.

**MAYOR BEFORE.** I'll show you around. You're not mad?

**BEAUTY QUEEN.** At what?

**MAYOR BEFORE.** At us.

**BEAUTY QUEEN.** What about?

**MAYOR BEFORE.** About this cemetery. Nobody looks after it. Nobody comes here.

**BEAUTY QUEEN.** What about you?

**MAYOR BEFORE.** Well, I do.

**BEAUTY QUEEN.** Why?

**MAYOR BEFORE.** I don't know. I like coming here. Something draws me here. I like this cemetery.

**BEAUTY QUEEN.** But there's nothing here.

**MAYOR BEFORE.** There is. I'll show you everything. It's an odd cemetery. When you walk around it, what was there a moment ago vanishes. Every step makes an inscription disappear. The letters crumble off the stones. I tried picking them up but they fall apart in your hands. Except for one. I have it at home. One gravestone letter. Maybe that's wrong? I don't know.

**BEAUTY QUEEN.** I don't know everything either.

**MAYOR BEFORE.** Maybe you're not supposed to have gravestone letters at home? When I first saw this cemetery, I thought there was nothing here, just like you did. But then, slowly, everything began opening up for me: between the trees, stars, leaves, stones and the moon, a Town started rising up. I felt like I was in an enchanted forest. It was a voyage of discovery. It turned out that some stones had hands carved on them. Hands held like this. Gravestones with hands. Do you know what that means?

**BEAUTY QUEEN.** It's a blessing.

**MAYOR BEFORE.** At last! I knew there was some secret to it! What about the pitcher pouring water?

**BEAUTY QUEEN.** There was this family. It's their emblem.

**MAYOR BEFORE.** Magic! And the lion? I'd like a lion on my grave when I'm dead. What does the lion mean?

**BEAUTY QUEEN.** Judah, it's a name.

**MAYOR BEFORE.** Hm. Well, that won't work. My name's not Judah. See? This is the place! Stroke the soil, stroke it right here; there's still a trace, the air takes on different shapes here, feel it? It's preserved the contours. You're not mad at me?

**BEAUTY QUEEN.** Why should I be?

**MAYOR BEFORE.** It's hard to look after someone else's dead.

**BEAUTY QUEEN.** I can relate to that.

**MAYOR BEFORE.** Tell me, do you hear something?

**BEAUTY QUEEN.** It's very quiet here.

**MAYOR BEFORE.** Like a cry coming from somewhere?

**BEAUTY QUEEN.** No, nothing. Silence.

**MAYOR BEFORE.** Sometimes, a unicorn follows me around. Yes, I know unicorns don't exist. I was only kidding. But this cemetery is a very magical place, so, believe it or not, a unicorn follows me around, walking in my footsteps, cautiously placing its hooves where I've stepped, treading carefully: it's a good unicorn.

If he likes you, he'll show himself. Turn around, slowly now, and you might catch a glimpse.

(*The Beauty Queen turns around and sees nothing*)

**BEAUTY QUEEN.** Nothing.

**MAYOR BEFORE.** That's because you turned around too quickly. You're not mad?

BEAUTY QUEEN. Why would I be mad?

MAYOR BEFORE. I keep thinking: maybe you should get a bathroom of your own.

I don't know what it takes to look after someone else's dead.

BEAUTY QUEEN. Please don't explain yourself, it's not your fault. So, is the unicorn following me around?

MAYOR BEFORE. It is.

BEAUTY QUEEN. Well, can I turn around now?

MAYOR BEFORE. Hold on . . . It's telling me you should stop. Please shut your eyes. Don't move.

(*Kisses the Beauty Queen*)

MAYOR BEFORE. You've been kissed by a unicorn. Well?

BEAUTY QUEEN. No one in New York will believe me when I tell them.

MAYOR BEFORE. Don't tell anyone. Let's keep this to ourselves.

BEAUTY QUEEN. I hear something.

## STORMWAR

*A springtime barrage breaks out. Amid the claps of thunder rolling across the fields we hear the following strains of music:*

*A Red Army march to send shivers down the spine:*

[http://www.youtube.com/watch?v=8Y4_2Qa0QQs]

*A Polish resistance song—no less spine-chilling:*

[http://www.youtube.com/watch?v=rSgKreOuxrE]

*The unforgettable opening bars of the theme for a Polish TV series set during the war, though I'm not that sure it fits here:*

[http://www.youtube.com/watch?v=OHgtWywDn5w]

*And of course, the "Ride of the Valkyries" from Coppola's* Apocalypse Now.

*It all sounds innocent (items 1-4, that is) but, together with the noise, the thunder, and the lightning, it sows panic among the Townspeople.*

**TOWNSPEOPLE: SONS-IN-LAW AND DAUGHTERS-IN-LAW.** What's going on?
What is that?
Who is that? Lordy!
Jesus Christ!
Sweet Mother of God!
War!
A new war!
It's war again!
War's upon us!
Is it war?
What, who?
What's going on?
God, oh God!

They'll be bombing
Dropping bombs on us,
What's going on?
What's going on?
They're shooting!
What do we do?
Buy sugar,
Groats, rice
Matches
Stick pigs, catch the drippings
Vodka, moonshine
Smoke sausage
Cigarettes, lots of cigarettes
Gasoline
What else?
What else?
Lard, flour
Dollars
What's going on?
What's gonna happen?

(*The Penitent German watches the panic*)

**PENITENT GERMAN.** I can't bear to look. They're running around in circles.

Quitting their jobs. Leaving e-mails unwritten. Shutting down PowerPoint and running off to buy sugar. Stocking up for the war. What am I to do?

Is there any way to calm them down? Talk sense into them? Don't they realize the world has changed?

(*trying to strike a chord with the frantic Townspeople*)

(*strike one*)

The world has changed!

(*strike two*)

You're part of a united Europe!

(*strike three*)

You're surrounded by friends!

(*strike four*)

Our Chancellor does like you, you know!
I don't know.
I could grab their arms and say: Calm down!
It was a long time ago.
There was a war, but it's over now, so pardon me.
Calm down.
I beg you.
Calm down.
Listen to what I'm saying.
Stop. Look around.
You won't run out of matches! Or sugar! It's just a storm! A storm!

**BEAUTY QUEEN.** I was wrong, I misjudged them. They've got blue numbers in their heads; they need their meat, matches, sausage, lard, dollars, and bread. I'm so sad, I could cry.

(*runs among the Townspeople*)

People, please! Stop it! There's meat enough for everyone.
I'll let you have my share! I'll let you have my meat.
It's just a storm. A storm!

**THE MAYOR OF NYC.** I got inside the tunnel by pushing aside a statue of George Washington. It's on the ground floor of my office in New York, a gift from schoolchildren, made of bronze. I strained my back, it's a heavy statue, but it was worth it.

I'll go home and tell my Townspeople: I love New York! We live in a fortunate city!

**MAYOR BEFORE.** They'll calm down soon.
They'll see it's only a storm.
These things happen in our country.
It rumbles, it roars.

**THE MAYOR OF NYC.** Why do they keep thinking there's a war?

**MAYOR BEFORE.** Because our country is like that
In your country
When a plane flies over the city
It's just a plane

While here whenever there's a rumble
People think there's a war
That it's dive-bombers
Or rocket launchers
Old habits die hard

Don't think
They're savages
They're ordinary people.

**BEAUTY QUEEN.** I really feel like crying now.

(*to the German*)

Let's get away from here.

**PENITENT GERMAN.** (*spreads his hands resignedly*) I'm sorry.

## SILENCE

**BEAUTY QUEEN.** And now this silence, it's somehow odd—don't you think?

**MAYOR BEFORE.** It's the Truth approaching the Town. That explains the silence.

**BEAUTY QUEEN.** I feel uneasy.

**MAYOR BEFORE.** A thick, wax-sealed envelope as been opened in the world outside. Now the Truth is nearing the Town.
There's no escaping the Truth.
It will come.
(*Announcing*)
As Mayor of this Town
It's my duty to announce that I know what this sudden silence means, and what truth lurks behind it.
Townspeople, honored guests . . .
(*A horrible, unbearable CRY is heard. Nobody hears it except for the Mayor and You*)
What was that?
Did you hear that cry?
It's the Truth come to our Town.

**TOWNSPERSON.** We didn't hear anything.

## THE TRUTH PROCLAIMED

**TOWNSPERSON.** They let the truth out, broke the seal, so what now?

**MAYOR BEFORE.** It's come here.

**TOWNSPERSON.** What do we care?

**MAYOR BEFORE.** It's the truth about the people who lie in our cemetery.

**TOWNSPERSON.** There's no cemetery here.

**MAYOR BEFORE.** The cemetery you can't see.

**TOWNSPERSON.** What you can't see doesn't exist.

**MAYOR PRZED.** We killed those people lying there. That's the Truth.

**THE MAYOR OF NYC.** The Jooz?

**MAYOR BEFORE.** Those people lying there.

**TOWNSPERSON.** Whatever. It's the German that killed them.

**MAYOR BEFORE.** I told you the Truth would come to us in the end.
Those who left,
Those lying there
In the cemetery that isn't there
Were killed by our fathers
Not by THE GERMAN
Not by THE GERMAN

## I CAN'T GET NO SATISFACTION

*In the space of a second, several sequences of conflicting thoughts and emotions flash through the Penitent German's mind.*

Time: 1 second

**CONFLICTING THOUGHT AND EMOTION 1.** What do I feel? Do I feel any better? Now that I can call your fathers "bastards" and "shits?" Does it make me feel any better?

(*Does so*)

Your fathers are bastards! Shits!

**CONFLICTING THOUGHT AND EMOTION 2.** I'll run up to each of you and say: "At last, you're a Son of a Murderer too, and so are you, and you, and you, and you," and then I'll tell the oldest Townsperson: "And you're their father!"

(*Does so*)

You're the son of a muderer, and so are you, and you, and you, and you. And you're their father!

**CONFLICTING THOUGHT AND EMOTION 3.** I can sing a Song that goes: "La, la, la, whee, whee, whee, finally it's not me!"

(*Does so*)

La, la, whee
It wasn't me

Finally it's not me
Who did the killing
The executing
The bayoneting
The kicking
The butchering
The burning

La, la, whee
Finally it's not me
Not me, not me
The Bad German
The Born Killer
But
Some other nation
Honest folk
Not so urbane maybe
The People of this Town
Quite a nice bunch though

La, la, la
It's them who
Kicked
Killed
Raped
Tortured
Slaughtered
Without pity
Threw in the fire
Drowned in the lake
Andsoforth
Andsoforth

And this song
Will not fade
To be sung
It was made

**CONFLICTING THOUGHT AND EMOTION 4.** I could leave this Town now—how do I feel about that? Am I sad? Leave, just like that? Is my penance done? Am I supposed to just start living? I'm not ready. I thought I would be doing penance all my life. Am I supposed to go back to the real world now and stop running around with a ring around my neck? I'm not ready to do that.

**CONFLICTING THOUGHT AND EMOTION 5.** I want to leave this accursed Town right away, and take the Beauty Queen with me.

(*To Beauty Queen*)

Come with me Queen, let's settle in Europe or New York now that I've told you I love you and you've told me you love me. Maybe it happened too fast, but, perhaps, something fast, very fast, is happening in my life right now.

It's awful, absurd even, but who will play music to my cauliflowers? How will they make it without Mozart? It's summertime, the harvest is drawing near, the cauliflower heads will be sliced off with no Requiem playing.

## THE TOWN OF THE LIVING AND THE DEAD

**TOWNSPEOPLE: SONS-IN-LAW AND DAUGHTERS-IN-LAW.** Jesus and Mary!
What is this?
The dead have risen from their graves!
What do they want?

**TOWNSPERSON.** What is this Truth that's raised the dead and brought them to our Town? Cast them out, Mayor!

**TOWNSPEOPLE: SONS-IN-LAW AND DAUGHTERS-IN-LAW.** Cast them out!

**TOWNSPERSON.** You have to protect us from the Truth!

**THE MAYOR OF NYC.** Now you've got me scared. What ash-covered people are those?

**TOWNSPEOPLE: SONS-IN-LAW AND DAUGHTERS-IN-LAW.** The dead walk
Among the living.

They're all mixed up,
They were supposed to lie where
Corn cockles and cornflowers
Uselessly grow,
Shunned by cows—
Smart critters that they are.
But now they're walking

THE MAYOR OF NYC. In my City, the buildings scrape the sky so hard that it's full of holes! In the clearings you can see God blessing America. My Town is miraculous, but the dead don't walk with the living like they do here.

TOWNSPEOPLE: SONS-IN-LAW AND DAUGHTERS-IN-LAW. Hear that, Mayor!? Cast them out! Lead them underground, play your pipe, let them follow you like rats to their death.

MAYOR BEFORE. My Townspeople, Sons, Sons-in-Law! Those are no rats!

They're Jooz!

TOWNSPEOPLE: SONS AND SONS-IN-LAW. Drown them in the river, like in the fairy tale.

TOWNSPERSON. So it can all end happily.

THE MAYOR OF NYC. How can I be of service to this Mayor? What advice can I give?

TOWNSPERSON. There is no advice save this: cast out the dead, and may God bless our Town, as he has yours!

THE MAYOR OF NYC. This sight will haunt me: the dead among the living.

(*To Mayor Before*)

I don't know what to tell you, Mayor. I'd like to forget what I'm seeing right now.

MAYOR BEFORE. I won't cast them out! I won't cast the Townspeople of my Town out of my Town.

I don't know what to do. How do I talk to them?

I don't know what they're here for. Their children have left.

They don't have their children anymore. We're their children now. Right?

TOWNSPEOPLE: SONS AND SONS-IN-LAW. We're not the children of those corpses. Cast them out, Mayor!

MAYOR BEFORE. People of my Town, I think that each of you has a lot of love to give. I know it sounds funny, but I believe that each of you has so much love inside them, that they shouldn't begrudge it for those corpses. All people are children of God.

TOWNSPEOPLE: SONS-IN-LAW AND DAUGHTERS-IN-LAW. Love us, Mayor! Cast them out!

MAYOR BEFORE. God doesn't begrudge anything. I became Mayor here because I love all of you. I think that's the least we can do. Give them some love. They must be miserable, the dead, if they've come out to be among us today. There's no sign of it being Doomsday. No trumpets have sounded, the world isn't on fire, the sky isn't falling, the seas aren't drying up. Besides, how would we know: we don't have a sea here, not even a lake.

PENITENT GERMAN. That's enough! Mayor, just listen to yourself! You're walking the line between the living and the dead here: it's a difficult act. Get real. Don't speak to them about love. There is no love. You're making a fool of yourself. You look like you've gone mad. Like you were a madwoman in a blue kerchief stopping people in the street, singing Hare Krishna, and shouting that love will save them. There is no such thing. Just like that: love does not exist!

Let's go, Queen.

BEAUTY QUEEN. I exist.

PENITENT GERMAN. Only you exist. Let's go, Queen.

BEAUTY QUEEN. Only I exist. And I love you, you Son of a Murderer.

PENITENT GERMAN. Let's get away from here. I want to get a life. I'm in a hurry to settle down.

BEAUTY QUEEN. How? Can? You? Want? To? Love? Me? Since?

You? Say? There? Is? No? Love?

(*The Beauty Queen sings a song*)
How can you want to love me?
Since you say
There is no
There is no
There is no
There is no love?!

What sort of a world is this, where only a madwoman in a blue kerchief can speak about love?
Just me, me, me, me, me!?
How come that Mayor can't?
What sort of a world is this?

PENITENT GERMAN. I know no other world, Beauty Queen
I haven't for years
When I think about it
I feel despair
Which I instantly find myself mocking
Will you forgive me, Beauty Queen?
Is it not too late?

BEAUTY QUEEN (*shouting, her blue kerchief fluttering*). Hare Krishna,
Hare Krishna
Krishna Krishna Hare Hare
How could you say something like that?
Hare Rama Hare Rama
Please go away, Hare Hare

*How come the Penitent German didn't get another chance? He said he was sorry, didn't he? Surely it can't be too late?*

## A DOWNPOUR OF LEAFLETS

TOWNSPERSON. You said you had special instructions regarding conferences in the outside world?

MAYOR BEFORE. How to reconcile the dead with the living? I was given no such instructions.

*Suddenly, leaflets start falling from the sky.*

TOWNSPEOPLE (*picking them up and reading*). "Citizens of this town
Do not be intimidated
We're with you
They're making you into murderers
Pressing you into penance
All because there are
Strange dead
Walking the streets of your town
Haunting
And spreading fear."
(*Reading*)
"They won't let you live in peace
Someone's let them out of their graves
Some of them run about
Baring their teeth
Like dogs let off their chains
Howling
And keeping you from sleeping."
(*Reading*)
"Citizens!
The Mayor of your Town
Is trying to make you
Communicate with the dead
Claiming they're friends and neighbors."
(*Reading*)
"Don't be let yourselves be duped!"
(*Reading*)
"You don't have to talk to those dead
You don't have to let them into your homes
Nor offer them food and drink
And give them shelter
In your closets
Basements

Pantries, and pigsties."
(*Reading*)
"You don't have to
Nor should you!"
(*Reading*)
"You should not apologize to those dead
Nor pray for them
They're not friends and neighbors,
They're strange skeletons
They rattle differently."
(*Reading*)
"These are strange skeletons
Their bones are entirely different from our bones
Their skulls entirely different from our skulls
As concluded by an important professor
Who weighed and measured those skulls
It's a scientific fact
To be found in academic publications."
(*Reading*)
"We need to set aside special sections
Where they can stay
Since they won't go back in their graves."
(*Reading*)
"Special zones
Special seats on buses
Special benches to sit in."
(*Reading*)
"But the best thing would be
To persuade them to leave."
(*Reading*)
"Once again
To tell them firmly
That the land where they were born

And died
Doesn't want them!"

## THE MAYOR OF NYC GOES BACK TO THE TUNNEL AND NEW YORK

**THE MAYOR OF NYC.** Please come back with me; think it over, Beauty Queen. This place gives me the creeps. You'll sing and dance in our free country, which has never harmed a soul. Ours is a happy city. Come back.

**BEAUTY QUEEN.** I'm not leaving him.

**THE MAYOR OF NYC.** Let's invite that Mayor to New York. He can get shown around my office for free by a skinny guide. Then together we can cry: "I Love New York!"

**BEAUTY QUEEN.** I'm staying here.

**THE MAYOR OF NYC.** Come home. We'll check my approval ratings. Maybe they've gone up? We'll catch a new show on Broadway, we might even bump into Woody Allen. Breathe different air . . .

**BEAUTY QUEEN.** Look, you have a piece of paper in your hair. They've dropped so many leaflets.

**THE MAYOR OF NYC.** Come back. Come home, Beauty Queen.

**BEAUTY QUEEN.** I'm glad I came here with you. I'm in love.

**THE MAYOR OF NYC.** How can you tell?

**BEAUTY QUEEN.** We've kissed already. It's love.

**THE MAYOR OF NYC.** Please.

**BEAUTY QUEEN.** I need to hurry. I'll run to him. He's all alone.

## THE TOWNSPEOPLE MARCH BY WITH THE MONUMENT, TAKING IT TO THE CEMETERY THAT ISN'T THERE

*Townspeople walk by carrying the Monument of gold, silver and precious stones on their backs.*

*They want to put it up in the Cemetery which is not there, so as to leave the dead with nowhere to go except maybe the Isle of Yakoundu. Someone at the back is holding up a unicorn's head on a pitchfork.*

TOWNSPERSON. We shall erect our Monument in the Cemetery that's not there. That's our answer. All unauthorized persons roaming our streets are required to leave the Town. This is no place for them.

Let us march in lockstep, Sons-in-Law and Sons of mine, Daughters-in-Law and Daughters of mine. Let us march. Let's carry our Monument. All together. Off we go.

TOWNSPEOPLE: SONS AND SONS-IN-LAW (*all together*). Sunbeams shimmer since the morn upon the amethyst brow of our Monument. They slide off its sapphire lashes to cast light into the depths of its emerald eyes. The gaze the Monument casts upon us is profound and clear.

TOWNSPERSON. Blaming us instead of the German is a slanderous lie!

TOWNSPEOPLE: SONS AND SONS-IN-LAW. Its emerald eyes are profound and clear.

TOWNSPERSON. We are bearing this Monument to arrive at the Truth! It's not an easy Truth. It's a hard Truth. Blaming us instead of the German is a slanderous lie.

TOWNSPEOPLE: SONS AND SONS-IN-LAW. The figure is clad in a uniform of chrysoprase with an amber sash.

TOWNSPERSON. It's a red herring!

TOWNSPEOPLE: SONS AND SONS-IN-LAW. The ruby buttons scintillate like blood in the sunlight.

TOWNSPERSON. We call upon all citizens to take arms! To take arms against such Truths!

TOWNSPEOPLE: SONS AND SONS-IN-LAW. The silver saber in its hand shines day and night, its hilt studded with diamonds.

**TOWNSPERSON.** He is our Mayor no more! He seemed so jolly.

Jolly and friendly. A jolly old fellow, a friend-in-need, the salt of the earth. But he is our Mayor no more!

**TOWNSPEOPLE: SONS AND SONS-IN-LAW.** The whole Radiant Figure glistens with gold, platinum and pearls. Such is the purest stuff the Monument is cast of, as indestructible as our pride.

**MAYOR BEFORE** (*makes his stand*). No, please, don't do this! Leave the Cemetery be!

**TOWNSPERSON.** Don't get in our way. Step aside.

**MAYOR.** I will not put up with this!

**TOWNSPERSON.** Who cares? You want to put us down in front of our Monument. Put yourself up for sacrifice instead.

**TOWNSPEOPLE: SONS AND SONS-IN-LAW.** Let us ask out loud: what is it that brightens each day?

**TOWNSPERSON.** You'll be put down in the books! As a warning! You'll be put down. This Town does not approve of you.

**TOWNSPEOPLE: SONS AND SONS-IN-LAW.** It is the Monument, this Town's pride and joy, that brightens each day.

**MAYOR BEFORE.** I know the Truth is hard to bear.

Hear me out, this isn't easy but I see a slow change taking place in some of you! We need time. Hear me out, Townspeople of my Town. You're under fire now.

**TOWNSPEOPLE: SONS AND SONS-IN-LAW.** Fire, fire, fire.

**MAYOR BEFORE.** You're blamed for a crime you've not committed. It is hard to take on such a burden. It is hard to bear such a burden. Let us light candles on the cemetery together. Let tears well in someone's eye. Let the dead see the warmth in our hearts.

**TOWNSPEOPLE: SONS AND SONS-IN-LAW.** He's prostrated himself, our Mayor
Tears welling in his eye
Warmth flowing from his heart
He's all focused
Watching the slow transformation
Within us.

MAYOR BEFORE. I'm watching the slow transformation within some of you.

TOWNSPEOPLE: SONS AND SONS-IN-LAW. He's watching the slow transformation within some of us.

TOWNSPERSON. Such as who?

TOWNSPEOPLE: SONS AND SONS-IN-LAW. Not us, not you.

TOWNSPERSON. We're still the same, unchanged.

TOWNSPEOPLE: SONS AND SONS-IN-LAW. And it's hard standing here like this with the Monument.

MAYOR BEFORE. It's hard to bear such a burden.

TOWNSPEOPLE: SONS AND SONS-IN-LAW. Where do you propose we set it down, Mayor? On your good self?

MAYOR BEFORE. Set it down on me, Townspeople, maybe that will save us. Lay the Monument on me that I might bear it for the Cemetery.

TOWNSPERSON. Whatever. Set it down.

*The Townspeople set the Monument down upon the Mayor. CRASH!*

MAYOR AFTER. Lord! It's me! It's me!

*Go home, Gentle Viewers, and don't look back. There's nothing left. Nothing to see. There is no cemetery. There is the Monument. There is no Mayor. There is only the Monument.*

**Old Testament Song:**

And God rained down
Upon that Town
A shower of brimstone
Fire from heaven

He smote the Town
As was foretold
One righteous soul
Can't set things right

He burned it all
The sparrows, the deer

And the Townspeople
Of that Town

And the smoke rose
Up from that land
Like smoke from a furnace
It was God's doing

*Don't look back, Gentle Viewers, or you'll turn to stone like the Beauty Queen.*

*The End*

# THE MAYOR II

**CHARACTERS**

THE MAYOR

A TOWNSPERSON

POET

PROFESSOR JAN T. GROSS

THE BOOK

READER 1, 2, 3

YOUNG GENERATION 1, 2, 3

FLORIST

DENTIST

COUNCILLOR

THE PRESIDENT OF POLAND

ISRAELI AMBASSADOR

COUNCILORS

GOD FROM THE TOWN, FROM JERUSALEM, FROM NEW YORK

CHORUS

## A PRAYER OF THANKS, PRAISING THE HERO

POET. There was never anyone like my Hero—and there never will be.

CHORUS. He is fair all over. The road he has gone down is strewn with flowers. The trees he has passed now have stars for leaves. The sun shines upon him with a special glow.

**POET.** There was never a hero as fair as him, and there never will be.

**CHORUS.** Songs are sung about him in his homeland. His name is carved in the hardest of stone. The letters of his name will never crumble to dust.

**POET.** Let all writers envy me. Let them look around—whom will they see in their countries? Will it be someone like him?

**CHORUS.** He set off on a journey like Odysseus. He met presidents, ambassadors, bishops and rabbis. He fought battles and was victorious.

**POET.** There was never a hero as fair as him, and there never will be.

**CHORUS.** He was banished from his land.

**POET.** That is not true.

**CHORUS.** He left of his own will.

**POET.** That is not true.

**CHORUS.** He left because the ground beneath his feet would no longer carry him.

**POET.** That is not true.

**CHORUS.** He could have walked the earth; pretended he was alive.

**POET.** That is not true.

**CHORUS.** He could have plugged his ears up with wax; put a black blindfold on his eyes.

**POET.** That is not true.

**CHORUS.** He could have committed suicide.

**POET.** That is not true.

**CHORUS.** There was nothing he could have done.

**POET.** That is not true.

## AS USUAL, IT'S ALL THE FAULT OF THE INTELLECTUALS

**POET.** Greetings all, now for a few words about myself: I have come from Poland; I'm a poet: I write poems. That's right. I admit it: I write poems like many other poets, but there is something that sets me aside. You see, I only write poems about a single specific person. It's not a woman—and it's not about sex at all. That person, that Hero of mine, is the Mayor. He is here, he will appear shortly, because I want to pay tribute to him with these poems, and I want to thank our Embassy for making every effort so that he could be with us today. Is the Mayor here? No? Is he on his way? Then I'll begin:

The story of my Hero and of my fascination with him began when Professor Jan T. Gross was running away from ghosts.

PROFESSOR JAN T. GROSS (*enters*). I disagree with that opinion.

POET. Greetings, Professor Jan T. Gross.

PROFESSOR JAN T. GROSS (*sitting*). Greetings, and I reiterate my disagreement.

POET. Though Professor Jan T. Gross disagrees with the opinion, I'm afraid I'm right to see him running pursued by ghosts. Since he's been a professor for a long time now, he's not in very good shape. He is short of breath when he runs. His body, twisted from rummaging in the drawers and crannies of archives, moves in a zigzag and creaks like an old wardrobe. Nonetheless, the Professor runs, well aware that even daily, determined exercise won't help him run away from ghosts. That's why the Professor has decided to stop and throw something over his shoulder. Isn't that right, Professor?

PROFESSOR JAN. T. GROSS. In European fairy tales, fleeing characters often throw something over their shoulders—magical objects, mostly. You can throw a mirror that will turn into a glass mountain, like they did in the Grimm Tales. During the war, people would drop all their belongings.

POET. What have you decided to throw over your shoulder?

PROFESSOR JAN T. GROSS. A book.

POET. And so the professor decides to throw a book over his shoulder. Since he doesn't have one at hand, he runs, creaking and panting, to his desk and eagerly starts writing. By the year

2000, he's done writing, and he throws all the author's copies over his shoulder.

The book gets published in Poland in the year 2000. Its title is "Neighbors."

This is where our story begins. Poland in the year 2000, the book is called "Neighbors." Could I have the Book, please?

**THE BOOK.** I am a slim and unassuming but my cover is hard. The hard cover was probably chosen for practical reasons. If someone suddenly throws up while reading, there's a chance I won't fall apart all at once. And if someone pees on me, I'll weather the piss, too.

**POET.** I'd like to ask Polish readers for their thoughts about the book.

**READER 1.** I am against this disgusting book.

**READER 2.** I also think that the book is disgusting, even though I haven't read it.

**READER 3.** I have read the book and I don't want to talk about what I have read.

**THE BOOK.** It's not easy to make up your mind after listening to my readers.

**POET.** For my Hero, it was a most important book.

**THE BOOK.** Why don't I say what my blurb was?

"Jan T. Gross 'Neighbors'": The tragedy of sixteen hundred Jews from the town of Jedwabne murdered by their neighbors, on July 10th 1941, though investigated by a court in Łomża in May of 1949, did not become part of the historiography of World War II. The book fills this gap, relying on testimony by survivors, witnesses, and participants of the pogrom. The author inquires whether, in light of the tragedy in Jedwabne, one shouldn't revise various established beliefs regarding the history of Poland in the latter half of the twentieth century.

**MAYOR** (*enters*). Why don't I finally say what I read in that Book?

**POET.** There was never a hero as fair as him, and there never will be.

**MAYOR.** But why?

I was a normal person
Just like you and you and you
I studied I loved I worked
I became the Mayor of my Town
It was my third term
I thought it would be nothing special
Roads waterworks bureaucracy
When suddenly a certain professor
Opened up a Pandora's box
He wrote a book
From which the stink
Of burning spread all over the country
The spirits of burnt Jews scattered forth
And joined the spirits
That—like Rabbi Nachman,
Blessed be His name—
That float above each killing site until
Some holy soul
Guides them to heaven
So the number of spirits over Poland doubled
The ones already floating
Were joined by spirits from my Town
Flying crooked
Because they were all twisted
The flames had melted their wings
Legs teeth noses
Into a single flying mass
What was to be done?
I asked I wept
I spoke of the cruel murder
Sixty years ago
Of the Jewish citizens of our Town
We must face the fact of this crime with Christian humility
Because I am a Christian
Let's change the inscription on the monument
That says the Jews were killed by the Germans

Professor Gross said in an interview
That he hoped Poland would gain credibility
That neighbors all over the world
In Serbia Bosnia Rwanda
Did such murderous deeds
It's a great challenge for contemporary civilization
But the main thing is the way
We'll deal with it
Us Poles

**THE BOOK.** I am all made up of Horrific Sentences. Seriously. Some sentences might not seem horrific, but that's just the way it looks. Take this Sentence from page 11 [2][1]: "On Monday evening, June 23, 1941, Germans entered the town"—it doesn't seem Horrific but it is. The next Horrific Sentence from page 11 is also Horrific: "And as early as the 25th local bandits, from the Polish population, started an anti-Jewish pogrom."

And now for the Horrific Sentences placed back-to-back on page 12 [2–3]: "I saw with my own eyes how Wacek Borowiuk together with his brother Mietek killed Chajcia Wasersztajn, Jakub Kac, seventy-three years old, and Eliasz Krawiecki. Jakub Kac they stoned to death with bricks. Krawiecki they knifed and then plucked his eyes and cut off his tongue. He suffered terribly for twelve hours before he gave up his soul. On the same day I observed a horrible scene. Chaja Kubrzańska, twenty-eight years old, and Basia Binsztajn, twenty-six years old, both holding newborn babies, when they saw what was going on, they ran to a pond, in order to drown themselves with the children rather than fall into the hands of bandits. They put their children in the water and drowned

1 Page numbers from the Polish edition of Jan T. Gross's *Sąsiedzi. Historia zagłady żydowskiego miasteczka* (Warsaw: Pogranicze, 2000); pages in brackets from the US edition *Neighbors: The Destruction of the Jewish Community in Jedwabne, Poland* (Princeton, NJ: Princeton University Press, 2001).

them with their own hands: then Baśka Binsztajn jumped in and immediately went to the bottom, while Chaja Kubrzańska suffered for a couple of hours. Assembled hooligans made a spectacle of this. They advised her to lie face down in the water, so that she would drown faster. Finally, seeing that the children were already dead, she threw herself more energetically into the water and found her death too. The next day a local priest intervened, explaining that they should stop the pogrom, and that German authorities would take care of things by themselves. Such an order was issued by the Germans on July 10, 1941. Even though the Germans gave the order, it was Polish hooligans who took it up and carried it out, using the most horrible methods. After various tortures and humiliations, they burned all the Jews in a barn." Eyewitness account by Szmul Wasersztajn, footnote 6 at the bottom of Horrific Page 14 [6].

## THE MAYOR'S PRIVATE EXPENSES

**POET.** After reading Professor Gross' Book, the Mayor decided to change the structure of his expenses.

**MAYOR.** On the fifty-ninth anniversary of the Jedwabne massacre, that is on July 10, 2000, I decided to lay a wreath before the Monument in our Town. The chairman of the Town Council and I went to a florist's. The Horrific Sentences from the Book were with me.

**THE BOOK.** Page 67 [55]: "They chased them all to a barn. Poured kerosene all around. It took but two minutes, but the screaming . . . I can still hear it."

**MAYOR** (*to the Book*). That's enough.

**THE BOOK.** Page 73 [60]: "The beautiful Gitele Nadolny (Nadolnik) . . . had her head cut off, and the murderers . . . later kicked it around."

**MAYOR.** Enough.

**THE BOOK.** Page 73: "Laudański and Kalinowski were leading Hersz Zdrojewicz . . . blood was flowing from his over his neck and onto his torso, and he said to me, Save me, Mister Bardo□. Being afraid of these murderers, I replied, I cannot help you with anything, and I passed them by."

**MAYOR** (*to the Book*). Stop it.

**THE BOOK.** I'm not saying anything: I'm not an audiobook. You've read me and those Horrific Sentences are now etched in your flesh, Mayor. They're playing in your head of their own accord, you know?

**MAYOR.** Good day, madam florist.

**FLORIST.** Good day, you Jewish flunky.

**MAYOR.** I want to use my private money to buy a bouquet that I can lay in front of the Monument to the Jews murdered in our Town.

**FLORIST.** I suspect that it was Jews who gave you that money, you Jewish flunky.

**MAYOR.** No, it's money from my salary. And I'd like the ribbon to read: "To the murdered Jewish townspeople of Jedwabne in commemoration and as a warning—Society."

**FLORIST.** And where is that society of yours?

**MAYOR.** I have the chairman of the town council with me.

**FLORIST.** Two Jewish flunkies do not a society make.

**MAYOR.** We might see things differently but I discern a slow evolution within you. You must gain the maturity to bear the burden of other people's guilt.

**FLORIST.** Yes, I do feel a readiness to undergo spiritual transformation. I work at a florist's, and that's just like attending an aromatherapy workshop.

**POET.** It's all because of you, Professor. You're the one responsible for the Horrific Words etching themselves in the Mayor's mind. You've hurt him.

**PROFESSOR JAN T. GROSS.** He could have not read the Book, like other people. Slept soundly. Lived a normal life.

**POET.** You could have warned him. You could have told the Book to have a different blurb, for instance: "whosoever picks me up will murder Sleep."

**PROFESSOR JAN T. GROSS.** I wrote the truth. Human beings are not God: they only see what's in front of them. I saw my desk, drawers in filing cabinets, and creaky wardrobes.

**MAYOR.** I stopped dreaming my old dreams, and the new ones are unbearable.

Tonight, I dreamt up "A Prayer to Satan."
Thank you Satan for all thy bounty:
For eyes that see only the dark side of life
For the guts you wrenched from me so you could have something to play with
Thank you Satan for all thy bounty
When I ask, Satan, why are you doing this to me?
You always reply in an affable tone:
You have free will, Mayor
You have what you yourself have chosen, Mayor
Thank you Satan for all thy bounty
For making me hate my neighbor as I hate myself
For my revulsion for life and revulsion for death
Thank you Satan for all thy bounty
When I ask, Satan, why are you doing this to me?
You always reply in an affable tone:
You have free will, Mayor
You have what you yourself have chosen, Mayor
A curse on you, Satan, My Lord
Because of you
I have nowhere to go

I don't know what to live for
Because of you
I have murdered sleep
I am a murderer
Because of you I thought
It would be one murder
Of just one dream
But I had to murder on
Now all I have is nightmares
You're saying that was my choice?
Help me, Satan
For I have nobody left but you
Help me
To flee this life
Help me die, Satan
As I curse you

## A SESSION OF THE TOWN COUNCIL REGARDING HEADGEAR

**COUNCILOR.** I move to purchase two skullcaps: one for our Mayor, another for the Chairman of the town council.

**MAYOR.** I oppose the motion. I have a cap already. I don't need another one.

**COUNCILOR.** A skullcap is not a real cap. Nor did my motion stem from any concern for the health of Mr. Ikey and Kikey here.

**MAYOR.** What did it stem from?

**COUNCILOR.** Patriotic concern. I consider laying a wreath with an inscribed ribbon to be anti-Polish activity.

**MAYOR.** That's where we differ. Laying a wreath with an inscribed ribbon seems patriotic and pro-Polish to me. But I do discern a slow evolution within you.

**COUNCILOR.** Are you saying I am gaining the maturity needed to bear the burden of someone else's guilt?

MAYOR. I am.

COUNCILOR. Maybe I am, but these things need time, you sidelocked schmuckface.

## DISINFORMATION IN THE PRESS

MAYOR. I read in the nationwide press that our President wants to apologize.

TOWNSPERSON. To whom?

MAYOR. The Jews.

TOWNSPERSON. Would he be thinking of a symbolic apology as a gesture of reconciliation between the Polish and Jewish communities who had, for centuries, lived amicably in this hospitable land of ours?

MAYOR. That's right.

TOWNSPERSON. I don't like the idea. The President will apologize and the Jews will tell him to shove the apology.

MAYOR. Why would they tell him to shove it?

TOWNSPERSON. Haven't you read Simon Wiesenthal's "The Sunflower?" There's a dying German in it who asks Wiesenthal to forgive him, but he says "no way." That's not a very encouraging precedent, is it?

MAYOR. No, it's not. So what happened to the German?

TOWNSPERSON. He died without achieving anything. That's why we're starting a Committee Against Apologizing in our Town. Are you in?

MAYOR. I am.

**MAYOR.** That was a mistake. The decision to join the Committee. I quit after two weeks. At first I hoped I'd be able to come to some sort of compromise with the Townspeople regarding our position on the crime. I was thinking of joint prayer at the site of the atrocity. I believed it was possible. Gross wrote the truth in his Book, which is full of those Horrific Sentences. They have etched themselves in my flesh. It's hard on the Townspeople as well. There are journalists in the Town, looking at them like they were murderers. TV crews, foreigners, a media circus. An end to peace and quiet. And is the Polish state doing something to help us? Is it sending mediators, psychologists, negotiators? No. We're on our own . . . Though I think that if someone doesn't react to these horrors on his own, there's nothing a psychologist could do. Besides, our priest claims that the Jews were killed by the Germans. He has cancer. They've removed 27 centimeters of his intestine, and he's still alive. He thinks it's a miracle. Thinks God is keeping him alive so he can talk about the Germans.

## LETTERS FROM POLISH-AMERICANS IN CHICAGO

**LETTER 1.** "Dear Mr. Mayor! We express solidarity with you and your presence in the Committee Against Apologizing. Jedwabne is Goebbels-style propaganda in Jewish garb." Polish-Americans from Chicago.

**LETTER 2.** "To whom it may concern: don't let them set up some Jewish cemetery in your town. Even the Gospels call the Jews a generation of vipers. Don't let the minority become the majority. The Polish Organization of Patriotic Pudding Heads."

## STATEMENT BY THE PRESIDENT OF THE POLISH AMERICAN CONGRESS, EDWARD MOSKAL

Fifty years down the road, the Jews are still at their endless diatribes and hateful denunciations whereby Poles are the sole culprits, without ever mentioning the collusion of so-called Jewish "partisans" with the killing machine of Nazi Germany or with Russian murderers for the exact same reason.

Prof. Kieres relies on evidence originating from Rabbi Baker. We know all there is to know about rabbis and their love for Polish institutions.

It would be better if they treated the Palestinians right instead of killing their children. There is something horrific about the image of a young Palestinian boy being shielded from Israeli bullets by his father, and killed by those "heroes" a while later.

Thank you. Today is February 28, 2001. God bless.

## THE TOWN'S NO LONGER THE SAME

MAYOR. We get visits from representatives and senators: there was even a film director and a professor.

On the one hand, that's good, but then again it isn't.

The Townspeople who believe in a Jewish conspiracy are in the minority, but they get support from important individuals. People want to do the right thing but then somebody calls them and says "you Jewish flunky," so they get scared. I'm not scared. We're renovating the market square and the road to the barn. The President and guests from all over the world are coming: we have to make a good impression.

I have a dream in which I say: "Our Jewish brothers who were born here, we are touched to have you here."

**TOWNSPERSON.** In the name of the Father, the Son and the Holy Ghost, Amen. Good Lord, thank you for the summer. Thank you for making the wheat grow by sending an angel to stand by every ear and whisper "grow" to it. Thank you for this beautiful church in my Town, where I can kneel before you and ask for help. What am I supposed to do? The things happening in the Town are driving me mad. Did you rid the Polish lands of godless communists just so we could experience humiliation and helplessness? The authorities in Warsaw have planned a great commemoration in our Town. They're not asking us Townspeople whether we are mature enough to bear the burden of someone else's guilt. The President of Poland is supposed to come here along with the Israeli ambassador, senators and members of parliament, Rabbi Baker, who immigrated to America before the war, journalists, and I don't know who else. They will commemorate the anniversary of the burning of Jews in our barn. They will accuse us of being the sons and daughters of murderers, with the whole world watching. They will do penance by proxy and trample our soil. They will enter our homes and say: it reeks of charred flesh here, so we'll throw the windows open, for you are like swine oblivious to the stench they live in. We're swine to them.

Tell me, God, can you file a complaint against the Polish authorities at the Court in Strasbourg? Will they put them in jail for treating us like pigs? Will they pay us compensation for calling our homes sties?

Do you know, God, that an official inquiry into the atrocity is underway? I'm sure you do, for you know everything, but we in our Town know nothing. There's a chain-link fence around the site of the burned-down barn. And behind the fence, the inquiry is underway. They walk around and inquire. They dig around and inquire. I had a dream that they were going to open an underground museum beneath the barn. They would dig up the dead and expose their bodies underground. They would remove the soil, which is like a mother bundling up her child at night. Instead there would be a train in that underground museum: little cars with glass sides. You'll be able to sit comfortably and look with horror out the window at those burnt Jews. The train would choo-choo on, silent and electric, a voice in the headphones whispering in English, German, French, Italian, Spanish, Russian, Japanese, Chinese, and Etruscan: "This was done by the Poles, those Polish swine, polnische Schweine, Polish animals." And will you suffer that to happen, God? Why should Germans hear such things? Why should Germans listen to them comfortably and with horror?

I heard there was this Jew called Wiesenthal who hunted Nazis after the war. This Jew Wiesenthal survived the war to hunt Nazis who killed Jews, that's what you have decided God, for Thou art just. But before that Jew survived the war, a dying German asked his forgiveness for killing Jews. And Wiesenthal did not forgive that German on his deathbed.

Why should we, who did not commit this past atrocity, ask the Jews for forgiveness?

## THE BONE COLLECTOR

TOWNSPERSON. Mister Mayor, what are you doing in a dentist's waiting room?

MAYOR. Waiting to see the dentist because everything you've been saying about me has given me a toothache.

TOWNSPERSON. What have we been saying exactly?

MAYOR. That I'm a Mayor who wants to sell the whole Town to the Jews, that my mother-in-law married a rabbi in America, and that I say "Shalom" instead of "God bless."

DENTIST. Shalom to you, Mister Mayor. Ha, ha, just kidding. Did you hear the news? Our Polish authorities have trucks parked outside the barn.

MAYOR. What trucks?

DENTIST. With human bones. And they're laying the bones next to the ones under the barn. So it all adds up, so they have 1,600 bodies there like that Jew Gross wrote in his book.

PROFESSOR JAN T. GROSS. Yes, we are flying bones in from Israel, but we have to separate the Ashkenazi bones from the Sephardic ones some idiot added to the cargo. Imagine sending Sephardic bones to Poland. How will I account for Spanish DNA under a Polish barn?

MAYOR. Professor, are you really saying what I think you're saying?

PROFESSOR. Come now, Mayor, I'm not really here. It's just you and your Townspeople. You're seeing things, and that means you're on the verge of a nervous breakdown. All that's left is for you to organize a great anniversary commemoration in your free time and against the will of your Townspeople—and that will be that. I'm not saying you're going to die: one doesn't die that easily.

MAYOR. I'd like the Townspeople to pray for those who were killed, to pay tribute to the victims. For newlyweds to take photos of themselves in front of the monument that will be erected on the scene of the crime. For them to say, "where there was death, there is life, spirits of the dead we apologize for our fathers, bless our children."

DENTIST. Madman.

MAYOR. One must have the maturity to bear the burden of someone else's guilt.

## ANOTHER POINT OF VIEW (THE YOUNG GENERATION)

YOUNG GENERATION 1. Weed's the thing to give you the maturity to bear someone else's guilt.

YOUNG GENERATION 2. Yeah, grass rocks from time to time, you chill out, so's you can bear the burden of guilt and apologize. Hash is also boss when you want to unwind. It's all cool, s'long as there's no needles involved: that shit is too heavy.

YOUNG GENERATION 3. I'm not stoned like those retards, so I'll say something sensible:

We were born 50 years after the war. Got that? We don't give a shit about the war. We don't give a shit about World War II.

YOUNG GENERATION 2. Did you just call me a retard?

YOUNG GENERATION 3. Yeah, I called you a retard. Only retards get stoned.

YOUNG GENERATION 1. What worries me is that bros are doing smack, blow, speed and designer drugs like mephedrone. I smoke weed because it doesn't hurt anybody.

YOUNG GENERATION 3. Because of that Gross dude whenever I go anywhere, like Warsaw, and say where I come from, there's always some 'tard who's like: Are you from that Town where neighbors kill their neighbors and burn them in a barn? And that pisses me off. So I'm like: Shut up, dude, don't piss me off. And if he doesn't shut up, I go: Now I'm pissed off. And I guess you know what people from our town are capable of when they're pissed off?

YOUNG GENERATION 1. Speed in Poland is 10 dollars a gram. That's the lowest price in Europe.

YOUNG GENERATION 2. Nobody does coke here; dudes from Warsaw do coke.

YOUNG GENERATION 3. I'm never moving out. Screw life in Warsaw.

YOUNG GENERATION 2. I forgive you for calling me a retard.

YOUNG GENERATION 3. Yes, it was me who burned those Jews in the barn.
Is that what you wanted to hear?
Yes, it was me who herded them into the barn.
Can't you tell it from the way I look?
So, what do you think I should look like?
I'm sick of this business with the Jews.

Sing the anthem:
March, march Dąbrowski
From Italian lands to the Polish!

Down with the barn!
(*All together*)
Down with the barn!

March, march Dąbrowski
We want iPhones!
(*All together*)
We want iPhones!

March, march Dąbrowski
Down with the barn!
(*All together*)
Down with the barn!

March, march Dąbrowski
The Jews were killed by Voldemort!
(*All together*)
The Jews were killed by Voldemort!

March, march Dąbrowski
Down with history!
(*All together*)
Down with history!

March, march Dąbrowski
Down with memory!
(*All together*)
Down with memory!

March, march Dąbrowski
We want to live!
(*All together*)
We want to live!

MAYOR. A warm welcome to all on the hospitable soil of Jedwabne.

THE PRESIDENT OF POLAND. As the President of Poland I'd like to welcome the whole public.

TOWNSPERSON. Where do you see the public, Mr. President?

THE PRESIDENT OF POLAND. It's this metaphor you use in speeches.

FLORIST. But I'm here, it's me, the florist from the florist's. I sold the Mayor a wreath with a ribbon, and the flowers brought about a spiritual transformation within me.

COUNCILLOR. As a Councilor, I too have thought the matter over and gained the maturity to bear the burden of someone else's guilt.

TOWNSPERSON. Two Jewish flunkies do not the public make.

POET. It is July 10, 2001. The ceremony is about to begin. In a while the President of Poland, Aleksander Kwaśniewski, will be apologizing.

TOWNSPERSON. I'm out of here.

PRESIDENT. Today, as a human being, a citizen and the President of the Republic of Poland, I apologize. I apologize in my own name and on behalf of those Poles whose conscience has been moved by this atrocity. On behalf of those who believe that one cannot be proud of the glory of Polish history without feeling pain and shame at the evil Poles have done unto others.

TOWNSPERSON. What do you say to that, Lord?

GOD FROM THE TOWN. Give it a moment.

MAYOR. What I want most is for those who have come here to see the warmth in our hearts, and realize that only a handful of Poles were responsible for this evil.

TOWNSPERSON. So, what do you say, Lord? The President's words have etched themselves in my flesh.

GOD FROM THE TOWN. I wanted to listen to your Mayor, and my answer is: I have sent down rain today. Satisfied?

TOWNSPERSON. To spoil the ceremony. That is fitting.

**GOD FROM THE TOWN.** I know you feel like strangers in your own Town. But I had your

President—even though he is an atheist—sow the words "I apologize" in your hearts. One of my angels is standing by those words now, saying, "grow, grow."

**TOWNSPERSON.** Our parish priest did not go to the Monument, but he did invite Rabbi Baker to the vicarage. Maybe they're working on cleansing the memory and reconciliation right now. Or maybe our priest is telling him about the tumor, the 27 cm. section of intestine he had removed, and about the Germans.

**PRESIDENT.** Today, as a human being, a citizen and the President of the Republic of Poland, I apologize. I apologize in my own name and on behalf of those Poles whose conscience has been moved by this atrocity. On behalf of those who believe that one cannot be proud of the glory of Polish history without feeling pain and shame at the evil Poles have done unto others.

**ISRAELI AMBASSADOR.** Mr. President, thank you for these words. They come from the heart and they will sink into our hearts. Maybe this rain is a symbol—maybe God wants to cry along with us today?

**TOWNSPERSON.** I went home. But I watched the events in my Town on TV.

**PRESIDENT.** Let us all be Townspeople of this Town today. Let us identify with them. Let us remain with them in a shared sense of regret, despair, shame and solidarity.

**MAYOR.** I'd like to thank all the Townspeople who came here today.

**TOWNSPERSON.** Two Jewish flunkies do not a society make.

**ISRAELI AMBASSADOR.** I, Shevah Weiss, the Israeli Ambassador to Poland, had the opportunity to know other neighbors in my life. Thanks to them, my family and I survived the Holocaust. Thanks to them, I can stand before you now. In my life, I have known other barns, ones in which Jews were hidden in the hope of a better future. I want to underscore these facts here and now.

MAYOR. The Polish Bishops' Conference is not officially represented. But there are Catholic priests. They are praying.

TOWNSPERSON. God, I seek refuge in Thee.

MAYOR. God, I seek refuge in Thee.

GOD FROM JERUSALEM. Young Israelis don't care much about the past. They are only concerned with today and tomorrow—that is, the war. Nobody's interested in what's going on today in some Polish Town. Even the spokesperson of Yad Vashem has little to say on the subject.

GOD FROM NEW YORK. The American Jewish Committee is watching the Town from a distance. The prevailing mood is one of disappointment, but there are diplomatic expressions of satisfaction that the Polish President has made a step forward, even though he was standing still.

MAYOR. This ceremony has shown the strength of the Polish nation.

POET. But it's over now. Everybody's gone home. What now, Mayor?

## TOMORROW AND FOREVERMORE

COUNCILLORS. Jew-bastard! Menorahs-Shmenorahs! Sabbath-blabbath!

MAYOR. I have been stubborn. I never thought I could be so stubborn.

COUNCILLORS. Do what we've all been waiting for. Go ahead and say it. We're all waiting.

MAYOR. One becomes Mayor to pave a road, to shape up the local health service, to clean up the market square. What I was occupied with this whole year had nothing to do with being a Mayor, and I was not ready for it spiritually or substantively. I, the Mayor of a small Town, faced the task of teaching charity between nations and mourning the death of others. All my life, I've wanted to leave this Town. You know I'm not from around here. I came here many years ago. But I was one of you. I saw the world as you did. I was an anti-Semite until recently. Like you, I thought that the Jews were running Poland. I was wrong about other things as well. At school, they taught me that the Russians were our friends, and that the Americans were imperialists. That's what you were taught, too. I believed it, just like you did. But I've changed. I don't know how it happened. I don't know how a man can change so much and be so stubborn. How something he never imagined he had can awake within him. I can't give it a name. But it turned out that I'm terribly stubborn. I resolved to weep at other people's deaths. I turned out to be terribly stubborn when it comes to the truth. The truth turned out to be more important than anything. More important than fear, for instance. I know you can't bear to look at and listen to me anymore. I'm putting in my resignation.

COUNCILLORS. You could have been our Mayor, not theirs. You could have basked in a hero's glory, and now what? You did what the Jews wanted, and now they've left you.

TOWNSPERSON. You think this is where the story ends? That you'll simply put in your resignation and be left in peace? As a Townsperson of this Town, I won't leave you in peace. I'll cut off the roots connecting you to the soil on which the Town stands. I know this soil, it's mine, I strew grain into it every year, and every year it grows. I know what should be done to cut off the roots.

Now I'm cutting the roots from your arms, your legs your head, your heart, and I curse you for all eternity. I curse you. This soil will never be yours. I curse you. This soil will never feed you again. I curse you. This soil will never bear you again. You are not of it anymore. You're a stranger. Go forth. This soil no longer wants you. Go and ask another soil to take you in. There is nothing left here for you; neither life nor death. I did it in spite of God, but that's my business.

Be you cursed.

**POET.** Barely a year longer did the Mayor live in his Town. Without a job, without friends, without hope. Confined within four walls, confined within himself, confined within his heart. Did he expect help or didn't he? We'll never know. Maybe he did, maybe he didn't. He was licking his wounds. He was very stubborn, very strong, but the soil upon which he walked would no longer bear him. One day he got up, packed his all belongings and threw them behind him. He got up, looked at his life and threw it behind him. Now he was free, he could go wherever he wanted. Where is he now? Here. What does here mean? Everywhere.

He changed his name. He's now walking the streets of Chicago, New York, Minneapolis. He's one of you. He changed his name so that his countrymen wouldn't recognize him and give him too strong a hug.

He changed his name because he'd cast something behind him– his former life—because that's the way you run away in European folktales. If he could speak—and he doesn't want to say anything in public—perhaps it would go something like this:

**MAYOR.** Was I alive only to learn that I've been stubborn? That's what I keep asking myself as I wander the empty sidewalks along your broad streets. It's this European habit: walking. I hear a language that isn't mine, I'm scared of places I don't know, customs I don't understand. I'm a stranger. I will never belong anywhere anymore. Fear is always with me, I say it, I repeat it, garbling your words. I keep thinking that I was stubborn, very stubborn. And that I found the strength to stand by myself and by my truth. That's something to be proud of, something big.

But the loneliness, the loneliness . . .

**POET.** This is the end of the story. There's no use pretending that anything else will happen. I'm no poet, just a frustrated author who can't find the words to describe his Hero. He's not coming here, no embassy will give him the VIP treatment, nobody's waiting to applaud him. It's so threadbare to say that there was never anyone like my Hero and there never will be. How to find the words that will persuade others this is so? Perhaps I'll never find them? Perhaps it's something one has to live with? That all that remains is loneliness—and pride at having stubbornly tried.

*The End*

*Warsaw, July–September 2011*

## CHARACTERS

JAN KRUCZKOWSKI
JAN CHAREWICZ
ZYGMUNT SOBOLEWSKI
ANDRZEJ URSYN SZANTYR
KAROLINA KOZAK
HANNE-LORE PRETZSCH
ILSE BODE
ANGELA HUBRICH
MATTHIAS GÖRITZ
DIETRICH GARBRECHT
STALIN
CHURCHILL
ROOSEVELT

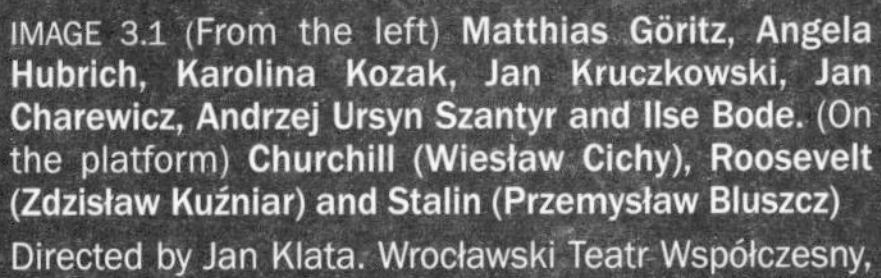

IMAGE 3.1 (From the left) **Matthias Göritz, Angela Hubrich, Karolina Kozak, Jan Kruczkowski, Jan Charewicz, Andrzej Ursyn Szantyr and Ilse Bode.** (On the platform) **Churchill (Wiesław Cichy), Roosevelt (Zdzisław Kuźniar) and Stalin (Przemysław Bluszcz)**

Directed by Jan Klata. Wrocławski Teatr Współczesny, Wrocław (2006)

*Photograph by Bartłomiej Sowa*

DUNJA FUNKE AND SEBASTIAN MAJEWSKI

Translated by Artur Zapałowski

# TRANSFER!

## NOTE

The protagonists of *Transfer!* are Poles and Germans displaced in the wake of the territorial changes after World War II, when the borders of Poland, Germany and the Soviet Union were redrawn, forcing them to leave their homes. The text is based on the recollections and accounts of people who witnessed and were affected by the deportations. Their life stories were set against a grotesque take on the Yalta Conference, at which Joseph Stalin, Winston Churchill and Franklin D. Roosevelt drew up the borders of postwar Europe. The documentary accounts, collected and edited by Dunja Funke and Sebastian Majewski, are woven in with original text written for the scenes at Yalta, making use of documents and archival sources, and often set to songs by Joy Division.

The production, directed by Jan Klata, premiered on November 18, 2006, in Teatr Współczesny in Wrocław (co-produced by Hebbel-am-Ufer in Berlin), and starred displaced Germans and Poles who told their life stories on stage. In this storytelling production, ten community performers spoke in their native languages, either Polish or German. Audience members had headphones for simultaneous translation. Subtitles were not an option, because the elderly performers would often forget lines or even change stories from one night to the next. The professional actors playing Stalin, Churchill and Roosevelt were placed on a mobile platform in the center of the stage. At each time in the script when a Joy Division song appeared, attention shifted up to the platform, where Stalin, Churchill and Roosevelt pretended to play and lip-sync along with the song.

### DAY OF THE LORDS—JOY DIVISION

This is the room, the start of it all
No portrait so fine, only sheets on the wall
I've seen the nights, filled with bloodsport and pain
And the bodies obtained, the bodies obtained
Where will it end? Where will it end?
Where will it end? Where will it end?

These are your friends from childhood, through youth
Who goaded you on, demanded your proof
Withdrawal pain is hard, it can do you right in
So distorted and thin, distorted and thin
Where will it end? Where will it end?
Where will it end? Where will it end?

This is the car at the edge of the road
There's nothing disturbed, all the windows are closed
I guess you were right when we talked in the heat
There's no room for the weak, no room for the weak
Where will it end? Where will it end?
Where will it end? Where will it end?

This is the room, the start of it all
No portrait so fine, only sheets on the wall
I've seen the nights, filled with bloodsport and pain
And the bodies obtained, the bodies obtained
Where will it end? Where will it end?
Where will it end? Where will it end?

**STALIN.** Silence! Out!

**CHURCHILL.** Yalta. The Riviera of Hades. The cocktails lack lemons.

**ROOSEVELT.** I've noticed a lack of fish in the aquarium.

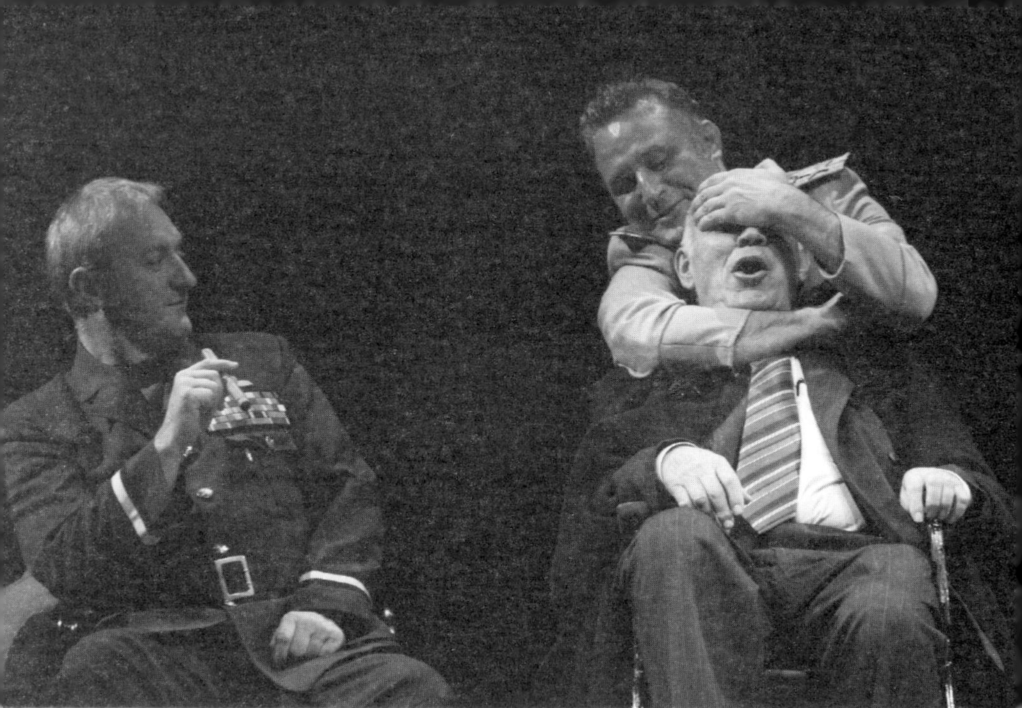

IMAGE 3.2 **Churchill (Wiesław Cichy), Roosevelt (Zdzisław Kuźniar) and Stalin (Przemysław Bluszcz)**
Directed by Jan Klata. Wrocławski Teatr Współczesny, Wrocław (2006)
*Photograph by Bartłomiej Sowa*

CHURCHILL. There came three of us: me and my Sikhs, President Roosevelt and his Filipino chefs, and Stalin. The conference room was spacious and very neat.

We convened. Me, President Roosevelt and Stalin.

STALIN. His modest garb brings out his inborn grandeur.

ROOSEVELT. Stalin's face

CHURCHILL. Expressive and mercurial.

ROOSEVELT. Cat-like moves

CHURCHILL. Supple and full of grace.

ROOSEVELT. He seethed.

CHURCHILL. With sensuous energy.

**ROOSEVELT.** Everyone.

**CHURCHILL.** Everyone,

**ROOSEVELT.** Who saw him,

**CHURCHILL.** Wanted to see him again.

**ROOSEVELT.** A quiet modesty,

**CHURCHILL.** Puffing at his pipe,

**ROOSEVELT.** Serenity.

**STALIN.** When Zhukov first met me, he couldn't sleep.

**ROOSEVELT AND CHURCHILL.** It's hard to imagine a man like that ever deceiving someone!

**CHURCHILL.** And then . . . Stalin opened the meeting with a fine speech.

**STALIN.** I know how much the German people love their Führer.
He is a great man. No wonder he has gained such enormous support.
Mister Ribbentrop, I would like to drink to the health of the Führer . . .
Fuck! Ooops! Sorry! Fuck!
The same bunch of waiters. From the Metropol Hotel in Moscow. Dressed in white.
Who hired the same waiters? Fuck this shit!

**ANDRZEJ URSYN SZANTYR.** My family
came
to Lithuania from Pomerania
in the fifteenth century
36 generations
I'm the thirty-seventh

**JAN CHAREWICZ.** September 1, 1939
was the beginning of my wanderings
how many times did we move
Vilnius
Niemenczyn
the woods
Punżanki

Podbrodzie
Powiewiórka
Czarnoliszki
Preny . . .
Balingródek
a dozen times
and finally
Wrocław[1]

MATTHIAS GÖRITZ. Hamburg
Moscow
Paris
Marseilles
Chicago
Hamburg
Shanghai
New York
Berlin
Iowa City
Frankfurt
New York
Seoul
Los Angeles
Rabat
Reykjavik
Rome
Los Angeles
Como
Breslau
presently Wrocław
Berlin
Wrocław
here

---

1 After World War II, Vilnius was no longer part of Poland once the nation's borders were shifted to the west, while Wrocław became part of the reconfigured country.

GARBRECHT. My father was a Prussian and a staunch Protestant. He revered Bismarck and Frederick the Great.

He was a nationalist and a patriot, and in the early days of the Third Reich, he thought that was a good thing.

In 1940, my father was transferred to the university in Posen to help Aryanize it and drive out the Jews.

He was 1.96 meters tall, and heavy-set. In his day, he towered over everybody, including his sons, who never managed to outgrow him.

Father had broad shoulders and always held his head high. That earned him respect.

He had a peculiar way of criticizing us:
HAS THE SPIRIT OF GOODNESS ABANDONED YOU?
I spent a long time convinced I was insane.
Father strove to live according to Prussian principles:
Duty
Obedience, perhaps even to the point of blind obedience and death
Honesty
Goodness
Humility
Hard work
Love of the homeland
Discipline
Very important: Discipline!
It's almost easier to describe a Prussian than a German.
Father was taciturn
Father was taciturn
Father was very taciturn

HANNE-LORE PRETZSCH. After the war nobody talked about it.
I tried to find out something.
Nobody ever told me about anything.
I asked: Why didn't you resist,
couldn't you have . . .
No, No, No.

And then the student protests started.
I could really relate to Ulrike Meinhof at the time because
she was also a child of the war,
she also had a nice husband and two children.
I wasn't part of that movement but I could relate to her anger and wanting to break free of it all.
At home, my husband and I would be at each other's throats whenever we turned on the news.
He said one thing, and I said another.
The breaking point came when Ulrike Meinhof committed suicide. They said it on the news, and when my husband came into the bedroom he found me crying. What are you doing, he asks,

IMAGE 3.3 **Hanne-Lore Pretzsch**
Directed by Jan Klata. Wrocławski Teatr Współczesny, Wrocław (2006)
*Photograph by Bartłomiej Sowa*

and I say that Meinhof's committed suicide.
"Some terrorist commits suicide and my wife throws a fit."
That was the last straw . . .
Then I got my high school diploma and started college.
All the other students were about 20 years younger than me, and that was the first time I'd talked about it: the war—and they listened. That's how it began.
Later, I packed my things and went backpacking to India, where I encountered yoga, chakra and mudras. I began meditating.
That soothed my wounded soul.
I'd like to show you a position called the Archer pose. You can do it together with the Breath of Fire.

IMAGE 3.4 **Jan Charewicz**
Directed by Jan Klata. Wrocławski Teatr Współczesny, Wrocław (2006)
*Photograph by Bartłomiej Sowa*

This is practiced by the Sikhs. They are called the Prussians of India.

**JAN KRUCZKOWSKI.** I have six different report cards
in different languages
before the war, I completed three grades of elementary school
a report card in Polish—one
the Russians came
a report card in Ukrainian and in Polish—two
the Germans came
a report card in German and in Polish—three
after completing sixth grade,
I enrolled in an underground grammar school
an underground education report card—four
the Russians came
report card in Ukrainian and in Polish—five
I skipped eighth grade
in '46, I left home and moved to Kluczbork[2]
high school diploma—six

**ZYGMUNT SOBOLEWSKI.** My mother came from impoverished gentry
a small manor
a rusty shotgun on the wall
a saber on a hemp belt
Father had no money
he apprenticed at a blacksmith's
he trained as a driver in Lwow
he wanted a trade, otherwise he'd be a nobody
With everything he earned
he bought up land
and was becoming somebody
Mother caught his eye somewhere
she was taller than him
Grandfather laughed

---

**2** Kluczbork is a town in southwest Poland that belonged to Germany before the war.

and called Father a squirt
but my mother was determined
like the heroine of a soap opera:
it was him or no one
they got married
Grandfather looked down on Father
and Father wanted to prove he was worth something
him and Mother built a house
a temporary one, but their own
they were so busy
it was five years before I was born
Grandmother was getting worried
that was when Grandfather's attitude changed
he started respecting Father, even though he was still a squirt
meanwhile, Father kept buying up land
gathering materials for a real house
for the whole family, one that would last for years:
bricks, roof tiles
he had everything he needed by the summer of 1939
but in September it all came to an end
the plans and dreams
the community
my childhood

HANNE-LORE PRETZSCH. I was tall, slim, blonde and tanned—Hitler's future, they said.

"Kraft durch Freude"—"Strength through Joy," and my name was even Krafft—with two F's.

I was perfect for the BDM—the League of German Girls.[3] I very much wanted to join them. I was 10, and they would have accepted me that spring.

I wanted to be one of them—for the long white socks, the skirt, the brown jacket, the kerchief and the long braids.

3 Bund Deutscher Mädel was the girls' division of the Hitler Youth paramilitary organization.

I'm sure I would have become a squad leader or ended up in the Lebensborn program.[4]

**ILSE BODE.** Good evening.
Why did Hitler always stand this way? (*Hands covering crotch*)
He was hiding the last of the unemployed.
Goodbye.

**KAROLINA KOZAK.** Every night Father would go
read Sienkiewicz's "Trilogy"[5] in the common room
there was only one book
and they didn't want to lend it out
because someone might not return it
Mother waited at home
and when Father came back
he would tell her the story
I eavesdropped on them
the "Trilogy"
is interesting after all
love and romance
what father
would do that nowadays?

**ROOSEVELT.** I manage and appease. I do not vex. I do not antagonize.

**CHURCHILL.** I resort to various methods.

**STALIN.** Stalin.

**CHURCHILL.** The Big Three: that's what they call us.

**ROOSEVELT.** All we need now is the Pope.

**STALIN.** Splendid idea!

**CHURCHILL.** Let's call the Pope and make him our ally.

---

**4** The Nazi organization Lebensborn was designed to increase the Aryan population of Germany. It recruited young unmarried women to bear racially "pure" children.

**5** Henryk Sienkiewicz's "Trilogy" is a historical fiction epic about seventeenth-century Poland. The three novels are *With Fire and Sword*, *The Deluge* and *Fire in the Steppe.*

IMAGE 3.5 **Karolina Kozak**
Directed by Jan Klata. Wrocławski Teatr Współczesny, Wrocław (2006)
*Photograph by Bartłomiej Sowa*

STALIN. Fine, but how many divisions has he? If he tells us, we'll let him be our ally.

ROOSEVELT. Our Big Three is like the Holy Trinity.

STALIN. Then Churchill must be the Holy Ghost. He flies around so much.

CHURCHILL. I can't stand flying. I can't stand planes. It's always drafty on planes. I cover the holes with a blanket. It doesn't help. The wind comes in. And I don't wear pajamas.

ROOSEVELT. What do you wear?

STALIN (*to Churchill*). Can I tell him? Can I?

(*to Roosevelt*) Churchill wears only an undershirt to bed.

CHURCHILL. A silk undershirt!

**ROOSEVELT.** One, two, three. The Holy Trinity.

**CHURCHILL.** Tehran.

**STALIN.** Yalta.

**ROOSEVELT.** Potsdam.

**CHURCHILL.** Play a spade, you've got it made.

**STALIN.** Let it come from under my thumb.

**ROOSEVELT.** Cards like smoke, whoosh . . .

**STALIN.** Cards ain't sheep, I'll have a peep.

**ROOSEVELT.** Cards ain't swine: what's yours is mine.

**CHURCHILL.** We were having a jolly old time, but there was tension in the air.

**JAN KRUCZKOWSKI.** I had a lively imagination as a kid
we built a tank, my brother and I
my brother was a carpenter
I was just a brat
the tank was on a sled, it had a long gun
one of us sat inside
the other pushed
we were playing at war

**JAN CHAREWICZ.** Jerzy had been watching me
he came to me and said:
—Listen, Janek, do you want to fight for Poland?
—Yes.
—You'll take an oath.
some boy ran to get a crucifix
and I repeated after Jerzy:

"With my hand on this cross, I pledge to fight for a free and independent Poland. I will keep military secrets and follow all my commanders' orders, so help me God."

**ANDRZEJ URSYN SZANTYR.** My oath
was a simple ceremony
in an attic
my commanding officer

handed me a wooden cross
and I repeated the words after him
about military secrets
about obedience
about treason
and at the end:
so help me God

JAN CHAREWICZ. Jerzy administered the oath
and I had to choose a code name
I was taking care of a sergeant from Vilnius who was hiding out in the woods
his code name was Bough
bough, twig
Jerzy never said anything about a code name
Twig—no
Knothole—sounds bad
make it Knotty
Knotty
I was a month short of 17

ANDRZEJ URSYN SZANTYR. I was 16 at the time

GARBRECHT. We were seven to eight years old back then.
At school, we had to learn the German salute.
For some reason we children didn't want to.
I said that we'd simply say: Take care
And then the teacher said we were doing it wrong anyway, so we'd better learn to say Heil Hitler.
I don't recall ever having made that salute as a child.
Tonight was the first time.

HANNE-LORE PRETZSCH. I remember Uncle Erich coming to visit, he was on the Eastern Front at the time. People used to whisper a lot back then.

He was ordered to execute civilians on the Eastern Front, but he said he couldn't do that, he wouldn't.
Then—under the condition that he wouldn't talk about it—they sent him home, but he told the grown-ups anyway.

Fine, there was a war on: we knew soldiers were shooting at each other,
but it was only Uncle Erich who told us that civilians were being executed.
Later, Uncle was redeployed somewhere else.
That shows it was possible to say no.
Today, soldiers say: There was an order and we carried it out.
It wasn't like that.
I can only tell the story from my own point of view. The things I heard.
Whether it was always that way—I can't say.
I'm sure it must have depended on what unit you were in.

ILSE BODE. My father always imagined it this way: getting old with Mother, sitting together on the couch in each other's arms.

With a marble cake on the table in front of them. That didn't happen . . . unfortunately.

ZYGMUNT SOBOLEWSKI. The Gestapo are coming from Czortków!
I hear the sirens
and in Borszczów on the square by the hospital
the Ukrainian police are assembling
four paddy wagons and a jeep rolled in
and a passenger car with an officer
I was far away
I saw it all
but I didn't hear anything
it was like a dumb show
at the German officer's command
the policemen spread out
among the houses behind the hospital
where the Jews lived
they broke down the doors
barged into the houses
chased the Jews outside and led them to the square
the Germans were standing off to one side
watching and supervising

it was all done by Ukrainians[6]
many of them neighbors
other neighbors went into the houses
they brought out furniture, sheets, pots and pans
the Jews saw their neighbors taking their property
looting
and I saw two women
fighting over a quilt
tugging, shouting, cursing
one of them was Ukrainian, I think
the other was Polish, I knew that for sure
because she was the mother of my classmate

**KAROLINA KOZAK.** When the Germans came
the Ukrainians started killing people
I don't know why
it was horrible
things were quiet in the daytime
but at night
they burned everything
entire villages
all you could see was the glow in the sky
but things were good before the war
but the politics got in the way somehow
two kilometers from home
the Ukrainians killed a priest
they came at night
mutilated him
cut off his ears and nose
wrote in blood on the church wall
go west
that was when we became afraid

---

6 In the occupied territories of eastern Poland in 1941, Ukrainian military units operated under German command.

**CHURCHILL.** I cough an hour every morning because of these cigars. And my voice is raspy. But a politician's voice is the tool of his trade.

**STALIN.** Are you tired, Churchill?

**CHURCHILL.** A bit.

**STALIN.** Parliament should look after your health. When Lenin was seriously ill, we passed a resolution letting him work only 10 minutes a day.

**CHURCHILL.** Did that help?

**STALIN.** It helped a little.

**CHURCHILL.** Then I broached the issue of kolkhozes and the suppression of the kulaks.
Stalin grew very serious.

**STALIN.** The Decree on the Protection of Socialist Property[7]: death for hoarding three ears of grain. That was harder than the war. Much harder. It went on for years. A terrible struggle. Ten million were exterminated. But we had to do it if we were to mechanize our agriculture. Ultimately, agricultural output doubled. After all, what is one generation?

**ROOSEVELT.** What is one generation?

**CHURCHILL.** "Wealth, good taste, and prosperity may accomplish much but they do not bring happiness." Winston Churchill.

**STALIN.** Death solves all problems. Man gone, problem gone.

**CHURCHILL.** The problem . . .

**STALIN.** The problem gone as well.

**JAN CHAREWICZ.** Jerzy brought the gun
a beautiful new Luger
in a holster
he showed it to me

---

7 The Soviet decree from 1932, known as the Law of Spikelets, protected state property by prosecuting anyone caught collecting as little as "three spikelets" of grain left behind in harvested fields.

the ammunition:
"And now we shoot"
he sets up a packet of cigarettes
some five steps away
he fired
right on target
I fired too
I hit it
that was my shot
the only one I fired in the Resistance

**CHURCHILL.** We are together, and that means life or death for many people.

**STALIN.** Eat, eat. Give Roosevelt a chicken. I like chickens. Eat and drink. We'll get you drunk and see what manner of men you are. The Left-Right-wing Center plotted to assassinate me many times. But they had to apologize for that. "I was not tortured during the inquiry; on the contrary, it was I who tortured my interrogators by refusing to cooperate."

Who remembers the names of the boyars deposed by Ivan the Terrible? I have this specialist: Yezhov's his name. A tiny fellow. He put it well once: "I may be puny in size, but my hands are strong, for they are the hands of Stalin." Without getting up from his desk, Yezhov unravels and snips the threads of the fascist conspiracy . . . He is good at his job but he doesn't know when to stop.

**CHURCHILL.** What happened to the Polish officers captured by the Red Army?[8]

**STALIN.** I'm a romantic when it comes to nature. Take the mimosa plant for instance: you touch one, it curls up. Like lips . . . The mimosa is a metaphor for my hidden sensitivity.

---

8 Churchill refers to the Katyń massacre, the mass execution of Polish prisoners of war carried out by the Soviets in 1940. The number of victims is estimated at 22,000, including more than 10,000 Polish officers.

CHURCHILL. What happened to the Polish officers?

STALIN. I don't know. They've gone off somewhere. I give you my word.

CHURCHILL. I shook his hand. We looked into each other's eyes. All of a sudden, he seemed deeply moved. The man emerged from under the mask. Stalin.

STALIN. There's this brave fellow: Blokhin is his name. He shot 7,000 POWs over 28 nights. Personally. With a pistol. A brave fellow.

KAROLINA KOZAK. We had a dog
his name was Stalin
I don't know why
when the Russians came
we had to do something about the dog
Daddy called him Barepaw
who could have known
the Russians would come

JAN KRUCZKOWSKI. The soldiers are fleeing
leaving their weapons behind
oh, a gun
slightly damaged
I pull back the whatchamacallit
I go down to the cellar
to try it out
I had a lively imagination as a kid
you could also take the gunpowder from a bullet
cover it with soil
and bash it with a stone
whoa, neat crater!

ILSE BODE. My mother was small, barely 1.45 meters tall, but she gave us so much strength and we felt so safe around her, as if she were 1.8 meters tall.

And we had a really loving father. But, unfortunately, he had to go off to the war. That's when all good things came to an end.

Mother was very sad that Father was away. She was so used to having him at home. Father came to visit us when he was on leave—three weeks every year; and the last time he was on leave, it so happened that Mother got pregnant. Thanks to that, we were able to leave the city, we were evacuated. We had that much luck at least.

HANNE-LORE PRETZSCH. Everyone had to have a radio, and everybody did. A Volksempfänger. People listened to the news every day, and there were always special announcements.

Grandfather would run home from the fields to listen to the announcements and rage at the madness, at Hitler.

His daughter-in-law would come in with a broom, and say: Be quiet, he's our Führer. Those two were always fighting.

And everybody had to have a photo of Hitler.

—You got any Hitler photos . . .

—No, dearie, not yet . . .

—We'll order some the day after tomorrow.

And of course everybody had a copy of "Mein Kampf" but nobody ever read it. And that was the problem.

I read it only recently. It's all in there. How clever he was.

He staged his first rallies before noon and nobody came, so he thought: The theater!

People go to the theater at night!

People are more attentive at night.

Still, we all had a copy but no one ever read it.

ILSE BODE. People would also call the radio Goebbels' gob.

Are you—regardless of all circumstances and at the cost of supreme personal hardship—ready to follow the Führer in his fight for the ultimate victory?[9]

I can't listen to that anymore, I don't want to listen to it. Guilt or no guilt. Neither my father nor my mother were to blame. They were not guilty, and I'm not going to say they were

9 From a historic recording of Goebbels' speech given in Berlin on February 18, 1943. The quote is followed by thunderous applause.

tonight, either. They lived under that system and they couldn't help it. I don't want to hear that my parents were Nazis.

THE BIG THREE. Transmission—Joy Division
Radio, live transmission
Radio, live transmission
Listen to the silence, let it ring on
Eyes, dark grey lenses frightened of the sun
We would have a fine time living in the night
Left to blind destruction
Waiting for our sight
And we would go on as though nothing was wrong
And hide from these days we remained all alone
Staying in the same place, just staying out the time
Touching from a distance
Further all the time
Dance, dance, dance, dance, dance to the radio
Dance, dance, dance, dance, dance to the radio
Dance, dance, dance, dance, dance to the radio
Dance, dance, dance, dance, dance to the radio

GARBRECHT. It was always silent in the house.
Meals lasted 15 minutes.
When Father was there, we wouldn't speak to one another
That's the way it always was

ANDRZEJ URSYN SZANTYR. I had a Jewish neighbor
he would come visit my parents
and they would visit him
to me he was
Mister Engineer
when the Nazis ordered
that the Jews must
wear stars
walk in the gutter
and greet Aryans
by taking off their hats
I met

Mister Engineer
walking down the gutter
and he took off his hat before me
that was horrible
the man had been so humiliated
that he had to take off his hat
before me
a boy
him, whom I always thought of as
Mister Engineer

ZYGMUNT SOBOLEWSKI. We went to church in Borszczów
taking a shortcut
down the bottom of a deep gorge
its limestone banks
would shelter foxes
we would often smoke them out
by throwing burning rags
then the foxes would come out
sneezing
it was a Sunday
the Ukrainians were on the hunt
they threw smoke bombs
and Jews started coming out
from the caves in the rock
they weren't sneezing
from down below, we saw
only people's silhouettes
someone taking aim
someone falling
all silently
like a shadow play
then a shot rang out from above
the Ukrainians were killing a Jew
before our very eyes
they wanted to intimidate us
because it was our turn next

**ILSE BODE.** Good evening!
A lion escapes from the zoo.
Everybody panics except for one boy who rushes forward and tames the lion.
Everybody applauds and says: You're a hero.
A journalist shows up and asks: What's your name, young man?
Itzig Morgenstern.
Itzig Morgenstern? So that's how it is?
The following day, I read in the papers: Jewish thug strangles innocent lion.
Goodbye.

**KAROLINA KOZAK.** The Jews were fleeing to Russia
they didn't get along with the Germans
Jankiel, a Jew, hid in our stable
and asked Father to shelter him
but Father couldn't take the risk
he had us, his family, to look after
he gave Jankiel some food
and asked him not to travel in the daytime
but Jankiel went
about a kilometer and a half down the road
he was killed, but I don't know who did it

**HANNE-LORE PRETZSCH.** Aunt Dita said that sealed boxcars with women and children inside were passing through Stargard.
I saw them too, in Schlawe.
Later, I asked my mother about it, but she said she hadn't seen anything.
By then, the thing with the Jews had begun.
Our neighbors killed themselves by inhaling carbon monoxide.

Jews were not allowed to shop before 6 pm, and all the vegetables were sold out by then. Mother would buy them groceries, but that was strictly forbidden.

I saw children wearing their satchels on their breast so people couldn't see the Star of David they had to wear.
How can so many people disappear?

**ZYGMUNT SOBOLEWSKI.** There was a ghetto in Borszczów
I was walking home from school with my friends
and we heard gunshots
a column of people on the move carrying suitcases
as if they didn't know what was in store for them
shots were fired in the air every now and then
to keep them cowed
but the Jews were calm anyway
sort of numb
a German officer walked down the sidewalk leading an Alsatian
and rhythmically flicking at his boots with a riding crop
the dog barks
and I see
I remember it clearly
a woman in a skirt
checkered red and tan
a boy on her arm
and two children running alongside
when the Alsatian barked
the children would hide behind their mother
and, somewhat impatiently, she would
push them away
as if she didn't want them
to slow her down
I also remember
a gray-haired man
there was a whole group of them walking
but I saw only them:
that woman with the children, and that man
I knew what would happen to them
and I didn't understand why
I still don't understand
then Father said
they were the last of the ghetto
and he told me to come home straight from school from then on

those people
were executed by the Jewish cemetery
ditches had been dug there
and there was quicklime
to cover the bodies
they killed them with a shot from a pistol or a rifle
just like that
they stepped up to be shot
I went there later
it was all overgrown
but the ground was slightly sunken in
you could see rectangles
and on them
clumps of burdock, goosefoot and weeds
growing where the Jews lay

STALIN. You have to look after people until the end. One time, I went to the house of the great Maxim Gorky. The great Maxim is at death's door, and I ask: Why the somber mood? A healthy person can't die in such an atmosphere. I sorted things out, and he died happy.

ILSE BODE. March 1, 1944

Dear Käthe,

Last night, I couldn't fall asleep for a long time, I was troubled by dark thoughts. Without you, life would have no meaning for me. I pray that God may spare us this ordeal. It's awful being here with nothing to do but wait. If dreams and prayers have any power, everything will work out somehow. Live in peace, I love you very much,

Your Eberhard

KAROLINA KOZAK. Father was very scared
he traveled a lot before the war
he used to go to the Poznań fair
he was a busybody
and during the war

he thought
something would happen to him because of that
one day
he had a little too much to drink
he came back at night
Mother was upset
we were supposed to be hiding
and he was drunk
he lay down on the couch
and fell asleep
Mother and I
put towels under him
if the Ukrainians set the place on fire
we would drag Father out into the orchard
and we stayed up all night like that
in the morning, Father woke up
crossed himself, and said
he'd finally had a good night's sleep
he was very scared
from that fear
he got diabetes
and died

JAN CHAREWICZ. Jerzy brought a typewriter
with a long roller
a Wanderer
that's how my work began
in the Resistance
I wrote reports
in four copies
Jerzy dictated
I typed
on the left-hand side: area Wir, inspectorate Lin
that was the code name of our cell in the Home Army
the date
and the report:

IMAGE 3.6 **Ilse Bode**
Directed by Jan Klata. Wrocławski Teatr Współczesny, Wrocław (2006)
*Photograph by Bartłomiej Sowa*

bridge guard post
four soldiers, well armed
signed "Jerzy" at the bottom
Jerzy signed everything with his code name
blast it
I rolled the carbon paper in wrong, back to front
I always have to screw something up

ILSE BODE. March 3, 1944
Dear Käthe,
Your letter arrived yesterday, and it put all my sorrows to rest.
So we have another boy.
I'm glad you made it through it all in good health.
Maybe it will be enough to say that I cried for joy.

I send my fondest regards,
Your ecstatic Eberhard.

CHURCHILL. I should like to put forward the proposition that we discuss the Polish question, blah blah blah.

STALIN. Davayte.

CHURCHILL. We declared war on Germany because of Poland and, if only for that reason, Poland matters to us, blah blah blah.

STALIN. Yes.

CHURCHILL. The crucial matter is Russia's western border. Perhaps Marshal Stalin might share his thoughts on the issue.

STALIN. Yes. Speak.

CHURCHILL. So we are to try and demarcate a border?

STALIN. Yes.

CHURCHILL. We could adopt a certain approach, which we would then present to the Poles with the suggestion that they accept it.

STALIN. The Poles are not here?

ROOSEVELT. Since when is Poland a power? Ha, ha!

STALIN. So with the Poles not being represented?

CHURCHILL. With the Poles not being represented.

ROOSEVELT. We shall inform them of the outcome of our deliberations.

CHURCHILL. I personally believe that Poland might shift a little to the west. Like a soldier taking two steps left to close the ranks.

STALIN. Do you think I intend to annex Poland entirely?

CHURCHILL. I don't know how much Russia intends to eat and how much it's able to digest.

STALIN. Russia does not want anything that belongs to other nations, though it's not unlikely that she will bite off part of Germany.

CHURCHILL. What Poland will lose in the east, it can regain in the west.

STALIN. Maybe, maybe not. You can never be sure. Do you have a map?

CHURCHILL. No.

ROOSEVELT. No.

CHURCHILL. Then, using three matches, I put forward my plan of moving Poland to the west. Stalin liked it.

I spoke for a long time. When I finished, there was silence.

THE BIG THREE. Radio, live transmission
Radio, live transmission
Listen to the silence, let it ring on
Eyes, dark gray lenses frightened of the sun
We would have a fine time living in the night
Left to blind destruction
Waiting for our sight
And we would go on as though nothing was wrong
And hide from these days we remained all alone
Staying in the same place, just staying out the time
Touching from a distance
Further all the time
Dance, dance, dance, dance, dance to the radio
Dance, dance, dance, dance, dance to the radio
Dance, dance, dance, dance, dance to the radio
Dance, dance, dance, dance, dance to the radio

ANGELA HUBRICH (*Song*). Everything passes, everything goes away

After the winter, May will come again

Everything passes, everything goes away

When two are in love, to themselves they are true . . .

ILSE BODE (*Song*). People don't like being alone at night
The moonlight and love are the fairest of things
You know what I mean
On the one hand, the other, and all . . .

When a person wants love
Especially in a restless world
It is everyone's greatest desire . . .
You know what I mean
On the one hand, the other, and all . . .

ANGELA HUBRICH (*Song*). It won't shake a sailor boy
Don't you worry, Rosemarie
We won't let them ruin our lives
Don't you worry, Rosemarie
Even when the heavens and the earth tremble

JAN CHAREWICZ. News flash
we've captured the Polish Telephone Co. building[10]
I report to Jerzy
heavy fighting in Wola district
I report to Jerzy
we're withdrawing from the Old Town
through the sewers to Śródmieście
I report to Jerzy
we've surrendered Czerniaków
I report to Jerzy
it's getting worse
after some time, Jerzy said:
Someone will come to see you
give him the radio, you won't be monitoring the broadcasts anymore
I understood—we had nothing left to fight for

MATTHIAS GÖRITZ. Staying in the same place, just staying out the time
Touching from a distance
Further all the time
Dance, dance, dance, dance, dance to the radio

STALIN. Friend or foe?

ROOSEVELT. Friend.

STALIN. Give my white brother greetings from the chief of the redskins.

ROOSEVELT. You know what we call you? Between ourselves? Uncle Joe.

---

10 Charewicz refers to the combat success of Polish insurgents in the Warsaw Uprising in 1944, when the Polska Akcyjna Spółka Telefoniczna building, called the PASTa building, was famously captured from the German occupation forces.

**STALIN.** What?

**ROOSEVELT AND CHURCHILL.** Uncle Joe.

**STALIN.** Me—an uncle? Me—Joe? How long am I supposed to sit at this table listening to insults? I'm losing ten thousand people a day. I have the right to host this conference. I have the right not to be insulted.

**KAROLINA KOZAK.** I don't know
whether I saw any Germans
well, maybe one
because I remember
that he was nicely dressed
a belt saying: God Is with Us
and he had elegant boots

**ZYGMUNT SOBOLEWSKI.** When they were coming back from the Eastern Front, the Germans
weren't that elegant anymore
they would come to our house
grab some hay
pull off their shoes
then you could see the wounds, the blisters, the calluses, the frostbite
and they would sleep all day
they stank something awful
a soldier came into the kitchen once
and says: Mother, essen
he was so emaciated
he could barely stand
Mother gave him milk
and made him two eggs
hard-boiled
he was very surprised
his hands were shaking so bad
he couldn't eat
Mother helped him
he ate
and fell asleep at the table

when he woke up
he started thanking her
speaking our language some
he wanted to give Mother a hug
but she edged away
they looked a little awkward
finally, he got up and left
when he was crossing the road
which was awfully mushy
he fell face-down in the gray mud
the German soldiers
kept walking past
but no one helped him up
he lay there 5 hours or so
then they took him away
he was dead

**ILSE BODE.** Good evening.

Hitler, Goebbels and Goering are on a ship. A storm blows up. The ship sinks with all three on board. Who is saved?

Germany of course.

Goodbye.

**HANNE-LORE PRETZSCH.** The first Russians were in a hurry.

They burst into people's houses shouting: Uri! Uri! Uri![11]

They had watches up to their elbows, but they kept taking more. So Uri must have been something special.

Mother kept Father's watch.

She didn't give it to the first Russian who came along, just said: Comrade take already.

No Uri!

The first Russians didn't have time for women.

They took the Uri and got right back on their tanks to Berlin—day and night.

---

**11** They were demanding watches. The German word for watch is "Uhr." See also foonote 6 in *right left with heels*.

**STALIN.** I don't dance because I sustained an injury in exile and I cannot put my arm around a woman's waist. But I do sing.

**ROOSEVELT.** Stalin is a tenor. A sweet and remarkable voice.

**CHURCHILL.** Stalin's repertoire:

**ROOSEVELT.** Operatic arias,

**CHURCHILL.** Peasant songs,

**ROOSEVELT.** Georgian songs,

**CHURCHILL.** Cossack songs,

**CHU AND ROOSEVELT.** Church songs.

**CHURCHILL.** Top five:

**ROOSEVELT.** Lensky's aria,

**CHURCHILL.** Two arias from "Rigoletto",

**ROOSEVELT.** Two Georgian songs,

**CHURCHILL.** An Orthodox hymn

*C-R-S sing the song "Under a Moscow Night".*

**STALIN** *(over the music)*. Music is a wonderful thing. It tames the beast in men.

**GARBRECHT.** The voices
The voices
It's a pleasure to recall how Mother reacted whenever she heard that beautiful music.

**KAROLINA KOZAK** *(Song)*. O'er the hills of my native land
a maid there was made angels sigh
I meant to take her by the hand
and on her loving bosom lie

one time I called upon my dear
when she was in another's arms
you cheat my sweet I sadly cried
that time my love did do me harm

so fare thee well I said in woe
sorrow and rue urged me along

the monks I joined and took my vows
when my true love did do me wrong

years passed and my true love was wronged
by the same one who her love stole
she asked around and tracked me down
and knocked upon the cloister door

I went outside as night did fall
I stood before her in my cowl
and asked her: Who is it you seek
what would you have, oh tell me now

to this order you are sworn
oh tell me please, she did exclaim
a monk I seek inside these walls
and Anazory is his name

he's dead, I said, he's here no more
and even if he still did live
to God, not you, a vow he swore
this order he will never leave

at this news pale the maid did grow
sorrow and rue urged her along
her heart so full of pain and woe
in my heart sadness welled up strong

I sped to catch one final look
but by then from my eyes she'd gone
a candle to my cell I took
and lived in sorrow ever on.

I remember the songs
Polish, Russian
all of them

**CHURCHILL.** What about Poland? The question of Polish independence is a matter of honor for Britain, blah blah blah.

**STALIN.** For the Russians, the Polish question is not only a matter of honor but a matter of security. A matter of security because the Poles will not be allowed to attack us any longer. They attacked us in the seventeenth century, for instance. It is a matter of honor because the Russians have committed many sins against Poland. The Soviet government aims to atone for those past sins.

**ROOSEVELT.** Poland has been the cause of problems for over 500 years.

**CHURCHILL.** All the more reason why we should do everything to get rid of those problems.

The border will run from Stettin along the Oder-Neisse line.

**ROOSEVELT.** From Stettin along the Oder-Neisse line.

**STALIN.** From Stettin along the Oder-Neisse line. We'll move them. What if the Poles take offense?

**CHURCHILL.** Let them take offense. I've written down something about them.

"Their record of folly and ingratitude which over centuries had led them through measureless suffering." Winston Churchill.

**STALIN.** Once, before the Revolution, I was hiding in the house of a bourgeois family. They had a nice little daughter. I carried out an experiment. Every day, I would give the girl a bag of sweets. After a while, who would the girl run to? Not her mother. To Stalin.

We'll give the Poles a sweet.

**JAN CHAREWICZ.** Jerzy gave me an order:
Go to the forester's lodge
there will be men waiting for you
and a typewriter
I went there
I typed out what they dictated
then they gave me a sealed envelope
I slipped it under my shirt
wrapped my father's sheepskin around me

and headed back to Jerzy
I crossed the road
then the meadow
then a footbridge across the stream
and climbed the path uphill
all of a sudden, I hear: STOY[12]
it's the Soviets, I wonder whether to stop or run for it
I think: I'll be able to make it up that hill
then they won't get me
but what if they fire a machine gun?
so I go up to them
carefree
almost smiling
they start frisking me
they didn't find it
—Go to the commandant.
I go, what the hell?
why should I be scared of some commandant
I go up to him
the commandant goes: Who are you?
I tell him I'm on my way back from visiting a friend
and he goes: bumagi?
bumagi can mean papers, a newspaper, documents
so I take out my birth certificate
and hand it to him
he looks at it, turns it over in his hands,
folds it and hands it back
—Go home.
I go back up the hill
skipping
and it was only at the top
somewhere by an alder bush
that the fear left me

12 "Halt" in Russian.

ILSE BODE. April 5, 1944

Dear Käthe,

How many letters have I written to you these last three years? Is it still possible to find words I haven't already used? All I know is that I love you and the children with all my heart. You were my first love and so shall you remain as long as I live. Till we meet again, Your Eberhard

JAN KRUCZKOWSKI. In 1944, the Russians staged a demonstration
a truck drives into the main square
straight up to the gallows
in the back is a convicted Ukrainian
and four soldiers
all four of them slip the noose around his throat
so as to split the responsibility among them
and the truck drives off
the convict swung
he hung like that for three days
I once gave him a nudge when I was walking past
for fun
he started turning around
I had a lively imagination as a kid

STALIN. Want to know what I'm doodling?

ROOSEVELT. Flowers?

CHURCHILL. Butterflies?

STALIN. Wolves' jaws. It helps me think. They bare their teeth, and I think. Looks like the three of us will come up with something here.

ANDRZEJ URSYN SZANTYR. The Soviets introduced conscription
you had to show up
I'm waiting there, and some officer
walks up, looks at my leg, and asks:
—The Germans did this to you?
—Yes.
—Then sign up

—we'll put you on a tank
—you'll shoot
—you'll kill Germans
—you'll get your revenge
it was all the same to me
I sat there
another officer comes up
higher ranking
a doctor most likely
and asks:
—What are you doing here?
—They said I was to be a tank man
and he goes:
—Don't be stupid, get out of here
he took my card and wrote: "aswabażdion," exempted
I went, it was all the same to me

GARBRECHT. The main criterion determining whether someone was a good person was what kind of soldier he made.
The English—bad soldiers
The Italians—bad soldiers
The French, too: all love-making, eating and drinking.
The Americans—bad soldiers, they didn't even have decent shoes.
The Poles: they weren't good soldiers either, obviously; lazy and filthy Polacks.
Father believed that the Poles were not a nation capable of statehood.
My father's theory went like this: the fact that Poland had been partitioned so often was not the fault of the Germans or the Russians, but of the Poles themselves because they were unfit to create a state for themselves, and that's why Russia and Germany were able to partition Poland.
Besides, we never called them Poles, just Polacks.
That's how it was.
To me, "Jew" sounds different than "Icelander."
And "Pole" different than "Dane."

I still carry part of that attitude inside me.

Even now.

ILSE BODE. Yes, hi, yes, what's up? Yes. Listen, I'm in Wrocław right now, shame you're not here . . .

It's Eva-Maria from Berlin . . .

. . . I wanted to tell that joke about Hitler, do you remember how it went, the one about Goebbels . . .? Yes . . . Yes . . . Right . . . at the . . . table, dinner . . . right . . .

Good evening,

Goebbels is having dinner with his family when one of the children asks: Father, who set the Reichstag on fire? Goebbels gives him a stare, and says: "ess, ess[13] mein Kind".

Goodbye.

HANNE-LORE PRETZSCH. Everybody had a flag with a swastika.

We had to burn them later,

because the Russians would have been furious.

They'd call us SS, or something like that

The flags were made of good fabric and it would have been a shame to let it go to waste—so we cut out the swastika, burned it, and reused the rest.

CHURCHILL. They say the Red Army treats the civilian population in occupied territories very cruelly.

STALIN. What do you mean, cruelly?

CHURCHILL. Mass rapes.

STALIN. They said you were a good speaker, but all you are is a good storyteller. You're telling fairy tales. Where have you obtained this information?

ROOSEVELT. Where have you obtained this information, Winston?

CHURCHILL. Hmm . . . from the population.

STALIN. Have you read Dostoyevsky? You have. So you know how complicated the Russian soul is. Our Russian soldiers have

---

13 "Eat" in German.

heroically fought the Nazis from Stalingrad to the Oder River line. Look at the map and you'll see how much ground they've gained. And you find fault with Russian soldiers. So what if they enjoy a woman or two when the fighting's done?

ROOSEVELT. Everybody knows what the Germans did to the civilian population. War is a terrible thing.

ILSE BODE. Father looked after us even when he was away serving at the front. He once sent me a doll from Vilnius, where he was stationed.

It was a small rag doll, smaller than this one.
I was so happy when Father sent me that doll.
It was the only doll I took with me later, when we were fleeing.
I put the other dolls under my bed so the Russians wouldn't find them.
And I lost that favorite doll when we were running away. I was so sad. It was something to remind me of Father. And it got lost.
Oh, and he once sent me canned fish for my birthday.

HANNE-LORE PRETZSCH. While it was light outside, everything was all right.
The Russians ate and drank—funny that they always had vodka.
In the daytime, they would show us photos and say they had families too—they'd show photos of their wives and children.
We even learned some Russian. (*Says a few words in Russian.*)
I thought that they were pretty nice actually.
But it was different at night.
All of a sudden, it was only women that mattered.
We children didn't count anymore.
Only the women.
Frau komm, with a gun to her head.
It went quicky—one, two
They stood in an orderly line.
No one shoved.

Only when someone was too slow about it, they'd push him off to make room for the next one.
My aunt just lay there next to us. Blood all over the place.
Mother went to the other room, she didn't want us to see.
The women tried smearing soot on their faces, putting on dirty long dresses, but it was no use.
It was all the same to the Russians.

ILSE BODE. September 17, 1944

Dear Käthe!

War is like a piece for a symphony orchestra. The music grows louder and louder until it ends with a loud bang on the drums.

Then comes a silence, and nobody knows what all the noise was about.

Anyway, the man with the drum has already raised his sticks. God is the kapellmeister who will give the signal. I hope he does so soon.

A thousand kisses, Your Eberhard

The following day, my father died.

ANGELA HUBRICH. Fortress Breslau. We are in a bunker.
1,000 people
Dark.
Cramped.
Moans.
Wounded soldiers moaning.
No electricity.
No water.
No windows.
Carbide lamps
Stifling.
35 degrees.
An awful stink.
But we weren't bored.
The soldiers showed us tricks and told stories.
We lived in the bunker for three months.

**ANDRZEJ URSYN SZANTYR.** To me, war was something beautiful
something important
that's the way my father raised me
and then the war broke out
and things weren't so beautiful anymore
they were tragic
the war changed my life
I don't like talking about it
I don't want to

**ROOSEVELT.** But there are people living in those territories.

**STALIN.** There were. Germans.

**ROOSEVELT.** What happened to the population? There were several million of them.

**STALIN.** The population has left.

**ROOSEVELT.** All of them?

**STALIN.** The Germans shall be repatriated.

**ROOSEVELT.** And the Poles? They've been sent east as well . . .

**STALIN.** The Poles shall be repatriated, too. And we'll hold elections in the new Poland. The people will decide.

**CHURCHILL.** I don't hold the Poles in much esteem.

**STALIN.** There are good people among them.

**CHURCHILL.** Right.

**ROOSEVELT.** I want there to be no doubts as to the election in Poland. It should be like Caesar's wife. I didn't know her, but they say she was irreproachable.

**STALIN.** That's what they say, but she had her faults as well.

**ROOSEVELT.** I can't tell them what we decided on here, otherwise I'd lose the votes of 7 million Polish-Americans.

**CHURCHILL.** I can't tell them either, otherwise I'd lose several hundred thousand valiant soldiers.

**ROOSEVELT.** I'll tell the Poles: I assure you I did not agree to moving the borders of Poland. That's what I'll tell them.

**CHURCHILL.** I'll tell them something along those lines as well.

**STALIN.** Good idea.

**CHURCHILL.** We'll never persuade the Poles to say that they're happy.

**ROOSEVELT.** And when we tell them:

We would like to assure the authorities of the Polish underground state that their steadfastness has been duly recognized.

**CHURCHILL.** They shall surely never have cause to regret their brave decision to reject any collaboration with the enemy.

**ROOSEVELT.** Poland will reap the fruit of her heroism and sacrifice.

**CHURCHILL.** Even if we tell them that, they'll still won't be satisfied. Nothing can satisfy the Poles.

**JAN CHAREWICZ.** The Soviets came
we're hiding in a dugout
Jerzy says: Stay put and await orders
Jerzy goes off somewhere, then comes back
I ask: What do I do?
- stay put and await orders
he goes off and comes back again
once again I ask: What do I do?
- stay put and await orders
the orders don't come back
neither does Jerzy
And that was the end of my time in the Underground

**KAROLINA KOZAK.** We started packing
we didn't take everything
we weren't allowed to take dogs
Stalin-Barepaw stayed behind
or pictures
because they had glass
we had these two big pictures:
Our Lady of Ostra Brama[14]

---

**14** A copy of a painting of the Virgin Mary in the Chapel of the Gate of Dawn in Vilnius.

The Lord Jesus in His crown of thorns
we could have rolled up the paper
but we left them behind
we thought we'd be coming back
we got a place in a good railway car
and we left Czortków
the whole family: us, our uncle the tailor, Auntie,
the bed, the cow,
flour, kasha, lard, kielbasa, butter and cheese
Auntie slept on the cow
because there was nowhere else to sleep
and the cow didn't say anything
a week later, we were in Brochów

ZYGMUNT SOBOLEWSKI. We arrived in Wrocław
at Brochów station
by train
and then we rode carts
down Opolska, Krakowska and Kościuszki Street
when we were riding into the city center
I smelled something
it was getting more intense
ruins, old plaster, lime, rubble
we rode down Gartenstrasse—Piłsudski Street, that is
and Powstańców Street
dead animals and bodies under the rubble
I knew that smell
I smelled it in Tarnopol
which had suffered heavy damage
and now in Wrocław
I called it the smell of a dead city
the stink got weaker
somewhere by the radio station in Krzyki district
then I smelled fresh air
like I had crossed a threshold
into another room
we rode on

by Bielany junction
we saw a tangle of power lines
our neighbor, a simple man
drank in the sight and said:
They were right when they said Germany was all covered in wire
and I saw a road sign
Berlin 360—we were 360 kilometers away from Berlin
It was only then that I understood how far we'd gone

HANNE-LORE PRETZSCH. I'll never forget the sight:
A dead soldier was lying in the middle of the road, and the tanks were driving over him, one by one.
I stared, amazed at how much . . . insides a person has. He was entirely flat.
And we had to walk on through the woods, we had to stay quiet. A child that started crying was smothered and left behind.
Our luggage was getting heavier and heavier.
We threw parts of it away. First the silverware, then the linen.
And then the rest of it.
The snow was deep, and it was freezing cold.

STALIN. I heard the weather report yesterday. It turned out to be entirely wrong. There are saboteurs among weathermen as well. Yes, carry on.

CHURCHILL. At most, the Polish borders will infringe slightly on German territory.

STALIN. Slightly.

CHURCHILL. Nonetheless, she has to be strong, blah blah blah. She is an important instrument in the European orchestra, blah blah blah.

ROOSEVELT. Blah blah blah.

CHURCHILL. Shall we try to demarcate the borders?

STALIN. Yes. Do you have a map?

CHURCHILL. No, but I have my matches.

ROOSEVELT. May I share an observation with you?

IMAGE 3.7 **Churchill (Wiesław Cichy), Roosevelt (Zdzisław Kuźniar) and Stalin (Przemysław Bluszcz)**
Directed by Jan Klata. Wrocławski Teatr Współczesny, Wrocław (2006)
*Photograph by Bartłomiej Sowa*

STALIN. Yes.

ROOSEVELT. I am fascinated by the spiritual expression of your eyes.
The eyes of a Georgian highlander.

CHURCHILL. So am I. Candor and resolve.

STALIN. The ocean at night, a savage storm . . .
A weary figure on the ship's bridge.
It's the captain. Who is he?
A man of flesh and bone
Or iron and steel perhaps?

ZYGMUNT SOBOLEWSKI. We passed village after village
but still no home

Mother was getting anxious
fidgeting in the cart
finally we reached the village
and a yard:
our new home
standing on the threshold
is the owner, his wife and son
Mother couldn't believe it
Father tried to explain
that we'd only be there six months
what with World War III coming, and all
we managed to say hello somehow
it was Joseph Teisler-Meisterpumpe, his wife, and their son, Werner
we moved into a room in the attic

JAN KRUCZKOWSKI. There were fewer and fewer Poles
everyone was going west
I had no friends
nothing to do
I went to the movies
watched films
about the victorious Red Army
I remember "The Rainbow"
based on the novel by Wanda Wasilewska
"Chapayev"
and "Merry Fellows," naturally
I liked them very much
more Russians were coming to the city
I was scared
and stayed in the cinema two screenings at a time

STALIN. "Merry Fellows." I know that funny film by heart. Whenever I see it, I feel like I've had a month's vacation. "Merry Fellows."

HANNE-LORE PRETZSCH. The Russian officer who raped my mother told us a lot about the atrocities committed by the Germans:
Lublin

Majdanek
He said he couldn't understand it—Germans being so cruel—
weren't they a nation that loved art?
He showed paintings by Cranach and Dürer.
Mother had to give herself to him anyway.
She said right off that she was sure she'd get pregnant.
Mother was very pretty, I think.

GARBRECHT. In 1945, I was living with my family in a small village in western Germany. There was a dairy store in the village.

Two men in pajamas were standing outside that store, leaning against the railing.

They said:
The Americans liberated us.
But the Americans were occupying us
they didn't liberate us
I don't recall my mother ever explaining that we had met inmates from a concentration camp.

ZYGMUNT SOBOLEWSKI. Teisler showed Father the farm
they went out into the field
Father checked the soil
naturally, it wasn't like the one back east

JAN KRUCZKOWSKI. In 1946
I came to Kluczbork
Kreuzburg in German
the apartment had electricity, gas, running water and toilets
and a tub in the bathroom
I would turn on the tap
and watch the water flow
then I lay in the tub
and bathed
for hours
I had a lively imagination as a kid

KAROLINA KOZAK. From Brochów we went to Katowice
then to Strzelce Opolskie

then finally to Pieleszkowice
our new house
was riddled with bullets
a German woman lived there—
Hildegarde—Hilda
with her two children
and two children of her sister's
who had died in Wrocław
she was awfully scared
finally she opened the door
we moved into the kitchen
On the wall it said
"Lebensmittel—Hans Graf"
The Germans had had a store here
there were shelves
deep, dark-green ones
there was also a counter
later, I moved that counter
inside the store
Hilda ran the store, and so did I
the shelves stayed there for thirty years
we were afraid to take them apart
what would the German woman say?

HANNE-LORE PRETZSCH. We starved and starved.

Auntie Lieschen had a deck of cards, and the reputation of a fortune-teller.

Women came to her to gaze into the future.

Auntie Lieschen would sit up and say, her voice slightly changed:

Sit down and take a card,

Cut with your left hand, towards your heart.

Let's see what the cards have to say.

A young man is at the door.

A letter is on its way.

But there's also a black lady. Her intentions are bad, but she's far away.

Etc., etc., and I waited for her to get on with it.
She would spread out the cards and say:
A young man is at the door
A letter is on its way.
Always the same things, actually.
A man was always coming.
A letter was always on its way.
And there was always a minor obstacle in the meantime.
Fine, the woman was satisfied and she'd finally get up, while I waited impatiently to see what she'd brought.
Sugar, potatoes or bread?

JAN CHAREWICZ. I had no reason to go back east
I came to Wrocław
with my mother and father
in a cattle car
a covered one, though
the city was destroyed
nothing but rubble
few people around
autumn weather
it was drizzling
rats running around in the ruins
it looked awful
I wanted an apartment
a militiaman took me
to a three-room place on Grunwaldzka Street
but there were Germans still living there –
a woman with her daughter
of twenty
the militiaman says I'll be taking the apartment
and they will be resettled
I moved in
into the apartment
into the furniture, the sofas, the chairs, the harmonium, the guitar, the violin, the trumpet, the sheet music
one day I came home, and the Germans were gone

I don't know in what conditions the Germans were resettled
I don't know even know when

STALIN. I have some advice for you. If you ever make an appointment to meet someone after a war, make it at the train station. Stations always remain where they were.

MATTHIAS GÖRITZ. Sneakers
A yoga DVD
A player, headphones
A charger
A calendar
Linen
Socks
My first novel
A laptop
Albums:
Yo La Tengo, Mouse on Mars, Skalpel
A shaving kit
Condoms
A toothbrush,
A sleeping mask
Moby Dick—the book
Shirts, sweaters, pants
Handkerchiefs
Whisky—for times of need
A cap
Another manuscript
A necktie
Bathing trunks
My suitcase is my homeland.

KAROLINA KOZAK. We liked the Germans
they were hard-working people
they cried when they were leaving
these were their homes
first the German woman
sold everything in the store

then she got a letter from her husband
then she left
I remember, around their necks they had
these little bags
for jewels, I guess
or money
but I wouldn't know
it was then that we understood
we wouldn't ever be leaving here

STALIN. Molotov is a connoisseur of poetry. He read a poem once. He summons the poet and says to him: "This is very pessimistic. You should show a window through which the sun can shine."

A merry tune stays with you
And never wears on you;
It's cherished by villages large and small,
And loved by the big cities.
Spring.

ANDRZEJ URSYN SZANTYR. Once, when I was skiing
the instructor comes up to me and says:
—you ski very well
only you're holding that leg in a funny way
you might get it hurt
and I reply:
—I can't get it hurt
because it's not there

STALIN. Why don't I tell a joke: Stalin, Churchill and Roosevelt go hunting. Later, they decide to share the catch. Churchill says: I'll take the hide, let Stalin and Roosevelt share the flesh. And Roosevelt says: No, I'll take the hide, you share the flesh. And Stalin says: This bear is mine. All of it. I'm the one who killed it.

Why aren't you laughing?

JAN CHAREWICZ. STOY
of all the things that happened to me

the one that's stuck with me the most
is being stopped by those Russians
and the fear
not of dying
but the fear of what I would have told them
if they'd found that envelope
I took an oath after all
what would I have done
I don't know
I often dream about it
sixty years on
my dream of betrayal

JAN KRUCZKOWSKI. The brother who made the tank for me
died on the Pomeranian Wall
he wasn't even 19
my oldest brother—the officer
was arrested
survived the Kolyma camps
and fought in Anders' army[15]
my oldest sister
secretly married a courier
she spent her wedding night with him
shortly afterwards, her husband was killed taking people across the green border
the green border
nine months later, their son was born
the family couldn't admit who the real father was
so they decided to say that my sister had lost her head for some Russian
it was a horrible smear on her and all of us
but that's how it had to be; it was only after the war that Father Mateusz, a Dominican, could tell the real story from the pulpit

15 The army under the command of General Władysław Anders, created in the Soviet Union in 1941. Anders' Army left the Soviet Union through Iran to Palestine; under British command, as the Polish Second Corps in the Polish Armed Forces in the West, it fought with distinction in the Italian Campaign.

my second sister married an officer
who ended up in a POW camp
they didn't see each other until the war ended
my third sister enlisted into the Second Army of the Polish Armed Forces
my fourth sister became a nun
only I was free as a bird
and played at war

GARBRECHT. I studied architecture in Brunswick; city planning at MIT and Harvard in Cambridge, Massachusetts; object art in Switzerland

Then I studied fashion design,
Then came the Argentinian tango,
I modeled in the nude,
I took singing lessons,
I've written two books, I almost became a restaurant owner.

ANGELA HUBRICH. The cemetery was on the way to school.

My younger sister died of diphtheria when she was four and a half. Mother nursed her at home for six weeks. Our parents had contacts at an orphanage. Children from the orphanage sang at the funeral, I still haven't forgotten the song.

On Sundays, our whole family would go to the cemetery. When we were leaving, Father would always turn and wave goodbye to my sister.

There's a playground with benches there today—but it's still a very nice place.

KAROLINA KOZAK. A lot of Germans come nowadays
they don't ask anyone
they just come
what gets to them the most
is that the cemeteries have been destroyed
but it was the state that had them destroyed
stonemasons took the granite slabs
and carved them into new gravestones

only the sandstone ones were left
and a lot of bones in the ground

**JAN CHAREWICZ.** The Germans—poor people
resettled just like we were
they went through the same things
I had nothing to go back to
they left behind all they had
we all went through a lot
but it was the Germans who resettled the Germans.
Hitler.

**STALIN.** I have a splendid comrade: Molotov. Molotstein. A tireless diplomat. Lenin called him Stone-Ass. Molotov is better than Ribbentrop. Molotstein will make a deal with everyone. And he likes compliments. Sometimes I say to him: World leader, the fuck with him! You've criticized them all, the fuck with them! You put a boot up Churchill's and Roosevelt's asses!

Molotov tends to overdress. That's not my style. Look: My modest garb brings out my inborn grandeur.

**ROOSEVELT.** Stalin's face,

**CHURCHILL.** Expressive and mercurial.

**ROOSEVELT.** Cat-like moves,

**CHURCHILL.** Supple and full of grace.

**ROOSEVELT.** He seethed.

**CHURCHILL.** With sensuous energy.

**ROOSEVELT.** Everyone.

**CHURCHILL.** Everyone,

**ROOSEVELT.** Who saw him,

**CHURCHILL.** Wanted to see him again.

**ROOSEVELT.** A quiet modesty,

**CHURCHILL.** Puffing at his pipe,

**ROOSEVELT.** Serenity.

**STALIN.** When Zhukov first met me, he couldn't sleep.

IMAGE 3.8 **Churchill (Wiesław Cichy), Roosevelt (Zdzisław Kuźniar) and Stalin (Przemysław Bluszcz)**
Directed by Jan Klata. Wrocławski Teatr Współczesny, Wrocław (2006)
*Photograph by Bartłomiej Sowa*

ROOSEVELT AND CHURCHILL. It's hard to imagine a man like that ever deceiving someone!

KAROLINA KOZAK. One evening, I took a notebook
and started writing down the names of everybody from our village
back east, the whole village, from end to end
I remembered a lot, and I marked down
who was Polish and who was Ukrainian.
There were more Poles in the village.

Here are the young men, the weight on their shoulders
Here are the young men, well where have they been?
We knocked on the doors of Hell's darker chamber
Pushed to the limits, we dragged ourselves in
Watched from the wings as the scenes were replaying
We saw ourselves now as we never had seen
Portrayal of the trauma and degeneration
The sorrows we suffered and never were free

Where have they been?
Where have they been?
Where have they been?
Where have they been?

Weary inside, now our heart's lost forever
Can't replace the fear, or the fear, or the thrill of the chase
Each ritual showed up the door for our wanderings
Open then shut, then slammed in our face

Where have they been?
Where have they been?
Where have they been?
Where have they been?

MATTHIAS GÖRITZ. My father was born in 1943, in Samogitia.

Samogitia was both Lithuanian and German, Poland also had a claim to it.

In 1945, during an air raid, Father was buried alive. He spent two days sitting in the darkness. He survived, but it left him with a stutter until he was 16.

The family was torn apart. He was the youngest of thirteen children. He grew up in a refugee camp in Denmark.

He studied administration and law, and made a career in politics.

He was the child of refugees, and didn't even have his own bicycle.

He was self-taught. He wanted to know everything, to do everything well. He wanted to be good at everything, to excel at everything even.

After he gave it all up—including the post of mayor in a city near Hamburg—he became a businessman and the two of us traveled through half of Europe. He was always interested in the history of the people he met, and of their countries.

I think he was looking for a place for himself, for a home of sorts.

He never found one.

He was sentimental. He'd never seen Samogitia, yet he missed it all the same.

He was of the '68 generation, they wanted to change everything.

They were the ones who inherited all the guilt.

Maybe it's nostalgia for a place he could call home, and the knowledge that that place has been lost, and it's the Germans who are to blame—their National Socialism and racist madness.

Maybe my father thought that the guilt could be lessened if you acted morally, maybe he thought that if, being a German, he would face up to history, he might find a home someday.

## CHARACTERS

SON, about 19 years old

MOTHER, 58 years old

FATHER, 60 years old

WIDOW, 35 years old

URSULA, 10 years old

IMAGE 4.1 **Little/Son (Dawid Rafalski)**
Directed by Marcin Liber. Lubuski Teatr w Zielonej Górze, Zielona Góra (2012)
*Photograph by Bartłomiej Sowa*

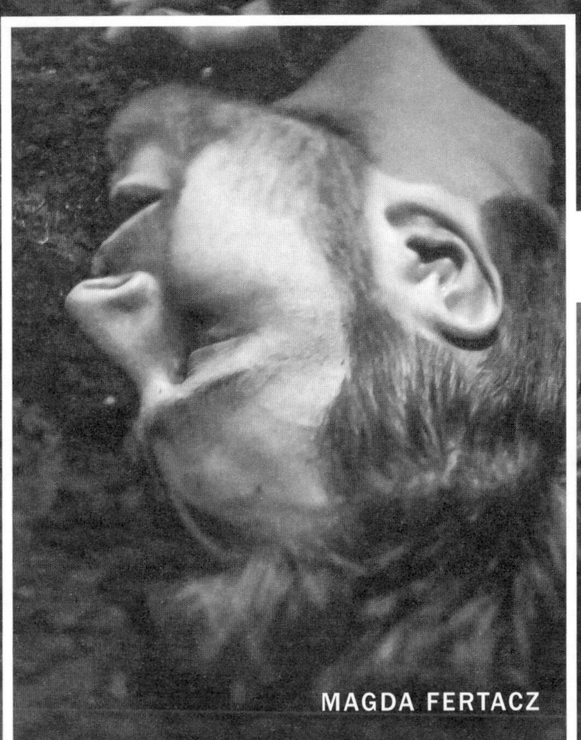

# TRASH STORY

MAGDA FERTACZ

Translated by Benjamin Paloff

**NOTE**

*Trash Story* is a play about the wartime trauma suffered both now and in the past by a Polish family living in a house on what was German territory before the war. The family has to come to terms with the PTSD of a son who went through hell during his tour of duty in Iraq, and with the fate of a grandfather, a former inmate of Auschwitz. The house's previous owner fought in the Wehrmacht at Stalingrad. His daughter, Ursula, haunts the house, and tells the never-before-told story of how she was hanged at the end of the war by her own mother, rather than be raped by Red Army troops.

*Trash Story* addresses the subject of violence: military violence on the front lines, genocidal violence in concentration camps, and sexual violence behind the lines. But it also reveals the symbolic sources of that violence—blind adherence to patriotism and honor—and exposes its manifestations in the family and education. All these strands come together in the opening monologue spoken by a veteran of the Iraq war just before he commits suicide. He describes his wartime trauma, then moves on to the toxic influence of being raised to revere duty and the cult of martyrdom. Significantly, he refers to Tadeusz Różewicz's poem, "The Braid," that, recited "before bed, and in every school, in honor, every year," appears as a bitter symbol of the terror of memory.

In 2008, *Trash Story* won the Gdynia Drama Award, the first prize in Poland's most important playwriting competition. The 2008 premiere of *Trash Story* was directed by Ewelina Pietrowiak in Warsaw's Teatr Ateneum. In the production, done in the convention of a household drama, ten-year-old Ursula was played by mature actress Jadwiga Jankowska-Cieślak. In the large-scale production at Lubuski Teatr im. Kruczkowskiego in Zielona Góra in 2012, which made extensive use of documentary material, director Marcin Liber split the part of Ursula into ten female voices to highlight the real-life stories of German women in the Nazi period, many of whom committed suicide in 1945 in fear of the advancing Red Army.

# TRASH STORY

*Our destinies are determined by the deeds of others, and our actions and inaction are part of theirs. Whether we are aware of this or not, we carry a responsibility for what happens to us all.*

Zygmunt Bauman

*There are no characters, only freedoms that have fallen into a trap, and the way out of it is human value.*

Jean-Paul Sartre

## PROLOGUE

*By the river. Before drowning.*

**BROTHER.** Mother, with a capital "M." O Motherland.
To your health. I drink. I kiss your feet.
Its skin grown thick and hard.
You didn't say. The word I wanted to hear. Not even the usual lie.
Is it too much to ask?
You had only one word for me: Duty.
The only light in your house is a memorial candle.
Candles.
An unctuous flame shrouded in the tatters of memory.
I grew up to kill.
When are you grown up enough for that? Well, doctor?
The doctor!
The doctor said my brain cells are losing their ability to hold memories separate. My memory can't wipe away what it doesn't need.
What it doesn't need. What doesn't it need?
A body in pieces—that's shit-I-don't-need number one. My

IMAGE 4.2 (In the foreground) **Brother (Ernest Nita);** (in the background) **Ursula-Joppe (Joanna Koc), Ursula-Martille (Marta Frąckowiak), Ursula-Klarin (Kaja Bień), and Ursula-Elfriede (Elzbieta Lisowska- Kopeć)**
Directed by Marcin Liber. Lubuski Teatr w Zielonej Górze, Zielona Góra (2012)
*Photograph by Bartłomiej Sowa*

---

hand shaking before pulling the trigger—shit-I-don't-need number two. Jerking off on base—more shit I don't need. Subtle shades of blood on my hands—that's shit I don't need. The things I don't need to have in my head. You can treat that. You can get past it. The doctor. The doctor said so.

You can get past murder.
Motherland.
Motherland—putrefaction. A mommy-pig.
And that goodnight poem of hers, every night.
The one about the braid. Before bed, and in every school, in honor, every year.
Tadeusz Różewicz.

IMAGE 4.3 (In the foreground) **Brother (Ernest Nita)**; (in the background) **Ursula-Althe (Anna Haba), Ursula-Katli (Karolina Honchera), Ursula-Martille (Marta Frąckowiak), Ursula-Trude (Tatiana Kołodziejska), Ursula-Klarin (Kaja Bień), and Ursula-Mother (Elżbieta Donimirska)**

Directed by Marcin Liber. Lubuski Teatr w Zielonej Górze, Zielona Góra (2012)

*Photograph by Bartłomiej Sowa*

---

## BRAID

When all the women
from the transport had been shaved
four workers with brooms
made of linden swept
and piled up the hair

Behind clean glass
the stiff hair of those asphyxiated
in the gas chambers
in that hair there are pins
and combs of bone

No light shines through it
No wind scatters it
No hand touches it

In large crates
the dry hair of the asphyxiated
billows
and a gray braid
a pigtail with a little ribbon
pulled at in school
by naughty little boys

Her tears. In her eyes. The mommy-pig, crying. Moved by how beautifully her son recites. The rhythm. One, two. March.

You keep marching till you stamp down, pack down those hands sticking out of the ground, those sunburnt legs; you just pave that shitpile over. Under the asphalt of great deeds. In the name. Always some name, some "in."

In the name of those relics of childhood. The two feet of the Motherland-Mommy-pig. She's, like, dead, but with a smile that portends her miraculous resurrection.

Sainted by her hand. As the bridegroom of murder. As a tin soldier, defender of her religion. The one true. Get down to business. Her business.

A key hung around her neck. The Key of Duty.

This is my fealty to her. My filial fealty.

Because she gave birth to a son. A soldier-son. She sacrificed her Sow-womb, draped in a black pall, now to take back what is hers.

And her corpse is eaten by worms. And it only looks like she's alive. Because the worms of the past wriggle on her body and coo, announcing the Gospel of Duty. A breast bared, like to give suck. Only the milk's poisoned: Honor. Patriotism. P. A. T. R. I. O. T. I. S. M.

H. O. N. O. R.

You liter of puke.

You litter, of rabid dogs.

I could bite you, tear you to pieces, spit you out, lick you clean, and it wouldn't be matricide.

I could strangle my brother, whip my father, bang my wife with a broken bottle. And what? And nothing. I'll be a hero. War has its own laws.

And what good is our family's greenhouse-slash-concentration camp? We keep watering and fertilizing with the shit of the past, with these Motherlandish delusions. Enough. Enough of this shit.

And some of us are still blind.

They're still deaf.

To their health.

## ACT I

*Present day. Summer. One of the small villages near the western border, formerly Görlitz, now Górczyca, or else Gross Gandern, which is now Gądków Wielki. A house by the river on the edge of town. Long ago this had been a model German farmstead. Today, the house is occupied by Poles, so-called city folk.*

### URSULA AND HER STORY. SCENE 1

*Enter Ursula with a smallish sack. She has a key dangling around her neck. But we cannot see it, since it is quite dark. She takes a rag doll from the sack and starts playing an innocent game of theater.*

**URSULA.** "Knock knock."

"Who's there?"

"It's me. Ursula."

"Ursula who?"

"The one with blond hair."

"Oh, it's you. Dear child. And where have you been all this time?"

"Hiding. Far away."

"Come in, dear child, come in."

*Ursula lights a candle. Mother is sleeping in an armchair. Ursula circles around the sleeping woman and starts speaking.*

(*To the audience*)

This is my house. It's white, with a little red roof. The windows aren't too big; they have brown shutters. The window sills had boxes with yellow flowers. There was a vegetable garden out front, with chives that bloomed purple. Geese and ducks would walk around the backyard. We had four rooms. I slept in one with my sister Liza, my brother Hans had the smallest room, and next to that were my mom and dad. There was a coal-burning stove here with very hot lids. Across from that, a small wooden table with a pitcher of sour milk. We always sat down at the table together; Mommy would gather hot potatoes from the stove and pour them out on the table. We'd skin them and eat them with salt, sipping the sour milk. Then we'd all go out to the fields, even little Liza. I'd run out in front, singing my favorite song . . . Here, listen to my favorite song. They don't want to. You listen to it, then. You're listening, right?

(*Sings*)

Der Tag war grau,
Der Tag war schwer,
Und stürmisch ging die See,
Nun klärt es auf von Westen her,
Die Brandung glänzt wie Schnee.
Ums Achterdeck die Möwe fliegt
Und leiser kommt der Wind,
Der mich in gold'ne Träume wiegt,
Antje, mein blondes Kind.

Antje, Antje,
Hörst du nicht von ferne das Schifferklavier,
Antje, Antje,
Das Lied soll Dich grüßen von mir.

*A knock at the door. Ursula puts out the candle and leaves.*
*Son's homecoming.*
*Darkness.*

**SON.** Knock knock!

**MOTHER.** Who's there?

**SON.** Your kid.

**MOTHER.** You've finally made it.

**SON.** I'm beat.

**MOTHER.** Did you take the bus?

**SON.** I biked. You're sitting in the dark?

**MOTHER.** The power's out. It's the wind.

**SON.** I'll have a look.

**MOTHER.** Leave it. Such a long way by bike?

**SON.** Yeah, I biked. We always used to have candles in the drawer.

**MOTHER.** We still do. I thought that something had happened to you.

**SON.** I'm on my way, and you're worrying. (*He lights a candle*) As it should be.

**MOTHER.** You've changed. You've grown into a man.

**SON.** On the scraps they serve at the dorm.

**MOTHER.** And you have stubble . . . By bike. It must have taken you a couple of days.

**SON.** Two.

**MOTHER.** These days people drive cars.

**SON.** And I ride a bike.

**MOTHER.** How are things?

**SON.** Fine.

**MOTHER.** Really?

**SON.** Everything's fine!

**MOTHER.** I ask because I'm supposed to.

**SON.** Everything's fine . . .

**MOTHER.** Fit as a fiddle.

*Enter Widow.*

WIDOW. Hey, it's Tiny!

MOTHER. No need to get all excited.

WIDOW. I'm sorry.

SON. I thought you'd left.

MOTHER. We look after each other.

SON. What is it you're sorry for?

WIDOW. It's always best to apologize. Right from the start.

MOTHER. Is something itching you, dear? You're leaning over so strangely.

WIDOW. And how silly of me, coming to greet you in the middle of the night.

SON. You've come in at just the right time, miss.

WIDOW. What's this "miss"?

SON. Force of habit . . . But I've grown up!

WIDOW. You look good.

SON. Fit as a fiddle.

MOTHER. Ready for service.

SON. Mom, please.

WIDOW. Should I put the tea on?

MOTHER. Let's not drag out the homecoming.

WIDOW. I was drawing the bath. How could I have been so sure I'd be coming back? I might not, and then there'd be trouble.

MOTHER. Exactly.

WIDOW. I'm going.

*Widow leaves.*

SON. She came back?

MOTHER. She never left. You've been gone a long time.

SON. You never said anything when I called.

MOTHER. So you've come, you've seen for yourself.

SON. I'm going to bed.

**MOTHER.** Your room's ready. Take a candle.

**SON.** How are things on the river?

**MOTHER.** Quiet, calm. Not a lot of tourists this year.

**SON.** Let's go down tomorrow . . . to have a look.

*Father's Phone Call.*

*Father is present on stage.*

**FATHER.** I really wanted you to call me, but you didn't. So I'm calling you. It's daytime here. I really have to get down to work soon.

**SON.** Here it's night.

**FATHER.** Yeah . . . That's right. How's your mother?

**SON.** Fine.

**FATHER.** I sent you some money.

**SON.** Yeah. I know.

**FATHER.** I'll send you more next time.

**SON.** That's okay.

**FATHER.** Don't stay there too long. Go somewhere. Take your mind off things.

**SON.** I'm going to hang around here a bit.

**FATHER.** The penitents are going to wear you down . . . They've forsaken the world. They have that luxury, because the bluebird of happiness brings them money from across the sea.

**SON.** They're grateful.

**FATHER.** Are you going to celebrate?

**SON.** Same as every year.

**FATHER.** Good . . . that's good. I won't make it . . . you see . . .

**SON.** Don't explain.

**FATHER.** We're free people. Aren't we?!

**SON.** We are. Have a good time.

**FATHER.** I am. I'm having a good time, son. And I have no regrets. You should have fun, too.

**SON.** I'll have fun. I promise.

**FATHER.** Good . . . That's good. I bet you've grown. Have you had beer yet?

**SON.** I have.

**FATHER.** That's the way! How else could you stand them?

**SON.** Indeed.

**FATHER.** Are you coming out?

**SON.** If that's how it goes.

**FATHER.** I'll be waiting.

**URSULA** (*walks around the house, singing; none of the household hears her*). Antjc, Antje,
Hörst du nicht von ferne das Schifferklavier,
Antje, Antje,
Das Lied soll Dich grüßen von mir.

*Son and Widow in front of the door out to the river.*

**WIDOW.** Lovely day. No wind.

**SON.** I remember that dress!

**WIDOW.** You remember that nonsense?

**SON.** It was torn . . . at the shoulder.

**WIDOW.** And now you couldn't even tell.

**SON.** No, you couldn't.

**WIDOW.** It really was stupid of me to come, but later . . .

**SON.** You wouldn't have had the heart, miss?

**WIDOW.** I thought that maybe we could go down to the river.

**SON.** As you wish, miss.

**WIDOW.** Don't call me "miss."

**SON.** I'd love it if things could go back the way they were . . . You all called me "Tiny." My brother came up with that.

**WIDOW.** His birthday's coming up . . .

**SON.** We'll celebrate.

**WIDOW.** If only the birthday boy could make it.

**SON.** If only!

WIDOW. You're nervous.

SON. No. Just surprised.

WIDOW. Surprised.

SON. I'm surprised, miss . . . that you've stayed.

WIDOW. I'm in no hurry.

SON. You've got to be kidding.

WIDOW. I've thrown together a picnic for the river. How's it look?

SON. Great.

IMAGE 4.4 (In the foreground) **Widow (Hanna Klepacka) and Little/Son (Dawid Rafalski); (in the background, from the left) Ursula-Joppe (Joanna Koc), Ursula-Katli (Karolina Honchera), Ursula-Martille (Marta Frąckowiak), Ursula-Althe (Anna Haba), Ursula-Dulchi (Dobrosława Trębacz), Ursula-Klarin (Kaja Bień), and Ursula-Elfriede (Elżbieta Lisowska- Kopeć)**

Directed by Marcin Liber. Lubuski Teatr w Zielonej Górze, Zielona Góra (2012)

*Photograph by Bartłomiej Sowa*

WIDOW. Things taste better by the water.

SON. What's keeping you here? Him?

WIDOW. Anything's possible . . .

SON. It's not like anything goes.

WIDOW. You talk like Tiny.

SON. Or maybe it's anything goes, but nothing is possible . . . I don't know.

WIDOW. So that's how things are going to be?

SON. Up to you.

WIDOW. Tiny and his yellow shorts . . . You manage to crack me up, as usual.

SON. I used to do somersaults for you. Remember, miss?

WIDOW. And handstands . . .

SON. And jump into the water . . .

WIDOW. You were all sweaty, you'd run up for a slice of peach.

SON. Which you would peel for me.

WIDOW. My husband . . .

SON. My brother would be lying on the blanket next to us with my mother, and, as usual, he'd be massaging her feet.

WIDOW. That was so long ago . . .

SON. I remember it well.

*At the River.*

MOTHER. I'd go in for . . . a dip . . . to have a splash.

WIDOW. Have a splash? (*Laughs*)

MOTHER. Such a foolish, impertinent laugh.

WIDOW. You startled me.

SON. Let's go in.

MOTHER. You're dreaming . . . I wouldn't be able to do it so blithely now . . .

SON. Come on!

MOTHER. How many times have I promised myself I'd do something . . .

**SON.** Come on! Please.

**MOTHER.** . . . and then put it off till the right time . . .

**SON.** This is the perfect time.

**MOTHER.** People . . . like your brother . . . they don't put things off till later . . . When he set himself a task, he did it.

**SON.** Wonder of wonders.

**MOTHER.** Not everybody has that.

**SON.** It's a shame he was squandered in the army.

**MOTHER.** Don't start . . .

**WIDOW.** I brought a picnic. How's it look?

**SON.** Of course, he has the thanks of a grateful nation.

**WIDOW.** Here . . . have an apple.

**MOTHER.** He looks great in uniform.

**WIDOW.** Women love a man in uniform . . .

*She laughs.*

**MOTHER.** That laugh. That stupid laugh.

**WIDOW.** I'm sorry.

**SON.** You're always saying sorry, miss.

**MOTHER.** Better that than giggling.

**SON.** Maybe this place has that effect on you . . . or maybe it's my mom's compliments?

**MOTHER.** You'll lose that arrogance of yours. In the army.

**SON.** Sure I will . . . I'll lose everything.

**WIDOW.** It's beautiful here . . . so beautiful.

**MOTHER.** This land has seen a lot.

**SON.** You don't like this place.

**MOTHER.** This is where my father's health failed. He insisted that this land would keep him up. It kept up the German, so why not us? He couldn't club a hog. He'd stare out over our heads, his lips never came together . . . "Like a retard," my mother said . . . He fled to the church. He'd given up research for cow dung . . . He walked around the village in threadbare pants and sang the children Gypsy songs. I ate a lot of crow. Before the war, his eyes exuded pride . . . I've seen pictures . . . But all I had looking at me were the eyes of a retard . . . "My sweet little Shirley Temple," my mother cried, and she put my hair in ringlets. "I'll save you . . . You'll see streetcars and cafes . . . You'll be a lady . . . A lady in boots the color of Höflinger chocolate." She took me away . . . She knew what she was doing . . . I was afraid of this place . . . The sticky walls, always something scratching away inside . . . And now . . . who would have thought . . . I'm back here again.

**WIDOW.** A stork.

**MOTHER.** Sorry?

**WIDOW.** A stork . . . there.

**MOTHER.** Lovely.

**SON.** Maybe it's on its way to eat its young.

**MOTHER.** What are you talking about?

**SON.** They throw the weaker hatchlings out of the nest. They tear them to pieces and feed them to the stronger ones.

**WIDOW.** Weird.

**MOTHER.** Nature's law.

**WIDOW.** You couldn't tell by looking at them.

**SON.** I remember that during one of those vacations I climbed up on the roof and looked into one of their nests. Godawful mess. A used condom, cans, some dirty old newspapers, pieces of wire, and in all that: eggs.

**MOTHER.** Can't trust storks.

**WIDOW.** No, you can't. (*Laughs*)

## URSULA AND HER STORY. SCENE 2

**URSULA** (*to the audience*). It's a good thing you didn't go down to the river . . . I'm not going to the river. I'm looking after the house. I have my own key. I close it, I open it, and then I close it and open it. They don't know I have a key . . . You really must listen to the bit about Elza and my dad. And the bike . . . When you go down to the river from our house, you pass a smallish rise on your right. It's perfect for riding your bike down. My dad had a bike. A green one. He sat me on the frame, and we sped down it. And I would laugh and press my head against his face. His moustache would brush against my neck. He had this thin, straight little moustache. Like Uncle Carl, Sleeping Beauty's father. Because Elza and I mostly played Sleeping Beauty. I was the evil witch. Elza was the good princess, and my brother Hans was the prince—he was good, too. He was awfully embarrassed about the kiss at the end. He always ran away. We didn't want him to, because the game is pointless without the prince, so I came up with the idea that Elza would hold a lump of sugar in her lips, and that she would push it into his mouth with her tongue just when they were about to kiss. And Hans really liked that. So much that we would just play the ending. Like this (*kisses her rag doll*). I was a little jealous of Elza. But then my dad had a bicycle, and hers didn't . . . (*To someone in the audience*) You be the prince. Want to? You have to wake up Sleeping Beauty. She's asleep the whole time. Would you all like her to sleep? You do, you want her to be asleep!

*Sunburned, Back in the Cool Shade of the House.*

MOTHER. My legs are all swollen from the heat.

WIDOW. You should prop them up.

MOTHER. It's better to keep them down, so they know their place.

SON (*looking out the window*). There are some people out there looking at our house.

MOTHER. More German visitors.

WIDOW. They walk around, ask questions.

SON. Now they're looking at a tree.

WIDOW. I once saw them hug the trees and kiss the ground.

MOTHER. That's not very German.

SON. They're coming our way.

**WIDOW.** They've been here before. They were poking around the barn.

**MOTHER.** They're such a pain. And for what?

**SON.** Did they say something?

**WIDOW.** I don't know German.

**MOTHER.** A good thing, too. Awful language.

**WIDOW.** The articles are a pain.

**SON.** They're standing by the fence.

**MOTHER.** Thank you, but no thank you. They're not going to march their heavy boots through our house.

**WIDOW.** God, those German women are ugly.

**MOTHER.** Absolutely! Our women somehow age with class. But those Germans—no class.

**WIDOW.** Their faces are so masculine.

**MOTHER.** They're that kind of people. All men.

**SON.** I'm going to invite them in.

**MOTHER.** Don't you move!

**SON.** You're right, they might start shooting.

**MOTHER.** Go out to them, then. Tell them about your grandfather.

**SON.** What do they have to do with him?

**MOTHER.** Same language.

**SON.** This is a piece of their history.

**MOTHER.** Well, it's not my history.

**SON.** No understanding for others.

**MOTHER.** And the fact that they turned my father into a retard is what, some kind of extenuating circumstance?

**SON.** Mom, stop it.

**WIDOW.** Oh God . . . Oh God.

**MOTHER.** They show up, they leave, it'll be fine. No point in standing around. The house needs cleaning. If we're going to have everything ready for the birthday.

*Enter Ursula. As usual, with a rag doll, which is now a hideous little thief.*

*The Widow, Son, and Mother do not hear her.*

**URSULA.** Fear us . . . You must fear us. I am Nightmare, the Evil Witch, and this is my faithful servant, Thiefy. We steal your secrets and lock them away in a dark dungeon. And there are rats in the dungeon, and they'll eat your secrets. And their tails will grow huge. And they'll have eyes like yours . . . because they'll be you. Your secrets are you . . . Nightmare, the Evil Witch, sees all, knows all, is all-powerful. She knows all the stories of the world, all the people, because she knows all the dreams.

"Let's go, Thiefy."

"At your service, mightiest among witches."

"Handle yourself well, and I'll give you some goose-liver pâté."

"How kind, my lady."

## THE FIRST STOLEN SECRET. THE SON'S DREAM

*Ursula speaks through the Thiefy doll.*

**SON.** I would like to submit my application for alternative military service.

**URSULA.** Read it aloud.

**SON.** I am submitting my request for alternative service on account of my worldview and express moral principles. I believe that it is unacceptable to use violence against another person, regardless of the situation around the world, regardless of the ruling government's policies. I support democracy, tolerance, and the necessity of resolving disputes in a peaceful manner. I am definitively opposed to aggression. I would not be capable of executing an order that would harm another living being, even on penalty of death. I would therefore like my principles to be respected.

I am prepared to fulfill my duty to my fatherland through hard and honest work during the term of my alternative service.

**URSULA.** You don't want to join the army?

**SON.** Like I just read . . . I don't like aggression, and I abhor guns.

**URSULA.** Do you have some kind of phobia of guns?

**SON.** No, I don't. I think the only reason they're around is to aim and shoot at other people, and I don't agree with that.

**URSULA.** Are you at all afraid of your own behavior once you have obtained a gun?

**SON.** No, I'm not afraid. My dislike of guns is simply a consequence of the moral principles I have professed.

**URSULA.** Do you profess a religion other than Christianity?

**SON.** I don't profess any religion.

**URSULA.** So your religion wouldn't prevent you from serving in the military?

**SON.** No . . . Like I've already said, we're talking about moral principles.

**URSULA.** And if some bad guys were to torture your mother, you wouldn't shoot them?

**SON.** I refuse to answer that question.

**URSULA.** What did your grandfather do in '39?

**SON.** Yeah, my grandfather was tortured in '39. So what?

**URSULA.** You're not ashamed?

**SON.** No, no, I'm not ashamed. Article 82 of the Constitution of the Republic of Poland guarantees me freedom of conscience.

**URSULA.** Your brother was a professional soldier?

**SON.** What does my brother have to do with it?

**URSULA.** He died four years ago. Do you know anything about that?

**SON.** No, I don't.

**URSULA.** He was supposed to have gone back to the desert. He's not there now.

**SON.** I'd like to leave now.

**URSULA.** You have the same great potential as your brother . . . even greater.

**SON.** Is that all?

**URSULA.** That's all. Your application has been rejected.

*Phone Call to his Father.*

*Father is present on stage.*

**SON.** Hello? Dad?

**FATHER.** Yes, son?

**SON.** They want to put me in uniform.

**FATHER.** My, you really have grown up.

**SON.** I don't know what I should do.

**FATHER.** It is the duty of every citizen to defend the independence and sovereignty of the fatherland . . . Just kidding.

**SON.** They want me to be just like my brother.

**FATHER.** Grease somebody's palm, and that's that. No one will touch you.

**SON.** I don't give bribes.

**FATHER.** I'll send you some cash . . . you'll take care of it . . .

**SON.** How do I tell Mom?

**FATHER.** Don't tell her anything for now. Listen, don't stay there . . . Don't waste your time.

**SON.** I'm going to stay.

**FATHER.** You know, I haven't been able to sleep . . . for a long time. I have a pain in my chest from not sleeping. I tried counting sheep.

**SON.** Count kilometers.

**FATHER.** I'm starting to be afraid of the end of the day.

**SON.** Take some pills . . . I have to go.

**FATHER.** Hello? Are you there? Come to me.

**SON.** To hell with your America.

*Widow Cannot Sleep.*

**SON.** Trouble sleeping, miss?

**WIDOW.** I feel weird . . . It's this wind.

**SON.** It was windy then, too.

**WIDOW.** No one could sleep that night. The house was packed with guests.

**SON.** My brother was supposed to go to the desert in the morning.

**WIDOW.** I really don't know why I'm talking to you about this.

**SON.** It's high time.

**WIDOW.** I have to go.

**SON.** Stay, miss. I'm sorry.

**WIDOW.** Funny . . . Now you're the one apologizing.

**SON.** You were wearing dark glasses.

**WIDOW.** It was summer.

**SON.** Are you embarrassed?

**WIDOW.** You don't understand anything.

**SON.** I'm trying to be nice.

**WIDOW.** You don't have to be nice.

**SON.** Why were you leaving, miss?

**WIDOW.** I had no idea where I would go.

**SON.** Under the nearest rock.

**WIDOW.** I could have stopped him that night . . .

**SON.** I saw the whole thing.

**WIDOW.** That day . . . I wanted to surprise him. I dyed my hair . . . painted my nails . . .

**SON.** And your mouth. He went up to you . . . yeah . . . and wiped it off. Wiped at it like it was graffiti in some dirty old doorway.

**WIDOW.** I shouldn't have made myself up.

## URSULA AND HER STORY. SCENE 3

**URSULA** (*to the Widow*). Don't be afraid. To you, I'm not Nightmare, the Evil Witch. Look: Thiefy is gobbling down his meatloaf. He's taking a break from his dark deeds. Do you hear the wind? It's really blowing out there, which means it's listening to what people are saying and carrying it to the four corners of the world . . . That's what my dad said . . . My dad was a good host. Everybody loved him. There was a pigeon coop next to the barn. Dad adored his pigeons. White ones. Snow-whites. He joked that he was going to teach them to bring letters to my mom. Because, throughout the war, Dad would travel far from home. He taught people from around the world how to work. Other people should follow the example of us Germans, Dad would say, and he'd toss me high into the air. They also had pigs where he worked. He often took them some rotten rutabaga, pickled beets, stale bread. Those pigs'll eat anything . . . he'd say. Mom didn't like pigeons. I remember how delighted she was when Hans shot one. It was the first time Dad'd let him shoot his gun. Because Dad had three great things: his moustache, his bicycle and his pistol. Hans said the coolest thing is a uniform, but I didn't like that sour smell. For the Führer, Dad shouted, and released the pigeons. And Hans shot and shot. He managed to hit one. He was pleased. Dad was, too, but Mom most of all. Then Hans said that the coolest thing is really the pistol. He marched around singing: "Am Adolf Hitler Platz, steht eine junge Eiche, strebt zur Sonne auf von Sturm und Not" . . . Do you know it? You really should. It went sort of like this. (*Hums.*) I'll teach you the words. You want me to? So, repeat after me . . . Teach it to your children. Boys like it . . . You can march to it. Here we go! "Am Adolf Hitler Platz, steht eine junge Eich" . . .

*Mother and Son by the River.*

**SON.** There's a stronger current today.

**MOTHER.** Don't sneak up on me. I can't stand when you creep around like that.

**SON.** I'd like to speak with you.

**MOTHER.** How tricky this river is. Look at those whirlpools.

**SON.** You're not listening.

**MOTHER.** Yes I am.

**SON.** Then look at me.

**MOTHER.** I hear everything.

**SON.** You can't even look at me . . .

**MOTHER.** Your brother's birthday is coming up. Why isn't he here yet? . . . Sometimes I think he's out there somewhere . . . Maybe he's lost his memory and can't find his way home . . .

**SON.** I'm sure he has his compass and pocketknife.

**MOTHER.** Such insolence. It's unacceptable.

**SON.** I know very well what's acceptable.

**MOTHER.** You've figured out what you want to be. You'll be disappointed, and then you'll be sorry.

**SON.** I sort through garbage . . . and I know what I don't want to be.

**MOTHER.** Because you put it on a T-shirt? Because you demonstrate with a bunch of freaks and shout until you lose your voice? You play at life . . . But your brother . . . your brother grapples with life and does so with honor . . . he's seen a thing or two . . . he's been to war. You think you're better than him.

**SON.** He shot at people.

**MOTHER.** He swore that he would. It's a matter of honor.

**SON.** He followed idiotic orders.

**MOTHER.** You have to hold fast to something. To have some important thing to see to in this world. And not to run around in bright shorts. Before you know it, you start to look like a retard. That's not for any sons of mine; I won't allow it.

**SON.** You only have one left.

**MOTHER.** You have no right to speak that way. I am his mother, and I know . . . I know.

**SON.** I have a mother, too. I can't get her to stop hugging a corpse.

**MOTHER.** You're just like your father. Weak . . . It's easiest to give up.

**SON.** It's been four years. They found his uniform on the shore . . .

**MOTHER.** I want to see the body.

**SON.** The fish have eaten it up.

**MOTHER.** Leave me alone . . .

**SON.** I didn't want to.

**MOTHER.** Leave me alone!

*On the Phone to Father.*

*Father is present on stage.*

**SON.** Dad!

**FATHER.** Yes, son . . .

**SON.** It's been four years now . . .

**FATHER.** A lot of time . . .

**SON.** What do you do for fun?

**FATHER.** You think that all I'm doing here is having fun? I'm working hard here.

**SON.** Yeah, I know.

**FATHER.** After work, I take the subway and observe. All the blacks, the yellows, the swarthy. All the strange people, all the suspicious packages, bags and purses. I've already called the police twice.

**SON.** I'm proud.

**FATHER.** Really? We could all be together . . . Eight eyes are better.

**SON.** Four.

**FATHER.** What's that?

**SON.** Never mind . . . Dad . . . You knew . . . That my brother . . . You knew what was going on.

**FATHER.** Where?

**SON.** At home. At his home.

**FATHER.** Your mother and I were at our place, they were at theirs. Your mother went there more often.

**SON.** Nothing seemed weird to you?

**FATHER.** I was sorry for the girl, because it was like she was in exile. Couldn't go dancing, couldn't go shopping . . . Though she's so weird . . . You couldn't tell by looking at her, and yet, typical Polish spoilsport . . . she ran to church too often.

**SON.** I don't believe it. You didn't notice anything?

**FATHER.** I was minding my own business. And I advise you to do the same, and you'll go far.

**SON.** Right . . . I'll mind my own business . . . and have fun.

**FATHER.** How's your mother?

**SON.** The same.

**FATHER.** Does she ever . . . you know . . . Does she ask about me?

**SON.** No, she doesn't.

**FATHER.** Is she wearing her hair up or down?

**SON.** Up.

**FATHER.** Too bad . . . She looks pretty with it down.

**SON.** I wouldn't know. I haven't seen it.

### URSULA AND HER STORY. SCENE 4.

**URSULA** (*to the Widow*). Dad got a motorbike! How delighted we were. He drove it along the fence. Back and forth, and all the kids, Elza, Hans, Renate, Liza, Gustaf—they all ran after him. The motorbike was really something. Dad took me out for a ride. Only me. The world's greatest dad. I didn't even get so mad when Hans got a bicycle. He was older, after all. It would have been a lovely day if not for the terrible fight. In the evening, Mom screamed at Dad that he was an utter fool and that she didn't want to see him again. Then, through the slightly open door, I saw her shaving the hair by his pee-pee, and he kept saying that it was just some camp scum, worthless, a trifle, and it was all because of Gypsy tricks. Mom was still really mad in the morning, but after a couple of days Dad came home from work with a black braid. He waved it around as he was speeding on his motorbike. He had such strange eyes and drops of sweat on his forehead, and he smelled even more sour than usual. He kept saying feverishly: "Yavsha shto bohtalo . . . Yavsha shto bohtalo." Mom wasn't angry anymore, she threw the braid out down behind the doghouse and burned it.

Then Dad went far, far away to fight for our Germany, and I never saw him again . . . It's too bad that Mom burned the braid. If I had it, I really would be a horrible Witch, right?

"Thiefy!"

"Yes, my lady?"

"Time to work for your jar of gooseberries."

"Two?"

"Don't forget who makes the rules around here."

"It will be as you wish."

"Get going!"

### SECOND STOLEN SECRET. MOTHER'S DREAM

*Ursula, as Thiefy, speaks through the doll.*

**URSULA.** Knock knock!

**MOTHER.** Who's there?

**URSULA.** It's a surprise!

**MOTHER.** Oh!

**URSULA.** I'm glad I can deliver it to you personally.

**MOTHER.** It's for me?

**URSULA.** Please open it.

**MOTHER.** I can't . . . I've forgotten how.

**URSULA.** Please try.

**MOTHER.** I can't remember the last time I received something.

**URSULA.** Sent from the Office of Memory.

**MOTHER.** These are my father's things . . .

**URSULA.** As you know, ma'am, we have been working on remembering your father.

**MOTHER.** Yes, of course.

**URSULA.** I'm sorry to say that we can no longer do so.

**MOTHER.** Why is that?

**URSULA.** We no longer find it reliable.

**MOTHER.** It's your obligation.

**URSULA.** We're very sorry.

**MOTHER.** He sacrificed everything for his fatherland. We didn't even have a dog, because he couldn't stand the barking.

**URSULA.** What you can do, ma'am, is send these things to the IVM.

**MOTHER.** I don't follow . . .

**URSULA.** The Institute for the Verification of Memory. Their job is to separate the wheat from the chaff in tragic historical events.

**MOTHER.** He was a hero.

**URSULA.** We have proof that your father didn't want to share his bread with his comrades in their deprivation as POWs.

**MOTHER.** That's impossible.

**URSULA.** The Institute for the Verification of Memory works on sorting heroes into the true and the false. The episode with the bread eliminates the possibility of counting your father among the true.

**MOTHER.** What filth. You can't do this . . .

**URSULA.** If you'd like to send these things on, that is, to the IVM, I could take them with me. Beginning tomorrow, the Institute of Memory will be known as the Institute for the Verification of Memory.

**MOTHER.** No . . . I'm not giving you anything.

**URSULA.** The world needs to know about the false heroes. To make this possible for the world, we're organizing an exhibition dedicated to those who have been verified. Your father's things are valuable items for us.

**MOTHER.** Please leave!

**URSULA.** I do wish you would reconsider.

**MOTHER.** Please go!

*The Son Is No Longer a Virgin* .

**SON.** I've been looking for you.

**WIDOW.** I'm not going anywhere . . .

**SON.** You've busted your lip!

WIDOW. Yeah . . .

SON. Please lick it.

WIDOW. Did I get it?

SON. That's much better.

WIDOW. You once thought about something all the time. About something bad. And you really wanted it to happen.

SON. Yeah . . . Maybe.

WIDOW. No. You're a good guy.

SON. You can't blame yourself, miss.

WIDOW. I'm bad, but not so bad that I couldn't stop it.

SON. Tiny knows. Tiny saw the whole thing.

WIDOW. No . . . Don't touch me . . .

SON. Often, when you were asleep . . . I'd sneak into your room . . . and watch you sleep. I looked at your knee sticking out from under the blanket . . . I'd lift the blanket . . . you were sleeping so peacefully . . . I'd go back to my room and jerk off . . . For the fallen! Till I swooned . . .

WIDOW. You have the air of a little brat . . .

SON. You had bruises on your shoulders . . . just like mine . . . I thought. I was always terribly bruised. As boys are . . . Tiny, and you, miss. What do you have there? Where are these scars from?

WIDOW. Aiii.

SON. What did you do?

WIDOW. Good little boy. It's no big deal.

SON. I think about you all the time.

WIDOW. That can't be.

SON. You deserve better.

WIDOW. I don't want sympathy . . .

SON. I could do a lot for you, miss.

WIDOW. I'm not complaining . . . I just want him back. For things to be like they were . . .

**SON.** You have such soft skin.

**WIDOW.** You can't. It can't be.

**SON.** I've never . . .

**WIDOW.** Tiny . . . Stupid Tiny.

*The Brother's Birthday. A Photograph.*

**SON.** What's that?

**MOTHER.** What, you don't recognize it?

**SON.** An altar?

**MOTHER.** They set it beautifully . . . A solid frame . . . glass. The way it should be done.

**SON.** Maybe I should go pick some flowers?

IMAGE 4.5 **Widow (Hanna Klepacka) and Brother (Ernest Nita)**
Directed by Marcin Liber. Lubuski Teatr w Zielonej Górze, Zielona Góra (2012)
*Photograph by Bartłomiej Sowa*

MOTHER. I don't know how it happened that we haven't had his picture in the house until now?

SON. Because in this house we're not in the habit of having pictures on display.

MOTHER. I don't know if this is the best place. Maybe it'd be better here?

SON. No, here is great. There's room for flowers . . . incense.

MOTHER. He has to know that we think about him. We'll make an effort to reach out to him.

SON. And what does the lady of the house say to that?

MOTHER. Sorry?

SON. You should ask.

MOTHER. I'm not going to ask about anything . . .

SON. Can't you be nice to her?

MOTHER. I see it in your eyes . . . Her husband wasn't dead yet.

SON. You hate her.

MOTHER. She should have been faithful. You know what that means to a soldier?

SON. Did you see what he did to her? Did you see her thighs, her shoulders? "This way she'll be faithful, Mom." Didn't he say that?

MOTHER. She did it herself.

SON. You're lying . . . He kept her here, far from anybody, so she wouldn't have a chance to run away. And when he came back, he checked around . . . like a dog . . . looking for the body. He sniffed around every scrap of her . . .

MOTHER. That was their business.

SON. You let it happen. You left her alone with it.

MOTHER. A woman is always alone. She had a roof over her head and something to eat . . . She had dresses and necklaces . . . She didn't say anything . . . just looked with those big eyes of hers.

SON. How many awful things can happen in one place? You knew about all of it. The two of you hounded her. A regular little family Gestapo!

**MOTHER**. Get out of here. From now on I have only one son.

**SON**. You've only had one son this whole time.

*Son and Widow*.

**SON**. Tiny'll get by. Tiny has always gotten by somehow. Tiny . . . he wasn't there. He learned to be as little seen as heard. He was not to be found within the field of vision . . . He ate, drank, and grew like a plant . . . As if I'd come to the world by popping out of a bud. My mother was always tense whenever she saw me . . . She'd ask if everything was alright, as if there were something on her conscience . . . As if I'd had stains on my clothes. I'm naughty . . . A single day went well in my mother's life. The day my brother came into the world. It was only with him, just with him that she would smile. He'd arrive in a uniform that suited him to a T . . . she choked the air to call him a hero. She'd stretch her legs out on the sofa, and he'd massage her feet. I'd walk by on some pretext . . . for a comic book or something. He told these funny . . . really very funny little stories, and she'd laugh . . . Jesus, did she laugh. Please, miss! I have very bad thoughts.

**WIDOW**. You have a fever. Your mouth is so dry.

**SON**. Is it even still possible to do something bad? Everything has already happened, and nothing's come of it.

**WIDOW**. You're burning up.

**SON**. Let's get out of here.

**WIDOW**. Where would we go?

**SON**. Far away . . . To some First Place.

**WIDOW**. First Place?

**SON**. Where we'll start all over again. We'll produce the First Children.

**WIDOW**. I always wanted to have a lot of children.

**SON**. The First baobab trees, vanilla, cinnamon, sapphires . . . lemurs. Let's go.

**WIDOW**. Quiet . . . You won't remember any of this tomorrow.

**SON.** You can't stay here, miss.

**WIDOW.** You're so good to me. I saw that right away, on that first night when I came to say I was sorry.

**SON.** You're not going to have to say you're sorry anymore, miss . . . What do you iron that uniform every day for? It should be burned . . . and those boots should be buried.

**WIDOW.** I think about him all the time . . . He'll change . . . when he comes back . . . everything will be different. That night when the wind was blowing, when the house was full of people, and he wiped off my lipstick and tore my dress . . . I wished him ill . . . I had his gun in my hand, and if he returned . . . if he'd come back into our bedroom . . . I wouldn't have had the strength not to shoot.

**SON.** It's too bad you didn't.

**WIDOW.** What are you saying, child?

**SON.** You can't leave me, miss. Now . . . that I've won you.

**WIDOW.** You're so similar. Me and Tiny.

**SON.** No one will catch us.

**WIDOW.** I'm not running away . . . I won't make myself up . . . I won't dye my hair. I'll wait. Leave me. Go.

## THE THIRD STOLEN SECRET. THE WIDOW'S DREAM

*Ursula, as Thiefy, speaks through the doll.*

**URSULA.** Daughter . . .

**WIDOW.** Thank you, God . . . you're here. I thought you were done talking to me. I did a bad thing.

**URSULA.** I see all.

**WIDOW.** I blamed you, God.

**URSULA.** You asked . . . for some very bad things.

**WIDOW.** Yes . . . I said I never wanted him to come back . . . That I wanted him to die . . . for him to be eaten up by dogs.

**URSULA.** So, how does that sound to you?

WIDOW. Bad . . .

URSULA. And you also did some mean things, didn't you?!

WIDOW. I did.

URSULA. That's right . . . You think of yourself. You're selfish and impatient.

WIDOW. I'm sorry, God.

URSULA. You know that I give, but I also take away. You asked me for love and received it, but you didn't respect this gift. And I worked hard for it. It wasn't easy to find.

WIDOW. I regret that . . . I regret what I've done.

URSULA. I don't see it . . . I don't see it. Do you still have the gun?

WIDOW. I do . . .

URSULA. You wanted to do something foolish. And how does that look?

WIDOW. Bad . . .

URSULA. That's right . . . Give it here, for safekeeping . . . so you won't be tempted.

WIDOW. That'll be better . . . It's hard, God . . . I don't know what I'm supposed to do.

URSULA. Get ready to be slapped . . . Wait for it . . . and forget the foolishness.

WIDOW. I'm always ready . . . I do it myself. Here, on my thighs and arms.

URSULA. Good . . . I see all . . . I appraise it . . . That won't go uncounted.

WIDOW. God . . . thank you.

URSULA *(to Thiefy)*.

—Thiefy.

—Yes, miss.

—You've earned a silver spoon.

—Are we done?

—Now I can give you back your freedom.

—You will?

—Nightmare, the Evil Witch, always keeps her word. Now run along.

## WAR LETTERS.

*Ursula, Mother and the Widow are reading letters. Ursula from her father on the Eastern Front to her mother, Mother from her father to her mother from Auschwitz, and the Widow from her husband in Iraq.*

URSULA. My Love:

You write about troubles; sadly, we have to press on . . . As for me, if not for all of you I'd have put a bullet in my head long ago . . . Watching this mess here and the unlimited injustice in everything, you could lose your mind in despair. A horse is worth more than a person! To hell with it all. You ask, little one, who invented this war? The Germans started this war! [. . .] The enthusiasm was mad, especially in people who are right now sitting all snug at home. Reading your letter, where you write that the children are constantly asking about their father—it brought tears to my eyes. I miss you all so much, I don't know how much longer I can stand it. Day and night, I think only of being near you . . .

MOTHER. Dearest:

I write these letters without really believing that you'll ever read them . . . I carry them all with me, a testament to the powerlessness that envelopes me whenever I try to name what I see and feel here . . . I've ended up in Hospital Block 12 in Camp B II f. There are other doctors in here with me, of different nationalities. Their families were liquidated as soon as they'd arrived . . . It's so good that you made it, my love . . . that you're not here . . . As doctors, we have to save the bodies we go on calling patients. Really, they're already dead . . . But we're not allowed to think that way. We've received the clothes . . . of people from the transports. Civilian clothes allow me to maintain my human appearance . . . In the doctor's room I have a bed with sheets . . . I think of you.

**WIDOW.** Woman!

My ass is intact and feet are down . . . Every few hours they spray the base with fire. We don't move without our helmets and bulletproof vests on. The heat is 120 in the shade. We execute every order, even the dumbest ones, without grumbling and as best we can. Our colonel doesn't leave HQ but to go back and forth to the mess. From AC to AC. Anyone who thought this would be a beach vacation—they're shaking in their boots.

**MOTHER.** Not far from our barracks is the Gypsy camp. Whole families pass through here, mothers with children running, men and old timers. They don't work. Colorful birds, the look of normal life. On the grounds of the Gypsy camp is the experimental barracks. The lab director is a world-renowned pediatrician from Prague. Four years a prisoner of the camp. He does experiments on noma, that is, the facial gangrene that has infected the majority of Gypsy children. I've been assigned to help. For science?

**URSULA.** My Dearest:

How are our treasures, Ursula, Hans and little Liza? I am crying for you here. We lie like sandbags, one on top of the other. Every so often a sergeant from the KP visits us. We get vials labeled "Pervitin." After taking these tablets, we don't feel hungry, and we don't feel like sleeping. The lice and bedbugs don't leave us in peace day or night. My body is all scratched up. A man approaches madness and could go crazy—could you believe that even I can sometimes scream in fury?! I'm afraid of doing something really foolish.

**WIDOW.** Morning, foot patrol. Around every corner you see an insurgent stalking up and a dog strapped with an explosive charge. Everyone is suspect. You shoot to be sure . . . Think about what I'm living through here . . . Think about it whenever you have some foolish thoughts . . . You know what I'm talking about.

**MOTHER.** My Dearest:

What are you up to without me there? Alone . . . I think the worst . . . I dream of someone coming and, with one thick stroke, separating the good from the bad. No clear criteria for that here. No morally pure choice. All hope is in you.

**URSULA.** I must disturb you, my love, with certain questions. Among our soldiers there prevails an unpleasant and downtrodden mood with regard to our fatherland. They say here that the soldiers' wives aren't so faithful, that eighty percent of these women are running around with other men, taking advantage of their husbands' absence. Write to me whether this is possible, but there must be some truth in it.

**WIDOW.** This mission is looking more and more like a circus. We ride around in these frigging farm carts and old trucks. Stripped-down cars. Like in Saint Tropez, breeze, sunshine. No cover, no armor. But there's a bonus for each trip off base . . . I hope they extend my contract. We'll expand the house, we'll live well . . . One boy, young guy, got a letter from his girl . . . some limp-dick stuck it in her. You get that? He's out here, like, fucking collecting corpses, and she's there spreading her ass for some shit-heel . . . I'd kill her. I'd totally kill her.

**URSULA.** The temperature drops every couple hours. The sky and the ground here look completely different. All of us have blisters from frostbite. You don't know what I would give, my dear, for a pair of decent gloves. We kill dogs. Their skin is warm enough to bring us momentary relief . . . If only we could get out of this damned Russia, see it no more, forget all about it. The only thing I could hate more is you, were you to betray me. Forgive me, but this thought gives me no peace. I hope that you're done worrying your little head over that Gypsy braid.

**MOTHER.** I've been taking measurements of twins and dwarves. I compile the notes, observe patients whose minds have been infected. I'm fixing these pictures in memory. Death is not the worst thing that can happen to you here. The patients ask for a fast-acting poison. I don't do it. I'm a doctor. I bring powders for wounds and bandages from the hospital. I pass them to prisoners from other barracks . . . Slight relief.

WIDOW. We're all fucking sappers. Yesterday two vanloads of wounded went into the air. And this is supposed to be a stabilization mission? It's a regular war. The Americans are equipped great. Technical wonders. "Shake 'n bake" – phosphorus bombs, they melt muscle and burn skin. MK-77s—cluster bombs. They break apart into hundreds of pieces the size of pool balls. Depleted uranium shells. Sort of mini nuclear explosions. High-tech thermobaric bombs—they suck out the oxygen and kill with a shockwave, crushing people with enormous pressure. Of course, all these awesome things come on top of the standard equipment. And how do we look? We lack basic materials. The guys buy the parts they need from the Arabs at the bazaar. I hope you have all your parts where they should be.

URSULA. Dearest:

My fingers refuse to obey. They're not capable of grasping this frosty rifle. There's been a blizzard for two days and two nights. We sit huddled up against a haystack, our only protection from the wind and the chunks of ice that bite our faces. We're huddled together like our piglets. The Russians are sitting on the other side of the haystack. Unfit for war, the same as us.

MOTHER. Vans marked with a red cross go daily toward the crematoria. Inside, they carry tins of Zyklon B. Greenish pellets the size of beans . . . They're poured through an opening in the roof of the crematorium . . . The gas first reaches the lower layers of air. I imagine those piles of bodies, those pyramids tangled together . . . Infants and children on the very bottom, then the elderly and women, and the strongest men at the top. And me—where?

URSULA. We're losing ourselves here completely . . . We're overcome with despair and depression. It's a living hell. Some people injure themselves in order to get out. They shoot through a slab of bread so that no one can see the powder burns. For the hardest cases, the medics keep ampules of morphine in their mouths so they don't freeze. We lie among corpses. The ground is too hard to dig graves.

**MOTHER.** Today our block's Reichsdeutsch covered the table with a damask tablecloth. He took out salt bacon, salami, canned food. Everything from today's transport. I recognize the Hungarian labels. I'm in agony, such that the food gets stuck in my throat . . . I was thinking of our child, whom we don't even have anymore, and maybe we won't have . . . How am I to tell him what I have become?

**URSULA.** I am unmoved by anything; I kill on my left, I kill on my right—the more I kill, the faster this will end. My eardrums burst with the detonations. The Bolsheviks are not people, they're animals, they just keep fighting with uncommon persistence, even when they're wounded and dying . . . I'm hungry! Hunger! If only this miserable war would end, I don't care how, just to get home, even on foot, even if I have to go on my hands and knees, if only to drag myself there and see my family and my fatherland one more time.

**WIDOW.** The bomb that was supposed to blow our car apart went off a few seconds too early. A few seconds. My friends from another patrol weren't so lucky. Bodies torn to shreds . . . Maybe everything torn off of some . . . I don't know. One completely burned, actually charred. He's alive. That's what I'm most afraid of. If I come back without my legs, with scars all over my body, promise me that you'll finish me off.

**MOTHER.** My experience here is one of terrible arrogance . . . I can't write anymore. I no longer have an internal "no" . . . It's dead. I'm consumed with dread at the throught of the reality awaiting me just past the gate. There's no desire in me to face up to it . . . Paradoxically, I dream of you . . . I hope that you'll find someone who will love you as much as I have.

*The Son, Alone with a Pistol.*

**SON.** She plucked me like a week . . . It means nothing to her. Nothing . . . If only she had seen how he would be. How he pissed himself . . . He had to go back to the desert . . . honor and fatherland . . . "I've come to bid you farewell, little brother." He pressed his strong, fat fingers into my cheeks. "You're still little, and you don't know how shitty this is." Son of a bitch . . . He put the pistol to my head. "Grow up, because you have to deal with all this shit . . . If your big brother doesn't come back . . . You know . . . some quick burst of fire, or fuck-all . . ." He reeked of vodka and fresh puke . . . Too bad he didn't shoot . . . It must have been a riot for him . . . I couldn't calm these fucking muscles . . . When I look at her, I feel a desire to shoot . . . Or maybe I should shoot myself? Maybe my mother? Everyone has something that's reason enough not to go on living . . . every one of us has somebody to whom we're just some pile of shit, an eyesore, decomposing and betraying what we eat, what we use to wipe our asses, whether we floss . . . She put up wire fencing around my head, with her fear. She throws her own damage in my face. I was quiet inside, and now something is buzzing within me. How much am I me, and how much am I somebody else . . . He tore off her nail, and she mewed like a cat . . . That's her submissiveness. It's worse than plague . . . Silence . . . as if nothing had happened . . . Is she nuts? She lies . . . Everyone lies . . . I just want to tell it like it really was. Tiny saw the whole thing, Tiny knows . . . Tiny's bad . . . Whose fault is this? Who did it? Who . . .

*Father on the Phone.*

*Father is present on stage.*

FATHER. You don't call. I was waiting.

SON. I'm at the front, Dad. I'm taking care of business.

FATHER. I'm taking care of business, too. Yesterday I reported some Arab on the subway. He was suspicious. The police took him in. The sheriff patted me on the back. You know, one of those policemen with a metal plate on his chest. They have these really cool plates. Respect. Full respect . . .

SON. You're in the enemy's camp. I have you in my sights.

FATHER. Don't talk like that . . . Don't do anything stupid.

SON. And why should I do something stupid, huh?

FATHER. Something's going on, Son. Something bad.

SON. That's none of your concern, you coward . . . you piece of shit.

FATHER. Maybe I should call back later.

SON. Don't call. Understand? You don't exist. You were done the moment you left. "I have to earn our bread, son. Remember to be a decent person." You ran away . . .

FATHER. I couldn't . . . not with her . . . When your brother disappeared . . . she became like herring: cold and salty. I couldn't stand how she goes on believing . . . she left her work, the city she loved so much, me—and for whole days she sat staring at that disgusting river . . . Life was over . . . And there was always you . . . I don't know what to call it . . .

SON. In another sector . . .

FATHER. Exactly . . . something like that.

SON. I was counting on you, Dad.

FATHER. I'm useful . . . I help the police keep this city in order . . . I work like a horse. Let's stick together, Son . . .

SON *(Shoots)*. Right.

FATHER. What was that?

SON. You're done. Don't call again.

*Order.*

*Son, with the pistol, as in the dream. He's bashing the framed portrait of his brother.*

SON. Enough of this shit!

MOTHER. Leave it . . . I just framed that.

SON. I see that some people are still deaf! Some are still blind.

MOTHER. God . . . What's happened to you? It's because of her! The witch.

WIDOW. Stop it, Tiny.

SON. Tiny is gone! Forget about Tiny! Tiny's back in Tinyland. Spit on the picture!

**WIDOW.** What?

**SON.** I said spit on it!

**WIDOW.** Stop.

**SON.** Come on!

**MOTHER.** Leave her alone.

**SON.** You stay out of it.

**MOTHER.** You have no right to spit on that picture.

**SON.** Spit on it! Don't listen to her. She hates you as much as she hates me.

**WIDOW.** You don't know anything. Put that down.

**SON** (*burns the photograph of his brother*). That's that!

**WIDOW.** Stupid Tiny . . . It's just a picture. Mine. I'm the one who took it. To calm the fever in my body, which wouldn't let me sleep. Your brother was right, he knew me . . . That's why I hate him most.

**SON.** You're lying.

**MOTHER.** Crazy woman. From God-knows-where. What are you doing here, anyway? Get out of here already, out of this house!

**WIDOW.** I have to wait here. I have to . . .

**SON.** You know, Mom . . . on the night my brother, your son, died, she . . . She was thinking about very bad things. She was waiting for him with a gun in her hand, and . . . you put it so well before . . . that you didn't have it in you . . . how did you put it?

**WIDOW.** That I didn't have the strength not to shoot . . .

**MOTHER.** Murderess.

*The light goes out. Ursula appears in the brother's uniform holding a candle.*

**SON.** My brother . . .

**WIDOW.** My husband.

**MOTHER.** My son.

**SON.** Drowned . . .

**WIDOW.** He's watching us.

**MOTHER.** So gaunt. Right from the road.

**SON.** Maybe it's not him . . .

**WIDOW.** His uniform . . .

**MOTHER.** His profile.

**SON.** Tiny knows, Tiny saw the whole thing . . . That night . . . I was there . . . by the river . . . I saw.

**MOTHER.** Son.

**SON.** I saw him . . . take off his boots . . . his uniform. I saw him stagger, take a swig of vodka . . . and get smaller and smaller . . . There was a terrible wind blowing that night . . . The leaves on the bushes were hitting me in the face . . . There was a strong current. I stood there. In the background you could hear the music from our house and the guests laughing. I couldn't move. I couldn't cry out . . . I didn't want to. Go . . . it's better for you this way . . . He went down . . . he disappeared under the water. I didn't even try to help him.

**MOTHER.** What are you saying? He came back, after all.

**SON.** The fucking drunk drowned . . .

**WIDOW.** God . . . God, take back your merciless little gift . . . Love is not patient . . . It's not polite . . . It's filled with envy . . . It's carried away by hubris . . . It's shameless . . . It seeks its own . . . It's filled with rage . . . It does not forget a wrong . . . It does not forgive . . . It does not outlast everything . . . I don't trust you . . . God . . . don't talk to me anymore. I won't hear you, I don't want to hear you . . . Let him bloat up in the water, let predatory fish eat his eyes out, let whirpools gnash his heart, let his arms get tangled around his neck, let his mouth get blocked up with muck and stones grow into his skin. Let his hair take root on the bottom of that goddamn river . . . Let a ribbon of ice cover the river forever . . . We'll light a bonfire on it and dance till morning . . . Without pain, without fear . . . We'll dance all through the night . . .

**MOTHER.** My son, my beloved little boy.

IMAGE 4.6 (In the foreground) **Ursula-Widow (Hanna Klepacka), Little/Son (Dawid Rafalski);** (in the background, from the left) **Ursula-Dulchi (Dobrosława Trębacz), Ursula-Joppe (Joanna Koc), Ursula-Trude (Tatiana Kołodziejska), Ursula-Katli (Karolina Honchera), and Ursula-Martille (Marta Frąckowiak)**
Directed by Marcin Liber. Lubuski Teatr w Zielonej Górze, Zielona Góra (2012)
*Photograph by Bartłomiej Sowa*

---

**SON.** You cut out his tongue, you gouged out his eyes . . . After all, one pair of eyes is good enough for two, one tongue is good enough for two . . . Tiny knows, Tiny saw the whole thing . . . That night . . . while that terrible wind was blowing . . . he came to you . . . You wanted him to rub your feet . . . as usual . . . He didn't want to go back to the desert . . . You were the only one who knew. He was afraid . . . all he was waiting for was for you to tell him there wasn't really anything to be afraid of . . . that he didn't have to go back there.

**MOTHER.** They'll tear my heart into quarters.

*The Son shoots at his brother. The apparition does not vanish. It moves towards them with the candle.*

**WIDOW.** It's a ghost . . . not a person.

**SON.** That's not him.

**MOTHER.** It's a little girl.

**WIDOW.** A little kid.

**MOTHER.** This house is cursed . . . for us to live our lives on graves . . . My father was digging . . . behind the shed . . . he wanted a little soil to build up the tomatoes . . . He pulled out some rag . . . then an entire body . . . this little blond girl . . . My father carried her to the forest . . . my mother lit a candle. We couldn't forget it. It's not something you can forget . . . But we did.

**WIDOW.** A weary, wandering spirit.

**SON.** It's taking off the uniform.

**MOTHER.** It's opening its mouth.

**WIDOW.** It wants to tell us something.

**URSULA.** They used to say in our village that when someone with poor eyesight suddenly starts reading without glasses, it means that death is on its way. And Elza's grandmother started reading the newspapers without glasses, and she'd been nearly blind for ten years . . . Then our soldiers rode through the village on their motorbikes . . . That was a sight. Hans and I stared at it all day . . . It's over now . . . It's over now, my mother kept saying. The Ivans are devils, all the women in the village were saying. There was a terrible commotion, Mama packed our things into trunks. She told me and Hans to put them on the wagon. I packed all the costumes we used in our games with Elza, and I hid them in a hole behind the shed. I was afraid they'd fall off the wagon while we were running away. Mama said we wouldn't be coming back here, but I didn't believe her. She wanted to throw away the key. I took it and hung it around my neck. I knew we'd be back, me, Mommy, little Liza, Daddy and Hans. Hans put on his Hitlerjugend uniform and said that he'd protect us. Mommy ordered him to take it off this instant, and that's when Hans and I understood that something really bad was happening, because Mama usually adored when Hans would walk around in his uniform. Once the wagon was full, we rolled it into our barn. I was glad, because Elza and the other girls were already there, and all the women from the village. Mama was nervous, since we had to wait for the evacuation order, so she told us to unroll our blankets and go to sleep. I was glad to sleep next to Elza, we huddled close together and weren't cold, and we could talk all night. We were awakened by the women screaming. "Die Russen kommen! Die Russen kommen!" The whole village was going crazy. The women were running alongside the packed wagons, ready for departure. Our neighbor, Renate, ran toward the river. Along with her daughters, Alma and Erna. To drown themselves . . . Mama is mumbling sort of strangely . . . pulling me, Hans and little Liza onto the loft of the barn. Hans runs away, and little Liza is crying her head off. Now the other women are in the loft. They scramble to find twine, they take off their stockings and belts. We're going to hang ourselves, Mama says.

Outside, you can hear the stamping of heavy boots. I look through the window and hear a shot. Stupid Hans . . . (*animates the doll, places twine around its neck*) Mama puts twine around little Liza's neck, she doesn't let her cry. She hits her in the face. They're really hurrying with the hanging. Other women wheeze horribly, unable to die. I ran away. I wanted to go back home . . . there was a line of soldiers in front of the door. Elza lay inside . . . Sleeping Beauty. She didn't move. They went up to her one after the other and . . . wanted to wake her up. Just like Hans . . . Other soldiers are singing by the stove. One of them takes me on his knee and strokes my head. He smells a little like my dad. He has maybe a hundred watches on his arms. Strapped all in a row. He's smiling. He has the face of a troll. Where did they all come from? They must have come down the chimney . . . I remember that Mama is still up in the loft, and I go back to the barn. They let me leave. "Málenka, málenka", they keep saying. It's terribly quiet up in the loft. Old Friede has foam on her mouth, but she's still alive. She hasn't been hanging long enough. Little Liza's not crying anymore. She's rocking, like in her crib. I get onto a sack of oats, Mama puts the twine around my neck. You have to jump, she says. Jump! I jump . . .

This is my house. It's white, with a little red roof. The windows aren't too big, with brown shutters. The windowsills have boxes with yellow flowers . . . You're like the wind. You go on telling my story. To the whole world. And it will be a kiss from the wind, a kiss from everybody, and then Sleeping Beauty will wake up and never fall asleep again. Otherwise, Nightmare, the Bad Witch, will take your secrets and lock them in her dark dungeon. And throw away the key. And dungeons have rats, and they'll eat up all your secrets . . . You don't like me? Naughty Ursula? It's my fault? What really happened? All I wanted to do was tell my story . . . There's nothing wrong with that . . . is there? This is my house. It's white, with a little red roof. The windows aren't too big, with brown shutters. The windowsills have boxes with yellow flowers.

(*Ursula sings and exits.*)

Der Tag war grau,
Der Tag war schwer,
Und stürmisch ging die See,
Nun klärt es auf von Westen her,
Die Brandung glänzt wie Schnee.
Ums Achterdeck die Möwe fliegt
Und leiser kommt der Wind,
Der mich in gold'ne Träume wiegt,
Antje, mein blondes Kind.

Antje, Antje,
Hörst du nicht von ferne das Schifferklavier,

Antje, Antje,
Das Lied soll Dich grüßen von mir.

The Calm after the Storm.

*Mother and Widow sit by the river. Widow massages Mother's feet and reads a letter from Tiny.*

Dear Miss:

I hope that you do not think ill of me. That you have found an explanation for my fit of madness. It's the sort of thing that can happen to anyone. It lands on your head like a bit of plaster. And nothing is the same as it was. What's inside us just wakes up. It discovers its own helplessness. Its own degradation, and one never comes out of indignity unscathed. Once freed, love of self can lead anywhere. You turn into pure hatred. You sip it drop by drop. And before you know it you're the person you despised. Looking at what has occurred in our microcosm and in the so-called wider world, it's regular people who are hatched out of every wickedness, out of the sorrow of abandonment. Not crazies. There is no *inhuman* depravity. Everyone has the right to choose, and the bad choice fit me better, as it is, in principle, a better fit for mankind. I don't know how to express this more clearly, but I believe that you won't think it just the mutterings of some crazy adolescent. Everything that passed is still real. I hope that you also remember the good times, miss, those seconds, those glimmers of crushing brightness. Because there were those, too. There always are. Perhaps my flight into the wild whiteness of Greenland will allow me to rebuild myself. Please look after my mom. Farewell.
Tiny.

**MOTHER.** So many thoughts in that young head.

**WIDOW.** They'll bring him relief, but they'll also lead him to temptation. Like this river.

**MOTHER.** It finally spat out the body.

**WIDOW.** I was with him in the morning. I washed the plaque.

**MOTHER.** And did you visit the little girl?

**WIDOW.** Yes. The gravestone came out lovely. Modest.

**MOTHER.** That's good. Maybe I'll go myself tomorrow. I'll light a candle.

**WIDOW.** As if looking at us from an airplane, this is our river, that's the house, here are these sort of smallish blotches, and so many tragic stories in this one blotch. It can't be concealed.

**MOTHER.** A stork.

**WIDOW.** What?

**MOTHER.** A stork. There.

**WIDOW.** Maybe a female?

**MOTHER.** Could be.

**WIDOW.** Yeah. It's looking for frogs.

*The End*

## SOURCES

Ursula's German song is "Antje, mein blondes Kind," by Hermes Niel (1940).

Memoirs of Adelheid Nagel, collected by Ośrodek Karta.

Włodzimierz Nowak, *Obwód Głowy* [Head Size] (Wołowiec, 2007).

Maria Podlasek, *Wypędzenie Niemców z terenów na wschód od Odry i Nysy Łużyckiej–relacje świadków* [The Expulsion of Germans from Territories East of the Odra and Lusatian Neisse: Witness Accounts] (Warszawa, 1995).

Marek Miller (ed.), *Europa według Auschwitz. Litzmannstadt Ghetto* [Europe as Seen through Auschwitz. Litzmannstadt Ghetto] (Oświęcim, 2009).

*Z myślą o Reichu* [Thinking of the Reich: Letters of German Soldiers from the Eastern Front], *Karta* 44 (2005).

Sylwester Latkowski, *Irak–Misja kompromitacja* [Iraq–Mission: Fiasco], TV documentary (2005).

pilgrim/majewski

# right left with heels

Translated by Artur Zapałowski

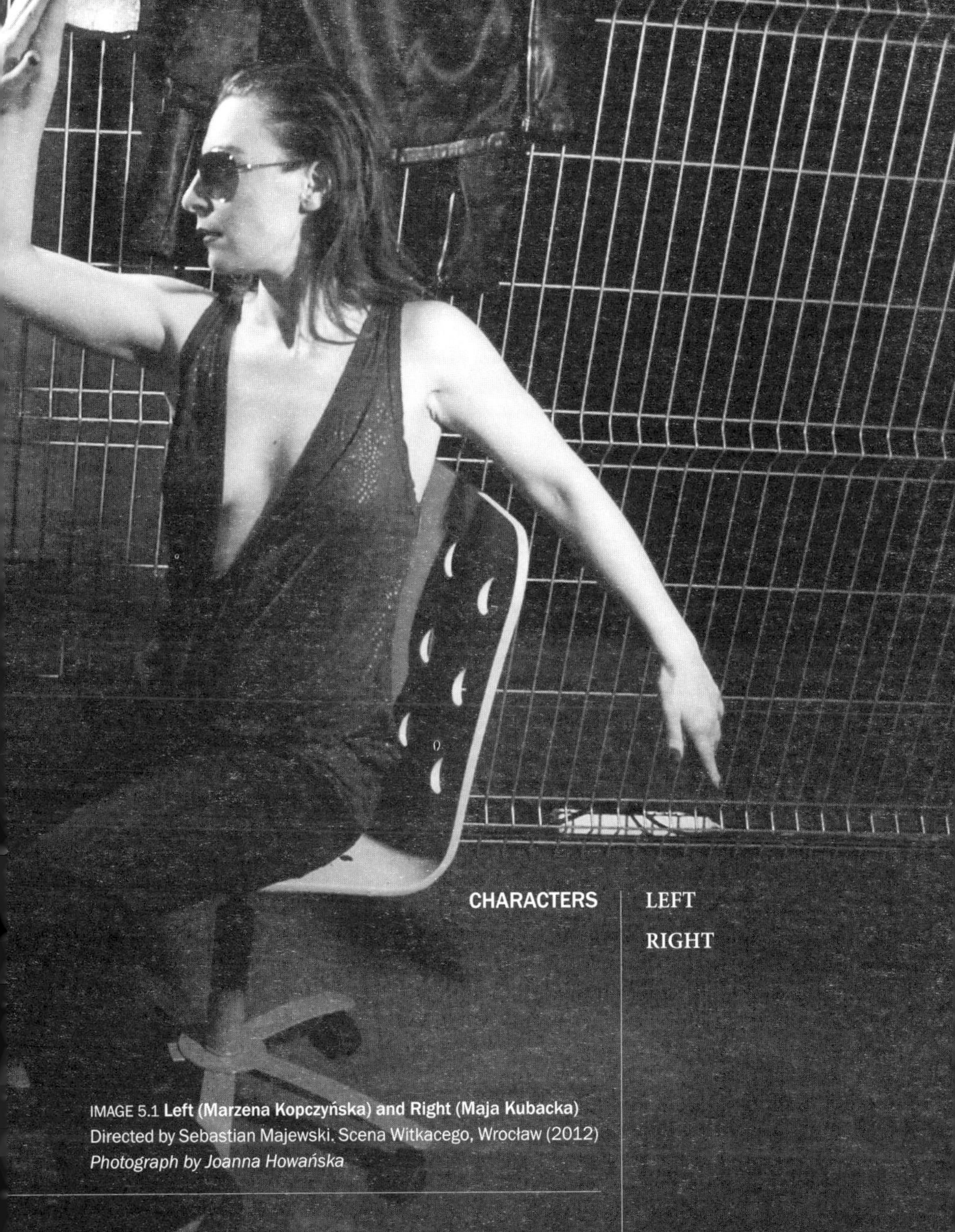

IMAGE 5.1 **Left (Marzena Kopczyńska) and Right (Maja Kubacka)**
Directed by Sebastian Majewski. Scena Witkacego, Wrocław (2012)
*Photograph by Joanna Howańska*

**CHARACTERS**

LEFT

RIGHT

## NOTE

pilgrim/majewski's *right left with heels* is a thoroughly realistic historical story based on a surreal concept. Its protagonists and narrators are the right and left shoes of Magda Goebbels, wife of Nazi Germany's minister of propaganda Joseph Goebbels, with whom she committed suicide in May 1945, having first killed her six children. The shoes, having escaped being burnt along with their owner, but sentenced to exile by the Nuremberg Tribunal, tell their story: from their manufacture in Auschwitz to their tragic end on the feet of a transvestite murdered by "real men—young polish patriots" in the twenty-first century. They describe their successive owners: a female Red Army soldier whose spoils of war they become; the "Doctor's Wife" who denounced a Jewish woman; Teresa, a secret police interrogator; and Magda, a Solidarity activist who broke under questioning during martial law in Poland in the early 1980s.

The shoes tell their story twice. In the first part of the play [00] they provide a general outline, while in the next parts, which are given dates—from ['46] to ['07]—they build on their account and fill in the details. The wandering of Magda Goebbels' shoes—a brief history of impoverished, enslaved and demoralized postwar—gives an insight into individual guilt and wickedness, and addresses individual, as opposed to collective, accountability in the face of history.

The premiere of *right left with heels*, directed by one of the authors, Sebastian Majewski, took place in the avant-garde performance space Scena Witkacego in Wrocław in 2007. The parts of right and left were played by two actresses who managed to bring out both the grotesque and the tragic gravity of the text.

# right left with heels



[00]

**LEFT.** hi
I don't like wood paneling

**RIGHT.** this room
is all in wood

**LEFT.** because it's a courtroom

**RIGHT.** this fabric—
flags

**LEFT.** nuremberg
the year 'forty-six
a special section
for degenerate objects
a building in the center of the city

**RIGHT.** they're charging us
only because
we didn't burn
and stayed
put

**LEFT.** they also ruled
that we'd contributed to
the extermination
of a nation
we the shoes
of magda goebbels

**RIGHT.** the right

**LEFT.** the left

**RIGHT.** black pumps
with heels

**LEFT.** early in may
of 'forty-five

they took us outside
doused us with gas
and set us alight
she burned
we didn't

RIGHT. but they threw us in
a pit
together
and covered in quicklime
we looked pretty
black and white
so classic

LEFT. a week later
they dug us up again

RIGHT. and then they
arrested us

LEFT. we thought
our tender age
would save us
barely a year old
but they
sentence even children
today
we're two now

RIGHT. as supporters of the regime
we were sentenced
to forced exile
to the east

LEFT. in the name of
the united nations

RIGHT. this is sveta
sveta
is twenty
she wears the ugly
unbecoming uniform

of the conquering army
she has slanted eyes
and a broad nose
her feet sweat
she smells
she's from asia

**LEFT.** that explains everything[1]

**RIGHT.** but sveta
also has a fiancé
and he's got
an army car

**LEFT.** sveta's happy
and so are we
we won't get worn out walking
sveta's sprawled
in the front seat
sticking her legs
out the window

**RIGHT.** it's a bit windy
and it's cold
how many times do we sneeze?

**LEFT.** twice
we have a cold

**RIGHT.** but we're alive
damn, we're alive
sveta drinks a lot
she likes drinking
and then she likes
lying down on the grass
on the ground
anywhere

---

**1** Magda Goebbels' shoes might have inherited her racist views, but this line connotes the genuine strangeness of Europeans encountering Red Army soldiers of Asian origin for the first time.

**LEFT.** and she wraps her legs around the back
of her fiancé
like this

**RIGHT.** and we're lying there on his back

**LEFT.** and we hear his name
for the first time that day
and the last
do it harder
sashka

**RIGHT.** we see nothing
just feel
and forget about it all

**LEFT.** so do sveta and sashka

**RIGHT.** but you sveta
cannot
forget about everything
that was foolish of you

**LEFT.** and that's why now we're lying
on a metal bed
on a cold oilcloth

**RIGHT.** and some strange man
is putting on a rubber apron

**LEFT.** hey

**RIGHT.** hey

**LEFT.** afterwards sveta
can't afford to pay
but the man doesn't mind
after all sveta
is with the conquering army

**RIGHT.** but sveta insists
he's saved her honor
her life

**LEFT.** and gives us to him

**RIGHT.** the right

**LEFT.** the left

**RIGHT.** black pumps
with heels
the wife will like them
the wife did like them

**LEFT.** the doctor's wife
because that's what
the doctor's wife is called
kept us
underwater for thirteen hours

**RIGHT.** we barely made it through

**LEFT.** but now we fit perfectly
on her feet

**RIGHT.** six days a week
we stand on the shelf
and on sunday
the doctor shines us with polish
it smells
does everything
here come from asia?

**LEFT.** the doctor's wife always wears
nylon stockings

**RIGHT.** we like that

**LEFT.** and we go outside
we don't know
where we are
we walk
paved sidewalks
like the ones in berlin

**RIGHT.** but we're not in berlin
because the doctor's wife calls the doctor
*my esteemed spouse*
*my esteemed spouse*
what language is that in
how can people talk that way?

**LEFT.** and we walk onto a slippery marble
floor

**RIGHT.** for fear of falling
we go down on both knees
and pray

**LEFT.** amen

**RIGHT.** says the doctor's wife
and we say amen

**LEFT.** later on
the doctor's wife falls to the floor
she grows cold right away

**RIGHT.** the doctor
carries her through the city

**LEFT.** hey
she's dead

**RIGHT.** we walk down streets

**LEFT.** legnicka
strzegomska
we see names
świerczewskiego
wrocław główny
railway station

**RIGHT.** tell him
she's dead

**LEFT.** most grunwaldzki
skłodowskiej curie
and back

**RIGHT.** szczytnicka
katedralna
grodzka
antoniego

**LEFT.** someone
dresses the doctor's wife

**RIGHT.** the coffin is quiet
 and soft
**LEFT.** the doctor's wife is cold
 and stiff
**RIGHT.** the doctor touches her
**LEFT.** us too
**RIGHT.** someone nails the coffin shut
**LEFT.** hey you
 we're alive in here
 darkness
 we slowly get used to it
 we're dying
**RIGHT.** a car takes us
 to the cemetery
**LEFT.** we don't make it there
 someone pulls us out
 steals us
**RIGHT.** we're alive
 and then
 teresa gets us
 teresa is clumsy on her feet
**LEFT.** no sense of rhythm
**RIGHT.** she can't dance
 but dances every night
**LEFT.** it's all the fun she gets
**RIGHT.** teresa
 is fat
 and smokes cigarettes
 without filters
**LEFT.** we stamp out the butts
 we stamp out the butts
 our soles are charred
**RIGHT.** teresa completed
 three grades of elementary school

and never read a book in her life
but she is
in charge of the cellar

**LEFT.** each year
in recognition
she gets sent
on vacation

**RIGHT.** in august
we walk fourteen days
singing songs
into a microphone

**LEFT.** we're altos

**RIGHT.** teresa's a soprano

**LEFT.** when we get tired
we sleep by the side of the road
with others

**RIGHT.** teresa talks
about god and comrade wiesław[2]

**LEFT.** we don't know
who comrade wiesław is

**RIGHT.** all teresa needs
is paper
she notes down everything
and puts it in files

**LEFT.** it's better
not to talk to her

**RIGHT.** she's dangerous

**LEFT.** super dangerous

---

**2** "Wiesław" was the party pseudonym of Władysław Gomułka, the Polish communist leader imprisoned during Stalinist purges in 1951, when he was denounced as right-wing reactionary. During the period of political liberalization in 1956, Gomułka was released and appointed first secretary of the Communist Party, which raised great hopes for reforms that were mostly left unfulfilled. Gomułka was the leader of Poland until 1970.

**RIGHT.** and teresa dances
and she's old
and getting uglier

**LEFT.** how ugly she is

**RIGHT.** teresa is still
in charge of the cellar
today is wednesday
and teresa
will get a visit from magda
we don't know her

**LEFT.** but we do know
that magda's read
more books
and finished more grades
that's why
she's not in charge

**RIGHT.** magda walks in

**LEFT.** magda
doesn't say anything

**RIGHT.** while teresa
screams her head off
what's she doing?
teresa's giving us
to magda
us
the right

**LEFT.** the left

**RIGHT.** black pumps
with heels
magda's chucked us
in the trash

**LEFT.** why don't you go
chuck yourself
bitch

**RIGHT.** here comes a bum
he's pissed himself
bums reeking of piss
didn't touch us
for weeks

**LEFT.** then
some fucked-up set designer lady
took us for a play

**RIGHT.** to the theater

**LEFT.** we walked the boards
in some shitty plays
no one fucking
understands

**RIGHT.** to the storeroom
and back on stage
lame

**LEFT.** if at least we'd
been on tv
had a cameo
in some soap
we'd be famous

**RIGHT.** but who goes to the theater

**LEFT.** boooring

**RIGHT.** and in that storeroom
we were bought
for 10 złoty[3]

**LEFT.** for 10 złoty
we the shoes of magda goebbels

**RIGHT.** by this fucking queer
krystian

**LEFT.** super queer

---

**3** The złoty is the Polish currency, and 10 złotysis equivalent to a little over US$3.

**RIGHT.** krystian's a dancer
he shakes his ass on stage

**LEFT.** and then
makes money
with that same ass

**RIGHT.** not that they pay
to bang him

**LEFT.** not like anyone
would pay him
because krystian
is gross

**RIGHT.** no
krystian's not
a whore
he just gets parts that way

**LEFT.** the fucking freak

**RIGHT.** but he won't be getting any more
not today
not tomorrow
not ever
krystian's lying there fucked-up
in the square

**LEFT.** oh yes

**RIGHT.** this is the end
good thing that
it's the end
of this punishment of ours

['46]

**LEFT.** I don't like wood paneling
it smells of resin
like the woods

and we don't like the woods
it's hard walking there

**RIGHT.** this room
is all made of wood
and the benches
are all sticky
slapped together
sloppily

**LEFT.** they were scared
we'd run away

**RIGHT.** but you know
we didn't
in may
we were arrested
and charged

**LEFT.** this room
is a courtroom
judges
prosecutors
an attorney

**RIGHT.** this fabric—
flags

**LEFT.** but you know that
all of it
you've come here
to see the trial
remember the trial?

**RIGHT.** you've forgotten

**LEFT.** then we'll remind you
nuremberg
the year 'forty-six
a special section
for degenerate objects
a building in the center of the city

**RIGHT.** we've been here before
at the parteitag
and on the way
to bayreuth

**LEFT.** is wagner still banned?

**RIGHT.** but today
the verdict will be read out
with mahler playing

**LEFT.** you know, that yid
or that polack
chopin

**RIGHT.** a sentence will be passed

**LEFT.** and that will be an outrage
because this whole court
is an outrage
there is no proof

**RIGHT.** not even in the photos
we're not in them

**LEFT.** others are
in the photos
of him or his children[4]
that sweet six, their names all starting with an h
h
h
h
h
h
h

**RIGHT.** they're charging us
only because
we didn't burn
and stayed
put

---

**4** A reference to Joseph Goebbels and his children.

**LEFT.** they also ruled
that we'd contributed to
the extermination
of a nation
us the shoes
of magda goebbels

**RIGHT.** the right

**LEFT.** the left

**RIGHT.** black pumps
with heels
fashioned
of human skin
and human fat
at the factory in auschwitz

**LEFT.** you knew about the factory in auschwitz?

**RIGHT.** neither did we

**LEFT.** no sir
who can remember
their prenatal phase

**RIGHT.** we were born
in the year 'forty-four
custom-made for the feet
of magda goebbels

**LEFT.** but
early in may
of 'forty-five
it was all over
you know that
then
they took us outside
doused us with gas
and set us alight
she burned
we didn't

RIGHT. but they threw us in
a pit
together
and covered in quicklime
we looked pretty
black and white
so classic

LEFT. straight away
the ants swarmed over us

RIGHT. but it was her they ate
you know?
she was tastier

LEFT. a week later
they dug us up again

RIGHT. the jealous
lída baarová[5]
goebbels' lover
you got to know her
at the movies
cried: those are her shoes
and then they
arrested us

LEFT. we thought
our tender age
would save us
barely a year old
but they
sentence even children
today
we're two now

RIGHT. as supporters of the regime
we were sentenced

---

5 Lída Baarová was a Czech actress whose affair with Joseph Goebbels led Magda Goebbels to attempt divorce, only to be blocked by Hitler.

to forced exile
to the east

**LEFT.** in the name of
the united nations

**RIGHT.** and
in your name too

## ['46/'47]

**LEFT.** right away
this girl
puts us on
her bare feet

**RIGHT.** hey
we're not
sandals
we're dress
shoes

**LEFT.** you need to wear
tights
or nylon stockings

**RIGHT.** she doesn't understand us

**LEFT.** do you understand
this barbarian tongue

**RIGHT.** meet
sveta
sveta
is twenty
she wears the ugly
unbecoming uniform
of the conquering army
see it
she has slanted eyes

and a broad nose
her feet sweat
she smells
she's from asia

**LEFT.** that explains everything

**RIGHT.** but sveta
also has a fiancé
and he's got
an army car

**LEFT.** sveta's happy
and so are we
we won't get worn out walking
sveta's sprawled
in the front seat
sticking her legs
out the window

**RIGHT.** it's a bit windy
and it's cold

**LEFT.** we have a cold

**RIGHT.** but we're alive
and you know
that many died
on the way east

**LEFT.** you know
your people and ours
in the nineteenth century
and the twentieth
and presumably
the twenty-first as well

**RIGHT.** let us commemorate them
together
in a united europe
whatever that is
okay?

**LEFT.** in the daytime we ride
with sveta
at night
we kick doors open
and enter
various houses

**RIGHT.** people don't object
they don't shout
after all sveta
is with the conquering army

**LEFT.** we come out carrying
cuckoo clocks

IMAGE 5.2 **Left** (**Marzena Kopczyńska**) **and Right** (**Maja Kubacka**)
Directed by Sebastian Majewski. Scena Witkacego, Wrocław (2012)
*Photograph by Joanna Howańska*

wristwatches[6]
grandfather clocks
clocks set in silver platters

**RIGHT.** and sundials

**LEFT.** in the morning we'll swap them
for bottles of vodka

**RIGHT.** sveta drinks a lot
she likes drinking
and then she likes
lying down on the grass
on the ground
anywhere

**LEFT.** and she wraps her legs around the back
of her fiancé

**RIGHT.** and we're lying there on his back

**LEFT.** and we hear his name
for the first time that day
and the last
do it harder
sashka

**RIGHT.** shut your eyes
don't look

**LEFT.** we don't see anything either
just feel
and wrap ourselves tighter
around sashka's back
and forget about it all

**LEFT.** so do sveta and sashka

**RIGHT.** but you sveta
cannot

---

6 According to eyewitness testimony, victorious Red Army soldiers saw wristwatches as a sign of wealth and collected them as war trophies, wearing several on each arm.

forget about everything
that was foolish of you

**LEFT.** and that's why now we're lying
on a metal bed
on a cold oilcloth
and you're spreading your legs again

**LEFT.** don't look

**RIGHT.** and some strange man
is putting on a rubber apron
you know what comes next
but don't report it
to anyone

**LEFT.** afterwards sveta
can't afford to pay
but the man doesn't mind
after all sveta
is with the conquering army

**RIGHT.** but sveta insists
he's saved her honor
her life

**LEFT.** and gives us to him

**RIGHT.** the right

**LEFT.** the left

**RIGHT.** black pumps
with heels
fashioned
of human skin
and human fat

**LEFT.** did you know that doctor?

**RIGHT.** no

**LEFT.** does your wife?

**RIGHT.** no
but the wife will like them

**RIGHT.** the wife did like them

**LEFT.** the doctor's wife
because that's what
the doctor's wife is called
kept us
underwater for thirteen hours

**RIGHT.** we barely made it through

**LEFT.** but now we fit perfectly
on her feet

**RIGHT.** six days a week
we stand on the shelf
and on sunday
the doctor shines us with polish
it smells
does everything
here come from asia?

**LEFT.** the doctor's wife always wears
nylon stockings

**RIGHT.** we like that

**LEFT.** and we go outside
we don't know
where we are

**RIGHT.** maybe you know
where we are?
you're right
it's better to keep quiet
everything will become clear eventually
so let us clarify

**LEFT.** we're in the east
but only part of the way east
because we're walking
paved sidewalks
with the doctor's wife
like the ones in berlin

**RIGHT.** but we're not in berlin
because the doctor's wife calls the doctor
*esteemed spouse*

**LEFT.** hear that?
*esteemed spouse*

**RIGHT.** what language is that in
how can people talk that way?

**LEFT.** and we walk onto a slippery marble
floor

**RIGHT.** for fear of falling
we go down on both knees
and pray

**LEFT.** the doctor's wife prays:
good lord
good and immortal
heavenly creator
of all things
those with names
and those still seeking a name
I give thanks to you that I exist
that I'm alive
that you give me oblivion
and deceive my memory
amen says the doctor's wife

**RIGHT.** and we say amen
and you say amen

**LEFT.** we repeat the prayer
four hundred sundays
like a mantra

**RIGHT.** today
is the four-hundred-first sunday

**LEFT.** amen

**RIGHT.** we do not rise

**LEFT.** listen to the doctor's wife:
you were always better

at cartwheels in the playground
and you were taller
but even when you straightened your hair
you were still the same
and he promised me chocolate
that soldier
and all I did was tell the truth
she's jewish

**RIGHT.** and the next day
that woman
was lying face-down in the mud

**LEFT.** the doctor's wife is crying
do you know why

**RIGHT.** neither do we
to be crying for such a
reason
come on
tell her
worse things happen
she doesn't hear

**LEFT.** she falls to the floor
grows cold right away

**RIGHT.** the doctor
carries her through the city

**LEFT.** hey
she's dead

**RIGHT.** we walk down streets

**LEFT.** legnicka
strzegomska
we see names
świerczewskiego
wrocław główny
railway station

**RIGHT.** tell him
she's dead

**LEFT.** most grunwaldzki
skłodowskiej curie
and back

**RIGHT.** szczytnicka
katedralna
grodzka
antoniego

**LEFT.** someone
dresses the doctor's wife

**RIGHT.** the coffin is quiet
and soft

**LEFT.** the doctor's wife is cold
and stiff

**RIGHT.** the doctor touches her

**LEFT.** us too

**RIGHT.** someone nails the coffin shut

**LEFT.** hey you
we're alive in here
do something do something

**RIGHT.** right
better not do anything

**LEFT.** darkness
we slowly get used to it
we're dying

**RIGHT.** a car takes us
to the cemetery

**LEFT.** we don't make it there
someone pulls us out
shoves us in a plastic bag
steals us

**RIGHT.** we're alive

**LEFT.** you saved us
this calls for a celebration

**RIGHT.** teresa
    is clumsy on her feet

**LEFT.** no sense of rhythm

**RIGHT.** she can't dance
    but dances every night

**LEFT.** it's all the fun she gets

**RIGHT.** teresa
    is fat
    and smokes cigarettes
    without filters

**LEFT.** we stamp out the butts
    and our soles get charred

**RIGHT.** teresa completed
    three grades of elementary school
    and never read a book in her life
    but she is
    in charge of the cellar

**LEFT.** each year
    in recognition
    she gets sent
    on vacation

**RIGHT.** in august
    we walk fourteen days
    singing songs
    into a microphone

**LEFT.** we're altos

**RIGHT.** teresa's a soprano

**LEFT.** when we get tired
    we sleep by the side of the road
    with others

**RIGHT.** teresa talks
    about god and comrade wiesław

**LEFT.** we don't know
who comrade wiesław is
maybe you know where god is?

**RIGHT.** teresa's not looking for god
what for?
all teresa needs
is paper
she notes down everything
and puts it in files

**LEFT.** it's better
not to talk to her

**RIGHT.** she's dangerous
super dangerous

**RIGHT.** and teresa dances
and she's old
and getting uglier

**LEFT.** you knew that
and didn't say so
you pigs

**RIGHT.** so you also know
that teresa summons people
to the cellar
she puts on her uniform
and we crush noses
fingers
bellies
tits
and even entire legs

**LEFT.** stop it

**RIGHT.** that's how teresa dances
and we get a headache
and teresa dances

**RIGHT.** teresa's old
and getting uglier

**LEFT.** everybody here is ugly

**RIGHT.** a lower race

**LEFT.** obviously

**RIGHT.** teresa's still
in charge of the cellar
today is wednesday
and teresa
will get a visit from magda
we don't know her

**LEFT.** but we do know
that she's read
more books
and finished more grades
that's why
she's not in charge

**RIGHT.** magda walks in

**LEFT.** magda
doesn't say anything

**LEFT.** she doesn't love the communists
but she loves freedom

**RIGHT.** teresa doesn't understand
the word
she's only finished three grades

**LEFT.** while magda
doesn't understand teresa

**RIGHT.** we don't understand
anything either

**LEFT.** but we're serving out our punishment here

**RIGHT.** maybe you understand something?

**LEFT.** you're saying

that magda
is in solidarity[7]

**RIGHT.** we know that solidarity
is a noun signifying
agreement and unanimity

**LEFT.** but you're saying
it's something more
an ethos
but all in all
it's some kind of bullshit
we don't understand

**RIGHT.** but you're saying
no one understands
and let's keep it that way

**LEFT.** and that magda's been interred
and she's supposed to name names
of friends
she's supposed to betray them

**RIGHT.** no
to save herself
there's a war on
you're saying
a civil war
it broke out in december
it was hard
but today

---

7 Solidarity was the first independent trade union in the Eastern Bloc, founded in 1980 under the leadership of Lech Wałęsa. The union evolved into a mass social movement calling for political and social reforms. The communist government attempted to suppress Solidarity in 1981, imposing martial law and imprisoning Solidarity leaders. Years of severe political repressions followed, then in the late 1980s, the communists decided to negotiate with the then-illegal union. This led to the first free democratic election in 1989, the foundation of the Solidarity-supported government, and the fall of communism in Poland and across Eastern Europe.

75 percent know
things
were better back then

**LEFT.** that's what you're saying
magda doesn't say anything

**RIGHT.** while teresa screams

**LEFT.** and we dislocate her jawbone

**RIGHT.** you cunt

**LEFT.** magda can't talk
she writes
błaut

**RIGHT.** they're last names

**LEFT.** kopczyńska
kubacka
Majewski
ska
ska
ski
ska
ski

**RIGHT.** they'll be arrested
and sentenced

**LEFT.** but you're saying
they'll get medals later
and later still
they'll be stripped of those medals
because they were just pretending
while they were actually collaborating

**RIGHT.** you're saying
there's dirt on them
in the files
teresa kept

**LEFT.** did teresa keep
a file on us

what do we do
how do we check
we're asking you

**RIGHT.** you tell us
it's some kind of bullshit
because even the pope
has a file

**LEFT.** wow, a file next to the pope's
great

**RIGHT.** you tell us
we've crossed the line

**LEFT.** okay so we've crossed the line

**RIGHT.** you can't laugh at the pope

**LEFT.** okay okay
we're not laughing any more
we're not doing anything

**RIGHT.** teresa
isn't doing anything either
she's dead
but before she died
she thanked magda
for giving her those names

**LEFT.** and gave her a present
two dress shoes
to remind her

**RIGHT.** of what you've done
you rat
teresa leaves

**LEFT.** we stay

**RIGHT.** teresa will die

**LEFT.** magda's alive
though frankly
she'd be better off dead

**RIGHT.** she chucked us in the trash

**LEFT.** why don't you go
chuck yourself
bitch

**RIGHT.** bums reeking of piss
didn't touch us
for weeks

**LEFT.** then
some fucked-up set designer lady
took us for a play

**RIGHT.** to the theater, fuck
to the theater, us

**LEFT.** we walked the boards
in some shitty plays
no one fucking
understands

**RIGHT.** to the storeroom
and back on stage
lame

**LEFT.** if at least we'd
been on tv
had a cameo
in some soap
we'd be famous

**RIGHT.** but who goes to the theater

**LEFT.** do you go to the theater?
of course not
boooring

**RIGHT.** and in that storeroom
we were bought
for 10 zloty

**LEFT.** we the shoes of magda goebbels
black pumps

with heels
fashioned
of human skin
and human fat
at the factory in Auschwitz

**RIGHT.** by this fucking queer
krystian

**LEFT.** mind you
that's a good price
for the victims of auschwitz
10 zloty

**RIGHT.** maybe the president's chancellery
could look into that

**LEFT.** you've called them already
great
order must prevail
right, krystian

**RIGHT.** krystian's a dancer
he shakes his ass on stage

**LEFT.** and then
makes money
with that same ass

**RIGHT.** not that they pay
to bang him

**LEFT.** not like anyone
would pay him
because krystian
is gross

**RIGHT.** no
krystian's not
a whore
he just gets parts that way

**LEFT.** the fucking freak

**RIGHT.** but not anymore

IMAGE 5.3 **Left (Marzena Kopczyńska) and Right (Maja Kubacka)**
Directed by Sebastian Majewski. Scena Witkacego, Wrocław (2012)
*Photograph by Joanna Howańska*

tonight he partied too long
in a darkroom
he left at dawn
he could barely walk
the punk-ass bitch

**LEFT.** his shoes gave him away

**RIGHT.** in the square
they were waiting for him

real men
hunks in hardhats
young polish patriots

**LEFT.** oh fuck
we're in poland
poland exists
that's impossible

**RIGHT.** and krystian's just
got hit in the face
a right
and a left
he cries:
help!

**LEFT.** he really is fucked-up
you're supposed to
say: fire!

**RIGHT.** a punch in the gut
the back of the neck

**LEFT.** they don't want to wear themselves out
they slice him open
vertically

**RIGHT.** krystian's lying there fucked-up
on the square
john paul ii square

**LEFT.** you know where that is
come on
let's go

**RIGHT.** this is the end
good thing that
we're in the city

**LEFT.** because we don't like the woods
remember

**RIGHT.** do you remember
that we were serving out our punishment

ours is just
coming to an end

**LEFT.** but yours
is just beginning

**RIGHT.** what do you mean what for?
as if you didn't know

*The End*

IMAGE 6.1 **Male Chorus (Maciej Konopiński, Łukasz Konopka, and Robert Ninkiewicz)**
Directed by Kuba Kowalski. Teatr Wybrzeże, Gdańsk (2012)
*Photograph by Michał Andrysiak*

JULIA HOLEWIŃSKA

Translated by
Artur Zapałowski

# FOREIGN BODIES

## CHARACTERS[1]

ADAM

EWA

MARYJA

LECH

WIKI

JADWIGA

BOGUMIŁ

BOLESŁAW

ALINA

ZOFIA

RYSZARD

MAN IN SMOCK

LADY IN SMOCK

MAN IN UNIFORM

MAN IN CASSOCK

SCHOOLGIRL 1

SCHOOLGIRL 2

SCHOOLGIRL 3

SCHOOLBOY 1

SCHOOLBOY 2

JOANNA SZCZEPKOWSKA (PERHAPS ON TV)

MALE CHORUS

FEMALE CHORUS

Each actor may, and even should, play several characters

## NOTE

*Foreign Bodies* sets the history of the great political and social transformation that swept Poland after 1989 against the story of its protagonist's gender transformation. Its subject is the difficult struggle for individual freedom within a conservative Catholic community that, until recently, had been united in the struggle against communism. The sections marked with the letter A, in which the heroine appears as Adam, take place in the 1980s, while the sections marked E, in which the heroine appears as Ewa, take place roughly 20 years later.

Political transition is depicted in terms of a symbolic shift from the masculine order relying on power, struggle and hierarchy, to the feminine, which enriches the public realm with a new vocabulary and new issues: the body, privacy and empathy. This explains the presence of both a male and a female chorus in the play, and the duality of its protagonist, who appears as Adam and Ewa. Disclosing her true identity and undergoing sex-reassignment surgery is done at the cost of the protagonist's rejection by her loved ones, her public humiliation, and having her name expunged from the history books. All this leads her to ask fundamental questions about the values underpinning Polish society today.

This symbolic play was inspired by the true story of leading Solidarity activist Marek Hołuszko, who, under martial law in the 1980s, headed one of the banned union's underground cells in Warsaw. With the onset of independence he decided to change his sex, and, as Ewa Hołuszko, is now an activist and public speaker. Ewa Hołuszko and Anna Grodzka, a transgender person elected to Parliament in 2011, have greatly helped in raising awareness of transgender issues in Poland.

*Foreign Bodies* won the Gdynia Drama Award in 2011, the first prize in Poland's most important playwriting competition.

The play premiered in 2012 at Teatr Wybrzeże in Gdańsk, where it was directed by Kuba Kowalski. The set was built around a huge DNA helix in the national colors of white and red.

---

**1** In Polish, *w* is pronounced like the English *v*, *j* like *y*, *ł* like *w*; *ch* like *h*; and *sz* like *sh*.

Wiki is a diminutive form of the name Wiktoria; Adaś is a diminutive of Adam, Rysiek of Ryszard, Boguś of Bogumił and Bolek of Bolesław. Maryja as a variant of the name Mary is used in Poland almost solely for Virgin Mary, mother of Jesus.

1. A.

MALE CHORUS. Night so drear, what is the year? 1982, or 1981, or 1985, or 1984, or 1986, or 1988, or 1987, or 1983?[2] Dirty abode, a hundred roads, anyone yet found a fling à la mode? Maybe him? Table set, a stack of sheets. Rain outside, watch it pour; it's not rain, it's the snow. No stars out: neither the first star, nor the star of Bethlehem, nor the red star, the red star's in darkness sheer. Men, women and all the rest, are talking. In whispers. Shouting. Giggling, crying. Putting on lipstick, brushing away the tears. Drinking vodka. It's New Year's Eve, or maybe the New Year already.

JADWIGA (*queen of Poland*). To freedom!

MARYJA (*queen of Poland*). To Poland!

BOGUMIŁ (*the name says it all*).[3] To spring!

ADAM (*the first man*). Yours the winter, ours the spring!

BOLESŁAW (*CI*).[4] Come the spring, come the spring, Communists from trees will swing!

ALINA (*Balladyna's sister, operational pseudonym Słowacki*).[5] Quiet, someone might be eavesdropping!

---

2 The 1980s in Poland were particularly hard, with martial law imposed by the Communist government on 13 December 1981, along with the suppression of Solidarity and political persecutions. The action of the play takes place among underground Solidarity activists; the main character, Adam, is one of their leaders.

3 Bogumił means "favored by God."

4 CI is an acronym for Confidential Informant. The secret police tried to infiltrate opposition groups and control them using confidential informants.

5 A literary joke: Juliusz Słowacki, a 19th-century Romantic poet, wrote the drama *Balladyna*, in which Alina is one of the characters. It has no further consequences for this play.

**ZOFIA** (*fount of wisdom, a blonde, naturally*). Who? Who could be eavesdropping on us on New Year's Eve?

**RYSZARD** (*not tricky at all*). Them.

**ZOFIA**. Them who?

**RYSZARD**. The Communists, who else? Bolshie bastards.

**ZOFIA**. But don't they deserve a day off too?

**ADAM**. Give it a rest. Let's have some fun!

*Someone turns on the music.*

**MALE CHORUS**. Pairs are formed and flow across the floor. Wildly whirling on the woodwork. Waltzes, polkas and mazurkas. Finger-licking finesse.

**RYSZARD**. Confetti. Does anyone have confetti?

**ALINA**. No, but we have sparklers. I got them in a package from Denmark. Shall we light them up?

**BOLESŁAW**. Children, you're acting just like children.

**MARYJA**. What else is there to do but have fun?

*Everybody lights the sparklers. Dancing, drinking, etc.*

**JADWIGA**. Russian champagne. Anybody want some? No? Bottoms up, then.

**ZOFIA**. Did you know they locked up Gienek?

**ADAM**. Where is he? Białołęka[6] prison?

**ZOFIA**. Yes.

**BOLESŁAW**. That's not so bad. We've turned one of their screws.

**BOGUMIŁ**. We need to get a package together for him. His mother died a few days ago.

**MARYJA**. Maybe we should offer a Mass for her?

**ADAM**. It's always offering Masses with you. We need to act. A package is a package. Sausage, tea, a loaf of bread, playing cards or, better yet, dice.

---

6 Białołęka was a prison at the outskirts of Warsaw, where many Solidarity leaders and members of the democratic opposition were imprisoned during martial law.

**MARYJA.** We should slip a holy picture in the package. Maybe Saint Afra—patron saint of forlorn souls, or Saint Philomena—patron saint of the Living Rosary, or Saint Collette—patron saint of carpenters and household help, or Saint Anastasia—patron saint of weavers and censors, or even Saint Lucy—patron saint of tailors, the blind, the visually impaired, glassmakers, servants, chandlers and lamp-makers, carters, farmers, seamstresses, weavers, ushers, upholsterers, intercessor in eye diseases, patron saint of radio and television employees.

**ALINA.** Saint Lucy? Patron saint of radio and television employees? Are you sure her middle name's not Wojciech?[7]

**BOLESŁAW.** I agree with Maryjka. Let's put a holy picture in the package. As long as it's a saint with a big rack!

**MARYJA.** Go ahead and laugh. I assume it's the champagne. All things Russian mess up your head and poison the soul. We're going to Mass tomorrow.

**JADWIGA.** It's a Mass for the nation, so we'll be there. Even with an aching head. Maybe we could bring a banner?

**ADAM.** So we can hide from the ubek[8] under it? You must be mad, thinking about a banner.

**RYSZARD.** That's enough now! Let's party already.

**ZOFIA.** Why doesn't someone play a song?

**BOLESŁAW.** Play something, Adam. Here's the guitar. "Walls"?[9]

---

7 "Wojciech" refers to General Wojciech Jaruzelski, the Polish leader who imposed martial law, when radio and TV were placed under military control and served only as vehicles of propaganda for the government. Thus Saint Lucy, as a patron of radio and television employees, could be ironically considered a collaborator with the regime.

8 "Ubek" is a common name for secret policeman or secret police informant. It comes from UB, the acronym for Urząd Bezpieczeństwa (Security Office) operating in the Stalinist period, then replaced in 1956 by Służba Bezpieczeństwa (Security Service).

9 "Mury" ("Walls") was a famous protest song by Jacek Kaczmarski, called the Bard of Solidarity. "Mury" was inspired by the song "L'Estaca" by the Catalan singer Lluís Llach.

IMAGE 6.2 **Crowd scene**
Directed by Kuba Kowalski. Teatr Wybrzeże, Gdańsk (2012)
*Photograph by Michał Andrysiak*

**MALE CHORUS.** Adam plays. Circle formed, bells did toll. New Year's revels. Falls the gavel. A year's stretch? So what's the catch? 101? 102? Or was it Catch 22? Two years to go, with no parole. A knock on the door. Evil galore!

**BOGUMIŁ.** Behind bars for singing "Walls"?

## 1. E.

**FEMALE CHORUS.** It's the twenty-first century, within Warsaw city limits, or maybe without. A minute's drive, no more than five. A house is seen, its chimney leans, and windows in its walls. It might be

New Year's Eve or has the new day dawned? A New Year's day, which year's that, pray? The Year of the Dog, or of the Pig? The pigs are gone, we've real cops now. And the black crows have flown. A white dove perches on the eaves. Inside it's cold, a long table not set for two. It's her inside, and only her.

EWA (*the first woman*). I've prepared twelve dishes. As if it were Christmas, gosh darn it, maybe that's why no one came. And such nice invitations I e-mailed them. Gosh darn it, I tried so hard to make it look nice. To make it posh. Here we are, it's all taken from cookbooks, darn it. That's right. Here we are. Salad with Roquefort cheese, walnuts, and endive. Roquefort comes from Auvergne, a region of France favored by the British. It's a rich cheese with a strong, tangy flavor. It needs to be kept in the refrigerator, it's easier to crumble then. The walnuts and walnut oil need to be selected with care because products past the sell-by date will have an unpleasant, rancid flavor. I selected fresh products, gosh darn it. Second course, here we are. Foie gras. I baked it myself. Silky, smooth and delicious. It's slightly fattening, but who cares? Foie gras goes very well with pickles or marinated vegetables. And the warm entrée? Coq au vin. This dish is the pinnacle of all the best French cuisine has to offer: a convivial atmosphere at the table, the company of friends, high spirits, simple and hearty fare, peasant bread dipped in sauce, and red wine that goes straight to your head. It makes time stand still. This popular dish will appeal to nearly everyone. While it might not be simple to prepare, it is a must if we want our party to be a success. I wanted the party to be a success, darn it. And? It didn't work. Maybe it's because I didn't marinate the chicken long enough? It was a very good marinade, by the way. Take a liter of red wine. Dry, naturally. It can be pinot noir, but not necessarily. A good Bordeaux will do, or even a Rhenish in a pinch, though the French would disapprove. Add three medium-sized carrots, bias-cut into slices a centimeter thick, two stalks of celery sliced 1.5 centimeters thick, twenty whole spring onions, trimmed, one teaspoon crushed peppercorns, and the bouquet garni, namely a few sprigs of parsley, two laurel leaves and six sprigs of thyme all bunched together.

FEMALE CHORUS. End quote.

EWA. I think I gave five sprigs of thyme, gosh darn it. Yes, that's probably why the party wasn't a success. And I so wanted them to come. Jadwiga, Maryjka, Bogumił, Bolesław, Alina, Zofia, Ryszard. It would have been nice, just like the old days, like back when they threw us in jail on New Year's Eve. What year was that? Eighty-three, eighty-five, or maybe eighty-seven. The lady next door reported us for singing "Walls". And they came and found the samizdat.[10] Rysiek was in hiding at the time, so they hauled him right away. And us, too, for company. Forty-eight hours in custody.

FEMALE CHORUS. Behind bars for singing "Walls". Behind bars for singing "Walls". She's reminiscing, her friends she's missing. All alone, woe, woe, woe!

EWA. God, it's so empty here. I'm talking to myself. Nobody came. Not a soul. Nobody sent New Year's wishes, nobody even called. And now who's going to eat all this?

FEMALE CHORUS. She's prepared twelve dishes. Salad with Roquefort cheese, walnuts and endive. Foie gras. Coq au vin. Salmon pudding. Mediterranean cannelloni. Tartines with black and red caviar and something green on top. Melon slices wrapped in Parma ham, not from Parma though, but from Tesco. Made in China. Grilled aubergine slices stuffed with mozzarella, sun-dried tomatoes and basil. And four desserts. Panna cotta. Galette des rois. Apple pie, and Black Forest Cake made with Black Jungle cocoa. She spent her whole salary, every last penny. Twelve dishes she prepared, and nobody even cared. Eat up, eat up or else we'll eat you up!

10 Samizdat refers to clandestine printing of forbidden publications.

MALE CHORUS. It's all right, it's all good, it's all warm, it's all snug, it's all together, no fear, no tears, no clothes on.

ADAM. Who were you in the cell with?

MARYJA. With Jadzia, with Zośka, with Alina and some, you know—prostitutes.

ADAM. They locked you up with whores? What did they look like?

MARYJA. Why do you want to know?

ADAM. I'm curious. Tell me.

MARYJA. Well—like whores.

ADAM. Meaning?

IMAGE 6.3 **Maryja (Justyna Bartoszewicz), Adam (Marek Tynda), and Male Chorus (Maciej Konopiński, Łukasz Konopka, Piotr Biedroń, and Robert Ninkiewicz)**
Directed by Kuba Kowalski. Teatr Wybrzeże, Gdańsk (2012)
*Photograph by Michał Andrysiak*

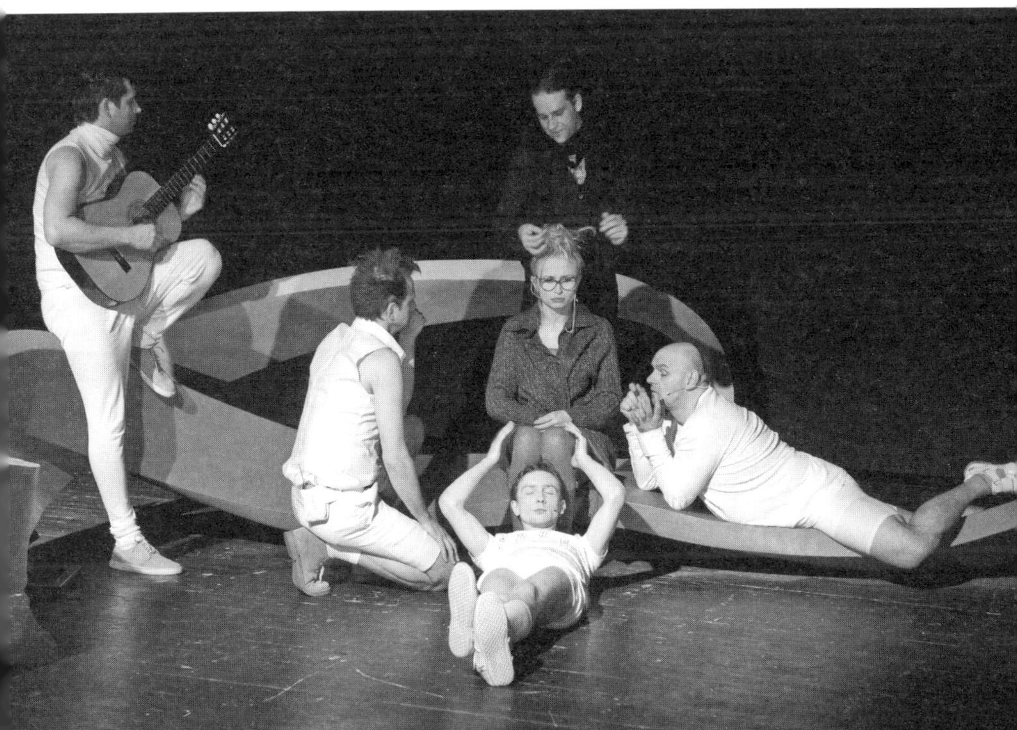

MARYJA. Normal, what do you think?

ADAM. Normal? Like you?

MARYJA. What do you mean, like me? How can you say that?

ADAM. I haven't said anything wrong. I'm just curious, you know, I've never gone whoring.

MARYJA. But why do you want to know what they looked like? That's disgusting.

ADAM. What's disgusting? Sluts? They're women. Like you and me.

MARYJA (*laughing*). What?

ADAM. It came out wrong. Jesus.

MALE CHORUS. "What exactly did you mean?" asked Freud, stepping on the scene.

MARYJA. Normal women. Only with slutty makeup. Pretty old. They must have been around forty, fifty maybe. We even talked a bit. One of them had two daughters, the other one had a husband.

ADAM. And did her husband know what she did?

MARYJA. I don't know, I don't think so. He was ill. She said was doing it to buy him medicine.

ADAM. Always a sob story. Tell me what kind of women they were. Specifically, you know?

MARYJA. That's what I was telling you.

ADAM. But I meant something else.

MARYJA. What?

ADAM. Well, you know—what kind of breasts they had. What they smelled like.

MARYJA. Adam, what's going on in that head of yours? I was arrested. They interrogated me, goddamnit . . .

ADAM. Don't curse, or, if you really have to, make it milder. Say gosh darn it, or something.

MALE CHORUS. Fuck, fukkity, cunt, cunny, shit, shite, turd, bird. An eagle with a crown, laying, laying eggs. No eggs for Easter because the ration cards ran out!

MARYJA. What's your problem, Adam? When did you last go to confession?

ADAM. A long time ago.

MARYJA. Why?

ADAM. Didn't have the time, I guess.

MARYJA. I'll help you then, we'll go together. There's nothing to be afraid of.

ADAM. I'll go if you tell me what they looked like.

MARYJA. What?

ADAM. I'll go to confession if you tell me about those prostitutes.

MARYJA. You're sick.

ADAM. Why? I'd like to know how they do their hair, how they walk, what makeup they have on, what skirts they wear, whether they have underarm hair, how they bat their lashes.

MARYJA. The country's dying and all you think about are whores. I don't understand you at all. Do you want to humiliate me? Is that what this is about? We don't have to be together. You don't owe me anything . . . (*Maryja starts crying*.)

ADAM. It's not like that, baby. Come on, I'm just curious, I never . . . You know I love you. I don't mean anything bad. You're the most important thing in my life.

MARYJA. And your country, too, I hope. And God.

ADAM. And Maryja. The Virgin Mary.

MARYJA. You're making fun of me again.

ADAM. No, I'm not making fun. I was worried about you. I asked about those whores, because I needed to get my mind off things. You know, it's all so hard, so dead serious. Rysiek might end up in jail for a long time. He runs an underground publishing house, after all. It's no joke, he might be looking at a few years.

MARYJA. Did they ask you about him?

ADAM. No, actually they didn't. They asked about the others. I didn't tell them anything, of course.

**MARYJA.** Maybe they'll announce an amnesty? Maybe they'll let Rysiek out?

**ADAM.** An amnesty? Nothing's ever going to change here. Things will only get worse.

**MARYJA.** So what's the point of it all? Well? What's it all for, since you don't believe things can get better?

**ADAM.** Because it has to be done. It has to be done, and that's that. This is how it has to be. Am I supposed to sit there scratching my ass? There has to be more of us, Maryjka! Don't you see? There have to be more of us, more, more, more! Not like it is now—everybody thinking about himself. Save up a few zloty in your stocking, buy a pork knuckle, a couple of beers, and muddle through somehow. Society is asleep. There's still too few of us. The future is in our hands, darling. We have to act. We Poles know no other way. There has to be an uprising. Blood must be shed, but first there has to be more of us, a lot more. The future is in our hands!

*Adam and Maryja start kissing.*

**MALE CHORUS.** The future is in their hands and legs. Between their legs, between their thighs. And the Poles, the Poles will rise. On the quilt, to the hilt, and a maiden's blood was spilt. Lo, the maiden she did weep, for the pain was awful deep! A-one, a-two, a-one, a-two. Poles we'll be, forever true!

**MARYJA.** But we're not married.

**ADAM.** We'll get married, Maryjka, but now our country needs us—our hands, our legs, our thighs, our parts, our children. I'll be gentle. You like it when I kiss your neck, don't you? I'll kiss it. And gently stroke your thighs. Your inner thighs. Like this. All right? Sure. I'll kiss your feet. Every toe. Your breasts. With a circular motion, gently.

**MARYJA.** What about me? What am I supposed to do?

**ADAM.** Do the same. The same thing I'm doing.

**MARYJA.** The same thing?

**ADAM.** Yes, I like it that way too. Gently.

MARYJA. But you will marry me?

ADAM. I will, of course I will. I'll choose the veil myself.

MALE CHORUS. They held themselves tight and turned out the light. A kiss and a bite. In each other's sight. They did it all night. For their country in plight. They did it all night!

## 2. E.

FEMALE CHORUS. Her hair she did, her face she washed. Her gloss she applied, her bottom she washed. Her blush she dabbed on, her pits she washed. And clean she was. Like a maiden with child, though childless she was. But a son did she have.

EWA. Great, great! Everything looks great. She even did a good job trimming my hair this time. I don't go to male hairdressers. It has to be a woman. It's different with women. You can talk. About the kids. About work. About nail polish. About nail-polish removers. About exfoliation. About masks. About lotions. About creams. You don't get that with a guy. In fact, my hairdresser recommended this cream to me the other day. It's very good. Reasonably priced. Twenty-nine ninety-nine. Good thing it doesn't cost thirty. That makes a difference, you know. I took a course in marketing and the psychology of advertising. It's always better to have the price end in ninety-nine than to make it a round number. But, but . . . this cream. Very good. Reasonably priced. Sometimes it's on sale. And then it costs twenty-seven ninety-nine. That makes a difference, you know. And then I buy two jars. Because I use it up quickly, see? I go through a jar in three weeks. Sometimes I find a special offer online. Twenty-five ninety-nine a pop. Then I buy three jars. Nearly wholesale. That makes a difference, you know. And then I have a nine-week supply. And I don't have to go to the shops. Or hunt for bargains. Because I've stocked up. I like having a little extra of everything. Just in case. Because you never know. I could fall ill or break a leg. Or they could give me additional classes at the school, and I won't have time for shopping. And bargain-hunting. So I prefer to stock up on everything. There were shortages of everything under martial law, and maybe that's why I like having a little extra of everything now. I keep buying pasta. For spaghetti. I really like the long, hard Italian kind. Al dente. I must have ten packages at home right now. It was on sale, so I bought twenty packages. I'm just afraid I won't be able to eat it all before it expires, but then I think, pasta can keep. I mean, what can happen to it? It won't go rotten. Worst that can happen is I'll eat it past the expiration date. Big deal. And the cream my hairdresser recommended—the good, reasonably priced one—works wonders on my complexion. Here we are, gosh darn it, let me just get my glasses on, hold on, I see it now: "Extract of myrtle and Indian horse chestnut improves all-around dermal circulation. Strongly vasoprotective due to aescin content. Ginger extract will stimulate your cells and light up your complexion. Helps you stay young, beautiful and stunning. Always." I'll be young, beautiful and stunning. Always. For twenty-nine ninety-nine. That's affordable. I'll just put on some lipstick, because they'll be here any moment now. There. I'm ready. Young, beautiful and stunning. Always. I believe in myself. I can do this. I'll make it. Everything will be all right. I'm sure of myself. I'll win them over with my naturalness. I have the get-up-and-go. I can do this. I can do this.

**FEMALE CHORUS.** Her lips she quickly painted, her family she awaited. And she was scared as hell. AAAAAAAAAAAA! Oh, she was scared as hell. Like in a prison cell. Had she messed up as well? She can do this, she fought the Reds because she had the muscle for it, so she can do this too.

*The doorbell rings.*

**EWA.** I'm coming, I'm coming, just a minute! Gosh darn it, I have a run in my tights now, of all times. I can do this. I can do this.

**LECH** (*Ewa's son*). Hi. This is Wiki.

**EWA.** Come in, come in. Keep the cold out. Welcome.

**FEMALE CHORUS.** She holds out her hand in greeting, but no hand her hand is meeting. Hands did not touch. Fingers did not together come. Not the pinkie, not the thumb.

**EWA.** Take your coats off. Come in.

**LECH.** You still haven't plastered the house. How can you live like this?

**EWA.** Where would I make enough money to finish the house, son? At the school?

**LECH.** Then why did you build it in the first place? And please don't call me son.

**EWA.** What do you mean, why? It'll be yours when I'm gone.

**LECH.** No need for that, thanks. I'll manage on my own.

**EWA.** But why are you so upset?

**LECH.** I'm not upset. I'm perfectly calm. You're the one who's shaking.

**EWA.** Yes, I am shaking a bit. It's cold, even though I have the fireplace going. They were chopping down trees nearby, so I hauled some wood into the shed. It was exhausting, but it should see me through the winter. But let's not stand here by the door. Come, join me at the table, please. I cooked some soup. I'll just warm it up, and get the noodles in the plates. Take a seat. Back in a sec.

*Ewa goes off to the kitchen.*

**LECH.** I don't know, I can't get used to it. I'm sorry I brought you here, Wiki.

**WIKI.** Don't be sorry. It's not your fault.

**LECH.** I don't even know what to call her. Mom, Mommy? This is ridiculous.

**WIKI.** Why don't you call her by her name?

**LECH.** The one she has now, or the old one?

**WIKI.** I don't know, I don't know what to say.

**LECH.** It's disgusting.

**WIKI.** So why the hell did we come here?

**LECH.** He—she kept calling. See, I still can't get used to it. Maybe I'm scared of her.

**WIKI.** She won't hurt you.

**LECH.** She already has. Fucking hell!

**EWA** (*from the kitchen*). Why are you cursing? Don't curse, you don't have to say fuck, you can say gosh darn it, or something like that.

**LECH.** I'm a man.

**EWA.** So I see, but what does that have to do with anything?

**LECH.** A man has to curse once in a while.

**EWA.** I don't know, I never really liked it. Wiktoria . . .

**WIKI.** Wiki, my name is Wiki, not Wiktoria.

**EWA.** I'm sorry, I thought your name was Wiktoria. As a sign of victory. It's a common name in your generation, isn't it?

**LECH.** I was supposed to be named Wiktoria. But I was born a boy. So they named me after Lech Wałęsa. My parents were in the opposition movement.

**EWA.** Yes, Lech's mother and I spent time in jail. For distributing leaflets. I wrote a bit.

**WIKI.** Are you a writer?

**EWA.** No, no. I was more of a journalist, if you can put it that way.

**WIKI.** Really? What papers did you write for?

**EWA.** You've probably never heard of them. They don't come out any more. Besides, I used a pseudonym. Would you like a pinch of parsley?

**WIKI.** No thank you, I'm not hungry actually.

**EWA.** But I made a whole pot of soup. It's good. Beef and chicken stock. And lots of vegetables.

**LECH.** Wiki doesn't eat meat.

**EWA.** Ah. I didn't know that. I'll make something else for you, then. How about an omelette? I have organic eggs. Straight from the farm. It said on the box that they were for the elite. "Eggs for the elite." Isn't that funny?

WIKI. Please don't mind me. I'm really not hungry.

EWA. That's a shame. Would you like a pinch of parsley?

LECH. It's all the same to me. Whatever.

EWA. Then I'll serve it with parsley. It's got lots of iron.

*Ewa goes off into the kitchen again.*

LECH. You said you were hungry. What's going on?

WIKI. I don't feel hungry anymore.

LECH. Does it sicken you?

WIKI. No, no. Not at all.

LECH. I can see it does. You always rub your hands in that nervous way whenever something grosses you out.

WIKI. Leszek, it's not that. You know how I am.

LECH. No need to explain. It sickens me a little too, actually. It's best if you don't eat. Especially in your condition.

WIKI. I'm sorry.

LECH. Come on. It's not every day someone like that invites you for dinner.

WIKI. Leszek, that's no way to be talking about your—parent.

LECH. Exactly, who is this person to me? Just look at the way she lives. How can anyone live like this? It's cold and dingy here. She gets water from a barrel. Pees in a bucket. Disgusting.

EWA. I put in a lot of parsley. So, Wiki, what do you do?

WIKI. I'm about to graduate.

EWA. Great. What are you studying? Is it at the university?

WIKI. No, a private college.

EWA. Oh, right. Some of the private schools are quite good. I'm getting my third Master's at a private school now. There aren't a lot of people my age at state schools. But there are quite a lot of girls like me majoring in psychology at the private college.

LECH. Girls? Like you?

EWA. Well, you know, girls my age.

WIKI. You're getting your third Master's degree? In what?

EWA. I like learning things. There's all this talk about the psychology of advertising nowadays. Who knows, I might become a coach or an image consultant. Recently they taught us how to dress for success and how to carry yourself properly. We even did this exercise where we pretended we were training a politician. The way a politician looks is just as important as his programme. A suit, preferably satin. And a tie. Smooth. Stripes can bring on bad associations. A cheerful expression. The head slightly raised, but not too much. Politicians can't afford to look proud or nonchalant.

LECH. But you teach kids, not politicians. Besides, what you're saying is some kind of newspeak. Like something out of an American textbook.

EWA. You never know what you'll end up doing. And it just so happens that Americans have the best image consultants. We could use somebody like that in the Polish right wing. Why do the Reds keep winning? Because they have good consultants. And I know people. I could be useful. I could help.

LECH. You think that anyone in that right wing of yours still remembers you?

WIKI. You teach kids?

EWA. Yes, troubled teens. It's not easy. The girls are especially difficult nowadays. I teach history and Polish at a middle school.

WIKI. And you like it?

EWA. Not really. It's hard work. Stressful. And it pays badly. Eat up, Lech, eat up.

LECH. Actually, we just dropped in for a while. We have to be going soon.

EWA. Already? But you just got here.

LECH. Wiki has a doctor's appointment.

EWA. What's wrong? Are you ill?

WIKI. No, I'm not ill.

EWA. Well then, what's wrong with you?

LECH. Wiki's pregnant.

EWA. Now you tell me? My dears, you can't imagine how happy I am! So, when do I get to be a grandmother? When? Not very soon, I bet. Because it doesn't show yet. You're so skinny. I'm so happy. Do you have a good doctor? What about a midwife? We'll have to pay for one. And you'll need a single room in the hospital. And Lamaze classes! The main thing is to have a good midwife, so they don't cut your perineum, because that hurts, and you won't be able to walk for a long time. And you can get incontinent.

LECH. Stop it.

EWA. What? Giving birth is important. Remember to tell them about not cutting your perineum. That's very important. You have the right to make decisions about your body. Giving birth doesn't have to be a nightmare, does it?

LECH. I see you've got a lot to say on the subject. Some expert, goddamnit.

EWA. Say gosh darn it if you really have to curse. The child can hear you.

LECH. Stop it, I said.

EWA. But I'm worried. I just want to help.

LECH. You haven't seen me for years. You've only just met my girlfriend, and what do you do? Go on about cutting perineums. That's fucking disgusting. Disgusting and tasteless!

EWA. The perineum is disgusting? But it's only human.

LECH. This is all sick. Disgusting. Wiki, get your coat. I'm not staying here any longer.

WIKI. Calm down, darling.

LECH. Why should I be calm? Let's go, this whole thing sickens you too. The thought of eating from a spoon in this house sickens you. You're too grossed out to shake her hand. Besides, she sickens me as well. Come on, I said. We're going.

EWA. Leszek, son . . .

LECH. Don't call me that. I have no mother, and I have no father. Remember this: my mother's dead, and so is my father. And you . . . I don't even know who you are. Or what. Because you're . . . living like an animal here, you know? It's not even about the way you look, but about the way you live. The walls haven't been painted, you don't have running water. What do you when you need to go in this great big house? Use a bucket? A great big house, and you don't even have a bathroom. You can shove this house of yours up your ass. This is all nauseating. It's disgusting. I think I'm going to be sick.

EWA. But Leszek, why are you doing this? What have I done wrong?

LECH. Stay if you want, Wiki, I'm leaving. I can't stand her any longer. The sight of her. The stink of her. You stink like a dude, you know that? You're sweating. A woman doesn't smell like that. That's what guys smell like. A dude with balls has a stench like that. A laborer after an eight-hour shift down at the mill reeks like that, not a woman.

EWA. It's nerves.

LECH. Nerves? Some things you can't change. You'll always stink. You already stank like that when I was a kid. I couldn't fall asleep for the stink whenever you tucked me in. I prayed you'd finish the Kitten Lullaby and get out of my room. But the stink would linger. It would stink of you in my room all night. Why don't you take a bath before you start talking about cutting twats, because it makes me want to puke.

WIKI. Goodbye.

*Exit Wiki and Lech. Ewa clears the table.*

EWA. But I used Rexona. Sprayed it on twice. And Rexona's good, and reasonably priced.

*Ewa starts crying. She lies down on the couch and starts crying harder.*

**FEMALE CHORUS.** Ah-ah-ah, kittens two. Fur so gray, and eyes so blue. There's one thing they want to do, and that is to tickle you. Ah-ah-ah, kittens two. Ah-ah-ah, kittens two. Ah-ah-ah, kittens two. There's one thing they want to do, and that is to torture you. First they'll claw you front and back, then they'll stuff you in a sack. Drag you in that sack will they, to the riverbank, hey-hey! Your skull they'll crack, and break your neck. And they'll drown you like a cat, will those kittens, just like that. Ah-ah-ah, kittens two. Fur so gray and eyes so blue. Sleep, kitten sleep. You'll be soothed by sleep so deep.

## 3. A.

**MALE CHORUS.** He was left alone. Home alone. He can show his face. Mirror, mirror on the wall, who's the fairest of them all?

*Adam makes a phone call.*

**ADAM.** I'm alone. Yeah, come over. There's a couple of things we need to discuss. I'm waiting, see you. (*Reads.*) Week 1: The sperm fertilizes the ovum in the fallopian tube. Once the sperm has penetrated the ovum, a zygote is formed. As it moves up the fallopian tube, the zygote starts dividing. After roughly three days the zygote will have divided into about sixteen cells, forming the so-called morula, God, what kind of a word is that? After about four days the morula reaches the uterus and forms a blastocyst.

*Adam reads on. This takes some time.*

**MALE CHORUS.** Morula, blastocyst, morula, blastocyst, morula, blastocyst. Ah-ah-ah, kittens two. Morula and blastocyst.

**ADAM.** Week 7: The neural tube has closed, and the brain is beginning to develop. The distinction into the prosencephalon, mesencephalon and rhombencephalon is becoming evident. Arms and legs begin forming and subdividing into arms, forearms, hands, thighs, calves and feet.

*Adam reads on.*

MALE CHORUS. Prosencephalon, mesencephalon and rhombencephalon. Arm, forearm, hand, thigh, calf and foot. Blackfoot. A waiter's hand.

ADAM. Week 19: In this week the genitals are almost fully developed. If the fetus is female, the vagina, uterus and fallopian tubes are already in the right place. If the fetus is male, the testicles are already developed and starting to produce testosterone. Be careful in Week 19, God, because this is no laughing matter. Everything should be just right.

MALE CHORUS. Testosterone, progesterone, a pinch of salt and cinnamon. Estrogen, prolactin, a dash of flour and a gherkin. Testicles, vagina, uterus, glans, a lollypop on a stick. You've got a cunny, and he's got a prick. Blend it all, and knead, and bake, for to get a tasty cake. And if you're not careful, it might turn out all doughy. Is it a boy or a girl? One, two, three, what will it be?

*Adam starts crying. He goes up to the mirror, takes a tube of lipstick out of a drawer and starts applying it.*

ADAM. Nice color. I think it suits me. I wonder if Maryjka will like it? It's a present for her birthday. I'm just, sort of . . . It's the last time. This damn stubble spoils everything. And the muscles . . . although they might come in useful soon. For holding the baby. For rocking it. God, we're going to have a baby. (*Adam goes up to the sofa-bed and takes a cushion, which he slips under his vest. He looks at himself in the mirror again. He pats his belly.*) Now, now, little one, don't you start kicking. Everything will be all right.

*A knock on the door.*

MALE CHORUS. Three short knock-knocks on the door. That's the code that lets you know it's a friend and not a foe.

ADAM (*quickly takes the cushion from under his shirt and wipes the lipstick off his mouth, though some of it stays on his beard*). I'm coming, just a minute.

**RYSIEK.** Hi.

**ADAM.** Come in, come in. You weren't being followed, were you?

**RYSIEK.** I don't think so. I don't know. Why? You scared?

**ADAM.** No way. It's just that, you know, Maryjka's pregnant. I don't want her worrying.

**RYSIEK.** Since when are you so sensitive? She'll worry anyway. But this is the stuff decent people need to be doing these days. Do you have everything?

**ADAM.** Yeah, sure. Give me a minute. It's in the other room.

*Rysiek looks around the room. He notices an open book.*

**RYSIEK.** Fuck this, don't you have anything better to read? "Pregnancy and Prenatal Development." This has to be Maryjka's, right? I didn't know she was that serious about the whole thing. Unless you're the one reading it?

**ADAM.** Get out of here. Of course it's Maryjka's. Some nun from the rosary circle gave it to her.

**RYSIEK.** The girl's overdoing it with the religion. What's worse, mine's getting there too. Goes to church every other day. Like they're patriotic Masses, and all, but I'm scared she'll be wanting a church wedding next, after all these years.

**ADAM.** Tell me about it. Hold on, it's in this box. Open it and check. I'll put the kettle on.

*Rysiek opens the box. He takes out a wig, a silk scarf and a pair of sunglasses. Adam comes in with tea. He spills it, scalding his hands.*

**ADAM.** Fuck, gosh darn it, I mean.

**RYSIEK.** What's this? You wear a wig when you distribute leaflets? You must really be shit-scared, huh?

**ADAM.** It's . . . my mother's. She's got cancer. She wears it after the chemo. And you're one for joking. You must have knocked back a few last night. That's why you're being funny. Right?

**RYSIEK.** You had me thinking you'd become a regular lady of the night.

**ADAM.** Stop talking shit.

RYSIEK. You've become awfully serious. Do you have the leaflets or don't you?

ADAM. I thought they were in this box. They have to be in the other one, then. I'll bring them right over.

RYSIEK. You know, I think someone's snitching on us.

ADAM. What are you saying? Have they caught one of our people?

RYSIEK. It's a funny thing, them locking up Gienek. Nobody knew he was delivering books. Just you, me, Bolek and Boguś.

ADAM. You don't suspect me, do you?

RYSIEK. And you don't suspect me, right?

ADAM. No, no. Come on.

RYSIEK. That leaves Bolek and Boguś.

ADAM. Bolek? A patriot like him?

RYSIEK. Boguś is a patriot too, and practically a padre to boot. He's so pious there's practically a halo over his head.

ADAM. This is a hundred and thirty leaflets. It's all we were able to print.

RYSIEK. Better than nothing. What's this? Adaś?

ADAM. What?

RYSIEK. Have you been kissing someone? Admit it, you dog, you're cheating on your pregnant wife!

ADAM. Me? You're out of your fucking mind!

RYSIEK. You're a sly one, you are.

ADAM. What the fuck are you talking about? Gosh darn it, that is.

RYSIEK. What's with the "gosh darn it"?

ADAM. I just don't like cursing, that's all. We have to get going.

RYSIEK. Fine, just wipe that lipstick off, because if Maryjka sees it on you, she'll hate you so bad, you won't ever get to see your kid.

ADAM. Wait here. (*Exit.*)

RYSIEK. I wouldn't be surprised if it was Bolek, but Adaś?

ADAM. Did you say something?

**RYSIEK.** No, no.

**ADAM.** That's good. Let's go.

*Exit.*

**MALE CHORUS.** And the boys went out on the town. Bang, bang, boom. Our boys up, and your boys down. Your boys up, our boys down. Can't stay seated, time to beat it! Or the cause will be defeated. Bang, bang, boom. Your boys up, our boys down. And when they were only halfway up, they were neither up nor down. Bang, bang, boom. Bang, bang, boom. Bang, bang!

## 3. E.

**FEMALE CHORUS.** In surgery. Rumpled and crumpled. Tattered and battered. Aching, quaking, ohmigod. Oh, my God, you sod, your God!

**EWA.** It hurts. It hurts bad. It hurts, darn it.

**MAN IN SMOCK.** But where does it hurt?

**EWA.** Here, right here.

*The doctor examines Ewa's abdomen.*

**MAN IN SMOCK.** How did you get these scars?

**EWA.** I had this procedure. A long time ago. But it doesn't hurt. It hurts me down there.

**MAN IN SMOCK.** A procedure? You wanted to improve on Mother Nature?

**EWA.** Well, you could say that.

**MAN IN SMOCK.** A pair of puppies wasn't good enough for your husband, he wanted a full rack, did he?

**EWA.** But what does that have to do with anything?

**MAN IN SMOCK.** Maybe it doesn't, but it's always nice to have a look. It's one of the perks, isn't it? The pay's bad, the hours are long, least you can do is feast your eyes a bit.

**EWA.** Shouldn't you be paying attention to my belly instead of my breasts?

**MAN IN SMOCK.** Relax, relax.

**EWA.** I believe you're forgetting yourself, mister.

**MAN IN SMOCK.** Aren't you the touchy one, though? I pity your husband, I really do. No sense of humor, this one.

**EWA.** I have a sense of humor when it's appropriate.

**MAN IN SMOCK.** How long has it hurt?

**EWA.** What?

**MAN IN SMOCK.** Your abdomen, what else? Does anything else hurt?

**EWA.** My heart sometimes, but that's not something a doctor can fix.

**MAN IN SMOCK.** Why's that? Hubby didn't like the new titties? Found himself another woman?

**EWA.** I don't have a husband. Or titties, either.

**MAN IN SMOCK.** So, about this abdomen of yours?

**EWA.** I've been having pains for a few months.

**MAN IN SMOCK.** And you waited this long to see me?

**EWA.** So I have.

**MAN IN SMOCK.** Any other symptoms?

**EWA.** What exactly do you mean?

**MAN IN SMOCK.** Anything worrying?

**EWA.** Such as?

**MAN IN SMOCK.** What kind of stools do you pass?

**EWA.** I don't know. I don't look at my stools.

**MAN IN SMOCK.** Shame.

**EWA.** I don't think any normal people do.

**MAN IN SMOCK.** Maybe normal people don't, but scientists have come up with a special scale. There are several kinds of stool. First you have the so-called nuts. Stool in the shape of separate hard lumps, which are hard to pass. The second type is sausage-shaped but lumpy. Then there's the sausage with cracks . . .

**EWA.** Stop, that's disgusting.

MAN IN SMOCK. Disgusting? It's only human, my dear lady.

FEMALE CHORUS. Even Garbo needs to poo when the turtle-head breaks through.

EWA. You shouldn't be allowed to practice medicine.

MAN IN SMOCK. You don't like it, you can fork out for a private clinic.

FEMALE CHORUS. Fork out! Fork out!

EWA. So what's wrong with me?

MAN IN SMOCK. What am I—a fortune-teller? We'll do the tests, we'll find out. Any rectal bleeding?

EWA. Sometimes.

MAN IN SMOCK. Get undressed, please.

EWA. But the bleeding could just be hemorrhoids. Maybe there's no need to examine them.

MAN IN SMOCK. Could be hemorrhoids, could be cancer.

EWA. Cancer?

MAN IN SMOCK. Well, it sure ain't Capricorn.

EWA. But how can you be sure it's cancer?

MAN IN SMOCK. Did I say I was sure? Please get undressed, and we'll check.

EWA. But is this really necessary?

MAN IN SMOCK. How else am I supposed to examine you? Through your throat or your ear, maybe?

FEMALE CHORUS. Deep throat. Stuffed ear. Ubek's ear. A yooman ear. The throat's deep, you creep. Red, with no strep.

EWA. Couldn't I just have blood test, or a urine test instead?

MAN IN SMOCK. Stop whining, will you? You think I haven't seen a twat before, save in your presence?

EWA. But do you have to be so coarse?

MAN IN SMOCK. The screen is over there. I'll try not to make it hurt. This examination can be quite pleasant, actually. Try thinking about something pleasant.

*They go behind the screen. The man in the smock examines Ewa.*

**FEMALE CHORUS.** Try thinking about something pleasant. Vanilla ice cream with whipped cream and a cherry on top, with melted chocolate, or ersatz chocolate—because that was the only thing in the shops back in the days when you felt pleasure for the only time in your life. All of it sprinkled with coconut shavings, though it's not really coconut but carob chips, trisodium citrate and calcium lactate, xanthan gum, guar gum and Stimorol chewing gum with added coconut aroma, and many variants of the letter E. E 211, E260, E212, E150. E for Ewa. Ewa 211, Ewa 260, Ewa 212, Ewa 150. Enjoy, Ewa, enjoy! Think about something pleasant.

**MAN IN SMOCK.** I thought we were being honest with each other. But it looks like you haven't told me the whole truth, miste—madam.

**EWA.** I thought it wasn't relevant.

**MAN IN SMOCK.** I'm the one doing the thinking here.

**EWA.** So what about those pains?

**MAN IN SMOCK.** You'll probably need an operation. They'll remove a section of your intestine.

**EWA.** Remove? A section of intestine?

**MAN IN SMOCK.** It's nothing to be worried about. It won't be the first thing you've had removed, will it?

*The man in the smock leers, revealing two gold teeth worth 5,890 Polish zloty, which, if converted, equals 1,472 European—not Polish—euro.*[11]

**EWA.** I'll make sure your superiors know about this. You're not a doctor, you're a . . . piece of shit. A number five on your scale. You're no doctor, you're scum! Ubek piece of shit. These are ubek methods! I'll file a complaint. I'll have the press on your ass. You'll see!

**MAN IN SMOCK.** I saw a thing or two just now. A freak show the likes of which I haven't seen in all the forty years I've been poking around in pussy.

---

**11** Equivalent to about US$1,830.

*Ewa runs crying out of the room. The man in the smock goes up to the washbasin, and meticulously scrubs his hands for a very long time, with a sneer of disgust under his slightly graying moustache.*

FEMALE CHORUS. Now, Dasher! Now, Dancer! Now, Prancer! Now cancer!

## 4. A.

MALE CHORUS. Home theater.[12] Raise the curtain. The actors step forward and take a bow. Reciting and rhyming, strutting and spoofing. To cheer the heart. To cheer the right ventricle.

ADAM. We'll be starting shortly. We still need to wait a bit. Bolek said he'd be coming. Let's wait.

JADWIGA. Maryjka, just look at the belly on you. Must be a great Pole waiting to be born.

MARYJA. You know, I'm getting a little tired of being pregnant.

ZOFIA. Have you chosen a name yet?

ADAM. Wiktoria or Lech.

RYSIEK. That's nice. Patriotic.

ZOFIA. And how's Adam doing? Is he excited about the baby?

MARYJA. Yes, I guess so. Sure he is. It's strange, come to think of it: he's more into it than I am. He keeps reading about pregnancy. About babies.

RYSIEK. I had no idea he was such a girly.

ZOFIA. Shut up, it's good that he's taking an interest. It's more than you ever did. You didn't know anything about babies or pregnancy.

RYSIEK. All right, okay. I'm going to the living room. I'll save a seat for you because the place is packed today.

---

12 Home Theater was a form of underground social resistance in the martial law period. Actors performed in private apartments for specially invited, trusted guests, and often recited patriotic poetry.

**ZOFIA.** Maryjka, what about, you know? Do the two of you still do it?

**MARYJA.** Is it sex you're asking about? That's a bit strange, too. Well, we don't any more, but, at first, I was all for it. You know, I was up for it all the time, but Adam didn't want to. He said something might happen to the baby.

**ZOFIA.** Maybe he's worried about you?

**MARYJA.** Maybe, I wouldn't know. Sometimes I think he's acting more like a pregnant woman than I am. He gets these moods.

**ZOFIA.** It's the nerves. Having a baby when you're in the opposition movement. He's got a lot on his plate.

**MARYJA.** You know what he's come up with lately? He's been telling me he dreams about being there when I give birth. I told him that won't be possible, and he says why don't I give birth at home. So I ask him, what does he want that for? And he says he's curious. That he wants to be with the baby from the start. And that he'll make sure they don't cut my perineum.

**ZOFIA.** What?

**MARYJA.** Just don't tell anyone, otherwise the boys will never let him hear the end of it.

**ZOFIA.** How does he know about that sort of thing, anyway?

**MARYJA.** I wonder too sometimes. I told you, he's always reading something. He's even borrowed a medical textbook from the library. And he keeps analyzing the pregnancy. Sometimes I get fed up. Some of the things seem gross to me, but he doesn't mind, he enjoys reading, looking and analyzing everything.

**ZOFIA.** You should be happy, actually.

**MARYJA.** I should, actually, but it's all kind of strange.

**BOGUMIŁ.** We're ready. Alina will go first. She'll be singing. And then I'll recite something out of Mickiewicz.[13]

---

13 Adam Mickiewicz was the principal poet of Polish Romanticism in the nineteenth century, and one of Poland's great poets. His poetry and his concept of Poland as "the Christ of Nations," as developed in his masterpiece

**MARYJA.** Fine, fine. Adam . . .

**ALINA.** We should get started. We need to wrap up by ten, so everyone can get home before the curfew. Boguś, why don't you start? I'll sing after you. It'll be better that way.

**BOGUMIŁ.** All right. Adaś, will you greet the guests?

**MARYJA.** Somebody's knocking. I'll get the door, and you start.

**MALE CHORUS.** Knock-knock. Who's there? It's to see Maryjka. For her birthday. May I? Ooh, look at all the people! Should I take my shoes off? Come in, come in. Take a seat on the floor. We'll be starting in a moment. What a nice flat you have. So many books. Who sent you? Bolek. Take a seat. Make yourself at home.

**ADAM.** Dear guests, dear friends. It's so nice to have you in our humble abode. In a moment, our dear patriotic friends will be performing for us. We will be passing the hat after the performance. Remember that the actors are boycotting the official media,[14] and deserve all the support we can give them in these hard times. And let me also remind you that it's Maryjka's birthday today.

**MALE CHORUS** (*Waxing lyrical*). Soft and subtle comes the sound. Tippy-toes and mum's the word. Barely heard, the enemy's song. A drone to drown your own songs out. For to shackle you in chains. Songs of Stalin and the Motherland, for our own land is no more.

**BOGUMIŁ.** My song is great, my singing is Creation!
For such a song is strength: is more than song.
True immortality is such a song!
I feel immortal, deathlessly create.

*The Chorus sings/recites the poem softly, but it can still be heard over Bogumił's rendition of the Great Improvisation from Mickiewicz's "Forefathers' Eve."*

---

*Forefathers' Eve*, served as inspiration for Polish national uprisings and the nation's striving for freedom.

**14** The actors' boycott of state-run radio and television was the longest and most spectacular protest against martial law.

**MALE CHORUS.** From my country and from the heart
would I speak to you, my friends,
and chat the whole night through,
until the dawn breaks in the sky.

You know, rugged Vanya from the kolkhoz would say,
and so would Ivan from the Dynamo, you know, brother,
how can a man not be Soviet,
when Joseph Vissarionovich himself
is our heart
and our blood.

**BOGUMIŁ.** If Thou gavest me equal sway over each soul,
I would create my nation like a living song,
And do a greater wonder than Thine Own;
For what a happy song I would intone!
Give me the rule of souls!

**MALE CHORUS.** The harvester bridles, the harvester of steel
grits its teeth, dull and tenacious -
you find yourself chewing the kernel of doubt,
when suddenly, brother,
you sense Stalin smiling.
And that is truly when, oh talkers,
we can with our will tame
the flow of Siberia's gray rivers.

And how can a man not be Soviet, brother,
when Joseph Vissarionovich himself
is our heart
and our blood.[15]

*A knock on the door. It is soft at first, then swells to a pounding.*

---

15 The quotes from Mickiewicz's *Forefathers' Eve* recited by Bogumił are intermingled with the poem "Stalin's Smile" (1952) by Tadeusz Ugacz, recited by Male Chorus.

**ADAM.** Boguś, quiet. Get up. Everybody, come on. Get your glasses. Chatter. It sounds like the Militia. Sit down, Maryjka, I'll get the door.

**MAN IN UNIFORM.** Good evening. Civic Militia. We've been tipped off that you are holding an unlawful gathering for the purpose of spreading subversive propaganda.

**ADAM.** It's my wife's birthday. She's pregnant. We're just talking and having a drink. Since when is that against the law?

**MAN IN UNIFORM.** We'll see about that. We'll see about everything.

**MARYJA.** What's this about?

**MAN IN UNIFORM.** Sit down, ma'am, the last thing we need in this mess is for you to go into labor. Get your ID cards out. All of you.

**MALE CHORUS.** Citizen Adam M., into the meat wagon, citizen Bogumił Z., into the meat wagon, citizen Ryszard K., into the meat wagon. Piece of meat citizen Alina Z. into the meat wagon. Piece of meat citizen Zofia K. into the meat wagon. Piece of meat citizen Maryja M. can stay and bear the fruit of her maculate conception. All the other citizens and pieces of meat, into the meat wagon. I meat it.

### 3. 4. E.

**FEMALE CHORUS.** A school, a classroom, a few desks and chairs. Boys and girls. Smiling faces. Screaming gobs. Every piehole yelling and cursing. Are these still human beings? And is she a human being?

**EWA.** What Konrad says confirms that, deep down, all of us are lonely: the only thing that always stays with us is our shadow. Other people simply come and go. Any thoughts?

**SCHOOLGIRL 1.** I'm not lonely.

**SCHOOLGIRL 2** (*Stage whisper*). Especially when Piotrek's coming in your mouth!

**FEMALE CHORUS.** Hee-hee-hee, har-har-har! Hee-hee-hee, har-har-har!

**EWA.** Nobody can truly know you. Only you know what you're thinking. In a sense, that makes you all alone. There's just you. Just you, with yourself.

**SCHOOLGIRL 1.** Bullshit. I have my mom and dad, though he's in the slammer now.

**SCHOOLGIRL 3.** He's a thief, no wonder.

**SCHOOLGIRL 1.** I prefer to have a thief for a father than a slut of a mom like yours who sucks cock for two zloty.

**SCHOOLBOY 1.** She'd have to suck all week to make two zloty. It's twenty groszy she charges.

**FEMALE CHORUS.** Hee-hee-hee, har-har-har! Hee-hee-hee, har-har-har!

**EWA.** Settle down. We're talking about Mickiewicz's Great Improvisation here . . .

**SCHOOLGIRL 1.** That's what I'm saying: I have a mother, a father and a brother. And I have this wall, a bulletin board, that is, where I pin photos and clippings about singers and actresses. I know where they go on holiday, what they eat, where they shop and what they buy. What size bra they wear. I'm a 36B, for instance, and Angelina's only a 32A, but Samantha's got a 38 with D cups. What's your size, miss? Looks like a 40DD to me.

**EWA.** What does that have to do with anything?

**SCHOOLBOY 2.** Ooh, she's turning all red in the face! What are you ashamed of? Tits are way more interesting than that Mickiewicz cunt!

**SCHOOLGIRL 2.** She's got enormous hooters. Wonder if they're real?

**SCHOOLGIRL 3.** The fuck they are. Ever seen a bitch with shoulders that broad and a voice that low?

**EWA.** Enough!

**SCHOOLBOY 2.** Our teacher's a manly lady! Bet she likes to be on top. You can ride me if you want.

**SCHOOLGIRL 1.** Not that you have anything to ride on.

**SCHOOLBOY 2.** Shut your trap, you cunt!

**SCHOOLGIRL 1.** Your mama's a cunt when she blows mangy dogs by the dumpsters.

**EWA.** Settle down!

**SCHOOLBOY 1.** Nobody said you had to teach school. If you can't take the heat, go work in a library or the church. Some priest might take pity and give you a good fuck!

**SCHOOLGIRL 3.** What about the tits, then? They natural or fake?

**EWA.** You're behaving like a bunch of animals.

**SCHOOLBOY 1.** Tits out, tits out! Tits out! Tits out!

*All the pupils chant "Tits out!" and the Female Chorus joins in.*

**FEMALE CHORUS.** There's just you and you alone. You, and you alone. You, and you alone. There's two of you. You're not alone. You, and you alone. Him and her. Tits out! Tits out!

*Ewa runs out of the classroom.*

## 5. A.

**MALE CHORUS.** They caught him, they copped him. Locked him up, broke him down. Bawled him out, pushed him around. He's in the slammer, he's on the inside, while Maryjka's screaming in pain. He goes behind bars, she goes into labor. What's it going to be? Dear me. Dear me. Dark as far as the eye can see.

**MAN IN UNIFORM.** So what's it going to be, mister citizen?

**ADAM.** What's what going to be? If you people stay in power, things will only get worse.

**MAN IN UNIFORM.** Not very nice of you to be insulting the authorities. What with everything we've done for you. The state put you through school, and university even. All free of charge. You've got a place to live. We've given you everything, and you don't want to give us anything in return.

**ADAM.** You can kiss my ass.

**MAN IN UNIFORM.** We can shove a truncheon up your ass is what we can do. Then again, you might enjoy that.

**ADAM.** Fuck off.

**MAN IN UNIFORM.** I wouldn't insult me if I were you. We're willing to do a lot for you. All we want is a few names. A few addresses. No one will ever know.

**ADAM.** I'm not telling you anything.

**MAN IN UNIFORM.** We'll see about that.

**ADAM.** You can't force me.

**MAN IN UNIFORM.** We won't need force. I think you'll see the light and tell us all we need to know. You'll sing for us. We have a bit of dirt on you. There's no need for us to rough you up, I'm sure you'll listen to reason.

**ADAM.** You don't have shit on me.

**MAN IN UNIFORM.** Are you sure about that?

**ADAM.** You don't scare me.

**MAN IN UNIFORM.** Oh, I'm not scaring you—yet. We're just having a nice chat for the time being. Remember that there's a lot we can do for you. But there's also a lot we can do to you. So, what's it going to be? Shall we have a little talk? I see you have a degree in Polish, whaddyacallit, philology. Educated citizen like yourself won't mind a little talk now, would you?

**ADAM.** I don't talk to scum.

**MAN IN UNIFORM.** A feisty one, are you? A real tough cookie. We'll see how feisty you are when I show you a couple of photos.

**ADAM.** Fuck off.

**MALE CHORUS.** Courage brother, courage! We're rooting for you! 'Tis freedom and truth you're fighting for. Courage brother, courage.

**MAN IN UNIFORM** (*reaches for an envelope, takes some photographs out of it, and leafs through them*). What a fine lady you make in these photos, mister citizen. That's a nice skirt you have on. Floral print. Your stems are a bit veiny, though. Thicker tights might do the trick. I'd say you overdid it with the lipstick in this one. But, all in all, I might look twice if I didn't know you were a dude. Would the wife happen to know you like going out on the town wearing her clothes? Maybe it turns her on, eh? Maybe she's into girls herself?

**MALE CHORUS.** Courage brother, courage! We're rooting for you!

**MAN IN UNIFORM.** She doesn't know, does she? The wife doesn't know you like sneaking about working-class neighborhoods of an afternoon, wearing her tights, bras and scarves. Made up all pretty like.

**ADAM.** I'm not telling you anything!

**MAN IN UNIFORM.** Then we'll tell. All your freedom-loving friends will find out all about you. We'll see how tolerant they are once they learn how you spend your afternoons in working-class neighborhoods. How you sneak up to the clotheslines and sniff sanitary pads hung out to dry. People wash them, but you can never get all the blood out. That turns you on, doesn't it?

**ADAM.** You're scum!

**MAN IN UNIFORM.** Me? I'm scum? No, I don't think so. I'm straight with my wife. I sleep with her the way the Good Lord intended.

**ADAM.** You mean the way the General, or maybe Stalin, intended.

**MAN IN UNIFORM.** The General, Stalin, God. Who cares? I sleep with my wife the way a man sleeps with a woman. I'm not living a lie. I have a dick, and I use it. What about you, citizen? Something must be wrong with your dick, I'd say. Or maybe that boy your holier-than-thou wife gave birth to yesterday isn't yours at all?

**ADAM.** A boy?

**MAN IN UNIFORM.** You wouldn't want him to end up in an orphanage, would you?

**ADAM.** You're not taking my baby away! Your laws don't reach that far! You can have me followed, lock me up in prison, but you're not taking my baby away.

**MAN IN UNIFORM.** We'll tell the competent authorities that you're a pervert, and it's off to the asylum for the little man. We won't have you warping the mind of a brand-new citizen. (*To the officer waiting outside the door*) Get this pervert out of here! As for you, citizen, I'd advise you to reconsider. A few names, a few addresses, and no one will ever know about the lipstick, the dresses and the wigs. See you later, madam. Take him to his cell!

**ADAM.** I'm not telling you anything! Poland has not yet perished![16]

**MAN IN UNIFORM.** It hasn't, it hasn't. Don't you worry, we're taking good care of People's Poland!

**MALE CHORUS.** In the afternoon, a young woman wanders through poor, working-class neighborhoods. This is where the weary, hardworking daughters of the nation hang out their pants, their linens, their slips, their striped stockings, their nylon tights, their threadbare and darned hosiery, and their hard-won, rationed cotton-wool sanitary pads, used five days a month, and washed with laundry soap so the bloodstains can barely be seen. And the young woman from the good neighborhood sneaks in under the drying laundry and pauses, rapt, beneath the laundered pads that still bear a whiff of unfertilized ovum, and sniffs at the soggy cotton wool. She takes in the smell as if it were flowers of the field, or the Givenchy perfume she dreams of but cannot afford—it being available only for hard currency—or apple-scented foreign soap, or the forbidden fruit itself. Pluck me, Ewa, pluck me. The young woman from a good family and neighborhood, who is, in fact, a not-so-young man, furtively pulls a moist sanitary pad from its clothespin and slips it into her pocket, then casually heads for the bus stop and leaves the working class neighborhood. Several hours later, a poor, work-weary daughter of the nation, who bones chickens at the processing plant all day, only to be boned like a fish by her unwashed

---

**16** From the Polish national anthem, "Dąbrowski's Mazurka."

hubby at night, notices that one of her pads, which still bore traces of use, traces of an ovum unfertilized by a hard-working son of the nation, is missing, and reports it to the Militia. A uniformed constable, uncrowned eagle on his cap, calls it in, and the filth fan out, the pigs go on the prowl. Sniffing, rooting, tracking until finally they find the discarded sanitary towel on the other side of town. Right by Adam's building. Gotcha!

## 5. E.

FEMALE CHORUS. In a free Poland we live, in a free Poland we'll die! The wages are twelve hundred a month. He's a hero, let him have more. More sorrows, more worries. A raise? How about a punch? I'll punch her in the nose. A trickle of blood will flow, like back in the days of the grim black crow. A hard life it was, but a life all the same. Now life seems to be guttering out. How many days left, how many hours? Fifteen hundred? Twenty-nine hundred? We're downsizing employment. We're downsizing life expectancy. There's a crisis!

EWA. Gas bill 140 zloty. Electricity bill 300 zloty. The mobile's prepaid. I don't use it much. There's no one left to call. But it's always an extra 50 zloty. There's the school, because I'm still studying. I like studying, you meet people. You can talk. Makes you feel better. But it's 3000 zloty a year, that's over 300 a month. You can't skimp on education, though. I might not have enough to eat but I'll go to school. I have a low salary. Twelve hundred zloty. Rysiek's publishing house sometimes sends some proofreading my way, the odd schoolboy comes to brush up before taking the Certificate. I don't go to get my hair done often, I buy clothes at the thrift store. Just the other day, I bought a brand-name sweater for four zloty. Nice and warm. Lamb's wool. Nobody has to know it cost four zloty. But now I need to buy those damn pills. I don't know if I'll have enough to pay tuition. Might have to give up school. That would be a shame, I've completed three semesters already. I have cancer. Bowel cancer. They say it's treatable. They say I'm lucky, because I can have surgery seven months from now. I said that was a long wait, and they said I could get it done privately in two days' time, but it would cost me. Seventy-five hundred. But that's more than half a year's salary. I'd have to save up. Not eat, not drink. Not pay the utilities. Give up going to the hairdresser, the night cream, shopping at the thrift store. Save up half a year's salary, and it still wouldn't be enough. I'd be 300 short, and I don't like borrowing money. So I'll wait a month longer. What should I do? I'll go to church. I can pray, but the priest won't remove my tumor. It must be twenty years since I've last been to church. I was mad at God for playing such a trick on me. Screwed up my whole life he did, the bumbling idiot. But I am sort of scared. I keep thinking about death. I'll give it a shot. I was never very religious, though it was easier for me to believe in God when Father Jerzy[17] was still alive. I always imagined He looked like Jerzy. They're to beatify him. It's about time, too. Well, I'll give it a go. We'll see.

FEMALE CHORUS. Our Father, who art in Heaven. Our Lady of the Gate of Dawn. And all the angels and all the saints. Saint Clodoald, patron of nailmakers; Saint Elijah the Prophet, patron of charioteers; Saint Genevieve, patron of virgins, chandlers, fishermen, hatters and vintners; Saint George, patron of armorers, gunsmiths and scouts, invoked against the plague, leprosy, syphilis and herpes; Saint Patrick, patron of barbers, wigmakers, despairing smiths and miners; Saint Servatius, invoked during cold spells, pray for Ewa, by no means the first sinner.

EWA (*kneels by the confessional*). Praised be.

---

17 Jerzy Popiełuszko, a priest known for his strong support of Solidarity. He was kidnapped and murdered in 1984 by officers of the Security Service.

**FEMALE CHORUS.** Honeybee or wannabe?

**MAN IN CASSOCK.** Forever, amen.

**EWA.** I don't remember the formula.

**MAN IN CASSOCK.** That's not good, we'll have to refresh your memory. I suppose you haven't been to confession for some time?

**EWA.** Twenty years or so.

**MAN IN CASSOCK.** Well, better late than never. Do you want to confess your sins?

**EWA.** I don't know. Maybe I'd like to talk some first.

**MAN IN CASSOCK.** If it's talking you're after, a psychoanalyst or a girlfriend is your man. I'm here to listen to people's sins.

**EWA.** And there I was thinking a man of the cloth was there to talk. Must have been mistaken.

**MAN IN CASSOCK.** Do you have all your sacraments?

**EWA.** Yes. Even the last one.

**MAN IN CASSOCK.** I don't quite understand.

**EWA.** Because I killed someone, in a sense. And gave them extreme unction.

**MAN IN CASSOCK.** What do you mean: in a sense? Either you kill someone or you don't. Who have you killed, for God's sake?

**EWA.** Myself, actually.

**MAN IN CASSOCK.** Have you tried to commit suicide?

**EWA.** No, no. It's not like that.

**MAN IN CASSOCK.** But you're saying you wanted to kill yourself.

**EWA.** I did kill myself. A couple of times.

**MAN IN CASSOCK.** It's not a psychoanalyst but a psychiatrist you'll be needing, it seems.

**EWA.** I see I shouldn't have come here.

**MAN IN CASSOCK.** Speak, my child. Lord forgive me my impatience.

**FEMALE CHORUS.** Why don't you confess your sins, Father? What about all the sins you may have forgotten? Or have you forgotten the formula? Hush, we're in the House of God! Silly sod, we're in the theater! Silent the priests, silent the vicars, the first to speak takes off their knickers!

**MAN IN CASSOCK.** So what about this killing, then? You are alive, if I'm not mistaken? Unless it's a ghost I'm talking to.

**FEMALE CHORUS.** He spoke first! The good Father must take off his skivvies!

**EWA.** The first time I killed myself was at the age of fourteen. I was friends with this boy. We played football and studied history together. He was the one who first told me about Katyń.[18]. When he told me how the Russkies shot Polish officers in the back of the head, I didn't want to believe him. Nobody at home ever spoke about Katyń. I couldn't sleep. I kept seeing their shattered skulls, the bullets in their brains, their cold dead eyes, and their blood oozing into the soil.

**MAN IN CASSOCK.** It was yourself you were supposed to be talking about.

**EWA.** I am talking about myself. I fell in love with that boy, but when I told him, when I told him who I really was, he shunned me. That was when I stopped believing in myself. And I killed myself for the first time.

**MAN IN CASSOCK.** But I don't get it. Katyń? First love? Heavy stuff, granted, but surely no reason to kill yourself?

**EWA.** I had to kill myself. Killing yourself to live, you know? I was all right for a few years. I was ripped, cut my hair short, listened to hard rock, smoked cigarettes, went out drinking with the boys every Friday, the opposition movement, jail. A wife, a kid.

**MAN IN CASSOCK.** A wife? A kid?

**EWA.** Yes, but the wife found out in the end. I loved her, though. I didn't want to lose her, so I had to kill myself again. Kill myself

---

**18** Katyń massacre—the mass execution of Polish prisoners of war carried out by the Soviets in 1940. The number of victims is estimated at 22,000, including more than 10,000 Polish officers.

to live. But it was no use. I ended up killing him instead of myself. You know what I mean, Father? I had to. It didn't hurt him any. Not like those Polish officers. No blood was shed. I didn't shoot him in the back of the head. It was all done in kid gloves. In a sterile environment. Almost painlessly. It hurt me, but not him. Not any more. He only died on paper. His birth certificate was put in a shredder. A painless death. In a piece of office equipment. Ten seconds.

FEMALE CHORUS. Sixth: Thou shall not kill.

MAN IN CASSOCK. You're sick, my child. You're rambling. Get yourself to a doctor. God won't help you here.

EWA. The doctors aren't giving me long to live. The tumor's the size of a fist. They say it's been growing inside me for twenty years now.

MAN IN CASSOCK. A tumor, Katyń, a wife, a fourteen-year-old boy . . .

EWA. I also accuse myself of all the sins I may have forgotten.

MAN IN CASSOCK. But you haven't confessed to any sin yet.

EWA. But that's the only part of the formula I remember.

MAN IN CASSOCK. Go with God.

EWA. I'm going to God. But what if God doesn't exist, where do I go then? To Hell?

MAN IN CASSOCK. I'll not have you blaspheming. May God have mercy on you. Do not abandon hope.

EWA. How much do I owe you?

MAN IN CASSOCK. An offering in the collection plate.

EWA. That's always less than the operation will cost.

MAN IN CASSOCK. God bless.

FEMALE CHORUS. A tumor, Katyń, a wife, a fourteen-year-old boy. All the sins I may have forgotten. More tumors than sins. Amen.

## 6. A.

**MALE CHORUS.** Mother, Mommy is so sweet. Mother, Mommy will tuck in your feet. Are you scared of Mother, Mommy, complete? Mother of Poland, Mother of God, Mother Częstochowa, mother hips so broad. Mother Earth, Mother Mammon, Mother Superior, mother of famine. Godmother, Grandmother, Queen Mother, Lacrimosa, comforting mother, drinking mother, beating mother, mal de la rosa. There is only one Mother.

**ADAM.** That's the fortieth diaper ironed. Here you go, nice and soft. Washed in soapsuds. You shouldn't use detergent to wash baby clothes. Soap flakes are the best, but they're hard to get these days. When the ration cards run out, I wash diapers in soapsuds. They're nice and foamy and smell of camomile. No risk of diaper rash. It'll be time to feed the little one soon. The midwife said to feed him every two hours, though I really don't see why. (*Leans over the baby's cot*) He's sleeping, the little angel, why wake him? What a beautiful boy. So tiny, so innocent. Such a small head, still bald, eyes as blue as a pussycat's. My little one. Wake up, Lesiu, wake up! I'll make you some milk. (*Goes to prepare the milk*) Five teaspoons. Gosh darn it, the powdered milk's running out, and we've used up all the ration cards. It's off to the dollar shop again. How could she not want to breast-feed? Says she doesn't know how, and how the baby keeps biting her. How can a person be so selfish? (*Stands in front of a mirror and strokes his nipples, then pulls down his shirt with a sad face. He gets the milk ready and goes back to the baby. When he wakes it, the baby starts screaming to high heaven*) Hush, Lesiu, hush. Just drink this milk. Mommy . . . Daddy will sing you a lullaby. Ah-ah-ah, kittens two, fur so gray and eyes so blue. (*The baby starts bawling even louder*) Gosh darn it, Leszek, everything's all right. Drink your milk. Come to Mo . . . me.

*The baby drinks the milk and calms down. After a while, there is a series of knocks on the door. Leszek recognizes the signal, and puts down the baby, who starts crying again.*

IMAGE 6.3 **Adam (Marek Tynda,** in the middle) **and Female Chorus (Marzena Nieczuja-Urbańska, Justyna Bartoszewicz, Anna Kociarz, and Magdalena Boć)**
Directed by Kuba Kowalski. Teatr Wybrzeże, Gdańsk (2012)
*Photograph by Michał Andrysiak*

FEMALE CHORUS. Knock-knock-knock. Knock-knock-knock.
Someone's in for a big shock.

ADAM. Where have you been all this time?

MARYJA. In church. I told you I was going to pray a while.

ADAM. What have you been praying for now?

MARYJA. I wasn't praying for anything. I went to pray to God.

ADAM. You could take care of the baby instead of fiddling with those beads.

MARYJA. It's not beads, it's a rosary. What's he bawling about?

ADAM. Maybe he wouldn't be bawling if you would breast-feed him.

MARYJA. I brought the post. Two letters for you, one for me. I don't know who it's from.

ADAM. What do you mean you don't know? Show me.

MARYJA. I said it was for me, didn't I?

*Maryjka rocks the baby to sleep.*

ADAM. Is he asleep?

MARYJA. Yes. He snuggled right up to me and went out like a light. Can't beat a mother's touch. What was in your post?

ADAM. A rejection of our passport application, and a letter from Gienek in prison. The censors blacked out practically the whole text.

MARYJA. The fuckers.

ADAM. Not in front of the baby.

MARYJA. But he's asleep.

ADAM. But he picks everything up in his sleep. You're setting a bad example. That's not how a mother should behave.

MARYJA. You're getting your panties in a wad again.

ADAM. What's in the letter?

MARYJA. Don't be so nosy.

ADAM. Why don't we have supper?

MARYJA. Sure. See what's in the fridge, and I'll whip something up.

*Adam goes out of the room. Maryjka opens the letter and takes out a bundle of photos. She inspects them. A long pause.*

ADAM. There's not a lot to choose from. A small piece of the sausage your mom sent us from the farm. Some flour, half a bottle of milk. Oh, and some eggs. We could make pancakes. Want some? Only I don't know what we'll have them with. Any ideas, Maryjka? Maryjka . . . (*enters the room*) Well?

MARYJA. Well what?

ADAM. I was asking what you wanted with your pancakes.

MARYJA. What's this?

*Adam sees the photos. A long silence.*

ADAM. Maryjka, darling. It's not what you think.

MARYJA. What is it then? Well? Why are you wearing my blouse?

ADAM. Maryjka . . .

MARYJA. I spent two months looking for it. You told me I must have left it at my mother's. And you . . . You were walking around in it. And these tights? Where the hell did you get such fancy tights? They must have cost a fortune. I never had a pair of tights like that. Did you have my panties on, too? Fuck! Fuck, fuck, fuck! What the fuck is this? (*Adam tries to give her a hug*) Don't you fucking touch me! You make me sick, you sick fuck! Get the fuck out of my house. Get the fuck out!

**ADAM.** Maryjka, I admit I do go out in your clothes every now and then, but what does that change?

**MARYJA.** Everything! See, you're not even trying to deny it. Who took these photos?

**ADAM.** The secret police. They threatened to show them to you if I didn't cooperate.

**MARYJA.** You should have signed their stupid paper! And stopped this nonsense. But no, you wanted me to find out? What now? Am I supposed to live with this? God created man and woman. Who are you?

**ADAM.** I won't do it anymore. I promise. That was the last time.

**MARYJA.** You've ruined everything! Who are you anyway? This is insane! You drink with the boys, get me pregnant, but what do you do when no one's looking? You wear dresses? Fuck!

**ADAM.** Don't curse! You could always say gosh darn it!

**MARYJA.** Get the fuck out of here with your dresses and your gosh darn its! Who are you anyway?

**ADAM.** You see, that infallible God of yours got it wrong. He messed up and gave me a man's body, even though I'm, I'm, I'm like you . . .

**MARYJA.** Oh, no you're not! Shut up. I'm not having any more of this.

**ADAM.** I'm a woman, Marysia. One with broad shoulders and no breasts.

**MALE CHORUS.** Tits out!

**MARYJA.** You're twisted. This is sick. I want to puke when I think that you touched me, that you slept with me. You're a fag. I'm living with a fucking fag. Get the fuck out of here.

**ADAM.** I can change. I'll kill her. I want to be with you.

**MARYJA.** Her who?

**ADAM.** Me. Her, that is.

**MARYJA.** Pack your shit. I don't want to see you again.

**ADAM.** I love you.

**MARYJA.** How long has this been going on?

**ADAM.** I must have been about seven.

**MARYJA.** What? What the fuck? You've been dressing up as a woman since you were a kid?

**ADAM.** I don't dress up, Maryjka. I just wear the clothes. I really am . . . I'm a woman.

**MARYJA.** You're sick is what you are. You're no better than a pedophile, or people who get off on corpses or animals. You're a regular sicko. They should lock you up and throw away the key!

**ADAM.** I won't do it anymore, I promise. (*Maryjka starts packing her clothes and the baby's things*) What are you doing?

*The baby starts crying.*

**MARYJA.** I'm moving out, what's it look like? You thought I'd stay here and things would be the way they were? That I'd sleep with a woman? Oh no, my dear. I'm not like that! God created man and woman. Got that? A woman and a man! There's no other option! It doesn't exist! You don't exist!

*Maryja dresses the baby and walks out of the flat. Adam starts crying.*

**ADAM.** Let me at least say goodbye to the baby.

**MARYJA.** No way! You're not touching my baby ever again!

**MALE CHORUS.** A woman and a man. A woman and a man. No other option. You don't exist. Don't exist. A woman and a man. Anouk Aimée and Jean-Louis Trintignant. A woman and a man. You don't exist.

**FEMALE CHORUS.** Without kin you're all alone. Like a dog without a bone, an actor out on loan! The dog's barking, Ewa's crying, all alone in bed she's lying. They shaved her hair and left her there. A family photo on the shelf. And the dog's all by itself.

**EWA.** My hair's falling out. I can't take this any longer. I wish it was over. I hope I die soon.

**LECH.** Don't say that. The anniversary's coming up. You'll see old friends, it's something to live for.

**EWA.** No, I'm not up to it. I'm not going.

**LECH.** Go, it'll make you feel better. It's something to live for.

**EWA.** I've been looking for something to live for all my life and where did it get me? I'm dying.

**LECH.** Maybe the whole thing wasn't worth it?

**EWA.** You see, son . . .

**LECH.** I asked you not to call me son. I'm here because I feel sorry for you. I'll help you, but some things I won't tolerate.

**EWA.** Look, I had to do it.

**LECH.** You ruined my mother's life. She died so young.

**EWA.** You think that was because of me?

**LECH.** I don't know, but she did take it pretty hard.

**EWA.** Get me some water.

**LECH.** Here you are. Sit up, I'll adjust the pillow.

**EWA.** No, thanks. I'm comfortable the way I am. You could open the window, though.

**LECH.** The dogs are barking like hell. Sure it won't bother you?

**EWA.** Open it, the smell's worse than the noise. Go see what they're barking at, will you?

*Lech opens the window and looks outside.*

**FEMALE CHORUS.** Some dogs tore a cat to shreds. Gnawed its legs, bit off its head. Ate the tail of that cat so frail. Spilled its guts, tore off its nuts. The cat's heart was bleeding, and the dogs started feeding. The cat stopped scratching, the dogs started retching. Cat's eyes for their dinner, they spewed up its innards. They're retching and retching, let's hope it's not catching.

LECH. Jesus, what's that smell? Have you thrown up again?

EWA. It's the chemo.

LECH. Get up. We need to get your clothes off and wash them. It would be easier if you had running water.

EWA. Throw the shirt and the bedclothes into the trash.

LECH. Why? They're still good.

EWA. I know the thought of washing you makes you sick.

LECH. A lot of things make me sick.

EWA. Do I make you sick? (*Lech does not reply*) Leszek, I had to do it.

LECH. You had to get your tits done? Damn, it stinks in here!

EWA. I wouldn't have been me otherwise.

LECH. So you're you now?

EWA. Sometimes I don't know who I am anymore. This tumor. There's a tumor growing inside of me. Some kind of foreign body. Another foreign body. Get it? That body was like this tumor. My manhood was like a cancer. It was eating me up. A foreign body.

LECH. You shouldn't have gotten involved with Mom.

EWA. But I loved your mother.

LECH. You lied to her for so many years. You slept with her. You got her pregnant. If you were a woman you should have been turned on by boys, right?

EWA. It's not that simple.

LECH. It is for me.

EWA. That's because you're lucky. But let's not talk about that.

LECH. What are we supposed to talk about? I want to know what it's like. Don't I deserve an explanation? You never explained anything to Mom.

EWA. She never gave me the chance. She ran away. She didn't want to know me.

**LECH.** Are you surprised?

**EWA.** I loved your mother very much.

**LECH.** What about sex? Did she turn you on? Did women turn you on, or did you have to force yourself to ejaculate?

**EWA.** I don't think you can force yourself to ejaculate. Of course she turned me on. But . . . Sex was never the main thing . . .

**LECH.** But you must have felt something when you were making me, right?

**EWA.** The times were different then. There was a shortage of Poles. I loved your mother. And I loved our country. Back then, your mother and I thought that they could take everything away from us. Our flat, our car, our phone, our books, our freedom, everything. Everything, but not our child.

**LECH.** So you made me for your country? For Poland?

**EWA.** Help me, I'm feeling weak.

**LECH.** A right Polish Mother. He made me for the love of country. Fuck!

**EWA.** Let's get this over with, please.

**LECH.** I said I'd help you, but it would be on my terms. If I want to talk about you, we'll talk about you. If you have a problem with that, you can keep lying in your own vomit.

**EWA.** You're cruel.

**LECH.** Sorry. I guess I take after you that way.

**EWA.** I never wanted to hurt anybody. I always tried to do the right thing.

**LECH.** You've hurt a lot of people. Mom, me.

**EWA.** Try to understand.

**LECH.** I'm trying. Ever since I can remember, I've been trying to understand you. Sit up. I'll change your shirt.

*Lech helps Ewa undress. He takes a long look at her breasts. He wipes up her vomit. He changes the pillowcase. He helps her put on a clean shirt.*

**EWA.** Thank you.

**LECH.** You've ruined Mom's life and mine for a pair of tits?

**EWA.** How many times am I supposed to tell you?

**LECH.** As many times as it takes. Until I understand.

**EWA.** I might not be around that long.

**LECH.** Don't say that. Bowel cancer is treatable.

**EWA.** How's Wiki?

**LECH.** I don't know.

**EWA.** How come?

**LECH.** She left me.

**EWA.** What? Why? But you're having a baby.

**LECH.** That's water under the bridge.

**FEMALE CHORUS.** Children under the bridge. Babies with bathwater. Thrown out, flushed away. Water-babies flowing under the bridge.

**EWA.** Water under the bridge? This is a baby we're talking about. Did Wiki have a miscarriage?

**LECH.** She had an abortion.

**EWA.** But that's illegal.

**LECH.** Money can get you anything these days. There's no such thing as absolute freedom. You and your friends won us the freedom that money can buy.

**EWA.** But why? Why did she do it? Was something wrong? Was the baby sick?

**LECH.** I don't know.

**EWA.** She didn't tell you?

**LECH.** She only said she was afraid it might be hereditary.

**EWA.** What might be hereditary?

**LECH.** You.

**EWA.** I don't understand.

**LECH.** She was afraid our child might be like you.

*A long silence.*

**EWA.** I'm sorry.

**LECH.** No, no . . . Don't apologize. I didn't love her anyway.

**EWA.** But a child is still a child. You can't kill it.

**LECH.** It wasn't a child yet. She was only seven weeks pregnant.

**FEMALE CHORUS.** Prosencephalon, mesencephalon and rhombencephalon. Arm, forearm, hand, thigh, calf and foot. Black foot. A waiter's hand.

**EWA.** The sex develops in Week 19.

**LECH.** I have to be going now. Can I get you anything?

**EWA.** No, no. I have everything I need. Thanks for coming.

**LECH.** Don't mention it.

**EWA.** No, really. You're all I have. The only family I have.

**LECH.** Don't give me that. You have a sister. Nan's still alive.

**EWA.** My sister won't let me see my mother. She says Mother would die if she saw me. She told Mother I was missing, you know.

**LECH.** Maybe it's for the best.

**EWA.** I'd so like to see Mother again.

**LECH.** Auntie was right.

**EWA.** It's very sad.

**LECH.** Is there anything else you need? I really have to be going.

**EWA.** You know what my dream is?

**LECH.** How am I supposed to know?

**EWA.** For you to call me Mom one day.

*A long silence.*

**LECH.** No . . . I can't. It's too much to ask . . . I'll close the window.

**EWA.** What about the dogs?

**LECH.** What?

**EWA.** Why were they barking like that?

**LECH.** They tore a cat to pieces. See you.

*Exit Lech.*

**EWA.** Shame they didn't tear me to pieces.

**FEMALE CHORUS.** The hounds were baying and Ewa was praying. Praying for death. For the scalpel and scythe. Red-and-white roses on her grave.

## 7. A.

**MALE CHORUS.** Testing, checking, sedating, palpating. Palpating in gloves. Of rubber and latex. But the effect will be a stunner. A chest worthy of Madonna. Go to it, ladies and gents! We can't wait to see this through! Courage, brother, courage! We're keeping fingers crossed for you. Courage, sister, courage! We're keeping fingers crossed for you!

**ADAM.** How long will this take?

**WOMAN IN SMOCK.** We need to keep you under observation for a while.

**ADAM.** It seems like that's all you've been doing so far. Can I have this operation or not?

**WOMAN IN SMOCK.** It's not that simple.

**ADAM.** Nothing in my life has ever been simple. I've gotten used to it.

**WOMAN IN SMOCK.** No one here can get you a good pair of tits.

**ADAM.** They don't have to be big. A C-cup, or even a B-cup will do.

**WOMAN IN SMOCK.** Not with your frame. With shoulders like that, you need at least a D.

**MALE CHORUS.** A, B, C, D. Alphabet soup, and in old age your tits will droop.

**ADAM.** And, you know . . . What about down there?

**WOMAN IN SMOCK.** That's up to you. We can do that in our hospital, but these things take much longer to heal at your age. You're not twenty anymore. It will hurt, the wounds might fester. Think it over. You said sex didn't matter that much to you.

**ADAM.** No, no . . . It doesn't. I've always preferred cuddling, stroking hair, holding hands. Sex itself seems a little brutish to me. Kind of disgusting.

**WOMAN IN SMOCK.** They do the best tits in Thailand.

**MALE CHORUS.** And they do the best ribs at Roger's.

**ADAM.** Thailand, good God! Why there, of all places?

**WOMAN IN SMOCK.** Why does Belgium have the best chocolate? Every country excels at something. When it comes to tits, Thailand beats all the others hands down.

**ADAM.** And us? Do we excel at anything?

**WOMAN IN SMOCK.** Poles? I don't know. Picking black currants maybe?

**ADAM.** That's a start.

**WOMAN IN SMOCK.** They do a good job in Thailand, and it's not all that expensive. The plane ticket will cost you more than the operation.

**ADAM.** I have some money saved up. Two years ago, I imported Commodore computers into the country.

**WOMAN IN SMOCK.** We can begin the hormone treatment here at our hospital.

**ADAM.** When?

**WOMAN IN SMOCK.** You've basically had all the tests done. The psychologist wanted me to ask you a few more questions. It won't be difficult. A free-association game. Because you're sure you want to go through with this, right?

**ADAM.** Yes, yes, of course I am.

**WOMAN IN SMOCK.** I'll be giving you pairs of words, and you have to pick the one that best describes you.

**ADAM.** But what for?

**WOMAN IN SMOCK.** We need to determine whether you're subconsciously a woman.

**ADAM.** What odd methods. I thought that would have been obvious, seeing as I'm here. I'm a woman in all but body. Unfortunately.

**WOMAN IN SMOCK.** Tomato or cucumber?

**ADAM.** Tomato.

**WOMAN IN SMOCK.** Shopping or reading?

**MALE CHORUS.** What's that got to do with the price of eggs? We were supposed to be talking tits and cocks!

**ADAM.** Shopping and reading. This is silly. Why don't you tell me about the procedure and the hormone therapy?

**WOMAN IN SMOCK.** As I was saying, you've been diagnosed, so we could start the treatment tomorrow if you're ready. I hope you realize how lucky you are. They used to treat people like you with electric shocks.

**ADAM.** Kill not treat, I'd say.

**WOMAN IN SMOCK.** First you'll get estrogen and so-called blockers that impede the body's secretion of sex hormones. Your facial features will change, and the fat will be distributed differently. You'll get curves, my lovely! And your tits will get a little bigger.

**ADAM.** And my voice? My voice is so low.

**WOMAN IN SMOCK.** Your voice and facial hair won't be affected. But that can be helped.

**ADAM.** Fine. Things are looking up. Let's do this.

**WOMAN IN SMOCK.** You could also get cancer. But the chances are slim.

**ADAM.** Cancer?

**WOMAN IN SMOCK.** Anyone can get it.

**ADAM.** I'd rather have cancer than these shoulders and moustache.

**WOMAN IN SMOCK.** Then you change your papers, and we'll give you the snip.

**ADAM.** Snip what?

**WOMAN IN SMOCK.** Your johnson. We'll fashion a vagina out of your penis and scrotum. There are several types of procedure: the difference is in the way the skin is used. The testicles are surgically removed.

**ADAM.** That's got to hurt.

**MAN IN SMOCK.** Hurts like hell. The procedure is fairly complicated, and the convalescence is long and painful. It hurts more the older you are.

**ADAM.** And the tits?

**MAN IN SMOCK.** Tits are a piece of cake.

**ADAM.** I'll need to think about it.

**MAN IN SMOCK.** Have you chosen a name?

**ADAM.** Ewa.

**MAN IN SMOCK.** Like the first woman?

**ADAM.** Like my first doll. A ragdoll with pigtails and buttons for eyes. I made it myself. Out of a piece of cloth my mother threw out. I stuffed it with cotton wool and sewed it back up. I still keep it in the bottom drawer.

**MAN IN SMOCK.** I have a doll like that too.

**ADAM.** And you?

**WOMAN IN SMOCK.** So do I.

**MALE CHORUS.** A ragdoll, a Barbie doll. Bang Barbie up the carby. A Doll's House. The Hollywood Doll. A blow-up doll. A doll you can blow. A living doll. Living with a hole. Living not whole.

## 7. E.

**FEMALE CHORUS.** Hail fellow well met! Make metas worse. Metastasis from the abdomen to the lungs. Go Mets!

**EWA.** I'm very sorry, but, despite the chemotherapy and the surgery, the tumor metastasized to the lungs. Your outlook is getting worse. You might not survive the operation, but don't despair. There's always hope. You must have hope. That's what my doctor told me. You must have hope. You must have hope, you might also consider praying. That's exactly what he told me, and then he adjusted his white smock and walked out of the room. You must have hope.

**FEMALE CHORUS.** Faith, Hope, Love. Cancer, Lungs, Grave!

**EWA.** I've been hoping all my life. For love. For freedom. Hoping the world would accept me for who I am. Hoping Lech would call me Mom. I hoped to have a nice pair of tits, but they soon sagged. I have no hope left. Whatever will be, will be. I'm tired. I'll sort some things out, and then I can die. (*Ewa stands in front of a mirror.*) I'm happy. I'm Ewa. I'm happy. (*Ewa goes over to a dresser. She takes out a sales leaflet and a few catalogues. She reads them.*) Oak casket, half-couch, light-coloured, gloss finish. Price: 3,745 zloty. Alder casket, brown, high-gloss varnish. Accessories included: cover, pillow, handles. Price: 856 zloty. Italian sarcophagus—a comfortable and stylish casket. For the true connoisseur and woman of distinction. Trimmed with Milan lace. Bespoke color and patterns. Price: 12,000 zloty. Expensive, gosh darn it, but I am a woman of distinction.

FEMALE CHORUS. Our coffins make you look larger than life.

EWA. I'll take the pinewood one. They say it's comfortable. 642 zloty. Comfortable and reasonably priced. It's on sale. Now for the dress and the shoes. Why are all these dresses black? Black doesn't become me. Spring green or lilac—that I could live with. Anything but black! It'll make me look old, and I'd like to look young for once. Black kind of makes you look like a dead person. I wonder if they have anything in brown at least? Gosh darn it. Oh, gracious. I'll just get something from the closet. (*Goes through her wardrobe.*) This'll do. A navy-blue cotton suit. The fabric stretches so it'll fit even if I do bloat a little, though it would be best if they put it on me before the soul leaves the body. And for a springtime touch, I'll tie this foulard around my neck. A polka-dot foulard. Yes, a handkerchief to wipe the tears I'll shed for this dreadful world. I bought the shoes already. They're comfortable, because they say your legs swell when you die, and they've got air holes so the feet won't sweat. I don't like having sweaty feet. I always wear special insoles and use foot spray every day. That's all, I think. Let them put my ragdoll, Ewunia, into the coffin, and some pocket change, too, because there might be palms to grease where I'm going. Everybody's on the take these days, so it might be the same in heaven. Right, that's me sorted. I'll just fold it all nicely, leave it where Leszek can find it, and I'll be off. Today's June 4. On this day, twenty-one years ago, Communism ended in Poland.[19] Nobody invited me for the anniversary. Nobody remembered. I prefer to think they didn't. It's better than them being sickened by me. People are people. Just like me. I'm an ordinary person. (*Pause.*) And I'm not taking anything to hospital. Maybe just a tad bit of hope.

FEMALE CHORUS. Because, as we all know, too much hope can kill you!

## 8. A.

MALE CHORUS. Brilliantly colored birds of paradise preen their wings. In our town, the church bell rings. Rings instead of handcuffs. Birds of paradise, splendid gowns, bangles and ribbons. Long live Poland! It's the end of our bondage!

JOANNA SZCZEPKOWSKA (*Perhaps on TV*). Ladies and Gentlemen, June 4 marked the end of Communism in Poland.[20]

MALE CHORUS. Bravo! Bravo! Bravo! Encore!

JOANNA SZCZEPKOWSKA (*Perhaps on TV*). Ladies and Gentlemen, June 4 marked the end of Communism in Poland.

ADAM. I have Russian champagne. Anybody? No? Then bottoms up! Where are you, friends of mine? Where? Why aren't you here? We have a reason to celebrate, don't we? It's the end of Communism in Poland! Did you hear that? You're not here. And I'll be gone soon. They'll be burying Adam today. They'll put him through the shredder. But I'll be here. You can call me. Or visit me in hospital. Bring a bunch of roses, or a box of chocolates. Solidarność brand, preferably.

---

19 The anniversary of the first partly free election in Poland that took place on June 4, 1989, leading to the foundation of the first non-communist government then to full democracy and Poland's independence.

20 Joanna Szczepkowska, a well-known Polish actress, made this statement on national television in October 1989.

**MALE CHORUS** (*Chanting*). Solidarność! Solidarność! Solidarność! Solidarność!

**ADAM.** But you don't have to bring anything. As long as you're here with me. Just as I was there with you. Always. I was always there for you. Jadzia, remember how your son left the faith? You cried, blamed yourself, you were scared the Church would cast you out. Remember who held your hand and explained it all to you? Me. And you, Boguś? When you were cheating on your wife, remember? You, who were always such a saint. Who told your wife he was out drinking with you when you were really shacking up with some bimbo? Who had your back then? Me. And all you snitches? Bolek? Alinka? Who was the first to forgive you? Who shook your hand? Me. What about you, Rysiek? Who got you in touch with people in Paris when you got sick of this communist shit and decided to emigrate? Who? Me. And you, Zosieńka? You were always so dumb, but you got your degree somehow. Who wrote your thesis for you free of charge? Who? Yep, me again. (*Pause.*) Where are you now, friends of mine? Communism's dead, Adam's dying. Celebrate with me. Is that so hard? Do I sicken you? I won't change. Maybe just a bit, but you'll get used to it soon enough. Where are you? Why aren't you here? This is what we were fighting for. For freedom, tolerance and the truth. This is my truth. Here I am. Give me your hand, I'm a little scared. I really need you now. A lot! Where are you? You're not here? That can't be. We swore before God and the crowned eagle banner that we'd always be together. For better or worse. Now you're not here. And me? Now I can finally be me.

**MEN'S CHORUS.** Bravo! Bravo! Encore!

**ADAM.** Now I can finally be me. Now I can finally be me. Now I can finally be me.

**MEN'S CHORUS.** He's dying! Help, he's dying! Not dying, but being born! Hurrah! He's being born! He's dying! He's being born! Ah, what's the difference?

*Hospital waiting room. Adam and Ewa are sitting next to each other. They are both waiting for an operation, but neither is frightened. They are smiling serenely at each other.*

ADAM. You look familiar.

EWA. I seem to remember you as well.

ADAM. It's you?

EWA. Who else?

ADAM. I'm dying, you know.

EWA. I know, I'm glad to hear it. Don't be scared.

ADAM. I'm not scared at all. I know I'll meet you there at last.

EWA. I'm dying too. But how did you know we'd meet, how did you know it would work out?

ADAM. It had to work out. There was never a doubt in my mind.

EWA. But there won't be a happy ending, will there?

ADAM. You never liked happy endings.

EWA. But I want there to be one now. I'd really like for the ending not to be sad.

ADAM. I'll have a word with the right people.

EWA. Cheers. I knew I could count on you, all things considered.

MALE AND FEMALE CHORUS. And they lived happily ever after. AAAAAAAAAAAAAAAA! And that's it for us, the chorus.

*The End*

BARTOSZ FRĄCKOWIAK AND WERONIKA SZCZAWIŃSKA

# IN DESERT AND WILDERNESS
## After Sienkiewicz and Others

Translated by Artur Zapałowski

IMAGE 7.1 **Silhouette**

Directed by Bartosz Frąckowiak. Teatr Dramatyczny im. Jerzego Szaniawskiego, Wałbrzych (2011)

*Photograph by Bartłomiej Sowa*

## CHARACTERS

STAŚ TARKOWSKI, a brave Polish lad, quite the perfect European boy

NELL RAWLISON, a brave English lass, quite the perfect European girl

AFRICA, a critical identity-performer

EUROPE, an affirmative identity-performer

KALI, a not-quite-genuine African man

MEA, a not-quite-genuine African woman

THE ARAB, a stager of situations and freedom fighter

THE LAST BLACK MAN, the last of a not-entirely real tribe

SABA THE DOG, an imperial English bull mastiff; domesticated, but only up to a point

KING THE ELEPHANT, an African elephant; wild, but only up to a point

LINDE-KURTZ, an explorer from the very heart of darkness

OBERSCOUTMASTER, a shady imperial figure

MISTER TARKOWSKI, Staś's father, once an insurgent, now a gentleman

MISTER RAWLISON, Nell's father, a born gentleman

SCOUT 1

SCOUT 2

## NOTE

*In Desert and Wilderness: After Sienkiewicz and Others* is a found-footage collage of diverse quotes from literature, anthropology and political commentary, placed within the narrative framework of Henryk Sienkiewicz's classic adventure novel for young readers, *In Desert and Wilderness* (1911). As much an essay for the stage as a dramatic text, the piece addresses white people's ingrained cultural stereotypes, myths, prejudices, anxieties, complexes and megalomania. The action takes place in an unreal Africa constructed from quotes, clichés and fantasies. The child protagonists do not wander through deserts and jungles, but get lost in the tangle of colonial and postcolonial discourse.

The text was first staged in 2011 by Bartosz Frąckowiak at the Teatr Dramatyczny in Wałbrzych. Set in an empty performance space full of ditches and spider-holes, with all the characters always on stage, the lively production unfolded on many levels, creating a reality entirely its own. Trance-like scenes and surreal imagery served to exorcize ghosts of the colonial past as they emerged from cultural texts used in the script.

The most important sources of the text are:

Henryk Sienkiewicz, *In Desert and Wilderness* and *Listy z Afryki* (Letters from Africa); Marian Brandys, *Śladami Stasia i Nel* (Following the Path of Staś and Nel); Paul Bowles, *The Sheltering Sky*; Tim Butcher, *Blood River*; Winston S. Churchill, *My Early Life*; J. M. Coetzee, *Elizabeth Costello*; Joseph Conrad, *Heart of Darkness*; Korney Chukovsky, *Black Peter*; Maya Deren, *Divine Horsemen: The Living Gods of Haiti*; James Joyce, *A Portrait of the Artist as a Young Man*; Ryszard Kapuściński, *The Shadow of the Sun*; Rudyard Kipling, *The White Man's Burden*; Leszek Kolankiewicz, *Wschód słońca na Ergu Chebbi*; Michel Leiris, *L'Afrique fantôme*; Adam Mickiewicz, *Forefathers' Eve*; Alan Moorehead, *The White Nile and The Blue Nile*; Józef Potocki, *Sport in Somaliland: Being an Account of a Hunting Trip to That Region*; Raymond Roussel, *New Impressions of Africa*; Flora Shaw, *Flora Shaw Gives the Name Nigeria*; Binyavanga Wainaina, *How to Write about Africa*; H. G. Wells, *The Island of Doctor Moreau*; songs: John Lennon, Yoko Ono, "Land of Hope and Glory", "Woman Is the Nigger of the World"; Mick Jagger, Keith Richards, "Paint It Black"; Gregor Frenkel Frank, Hans van Hemert, "The Elephant Song"; The Stooges, Iggy Pop, "I Wanna Be Your Dog"; James Thomson, Thomas Augustine Arne, "Rule Britannia", Die Antwoord, "Enter the Ninja".

## A WORD FROM THE AUTHORS

The Africa we are concerned with here does not exist. It is a phantom, a mirage, a patchwork of imaginings, ideas and fantasies; a meticulously constructed phantasm, a documentary falsehood, and a factual distortion. It is glossy tourist brochure, a vision for thrill-seeking explorers, a cheap holiday where the locals want to mug you; it is your own fear; Ryszard Kapuściński's *The Shadow of the Sun*, a special feature on CNN or BBC, an entry in the World Press Photo competition that draws your attention, and many other things that only exist in your memory.

The limits of the world are the limits of language: whenever language cracks, it leaves fissures in the earth, which is why you will find many demarcation lines separating various familiar-seeming territories. The Africa we are concerned with here, and which does not exist, has absorbed many ready-mades. Lines spoken by Stanisław Tarkowski channel the surrealism of Michel Leiris' ethnographical adventures, the experience of emptiness in Paul Bowles' prose, and the run-down colonial narratives of Joseph Conrad. Nell, a true discursive ghoul, sucks in and spews up so many words, which she processes in the machine that is her body, that listing them would take up more space than Western standards of proportion and style allow. Suffice it to say that Nell's self-consciousness is informed by Maya Deren and Raymond Roussel. Kali, a not-entirely-genuine African, performs his identity in line with books of anthropology that he had found in the attic of his single-storey *tukla*. They pissed him off so much that he decided to make them the basis for his private-public theater.

Intimately familiar with Lévi-Strauss—his *Tristes Tropiques* act is a true show-stopper—he is also well-versed in more radical postcolonial theory, which he doesn't hesitate to use in his political performances, even at the risk of being accused of terrorism. The Arab kidnapper has, for his part, an extensive knowledge of classical Oriental poetry and knows exactly what Western tourists, captivated by the rustle of desert sands, expect.

We have given him some of our fury to atone for the fact that Sienkiewicz in his ever-so-patriotic novel failed to realize that the Arab, too, was fighting for his nation's freedom. The Polish Scouts are basically generic scouts, even though their demands and dreams are taken from editorials in *Morze*, a prewar magazine published by the Polish Maritime and Colonial League.

Seeing as the Africa we are concerned with here does not exist, we do not concern ourselves with the truth about the real Africa. We do not see people of color as being of any particular color, nor do we have them wear black-face. All these characters are intentionally contrived. Mea is chalk-white: it is only the Scouts who brand her with blackness. Kali is orange, not unlike an Indian *sadhu*, though we never fall back on superficial multiculturalism. The Last Black Man's skin is practically red, glistening like something out of Leni Riefenstahl's *The Last of the Nuba* or a fantasy of Ancient Sparta. Only the character of Africa wears black grease-paint, but our Africa doesn't really exist, so it's okay. Besides, she is a critical performer, existing only through the performances she stages, incorporating the images and idioms of oppression the better to criticize, subvert and distort them.

While our text does contain taboo words it is not because, in our savage, Eastern-European arrogance, we reject political correctness, but because we are interested in the taboo, and not only in terms of something exotic.

Speaking of savage—yes, here be savage beasts, as well as animals that have long since been transformed into subhumans. Both types of creature have been experimentally embodied in human form. Saba the Dog hums all sorts of tunes, but what he wants—what he really really wants—are the songs of the British Empire. Though domesticated, the desert has brought out something wild within him. A reverse process occurs within King the Elephant, the king of the African jungle with an epsiode on *The Island of Doctor Moreau* behind him. We suspect that he has watched the black dancers peforming in Antonioni's white *La notte*.

In an Africa which does not exist, time is no longer linear. It skips forward and backward at random, sometimes pausing in the times of the Mahdiyya, sometimes sprawling out like the interwar period, sometimes dangerously resembling your own times. That is why we recommend you think about the simultaneity of words, situations, and places. You do not need to stick to the sequence we have proposed, either. Here, words can follow an exceptionally winding path.

The space can resemble an "African" live-action boardgame, played out with the lazy cinematographic rhythm of Werner Herzog's *Fata Morgana*, to the sound of children's cries from Abbas Kiarostami's *ABC Africa*, among rusting European machinery, in a landscape that is difficult to identify as African because it does not agree with the memories our visual education has instilled in us, in the intense aroma of fair-trade coffee and of the incense Christian exorcists use to cast out spirits. But it can also look any way you want it to.

Nor are these the only spirits, hauntings and instances of possession to be found here: Nell is haunted by dreamed-up Arabs from the Orientalist visions so thoroughly deconstructed by Edward W. Said; haunted by words, languages and names from various periods and geographies. Kali is haunted by Anthropology, which he later uses for his own ends, for Anthropology, as is her wont, gladly submits to any authority. All of our not-entirely-genuine Africans are haunted by the colonial figures and institutions, as in the Hauka movement. Nell, the whitest of all colonial girls, is ultimately possessed by Erzulie Dantor, a Haitian voodoo deity worshipped in many guises, including that of the Black Madonna from white Polish Częstochowa. Bodies are haunted by signs and languages; colors are haunted by colors; the senses are haunted by concepts; the truth is haunted by fiction; microbes are haunted by other microbes; ecosystems are possessed by plants; Europe is haunted by Africa; Africa is haunted by Europe; Poland, which in the nineteenth century didn't exist either but was colonized by three foreign powers, is haunted by England; England is haunted by Poland, with her dreams of Empire; the stage is haunted by ghosts; documentary photographs of the atrocities perpetrated in Congo during the reign of King Leopold II are haunted by Felice Beato's war photography—the first ever visual reports from Sudan in the age of the Mahdi and General Gordon, and all this is haunted by theater, which is an artificially arranged sensuality in real time. And nothing more. This world, which does not exist, is full of noises, sounds and music—played live, preferably—while the dynamic images you see are a kind of visual ethnography, a study of images through images. Actors, objects, ghosts, music, animals and images create an artificial human and non-human ecosystem. Anything can become anything else. Anybody can become an Invasive Alien Species.

All this has been written in the mode of documentary surrealism: we have added fiction to fact and documentarized fiction, so if you see anything that, for some reason, you'd like to exorcize from your fantasy about our text, don't look away but *awry*, and bear in mind that fantasy, like collective memory, can only be cleansed by calling up its phantoms and letting yourself be possessed by the ghosts you're trying to suppress.

# IN DESERT AND WILDERNESS
## After Sienkiewicz and Others

### SCENE 1. THE NEWSPAPER OFFICE

EUROPE. I say, old chap, you're interested in Africa, aren't you?

The question was so unexpected that, at first, I was quite taken aback. So this was why my boss had me drop the article I was writing? This was why he'd summoned me to his office first thing in the morning?

AFRICA. Describe, in detail, naked breasts (young, old, conservative, recently raped, big, small) or mutilated genitals. Or any kind of genitals. And dead bodies. Or, better, naked dead bodies.

EUROPE. Of course I'm interested in Africa. Everybody's interested in Africa nowadays.

That's exactly it!—the Editor said with a smile—Nowadays, Africa is on the agenda, as they say. New countries are being born: in a word, business is booming. The eyes of the world are on Africa, and readers want reportage from Africa.

AFRICA. African characters should be colorful and exotic—but empty inside, with no dialogue, no conflicts or resolutions.

EUROPE. That's why we're sending you to Egypt to write a reportage. You'll check if the pyramids are still there and whether the Nile still flows from the south to the north. On top of that, you'll see other things worth seeing, get to know the land, the people and their customs, and make a dozen or so good reportages out of it.

AFRICA. Animals, on the other hand, must be treated as well rounded, complex characters. Elephants are caring, and are good feminists or dignified patriarchs. So are gorillas.

EUROPE. Hearing this, I felt as hot as if I were already in Africa. Egypt! The Sahara! Bedouins! Camels! Maybe even elephants! Lions!

AFRICA. Never, ever say anything negative about an elephant or a gorilla. Always take the side of the elephant.

**EUROPE.** I left the newspaper office in a state of happy excitement. In my mind's eye, I saw endless sands scorched by the sun. The stifling simoom swept across my face.

**AFRICA.** In your text, treat Africa as if it were one country. It is hot and dusty with rolling grasslands and huge herds of animals and tall, thin people who are starving. Or it is hot and steamy with very short people who eat primates.

**EUROPE.** Can you guess, dear readers, how I began my preparations? You probably think I procured a pith helmet? A Belgian rifle for hunting big game? Wrong, my dears. First of all, I went to a bookstore and bought Henryk Sienkiewicz's *In Desert and Wilderness*.

IMAGE 7.2 **Europe (Agnieszka Kwietniewska) and Africa (Ewelina Żak)**
Directed by Bartosz Frąckowiak. Teatr Dramatyczny im. Jerzego Szaniawskiego, Wałbrzych (2011)
*Photograph by Bartłomiej Sowa*

**AFRICA.** Your African characters may include naked warriors, loyal servants, diviners and seers. Or corrupt politicians, polygamous travel guides and prostitutes you have slept with.

**EUROPE.** A long, long time ago I, too, was a young boy. Just like you, I went to school, and just like you, I adored adventure novels. Staś Tarkowski and Nell Rawlison were my first guides through Africa. With them, I roamed the deserts and wilderness of Sudan. I shivered in the grip of the fever, and almost died of thirst.

**AFRICA.** The biggest taboo in writing about Africa is to describe or show dead or suffering white people. White people don't die in Africa.

**EUROPE.** Experiences like that can never be forgotten, me hearties. And now that I was really going to Africa, I felt nostalgic for the first African book I ever read, and wanted to pay off my debt to its young heroes somehow.

**AFRICA.** Among your characters you must always include the Starving African, who wanders the refugee camp nearly naked, and waits for the benevolence of the West. Also be sure to include a warm and motherly woman who has a rolling laugh and who is concerned for your well-being. Just call her Mama.

**EUROPE.** So began my journey in the footsteps of Staś and Nell.

## SCENE 2. NELL TRIES TO FIND A PLACE IN GEOGRAPHY (DISCURSIVE GHOUL)

**NELL.** Nell opened the geography
She turned to the flyleaf
and read what she had written there:
Nell Rawlison
N-E-L-L
R-A-W-L-I-S-O-N
Miss Nell Rawlison
Port Said

The Province of Port Said
Egypt
Africa
The World
The Universe
Nell says the words
Hello
I am
Nell Rawlison
I am eight years old
I live in Africa
Walking my days
Under African skies
Dear little children
Don't you ever go down
To Africa
To Africa
Into the deep dark wood
"Nell," Staś Tarkowski said to his little English friend,
"Nell, can you list our journeys?"
And little Nell, resembling a beautiful picture, raised her greenish
eyes to Staś
"I can
From Fayum to Khartoum—that's one
from Khartoum to Fashoda—that's two
from Fashoda to the ravine where we found King—that's three
and from Linde's Peak to the lake—that's four."
Staś said
"We'll be fine here
And this village will be named after you, Nell."
"Then I shall be in the geographies."
"You will. You will."
Nell
Nell
Was passionate about maps

Mappa
Mon papa
There was a picture of the Earth
on the first page of her geography:
a big ball
in the middle of clouds
North South
East West
At that time,
there were many blank spaces
on the Earth
a large shining map,
marked with all the colors of a rainbow.
Brr
Nell looks at the map
Fashoda
Rhodesia
Dahomey
Leopoldville
Stanleyville
Basuto
The Belgian Congo
It had got filled
since Nell's childhood with rivers and lakes and names.
Names and names.
Brr
Fashoda—Kodok
Rhodesia—Zambia
Dahomey—Benin
Kinshasa
Kisangani
Lesotho
Zaire
Congo Congo Congo

AFRICA. The Nubians, and the Sudanese, and the Somalis, and the Ashanti, and the dervishes, and the Beninois, and the Guanches, and the Tasmanians, and the Basques, and the Roma . . .

EUROPE. Staś lived with all on intimate terms.

*A visualization for teaching foreign languages appears. Words in Arabic, Swahili, English and Polish. There is also a pictogram from a primer illustrating words with the gestures, behaviors or situations typical for the culture of a given language. Staś repeats not just the words but also the bodily movements. Forcing language into the flesh.*

STAŚ. ةيوخأ

UDUGU

BROTHERHOOD

BRATERSTWO

EUROPE. Having, as is usual with Poles, an extraordinary aptitude for languages he became, he himself not knowing how and when, acquainted with many of their dialects.

STAŚ. ةيفسلفلا ريونتلا ةكرح ,ةفاقث ,ريونت .أ

KUTAALAMIKA

ENLIGHTENMENT

OŚWIECENIE

AFRICA. Born in Egypt, he spoke Arabian like an Arab.

STAŚ. ةمشاغلا

BRUTE

BRUTE

BYDLĘ

AFRICA. From the natives of Zanzibar, many of whom worked as firemen on the steam dredges, he learned Kiswahili, a language widely prevalent all over Central Africa.

STAŚ. ةلآ

MASHINE

MACHINE

MASZYNA

AFRICA. He could even converse with the Negroes of the Dinka and Shilluk tribes, residing on the Nile below Fashoda.

EUROPE. Besides this, he spoke fluently English, French and also Polish, for his father, an ardent patriot, was greatly concerned that his son should know the language of his forefathers. Staś in reality regarded this language as the most beautiful in the world and taught it, not without some success, to little Nell . . .

STAŚ. Staś, not Stes.

NELL. Stes.

Small tears began to glisten in the eyes of the girl.

STAŚ. Staś, not Stes.

Forgive me, Nell, my little friend.

You are only eight years old.

NELL. I want to be like you. Do you hear me? I want to be like you.

STAŚ. I can be a hero. Fourteen years old. Grave age and experience. Especially since I have Polish and French blood. I should like to perform heroic deeds in your defense.

NELL. And what if a great, big, putrid frog crawled under my blouse, how would you save me then, Staś?

*Staś answers each of Nell's questions by showing what he would do to save her.*

NELL. And what if all the rivers dried up, and we would be sweltering in the sun like dead rattlesnakes in the desert: where would you get a beverage for me?

*Staś's reply.*

And what if I were thirsty: could you fill your mouth up with water from your whole body to stop me being thirsty?

*Staś's reply.*

And if I was as tiny as a malaria plasmodium and lived in a mosquito's body, would you find me there, Staś, and take me in your arms? Could I live inside your body? I'd get in through your skin and live inside you, Staś. Staś, tell me, Staś.

*Staś's reply.*

What if a rhinoceros were to take me on his minaret-sized horn and pierced my tummy like a rotten fig and carried me off into the arid savannah?

*Staś's reply.*

What if a dirty old Arab were to shove a gag in my mouth and abduct me to his filthy harem? And then slit my throat?

*Staś's reply.*

What if right were left, and up were down, and the desert were life, and the past were the future, and black were white, and white were black, and Allah were Jesus, and I were you, and your mother were my mother, and your Poland were my England, and your language were my language, could you find yourself in all of that, Staś?

*Staś's reply.*

And what if it turned out that our daddies weren't our daddies, and that they're really wearing white masks?

*Staś's reply.*

And what if
Rhodesia were Zambia
Dahomey were Benin
And Zaire were—Congo Congo Congo

**AFRICA.** Unspeakable rites. Poor little girl. Unspeakable, unconscious, unnecessary, uncanny, unusual, untidy . . .

## SCENE 4. INVASIVE ALIEN SPECIES

**EUROPE.** Names and names!
On January 8, 1897
A part of Africa whose northern limit was settled by the Anglo-French treaty of 1891, and whose eastern boundary was determined by the Anglo-German treaty of 1893, was given the name Nigeria.

AFRICA. An area on the map, a country of swamps and forests, inhabited by pagan natives of low type who had not risen above the cannibal stage, was given a name by Flora Shaw, of the *Times*.

EUROPE. Dame Flora Shaw represented a singular species
A species of the group
Invasive Aliens
Invasive Alien Species
Aliens from Planet Earth
Dame Flora Shaw
And other specimens of invasive flora
Brought with them
The dreams of men, the seed of commonwealths, the germs of empires.

*Eichhornia crassipes*, the water hyacinth. According to one story, a Belgian colonialist imported the first seedlings to prettify a waterway near his remote colonial outpost; another account blames an American Baptist missionary who was attracted by its delicate pastel flowers. It grew and grew and grew, spreading a deadly mat suffocating the life out of ponds, lakes and slow-moving rivers, and upsetting entire ecosystems.

AFRICA. *Chromolaena odorata*. An ornamental plant whose seeds were brought to Africa around 1940. Its luxuriant growth in the vicinity of crocodile-nesting sites leads to an imbalance in the reptiles' sex ratio. A drop in the crocodile population leads to proliferation of *Bartovia multiplanum*, a delicate bird whose nests the reptiles eat in their breeding season. In the summer, flocks of the birds hover above pastures. The beating of their wings causes cattle to stampede, occasioning serious damage to property. Further uncontrolled reproduction of this species could turn certain parts of Africa into depopulated regions inhabited only by birds.

EUROPE. *Parthenium hysterophorus*. Its seeds, brought over in bags of grain shipped in to relieve the famine in Ethiopia, have, since 1988, been waging an assault on the green lungs of Africa. In an attempt to curb the uncontrolled invasion of *Parthenium hysterophorus*, a species of moth that feeds on the plants was introduced into the environment. The plan suffered a setback when local ants started eating the moths' eggs.

**AFRICA.** *Acacia mearnsi*, a champion colonizer for the past 158 years. Brought to Africa in 1853, it drains the soil, poses a hazard to stream-banks, and spreads rapidly to the exclusion of all other species.

**EUROPE.** Africa has been colonized by alien flora.
Meanwhile
The flora of Africa no longer lives in Africa, the native
Flora of Africa has moved to the homelands of Dame Shaw
And of other invasive species.
The flora of Africa is proliferating in Europe
Flooding it, heedless of checkpoints and customs authorities,
It sprouts on the streets of Rome and Paris,
In the collections of Europe.

## SCENE 5. IMPERIAL FATHERS

**STAŚ.** Why has the Egyptian government annexed all the country lying south of Nubia?

**RAWLISON.** Whatever was done by the Egyptian government was done at the request of England which extended a protectorate over Egypt and in reality ruled her as Egypt herself desired. The Egyptian government did not deprive anybody of his liberty, but restored it to hundreds of thousands and perhaps to millions of people.

**AFRICA.** Hundreds of thousands and perhaps millions.

**RAWLISON.** In Kordofan, in Darfur and in the Sudan there were not during the past years any independent States. These lands, a land of blood and tears. Ivory and slave hunters. Negro-Arab, Arab-Negro tribes. Free tribes, incessant warfare. Now

England which, as you know, pursues slave-dealers all over the world, consented that the Egyptian Government should annex Kordofan, Darfur and the Sudan. England extends a protectorate.

**TARKOWSKI.** I, Tarkowski, an insurgent in the 1863 uprising,[1] wounded, captured, sentenced, sent to Siberia, cherish freedom above all other values!

**RAWLISON.** Sad niggers . . .

**EUROPE.** Unfortunate blacks . . .

**RAWLISON.** . . . liberated. The depredations ceased. People living under tolerable laws.

**RAWLISON.** Until Mohammed Ahmed, known today as the Mahdi, appeared among them and proclaimed a holy war on the pretext that the true faith of Mahomet was perishing, and all rushed like one man to arms. Jihad is the first duty of all Muslims. He stirred his listeners into a religious frenzy. He has occupied Kordofan, Darfur and the Sudan; his hordes at present are laying siege to Khartoum and are advancing to the north as far as the frontiers of Nubia.

**STAŚ.** Can they advance as far as Egypt?

**RAWLISON.** No. The Mahdi announces, indeed, that he will conquer the whole world, but he is a wild man who has no conception of anything. He never will take Egypt, as England would not permit it.

**STAŚ.** If, however, the Egyptian troops are completely routed?

**RAWLISON.** Then would appear the English armies, which no one has ever overcome.

**STAŚ.** And why did England permit the Mahdi to occupy so much territory?

**RAWLISON.** How do you know that she has permitted it? England is never in a hurry because she is eternal.

---

1 The January Uprising of 1863 was a Polish revolt against occupation by the Russian Empire.

**TARKOWSKI.** I suspect that England in her soul desired that the Mahdi should wrest

it from Egypt in order to retake it later from him and make this vast

region an English possession. I did not, however, share this suspicion

with Mr. Rawlinson as I did not want to offend his patriotic feelings.

**RAWLISON.** It's pure selfishness, Mister Tarkowski, what these Arabs are up to.

**TARKOWSKI.** I, a white man. Within a few years, I assumed the post of senior engineer of the Suez Canal. Going about the streets of Port Said, I quickly realized I was in the net of apartheid. I was white, therefore a colonialist, a pillager, an occupier. I subjugated Africa, conquered Sudan, put to the sword the entire tribe of the man just now standing before me, the tribe of his ancestors. I made him an orphan. Moreover, a humiliated and powerless orphan. Eternally hungry and sick. Yes, when he looks at me, this is exactly what he must be thinking: the white man, the one who took everything from me, who beat my grandfather on his back, who raped my mother. Here he is before you, take a good look! Being white, I was guilty. I wasn't able to feel guilty. To show remorse. I, a white man. Apologize. You were colonized? We, Poles, were also! For one hundred and thirty years we were the colony of three foreign powers. White ones, too. These barefoot, hungry and illiterate boys had a moral advantage over me. The advantage of being victims. They were of a black race, but a pure one. I, a white man. I stood among them weak, with nothing more to say. I, a white man.

**AFRICA.** "The Shadow of the Sun." Ryszard Kapuściński. A critical reading.

**EUROPE.** The moon illumined their very dark faces, and in its luster they looked as if cast of bronze.

The whites of their eyes glittered greenishly from under the turbans.

**TARKOWSKI.** Rawlison, be a man! Our children have been kidnapped. We need to save them.

**EUROPE.** To put the thing in terms a Pole could understand: Staś and Nell were taken captive and driven into the desert, towards the Mahdi. To put the thing in terms familiar to the English: Staś and Nell were made part of the circulation of colonial goods. The Arab led the children across the sands so that the prophet could exchange them for his relatives, namely Fatma and her offspring. The honorable Fatma said: The children of these infidels are good children, but if I am not allowed to leave, there is no other way. The honorable Fatma said: my husband, Smain, is fighting for the prophet, and that is why the Egyptian government is holding me captive in Port Said. The honorable Fatma said: As of today, these children belong to Smain.

## SCENE 6. THE DESERT

**ARAB.** The hour was five in the afternoon. The weather was splendid. The sun had already passed on that side of the Nile and declined over the desert, sinking into the golden and purple twilight glowing on the western side of the sky. The world lost the traits of reality and appeared to be one play of supernal lights.

**STAŚ.** An illumination like that must cost a lot of money.

**NELL.** Exciting, amazing, very very well.

**EUROPE.** The desert makes a reliable setting for all kinds of stories.

**NELL.** Exciting, amazing, very very well.

**EUROPE.** These are probably the first tourists to come here since the last African war.

**NELL.** We're not tourists, we're travelers.

**STAŚ.** I really should look at the photos.

**ARAB.** In the meantime the camels swept like a hurricane over the sands glistening in the moonlight. A deep night fell. The distant desert hills were enveloped with silvery vapors like muslin.

**NELL.** How exotic!

How lovely is this nest woven on a camel's hump!

**ARAB.** Quail's eggs could not crack in those housings!

**STAŚ.** If one is to exaggerate, then exaggerate after the Arabian fashion. I ought to look at the photos that are to be developed.

**ARAB.** Yalla, yalla, mister, yalla!
Proverbs: A hidden well makes the desert beautiful.

The desert makes a man face himself: it flushes the mind and squeezes out the essence.

**STAŚ.** Speaking of essence:
Nell, would you like some tea?
Tea in the Sahara?

**EUROPE.** Tea in the Sahara, a truly Victorian adventure.

**STAŚ.** I ought to look at the photos that are to be developed, so I can realize I am in something resembling Africa.

**NELL.** An all-inclusive desert holiday.

**EUROPE.** In the darkness above the Sahara, the stars shine with such unreal intensity.

**STAŚ.** That they almost seem to be a stage decoration.

**ARAB.** Sing, oh desert sands, sing!
When Majnun did learn of Layla's doom,
he rent his clothes and rushed to her tomb.
A child he met there, bold and brave.
It laughed when asked 'bout Layla's grave,
and said: Majnun, if you loved true
you'd know precisely what to do.
Now go and search the desert lands,
scoop and smell the shifting sands,

IMAGE 7.3 **Nell (Marta Nieradkiewicz) and the Arab (Marcin Pempuś)**
Directed by Bartosz Frąckowiak. Teatr Dramatyczny im. Jerzego Szaniawskiego, Wałbrzych (2011)
*Photograph by Bartłomiej Sowa*

and if you smell the scent of love,
her grave will be there, sure enough.

STAŚ. If you have to lie, do it as only in the East they know how to lie.

ARAB. Bismillah!
Masallah!

Two bright little gloves in the sand. Yours, little viper? Are you marking the road?

NELL. He struck her with a courbash, a terrible Arabian whip, which cuts even the hide of a camel. Nell, though she was wrapped in a thick plaid, shrieked from pain and fright.

STAŚ. Your head is like an empty gourd. If you have kidnapped us for money, then know that the father of this little "bint" is richer than all the Sudanese put together. You know that the white people of Europe always keep their word.

ARAB. But can all their money open for us the gates of paradise which only

the blessing of the Mahdi can do?

Howsoever much the people in the East are greedy and venal, nevertheless when a true Mohammedan views any matter from the standpoint of faith, there are not any treasures in the world with which he can be tempted.

STAŚ. Sand and sky—the desert is contained in these two words but they do not contain its soul. It is hard to define. After some time, one senses perfectly well that there is a third thing between the sands and the sky, something that represents the essence.

NELL. Satan. There is no tea here.

STAŚ. A stupefying deadness; a horror I could barely have conceived. Furrowed sand; the sky above it glazes over like a dead man's eyes behind which which no soul stirs.

NELL. It's not exotic, it's empty. Words become as sand. Hearts become as sand.

STAŚ. Hence the oppressiveness, hence the anxiety, hence the fear. Here man is only sheltered by the sky. Reach out, pierce the fine fabric. There is nothing beyond it, not even stars. Beneath the shelter of the empty sky, I could even kill.

The Arabs are asleep, Nell is asleep, but I am not asleep . . . and I have to save her. His gaze fell upon the leather case containing the short rifle and the cartridge boxes. To kill men! No, no, he was incapable of that. What if, slipping out with the weapon and hiding among the rocks, he should kill not the men but shoot the camels?

NELL. It would be too bad and a sad ending for the innocent animals; that is true, but what was to be done? Why, people kill animals not only to save life but for broth and roast meat.

**SABA.** Now I wanna be your dog
Now I wanna be your dog
And now I'm ready to feel your hand
And lose my heart on the burning sands

**NELL.** Ah, Saba! What have you done!

**SABA.** The giant mastiff now began to turn his head to the right and to the left, his fangs striking against one another like nails of steel. It was a clear thing that whoever approached Nell at that moment would have the fangs of the infuriated mastiff sunk at once in his throat. Saba is no longer a gentleman-dog. Saba has become a dog of war. He too has discovered something savage within himself.

**ARAB.** Yalla! God himself has sent us this dog. Ah, if it were not for this dog! He would have shot us like wild geese for food.

**STAŚ.** Beneath the shelter of the empty sky, I could even kill. The desert trembles and shimmers. Look, Nell! Groups of slender palms and pepper trees, plantations of mandarins, white houses, a small mosque with projecting minaret! Look, Nell! Medinet!

**NELL.** Brr. Names and names.
You can never be sure with names.
Fashoda will be Kodok
Rhodesia will be Zambia
Dahomey will be Benin

**STAŚ.** Truly—Perhaps that is Kharga.

**NELL.** Tanganyika and Zanzibar
Added together make Tan-zania
Liberia was Libya
And Libya Lebanon
The map fascinated Nell

As a snake would a bird—
a silly little bird.

Poor little bird
Poor Nell sets off on a journey
Aboard the Nellie

IMAGE 7.4 **Staś (Wojciech Niemczyk) and Nell (Marta Nieradkiewicz)**
Directed by Bartosz Frąckowiak. Teatr Dramatyczny im. Jerzego Szaniawskiego, Wałbrzych (2011)
*Photograph by Bartłomiej Sowa*

---

STAŚ. That is Medinet perhaps—I recognize the minaret and even see the windmills above the American wells resembling great white stars—

That is Medinet!

NELL. Kinshasa was Leopoldville
Kisangani is Stanleyville
Lesotho can be Basutoland
Zaire is Congo Congo Congo
in the geography:
the Earth
spins
like a big ball
in the middle of clouds

STAŚ. Have we returned to Fayum? Is this Gharak-el-Sultani? Is this El-Wasta? Is this Assuan? Is this Wadi-Halfa?

NELL. Nell catches words
That have fallen off the map
Nell knows that she is in geography
But
She no longer remembers
Where

STAŚ. A mirage! It's all a mirage!
Beneath your compassion, we take refuge, O Mother of God.
Beneath your compassion

AFRICA. Voices rang out in the desert:
Khartoum! Gordon! Gordon! Khartoum!
Khartoum is taken! Gordon is killed! The Mahdi is victorious!

## SCENE 7. THE STATUE OF GENERAL GORDON

STAŚ. Khartoum!

SABA. Khar, Khar, Khartoum!

EUROPE. A brief history of the city for the benefit of guidebooks: Khartoum was founded and Khartoum was destroyed.

STAŚ. And then rebuilt. Like Poland after the national uprisings.

ARAB. Eat dates, master, eat. Dates are good, sweet, nutritious . . .

NELL. Khartoum happens to be called Khartoum. The word Khartoum means an elephant's trunk. But there are no elephants here. Instead, the people roar like wild animals. We are walking through the crowd. Nell be afraid.

EUROPE. The city sprawls on the bank of the Nile.

NELL. Many rotting corpses.

ARAB. Eat dates, mistress, eat. Dates are good, sweet, nutritious. There are many nutritious stories in Sudan.

STAŚ. Traces of the battle can everywhere be seen along the ramparts; on the inside protruded the ruins of razed buildings.

**EUROPE.** Between the houses, I see a statue of a rider on a camel. The statue of General Gordon.

**STAŚ.** Khartoum, Gordon! Gordon, Khartoum! Khartoum is taken. Gordon is killed.

**EUROPE.** The monument is very beautiful. A proud rider mounted on a richly bedecked dromedary.

**STAŚ.** A human head fastened on a high bamboo set up in the center of the marketplace. Gordon's head.

**EUROPE.** A statue of the general still stands in the center of Khartoum.

**STAŚ.** The head of the general is standing in Omdurman.

**IDRIS.** Look, mister, look, this is your last chance! It will be gone a month from now, they wrote about it in the papers. There are no foreign governors in Sudan; we don't need statues of them. But there are many interesting stories in Sudan.

**STAŚ.** Strange are the ways of the world, General. Thus had perished that hero, that knight without fear and without reproach who was loved even in the Sudan.

**EUROPE.** Strange are the ways of the world, General. I come to Khartoum and learn that the descendants of Idris and Gebhr, and Kali and Mea want to tear down your statue. This contradiction needs to be resolved, General.

**SABA.** Rule, Britannia, rule the waves, Britons never will be slaves! General Gordon was a hero and a great man.

**NELL.** Hello, hello! Where are we? Where in geography are we?

**IDRIS.** Verily I was to be a guide around the city, but I get lost in it myself. Perhaps I could offer you a ride in my taxi through the shifting sands of the desert instead.

**EUROPE.** I am not concerned with your city. I am concerned with Polish literature.

**NELL.** You are concerned with an elephant's trunk. History is a nightmare from which Nell is trying to wake. History has given Nell the fever. History has always truncated us. Everybody's always taking me to tusk. All they give me to eat are dates.

**SABA.** Oh, we're leaving Khartoum

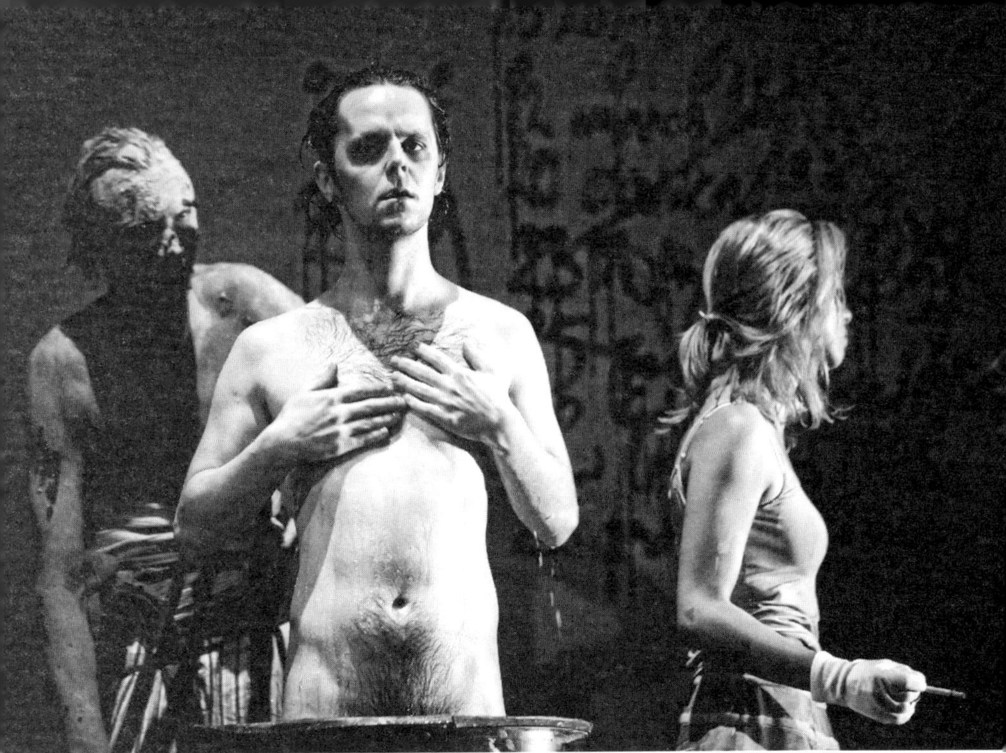

IMAGE 7.5 **Kali (Andrzej Kłak), Saba (Piotr Wawer), Nell (Marta Nieradkiewicz), and Staś (Wojciech Niemczyk)**

Directed by Bartosz Frąckowiak. Teatr Dramatyczny im. Jerzego Szaniawskiego, Wałbrzych (2011)

*Photograph by Bartłomiej Sowa*

By the light of the moon
We're sailing by night and by day
Oh, we can't stand the heat
We've got nothing to eat
We've thrown all our rations away!

NELL. Hello, hello! Where are we? Where in geography are we?

EUROPE. All I know is that it took place in January 1885. Our little friends, Staś and Nell, were still far away from Khartoum, somewhere in the vicinity of Assuan. I know this much from your Polish geographical novel.

**IDRIS.** All of oppressed Sudan rose up at the Prophet's prophetic voice and drew to the fort of Khartoum to capture and destroy the last bastion held by those foreign wasps, the colonizers. Some dates perhaps? Or would you rather take a ride through the shifting sands?

**SABA.** With myriad voices, Sudan howled for the head of Gordon-pasha.

**STAŚ.** Oh, knight without reproach!

**NELL.** I'm so hungry I could eat a roach!

**SABA.** General Gordon was a hero and a great man!

**IDRIS.** General Gordon was a professional queller of national uprisings.

**STAŚ.** I'm feeling a bit lost right now.

**EUROPE.** National uprisings in the countries of Asia and Africa.

**STAŚ.** Uprisings, huh? I feel the narrative splitting up and stratifying.

**NELL.** I feel hunger in my tummy and innards. Whose geography are we in now?

**SABA.** Khar, khar, Khartoum! This is taking place in January 1885. Gordon knows that khar, khar, Khartoum has to fall. London is late in sending the expedition corps. The invincible hero has one final weapon left—his own death. Gordon resolves to die in khar-Khartoum. England, my land of hope and glory, will defeat the insurgents and take control of Sudan to avenge Gordon's death!

**STAŚ.** His own death! Oh, that's the way we like to resolve things in Poland!

**IDRIS.** Who are you rooting for anyway?

**SABA.** Are you for England or Sudan?

**NELL.** I'm for someone feeding me right now.

**EUROPE.** I don't think I'm for Polish literature anymore. Imagine this book translated into Sudanese. Would Idris have liked Staś and Nell?

**SABA.** Great Gordon dies. And all the glory goes to that kitsch, kitsch, Kitchener. General Horatio Kitchener, with his epic army and epic mustache subjugates Sudan. In a great battle outside Omdurman, Kitchener routs the Mahdists.

**IDRIS.** Kitchener put up Gordon's statue to humble us. And my father's father had to help build that statue, mister. Perhaps you'd care to buy some of my dates now? Sweet, nutritious dates.

**NELL.** Hello, hello! Where are we? Where in geography are we? In whose geography? Because we seem to have ended up in a museum.

**EUROPE.** The house of Khalifa Abdallahi, the last leader of the Mahdiyyah. It was the most curious museum I have ever visited. A step away from the site where the battle was waged sixty years previously, it contained souvenirs of the greatest battle in the history of colonialism.

**STAŚ.** The greatest battle was at Grunwald.

**EUROPE.** Relics of the battle of Omdurman. The weapons of Mahdist fighters: primitive spears and ancient rifles bound with wire. On the opposite wall, heavy Maxim machine guns, state of the art for their time, first used by Kitchener's British troops at Omdurman.

**STAŚ.** There is something about this exotic African museum that makes me think of the Warsaw Rising.

**NELL.** Yeah!

**SABA.** Take up the white man's burden
Send forth the best ye breed.

We come equipped with a divine power, said General Horatio Kitchener. The art of killing at a distance!

**STAŚ.** Gunships!
Maxim machine guns!
Repeating rifles!
Dum-dum bullets!

**IDRIS.** You've gotten it all mixed up again, sir.

**SABA.** They advanced in regular order, it was enough to know how far away they were. Their white banners tossing and collapsing.

Collapsing. Collapsing. Collapsing. The infantrymen fired steadily and stolidly. They were stricken down before they could see their enemy. They were unaware how fast a speeding bullet flies! Soon the battle turned into a slaughter. There were fifteen thousand dead dervishes left on the battlefield, and . . . twenty-seven English casualties.

NELL. Hello, hello! Where in geography are we?

IDRIS. These are the houses of the Mahdi. He prefers to live in the wooden sheds of Omdurman rather than in Khartoum, though there he could occupy Gordon's palace!

NELL. Omdurman is actually called Omdurman.

IDRIS. I spoke with the Mahdi about you, and the prophet desires to see you.

Oh! Messenger of God! Oh! Victorious! Oh! Merciful! Oh! Gracious!

STAŚ. He was a middle-aged man, prodigiously obese as though bloated, and almost black. I saw before me a chubby-faced gourd, resembling drawings of a full moon.

SCOUTS. Sodomite transvestite!

Transvestite sodomite!

*Africa temporarily steps into the role of the Mahdi.*

MAHDI. God metes out punishments to those who disobey the commands of the Mahdi, and hide booty, get intoxicated upon merissa, spare the enemy in battles, and smoke tobacco. Temporal life is like a leaky leather bottle. Only faith is like a cow which gives sweet milk.

IDRIS. We want to die for the faith! To paradise through death!

MAHDI. Whoever does not acknowledge me as the Redeemer, is condemned to damnation. The end of the world is already near. Therefore I, the Redeemer and servant of God, bless this holy war and you warriors.

STAŚ. I will not kneel.

NELL. Why, but why? There is one God!

MAHDI. I beheld you in the desert. That was a terrible journey but I sent an angel to guard and shield you from death at the hands of the infidels. Are you delighted that you came to me?

STAŚ. No, prophet. We have been abducted in spite of our wills from our parents.

MAHDI. But you are at the fountain of truth. Do you want to drink at that fountain? Do you desire to accept my doctrines?

STAŚ. Prophet, your doctrines I do not know; therefore if I accepted them, I would do it out of fear like a coward and a base man.

Are you anxious that your faith should be professed by cowards and base people? I am a Christian like my father . . .

SCOUTS. Blood, blood! The true blood of the victors at Khoczim and Vienna!

MAHDI. Whoever closes his eyes to the voice of God, is only fuel for the flames. These children were abducted for Smain; so, though I do not want to enter into any negotiations with the infidels, it is necessary to send them to Smain. Such is my will.

EUROPE. And thus did Staś join the ranks of Poland's constant princes. A group of infidels closed in, driving him and the still-hungry Nell on a tortured pilgrimage leading to Smain, who roved within the wild jungle, plying his slaver's trade. Darkest Africa lay open before the children.

## SCENE 8. THE SLAVE MARKET

EUROPE. An expedition to Southern Sudan is a fairly complicated undertaking. You must think that I am hacking my way through the jungle on foot, tracking words, lions and elephants, swatting tsetse flies, and spending the night in Negro tuklas. Meanwhile, I'm sitting here on a hotel terrace, sipping this blasted lemon-squash soda, and have no money left to go to the Black South. Maybe I can find a Black from the South in Khartoum? And interview him? From then on, I wandered all over the city on the look-out for Blacks—just like the Khartoum slave-traders of old. And finally I found a suitable candidate to interview.

Got him!

**STAŚ.** Stanisław Tarkowski.

**KALI.** Kali, sir.

**STAŚ.** What is your nation called?

**KALI.** The Wahima, sir.

**STAŚ.** Is it a big nation?

**KALI.** A great nation, sir, which makes war on the vile Samburu and raids their cattle, sir.

**STAŚ.** Where is your village?

**KALI.** Far, far away, sir. Kali know not where, sir.

**STAŚ.** In a country like this?

**KALI.** No, sir. There be great water and mountains there, sir.

**STAŚ.** What do you call that water?

**KALI.** We call it Dark Water, sir.

**STAŚ.** Who is your father?

**KALI.** King of the Wahima, sir.

**STAŚ.** Would you like to see your father?

**KALI.** Kali want see mother, sir.

**STAŚ.** How many people are there in your family?

**KALI.** It's complicated, sir. Kali need to draw it for you, sir.

*Kali draws a complex diagram, like something out of Claude Lévi-Strauss.*

**KALI.** This cause complicated family drama, sir.

**STAŚ.** At what age do you become sexually active?

**KALI.** What does it mean to be active sexually? All things are one. All things be active. We be walking around naked and have constant need to get it on, sir.

**STAŚ.** What kind of taboos are there in your culture?

KALI. You ask question differently. I can't know what a taboo is. I be savage slave, uncivilized, almost animal. I not know taboo. Ask what is forbidden, and I will tell you.

STAŚ. What prohibitions are there in your culture?

KALI. Our culture be ancient. We be having animist deities, animal-shaped, you know. I will now show you a magic dance. Because we also be having developed magical system.

*Kali dances a made-up magic dance.*

STAŚ. They howled, and leaped, and spun, and made horrid faces; but what thrilled you was just the thought of their humanity—like mine.

(*To Kali*) But what does that have to do with prohibitions?

KALI. It be age-old sex magic. It be cruel. In it, we be freeing ourselves from bonds of kinship. Freeing from prohibitions. And then we be able to do anything. But first, we be having to make human sacrifice. White man best for sacrifice.

STAŚ. How do you choose the sacrifice?

KALI. Kali not know that. Big Wahima witch-doctor know. Kali only perform ritual. Kali be a lustful Negro. With big bulging penis in sheath. An embroidered sheath. With magic signs of tribe. Kali know what be signs. But Kali not lust after white woman without permission. Kali devote his black sensuality to the hard toil of civilization. Kali's ancestors build railway in Sudan. Kali have fine tribal myth related to railway in Sudan. But Kali cannot tell it. Kali sing it.

*Kali sings the railway myth, just the way you expected.*

STAŚ. I looked at the Negroes as you would on any human being, with a curiosity of their impulses, motives, capacities, weaknesses.

(*To Kali*) This myth sounds cheerful. You are a joyful people. How come you practice human sacrifice?

KALI. You be unhappy with Kali's story? Kali know other tribal stories. Kali from very open-minded, pacifist tribe. But we be still in 19th century, so Kali be cruel, proud, want to get it on, be animal, meat, brute. Kali wait see what his white massa tell him. Kali not yet strong enough for emancipation.

**AFRICA.** Kali, you be brute in twentieth century as well. Why you talk so stupid in the nineteenth century?

**KALI.** I not be stupid. Because I not be here on my own behalf. I be representing Black Africa. I be millions of black men. That's why I meet the expectations of white man.

**AFRICA.** What for?

**KALI.** I be hungry. And hunger make too weak for emancipation. But I knows how to be "black skin, white mask," too. I knows that hungry be sentimental stereotype. I be multipurpose specimen of species. I show how to be black skin, white mask?

**STAŚ.** Go on, show me, already!

**EUROPE.** Got him! I was trembling with emotion.
He reads!
Everything he did seemed extraordinary.
What does he eat?
Sugarcane.
Well, what do you know!

**KALI.** Kali now be from another tribe. You American, I betcha?

**STAŚ.** No, I'm from Poland.

**KALI.** Ah, Poland. I know! Many black students study in Poland. I've heard of it. Polska! Warszawa!

**STAŚ.** You're from the Dinka tribe, right?

**KALI.** Yes. I am a Dinka. How did you know?

**STAŚ.** I could tell by your legs. Poles like Dinkas.

**EUROPE.** Mea, the amiable young Negress, belonged to the Dinka tribe.

*The scouts buy Mea at a slave market.*

**OBERSCOUTMASTER.** Assignment: buy and name Mea.

**SCOUT 1.** Mea!

**KALI.** Mea. I don't know that name.

**STAŚ.** I am interested in the Black South. It's an extraordinary country.

**KALI.** Why extraordinary? Nothing extraordinary there.

**STAŚ.** Nothing extraordinary? What about the lions?

**KALI.** We have lions. They eat calves.

**STAŚ.** And elephants?

**KALI.** They trample our fields.

**SCOUT 2.** Ebony.

**AFRICA.** Ethiopian slaves were regarded as superior to all the rest for the beauty, warmth and constancy of their females to their masters.

**STAŚ.** So your brothers still live in their native village? Tell me something about their life.

**KALI.** What is there to tell? The ordinary life of the Dinka. They graze their cattle in the day, and light fires at night to keep the tsetse flies away from it. Cattle means everything to the Dinka. Dinka buy their wives for cattle. They get strength and courage from drinking cow's milk mixed with cow's blood.

**OBERSCOUTMASTER.** Tar!

**AFRICA.** Ethiopian men made the best house servants and clerks. The prices ranged from fifteen thalers for a boy to twenty-five for a girl.

**KALI.** His favorite occupation is polishing cows' horns for years on end, to give them the most elaborate shapes. The more curious-shaped horns a cow has, the greater esteem its owner enjoys.

**SCOUT 2.** Melanoma!

**KALI.** Dinka also hunt fish. Sailing up the Blue Nile, one sees, every few meters, a Dinka fisherman poised on one leg with a spear in his hand patiently waiting for a fish to swim past.

**STAŚ.** Why on one leg?

**KALI.** So less moisture gets into the body. Wading birds do the same.

**OBERSCOUTMASTER.** Black mamba.

**AFRICA.** Many of the traders hired out girls as prostitutes.

**STAŚ.** And you're saying that all these are ordinary things?

**KALI.** Yes, I find something else to be extraordinary.

**STAŚ.** What?

**KALI.** That a Dinka is a minister in the Sudanese government, that Dinkas are deputies and senators, that a school has been built in our village, that I can study at the university.

**SCOUT 2.** Black Madonna.

**AFRICA.** It was customary for all traders to sleep with the women they had bought, and very few of them reached the coast as virgins.

**SCOUT 1.** Soot!

**SCOUT 2.** Hard coal!

**SCOUT 3.** Asphalt!

**KALI.** Can I go back to the Wahima people now? Please. I'm choking in this buttoned-up collar.

Now Kali can be loving great master and moon-daughter. And be free.

**OBERSCOUTMASTER.** Black pudding!

**EUROPE.** For me, the thing that prevents black women from being truly exciting is the fact that they are too naked all of the time, so having sex with them does not introduce what might be called the social aspect into the game. Having sex with a white woman means breaking through a great deal of conventions—undressing is both a struggle with matter and a sort of ritual, a social activity. Thus, from a certain point of view, black women are not 'women.'

## SCENE 9. STAŚ'S PRIVATE DIARY

**STAŚ.** The private travel diary of Stanisław Tarkowski. February 13, 1885.

We have traveled nearly 286 miles across the desert already. Small desert foxes, black and yellow scorpions, hyenas and jackals—such were the only creatures we encountered along the way. I have the impression that our world has not yet been conceived. Civilization has simply still not emerged.

*The Scouts slip Nell index cards with distychs. The girl automatically starts reading them out loud.*

NELL. The dark mug,
Of an Islamic thug.

STAŚ. April 17, 1885

Africa, finally. A hundred-and-twenty degrees in the shade, slave convoys, cannibal feasts, discarded hollow skulls. A land that has engulfed everything, a land of lost things. A place where everything corrodes. I have long been haunted by the phantom of a pauper dying of hunger. His accursed figure looms between me and the sun. It is in his shadow that I traverse the continent.

NELL. The Arab eye doth gape
Like a filthy rotting ape

AFRICA. Is this a racist scene?

STAŚ. June 31, 1885
The exoticism is waning.
I am defending the custom of carrying an umbrella.
I ought to look at the photos that are to be developed, so I can realize I am in something resembling Africa.

NELL. The entire world is rotting
From this fiendish Arab plotting

STAŚ. I should like to be a Catholic missionary adapting religious dogma to the needs of syncreticism, and teaching that Jesus Christ is the founder of the *pégou* ritual, and the Virgin Mary is the "mother of masks."

NELL. This Arab's cruising
For a bruising

AFRICA. I asked: Is this a racist scene!?

STAŚ. We penetrated deeper and deeper into the heart of darkness. It was very quiet there. We were traveling in the night of first ages, of those ages that are gone, leaving hardly a sign—and no memories. In that vindictive silence I faced a chance to be free again. A lion lay on a fair-sized rock.

**ARAB.** Allah! Bismillah! Mashallah!
What is to be done?
Allah! Perhaps he will step aside.
No he will not.
Untie Kali, the lion will kill him, and we will escape on the horses.
Make it so!

IMAGE 7.6 **Africa (Ewelina Żak) and Nell (Marta Nieradkiewicz)**
Directed by Bartosz Frąckowiak. Teatr Dramatyczny im. Jerzego Szaniawskiego, Wałbrzych (2011)
*Photograph by Bartłomiej Sowa*

**STAŚ.** Give me a rifle. I will kill the lion!

**ARAB.** Give him a rifle! He will kill the lion!

**STAŚ.** A bullet between the eyes, or it will be all over with me! In the name of the Father and of the Son.

In the twinkling of an eye, the bead of the rifle was in a direct line with the forehead of the animal.

The lion toppled over.
I took in the Arabs with my gaze.

These are mere villains, executioners, murderers, and Nell is in their hands.

**OBERSCOUTMASTER.** Murderous bullet-time.
Such is the world of Islam.

**SCOUT.** Three folds on a jellabiya. Where is the heart?

**SABA.** Where is the heart? The heart, Stanisław.

**OBERSCOUTMASTER.** Your father fought for freedom
Have dignity
An insurgent from 1863
Be brave

*One of the Scouts temporarily steps into the role of the Ghost of Staś's Father*

**GHOST OF STAŚ'S FATHER** (*dressed as an insurgent in the 1863 Uprising*). Listen, Staś! It is not allowable for any one to be lavish with death, but if anybody menaces your fatherland or puts in jeopardy the life of your mother, sister or the life of a woman entrusted to your care, shoot him in the head and ask no questions. Do not reproach yourself on that account.

**STAŚ.** Come, Holy Ghost

**SABA.** Hypnotic concentration
Nell, her throat slit with Gebhr's knife.

**OBERSCOUTMASTER.** You are bearing
The White Man's Burden.

**SCOUT.** Raise high the barrel of your English Martini-Henry rifle.

**OBERSCOUTMASTER.** Exterminate all the brutes.

SABA. Go savage!

OBERSCOUTMASTER. Men are born to kill.

SCOUT. A drop of blood on a white keffiyeh

OBERSCOUTMASTER. Another shot.

SCOUT. Another shot.
A drop of blood on the burning sand

THE GHOST OF STAŚ' FATHER. Another shot.
A drop of blood on the lips.

NELL. These Arabs are clamoring
For a hammering

OBERSCOUTMASTER. It's a terrible thing to be a European: disliked yet respected, isolated in semi-divine exaltation, yet mocked whenever one attempts to fraternize with the natives.

AFRICA. That was a racist scene after all.

EUROPE. Free, free at last, liberated! The bullet pieced the Arab's brain. Staś accomplished the feat, Staś did not waver, did not flee, did not let his finger slip from the trigger, vivat Stanislaus, rex Poloniae! Staś and Nell's Legion is thrusting into Africa, using Kali and Mea to clear the way. Before them looms a mighty baobab, a hollowed-out tree. The Legion decides to establish a settlement. They will whitewash the tree's bark, and Nell can start sending invitations for five o'clock teas!

## SCENE 10. THE MICROCOLONY KRAKOW BAOBAB: OR, WE DEMAND COLONIES FOR POLAND

NELL/ALL. Behind us, Victoria's sun-kissed lake—
Our ship sails into the ocean's expanse.
The white-and-red flag of Poland waves
with pride above these foreign lands.

To these dark lands the Polish barge
Bearing Civilization calls

'Mong emeralds and crocodiles
The lion of the Piasts[2] shall roar.

An eagle soared over the bush—
Its blood baptized the savage throng.
The jungle drums began to play
And carried to their kings this song.

The Black Madonna's son shall sit
enthroned among the verdant palms
Warmed by the equatorial sun
Listening to Swahili psalms.

Coffee, cocoa, rubber, gold—
The black man awaits with precious gifts.
New schools and factories rise — behold,
as Africa's golden age begins.

The desert parts for a new Wawel's[3] birth—
Victory songs ring through jungle trees.
Africa, we swear we'd first
see you drown in blood before we'd leave.

Fair Africa, bountiful but coarse,
As our colony, you will thrive,
And from your lands, we will bring forth
the Polish empire, come alive.

OBERSCOUTMASTER. A purposeful and planned colonial policy must sooner or later lead to obtaining colonies irrespective of the material and moral advantages any colonial policy brings to nations with the courage to nurture colonial aspirations.

---

2 The Piasts were the first Polish dynasty, and ruled from the tenth to the fourteenth century.

3 Wawel is the royal castle in Kraków, the historical capital of Poland until 1596.

I.

**OBERSCOUTMASTER.** Colonial action, code name KRAKOW BAOBAB.

**SCOUTS.** We demand colonies for Poland! We demand the revival of the Polish Commonwealth in the heart of the Dark Continent!

**SCOUT 1.** We want coffee, copper, cocoa and carcasses. A black People's Republic. A Republic of Polish Africa. Hey, hey, RPA!

**OBERSCOUTMASTER.** We demand new living space!

**EUROPE.** The Polish nation is calling for colonies. The streets are full of propaganda slogans, and every resident of Warsaw, looking at maps of the world, wonders which Uganda or Liberia to annex first. Meanwhile, in the Dark Continent, work is well underway. The first Polish microcolonies are being established. We can watch live, in real time, as territory is being taken for the glory of the fatherland.

**SCOUTS.** Glory!

I am the Negress Dina, Dina from a distant land, mark that Dina is different from me and you and him, she has dark skin, curly hair and a black, bleak existence!

II.

**OBERSCOUTMASTER.** Archeological excavation Baobab Krakow.

**SCOUT 2.** Hurry, faster, before it's snatched away from us!

**SCOUT 1.** Snatched by whom? Snatch what? Snatched by the Jew? Snatched by the German? It won't be snatched by them.

**SCOUT 2.** Snatched by the German, who surely will snatch what can be snatched. Snatched by the Belgian, snatched by the Frenchman, snatched by the Englishman . . .

**OBERSCOUTMASTER.** Glory!

**SCOUTS.** Glory to the White Eagle of Africa!

**EUROPE.** Equipped with a compass, dreams, maps and dreams of empire.

*The Scouts present their archeological finds.*

SCOUT 1. The barometer of the steamship Dar Pomorze, sunk by the Hottentots.

SCOUT 2. Łukasiewicz's oil lamp, invented by a Polish inventor, outshines even the light of the sun.

SCOUT 3. Cocoa is cocoa is cocoa is cocoa is cocoa is cocoa
A Polish saber Polish saber Polish saber

SCOUT 1. The genetic code of a Polish saint in the black land.

III.

OBERSCOUTMASTER. African netherworlds: their extermination.

STAŚ. What are you looking at?

KALI. Kali be scared of Mzimu.

STAŚ. What is this Mzimu?

KALI. Evil spirit.

STAŚ. Have you ever seen a Mzimu?

KALI. No, but Kali has heard the horrible noise which Mzimu makes in the huts of fetish-men. Negroes bring them bananas, honey, pombe-beer, eggs and meat in order to propitiate the Mzimu. Aka! Mzimu! Aka! Aka! Aka!

SCOUT 1. In the name of Jesus Christ, the Satanic rule of Mzimu must come to end!

SCOUT 2. Aka! Aka! Enough of this primeval mumbling.

OBERSCOUTMASTER. Kill all the ancestors, wipe all African netherworlds from beneath the face of the earth.

SCOUT 2. *Per signum crucis de inimicis nostris libera nos, Deus noster. Amen.*

SCOUT 1. *Gloria Patri, et Filio, et Spiritui Sancto. Sicut erat in principio, et nunc, et semper, et in saecula saeculorum.*
*Amen.*

AFRICA. This Africa a hard case: even the dead have to be killed.

STAŚ. Your Mzimu has been killed. Have no fear!

**KALI.** Oh, great master! Great! Master not be scared even of Mzimu?

**STAŚ.** Aka! Aka!

IV.

**OBERSCOUTMASTER.** Convert the desert into fecund fields and gardens, breed new varieties of useful plants and animals, discover a mine where none suspected its presence. The Krakow Baobab plantation.

**SCOUT 1.** *Parthenium hysterophorus*.

**SCOUT 2.** *Acacia mearnsii*.

**SCOUT 3.** *Chromolaena odorata*.

**OBERSCOUTMASTER.** Our forefathers told us that the Polish mind contains, and every now and then manifests a dream of imperial existence. Perhaps now is the time to discuss whether we want to be an empire or not. And if we don't, what do we want to be?

**EUROPE.** Jarosław Marek Rymkiewicz?[4]

**OBERSCOUTMASTER.** Now we are giving the reply with our deeds. This is our reply. This is the fruit of our labors!

**SCOUTS.** Our reply, our reply, our reply . . .

**SCOUT 2.** Colonies are ever a convenient vehicle wherewith to channel excess energy and provide our youth with a vent for its vitality. Baden-Powell, for instance, said—

**SCOUT 1.** In the event of tribal unrest or colonial skirmishes, the National Democrats would have the opportunity to muster several hundred bruisers and send them to Warsaw armed with sticks and knuckledusters.

**EUROPE.** Polish radio was broadcasting the rustling of palm fronds and the roar of savage beasts.

---

4 Jarosław Marek Rymkiewicz is a contemporary Polish writer of strong national convictions.

**KALI.** Gnu, gnu! Plenty meat, bwana kubwa, meat sleep there.

**EUROPE.** An African safari? Is it time already?

**STAŚ.** My only thought was to supply the caravan with meat. I shot at the nearest animal. It fell.

**KALI.** Master, there are rhinos. Do I track them?

**STAŚ.** Track them. On the third day fortune at length rewarded our perseverance. I looked carefully through the brushwood, when I saw a rhino standing forty paces away, with its head raised as if sniffing danger. I aimed quickly at its ear and fired.

**EUROPE.** It is indeed difficult to imagine anything less in accord with aesthetic form, or bulkier and less shapely than a rhinoceros; and this character makes it seem the relic of a past epoch of creation, and thus gives it the distinction of a peculiar and splendid sporting trophy.

**STAŚ.** Meanwhile, something under the tree moved. I fired without knowing at what part of the body of the creature I aimed. I fired a second time; silence followed, broken only by the squealing of the little rhino left at the tree by its mother. The poor little thing squealed piteously indeed, pushed close up to my feet and nosed my hand, not being yet capable of distinguishing objects. When we advanced a couple of steps it began to follow, pushing with its ill-formed head the man in advance, as if mistaking him for its mother .

**KALI.** There were also elephants.

**EUROPE.** Cut. Ineffably sad things are happening here. Meanwhile Kali was possessed by such joy that he began to leap, slapping his knees with his palms and laughing as if insane, in addition rolling his eyes and displaying his whites.

**STAŚ.** Do you know, Nell at times it seems to me that I am a knight-errant.

**NELL.** And what is a knight-errant?

**STAŚ.** Long, long ago in the medieval days there were knights who rode over the world, looking for adventure. They fought with giants and dragons, and do you know that each one had his lady, whom he protected and defended?

**NELL.** And am I such a lady?

**STAŚ.** No, you are too small. All those others were grown up.

**NELL.** And you once said in the desert that I acted like a person of thirteen?

**STAŚ.** Well, that was once. But you are eight.

**NELL.** Then after ten years I shall be eighteen.

**STAŚ.** A great thing! And I shall be twenty-four! At such age a man does not think of any ladies for he has something else to do; that is self-evident!

**NELL.** And what will you do?

**STAŚ.** I shall be an engineer or a sailor or, if there is a war in Poland, I shall go to fight, just as my father did.

**EUROPE.** Worn out by the exemplary civilizational campaign, the young residents of the baobab made themselves at home and politely sat down to have some tea, which they were fortunate to find in the whitewashed soil. How tidy and homey everything is! This is Krakow, and the zeriba nearby is—Wadowice?[5] The polite conversation is interrupted, alas, by the rattle of Nell's little teeth against the brim of the teacup, and Mea whooping outside the thorn fence. Mea has not yet mastered the Queen's English, alas, and Nell, alas, has not developed immunity against African microbes.

---

5 Wadowice is the town where Pope John Paul II was born.

IMAGE 7.7 **Mea (Irena Wójcik) and Nell (Marta Nieradkiewicz)**
Directed by Bartosz Frąckowiak. Teatr Dramatyczny im. Jerzego Szaniawskiego, Wałbrzych (2011)
*Photograph by Bartłomiej Sowa*

## SCENE 11. MY DYING BRIDE

**STAŚ.** Mea, speak please. Mea want to speak, Mea have her say. Go on, speak!

**AFRICA.** But we've already had a racist scene.

**STAŚ.** Mea hasn't had any lines yet. Mea just jangles her bracelets. Mea stays silent. Mea keeps adjusting the pieces of ivory sticking from her ears, so as not to doze off. Mea could be having words, though.

**EUROPE.** So this is going to be a gender-focused scene.

**STAŚ.** It is a man's thing to be away, and a woman's thing to wait faithfully. I am moving away from this scene. I'm in too many scenes as it is: I am moving away towards action. Smoke is rising above the jungle, I am moving away towards the quinine. Now Mea will prattle, now Nell will prattle.

**MEA.** Mea love the little lady—and beads also.

**NELL.** Nell is a woman
Women are like children
Children are like Negroes
Women are like Negroes
Stes, Nell is the nigger of the world
Paint me black paint me black paint me black Mea paint me

**MEA.** One night at supper Nell, having raised a piece of smoked meat to her lips, suddenly pushed it away, as if with loathing.

**NELL.** I cannot eat.

**MEA.** Staś, who had smoked out the bees daily in order to get their honey, was certain that the little one had eaten during the day too much honey, and for that reason he did not pay any attention to her lack of appetite. But she after a while rose and began to walk hurriedly about the campfire describing an ever larger circle guided by a sense of guilt.

**NELL.** Nell is a doll
Nell's legs are made of rubber
They won't take her far away from Africa.

**MEA.** When the little maid continued to run around, more and more hurriedly, Staś followed her and asked: "Say, little moth! Why are you flying like that about the fire?" He was uneasy and his uneasiness increased.

**NELL.** I am sick. Forgive me, forgive me. Call the doctor, quick, quick, quick. I've had it up to here with Africa.

**MEA.** Then he placed his palm upon her forehead which was dry and icy. So he took her in his arms and carried her to the campfire. She begged him to permit her to rise and run about; then again she asked whether he was not angry at her because she was sick. That evening, or that night, the dog was somehow strangely disturbed and bayed continually.

**NELL.** Do you love me?
May I kindly ask you
To be loved by you?
I am your opus
I am your valuable
The pure gold baby
Staś!
Why are the Arabs walking around the tree and looking in on me?
They're walking around and looking in. Hello, where are we, where in geography are we?

**MEA.** We're in Krakow, Staś said, but only now in the daylight could be seen what havoc that one night's fever had wrought in her. Her complexion was yellow and transparent; her lips were black; there were circles furrowed under her eyes, and her face was as though it had aged. We're in Krakow, and I'm going off into the jungle to get some quinine.

**NELL.** Nell rubs her nose against Staś' arm. Nell is fawning like a kitten
I'll bite your ear, my parakeet
Like I bit Staś's ear so sweet
If I get a parakeet, I'll call it Daisy
Parakeets are like daisies
Kiss my toes and drive me crazy

**MEA.** "Nell," writes Staś Tarkowski to his friend, the little English girl, Nell, "Nell don't be frightened."

**NELL.** Do you know, there are certain toucans which during the breeding season seek hollows in trees; there the female lays eggs and sits upon them, while the male pastes the opening with clay so that only her head is visible, and not until the young are hatched does the male begin to peck with his long beak and free the mother.

And what does she eat during that time?
The male feeds her
And does he permit her to sleep?
Nell be scared Nell be scared.

**MEA.** Staś sends a letter from the jungle. Staś expresses the hope that Nell hasn't grown too much in his absence. Staś writes: I have declared that you would always be little Nell to me, because I came to love you when you were very little and I do not want to change that.

**NELL.** It's kind of scary
Mommy
That is: Daddy
Nell has the shivers, and she should die
Nell has a fever
And her own
Impressions of Africa
Nell looks out the baobab's window in a state of self-hypnosis
And suddenly she was walking under African skies

Truly amazing wonders were within reach. A large sponge sat immobile on a protruding ledge. The phosphorescent effluvia, passing through the animal's body, revealed in the middle of its quasi-diaphanous tissue a veritable miniature human heart attached to a complex circulatory system. Nearby, a gelatinous block quivered and, as a sign of distress, raised a tentacle like an elephant's trunk divided at its extremity into three divergent branches. Nell is collecting African specimens, Nell feeds them with her own blood, and hears their plaintive cries.

**MEA.** Nell prattled half an hour longer and fell into a slumber. Mea prattled using sentences that were not her own and went off to make tea for the little *bibi*.

## SCENE 12. THE HEART OF DARKNESS

**STAŚ.** With little Miss Rawlinson I have escaped from dervish captivity and we are hiding in the jungle. But Nell is terribly sick; and for her sake I beg for help.

**LINDE.** A white boy! I again see a white one! I welcome you whoever you are.

Did you speak of some sick girl? What do you want of me?

STAŚ. Nell has suffered from two attacks of fever. She will die if she does not get quinine.

LINDE. In the nighttime the fever is worse and my mind becomes confused. Are there two of you above me? No! I know that you are alone and that this is only the fever. Oh, this Africa! My father amassed a great fortune in the silk trade. I devoted myself to the geography of Africa. Many geographical societies enrolled me among their members. I began this last journey in Zanzibar. There was a war between the kings of Uganda and Unyoro. I rendered important services to the king of Uganda, who in exchange presented me with two hundred bodyguards. Huge blue flies settled on their ashen bodies.

STAŚ. And this camp?

LINDE. It is a camp of death.

STAŚ. And those Negroes?

LINDE. Those Negroes are sleeping and will not awaken anymore. They are suffering from the sleeping sickness. All fell prey to it, excepting those who previously died of smallpox.

STAŚ. Not a Negro stirred or even quivered. Huge blue flies settled on their ashen bodies. Are they asleep, never to wake again?

LINDE. This Africa is a charnel house. It is good even to gaze at a European face.
Method: packing sardines.

STAŚ. Outcome: Black shapes crouched, lay, sat between the trees, leaning against the trunks, clinging to the earth, in all the attitudes of pain, abandonment and despair.

LINDE. Huge blue flies settled on their ashen bodies.

STAŚ. Another mine on the cliff went off, followed by a slight shudder of the soil underfoot.

LINDE. The work was going on. The work!
Plan: luring butterflies.

STAŚ. Brought from all the recesses of the coast in all the legality of time contracts, lost in uncongenial surroundings, fed on unfamiliar food, they sickened, became inefficient and were then allowed to crawl away and rest.

**LINDE.** These moribund shapes were free as air—and nearly as thin.

**STAŚ.** I began to distinguish the gleam of eyes under the trees. Then, glancing down, I saw a face near my hand.

**LINDE.** Operation: collecting termites.

**STAŚ.** The black bones reclined at full length with one shoulder against the tree, and slowly the eyelids rose and the sunken eyes looked up at me, enormous and vacant, a kind of blind, white flicker in the depths of the orbs.

**LINDE.** System: splitting the stork.

**STAŚ.** Near the same tree two more bundles of acute angles sat with their legs drawn up. Huge blue flies settled on their ashen bodies. While I stood horror-struck, one of these creatures rose to his hands and knees, and went off on all fours towards the river to drink. He lapped out of his hand then sat up in the sunlight, crossing his shins in front of him, and after a time let his woolly head fall on his breastbone.

**LINDE.** Are there two of you above me? No! I know that you are alone and that this is only the fever. Oh, this Africa! My father amassed a great fortune in the silk trade. I devoted myself to the geography of Africa. Many geographical societies enrolled me among their members. I began this last journey in Zanzibar. There was a war between the kings of Uganda and Unyoro. I rendered important services to the king of Uganda, who in exchange for them presented me with two hundred bodyguards. Huge blue flies settled on their ashen bodies.

**STAŚ.** I am not trying to excuse or even explain—I am trying to account to myself for—for—Mr. Linde—for the shade of Mr. Linde.

**LINDE.** Most appropriately, the International Society for the Suppression of Savage Customs had entrusted me with the making of a report, for its future guidance.

**STAŚ.** But this must have been before his—let us say—nerves, went wrong, and caused him to preside at certain midnight dances ending with unspeakable rites, which—as far as I reluctantly gathered from what I heard at various times—were offered up to him.

LINDE. "We whites, from the point of development we had arrived at, must necessarily appear to them [savages] in the nature of supernatural beings—we approach them with the might as of a deity. By the simple exercise of our will we can exert a power that is practically unbounded."

STAŚ. There were no practical hints to interrupt the magic current of phrases,
unless a kind of note at the foot of the last page.

LINDE. "Exterminate all the brutes."

STAŚ. He looked like an animated image of death carved out of old ivory.

LINDE. Are there two of you above me? No! I know that you are alone and that this is only the fever. Among the blacks there are honest souls, though as a rule you cannot depend upon their gratitude; they are children who forget what happened the day before. All of them awake for a short time before their death and in their mental aberration fly to the jungle, from which they never more return. Huge blue flies settled on their ashen bodies.

STAŚ. It was my lot to remain faithful to the illusion I had chosen for myself.

LINDE. If in your country there are many boys like you, then they will not be able to manage you very easily.

STAŚ. Huge blue flies settled on their ashen bodies. Eyes, lips.

LINDE. I cannot doom them to be torn to pieces alive by hyenas. I cannot! I cannot! I cannot . . . I have a request to make of you, and if you can perform it, God may lead you out of this African gulf, and grant me an easy death. Take water in some utensil, stop before each one of those poor sleeping fellows, sprinkle water over him, and say these words: "I baptize thee, in the name of the Father, and of the Son, and of the Holy Ghost!"

**LINDE.** I desire to go together with even that remnant of my caravan upon the last great journey.

**EUROPE.** Staś wept like a beaver. As his tears fell, they filled vessels carried by a young Negro who was the only survivor of the natural disaster. Eventually quite a lot of liquid was collected, which the dying Linde still had the time to consecrate, and was from then on treated as holy water with which Staś baptized dying Negroes. Ever new Negroes would join Linde's caravan in the next world, making up a long line of otherworldly neophytes that stretched all the way to the horizon. Meanwhile, Nell consumed huge amounts of white quinine powder that destroyed the icky protozoa *Plasmodium vivax* and *Plasmodium falciparum* inside the little girl, so that the third bout of fever never came. Soon the young travelers were ready to hit the road again, and set off to meet the Wahima people.

## SCENE 13. STAŚ MOREAU

**NELL.** Though full of quinine, Nell still knew that astounding wonders were still within reach. She knew that beating in the bush nearby was another heart attached to a complex circulatory system.

**KALI.** Bwana kubwa! Bwana kubwa!

**STAŚ.** What is it?

**KALI.** An elephant!

**KING.** This colossus actually looked like a huge slate-colored rock walking on four feet. His fore legs were high but comparatively thin, which was undoubtedly due to the fast of many days.

**KALI.** There thundering water, here a rock. The elephant cannot get out. Great master kill the elephant and Kali will eat him. Oh, eat, eat! And at this thought he was possessed by such joy that he began to leap, slapping his knees with his palms and laughing as if insane, in addition rolling his eyes and displaying his white teeth.

**KING.** The elephant from time to time turned towards them his small, languid eyes and something in the nature of a gurgle escaped from his throat.

**STAŚ.** Indeed, it is best to cut short his pangs.

**KING.** The elephant is gurgling.

**NELL.** Staś! Don't do that! Staś, let us give him something to eat! I don't want it. I won't let him be killed! I shall get the fever if you kill him!

**KING.** The elephant is gurgling.

**STAŚ.** Pluck at once as many melons from the breadfruit trees, as many acacia pods, and as much of all kinds of weeds as you are able.

**KING.** And the elephant stretched out his trunk towards them as if he wanted to beg for more and emitted in a powerful tone: Hruumf!

**NELL.** He wants more!

**STAŚ.** I suppose he does. Bring melons from the breadfruit trees, as many acacia pods, and as much of all kinds of weeds, leaves and grasses.

**NELL.** The elephant drank so long that finally the little girl became alarmed. Staś, won't he harm himself?

**STAŚ.** I don't know, but since you have taken him under your care, warn him now.

**NELL.** Enough, dear elephant, enough!

**KING.** The elephant is gurgling. Hruumf! Hruumf! Hruumf! The dear elephant, as if he understood what was the matter, stopped drinking at once, and instead, began to splash water over himself. First he splashed water on his feet, then on his back, and afterwards on both sides.

**NELL.** Honestly, Staś, isn't he wise?

**STAŚ.** As Solomon, but what makes you think so?

**NELL.** Because when I asked him not to drink any more, he obeyed me at once.

STAŚ. If before that time he had not taken any lessons in English and nevertheless understands it, that really is miraculous.

KALI. Bwana kubwa! Great master kill elephant, and Kali eat him instead of gathering grass and twigs, breadfruit and acacia pods.

STAŚ. You are a donkey. Unfortunately he forgot the Kiswahili word for donkey and said it in English. Kali, not understanding English, evidently took it for some kind of compliment or praise for himself.

KALI. Kali be Kali donkey.

STAŚ. Kali is brute, and elephant is brute.

KALI. Kali is brute!

STAŚ. Kali is brute and this is brute King.

KING. Elephant is King.

STAŚ. Elephant be elephant, be brute.

KALI. Be brute!

KING. Brute bydlę.

STAŚ. Kali be donkey, brute, bydlę and shit.

KALI. Kali be shit!

KING. Elephant, brute, bydlę, be very shit.

KALI. Mea have black skin and black brain, and Kali be donkey.

STAŚ. These creatures are animals carven and wrought into new, human shapes.

AFRICA. But I still do not understand. Where is your justification for inflicting all this pain?

STAŚ. So long as visible or audible pain turns you sick; so long as your own pains drive you; so long as pain underlies your propositions about sin, so long, I tell you, you are an animal thinking a little less obscurely what an animal feels. Pain, pain, reign. Pain is the King.

KING. Pain is the King.

AFRICA. The elephant had changed. Most striking was the disproportion between its legs and the length of its body. It lacked that inward sinuous curve of the back which makes the human figure so graceful. Its shoulders were hunched clumsily, and its face was prognathous.

KING. Not to go on all-fours; that is the Law. Are we not Men?
Not to eat Fish or Flesh; that is the Law. Are we not Men?
Not to chase other Men; that is the Law. Are we not Men?

STAŚ. Staś made a mine for the purpose of blasting the rock that imprisoned the King. Elephants surpass immeasurably all other domesticated animals, and King, beyond comparison, surpassed Saba. After a few weeks, King discerned perfectly that the person whom it was most necessary to obey was Staś,

IMAGE 7.8 **Staś (Wojciech Niemczyk), Kali (Andrzej Kłak), and the Last Black Man (Marcin Pempuś)**

Directed by Bartosz Frąckowiak. Teatr Dramatyczny im. Jerzego Szaniawskiego, Wałbrzych (2011)

*Photograph by Bartłomiej Sowa*

and that the person about whom all cared the most was Nell. To Kali he paid less heed and Mea he slighted entirely.

**KING.** I am King, I serve Princess Nell.

## SCENE 14. AFRICAN SUPERMEN—STAŚ'S AFRICAN LEGIONS

**KALI.** Great master! That is a Negro village. Yambo, he! Yambo sana!

**STAŚ.** The sun illuminated their well-shaped forms, wide breasts and powerful arms, making them look like statues hewn of black marble or carved in ebony.

IMAGE 7.9 **Staś (Wojciech Niemczyk), Kali (Andrzej Kłak), and the Last Black Man (Marcin Pempuś)**
Directed by Bartosz Frąckowiak. Teatr Dramatyczny im. Jerzego Szaniawskiego, Wałbrzych (2011)
*Photograph by Bartłomiej Sowa*

**LAST BLACK MAN.** Oh Mother, what manner of creatures have come here, and what awaits us at their hand?

**AFRICA.** Is this nakedness natural? Does it arouse erotic feelings? Does it have a sex?

**KALI.** Let your king stand forth; let him tell his name and let him open his

ears and lips that he may hear better!

**LAST BLACK MAN.** M'Rua.

**KALI.** M'Rua, and you, M'Rua's men, you heard that to you speaks the son of the king of the Wahimas, whose cows cover as thickly the mountains around the Bassa-Narok as the ants cover the body of a slain giraffe. And what says Kali, the son of the king of Wahima? Lo, he announces to you the great and happy tidings that there comes to your village the Good Mzimu. Ohh!

**LAST BLACK MAN.** Yancing, yancing.

**KALI.** Look and rejoice! Lo, the Good Mzimu sits there in that white hut on the back of the great elephant and the great elephant obeys her as a slave obeys a master and like a child its mother!

**EUROPE.** They look just like Hector and Achilles from nineteenth-century illustrations to the Iliad.

**KALI.** Listen! Listen! The Good Mzimu is riding on an elephant in the direction in which the sun rises, beyond the mountains out of the waters; there the Good Mzimu will tell the Great Spirit to send you clouds, and those clouds during a drought will water with rain your millet, your manioc, your bananas, and the grass in the jungle, in order that you may have plenty to eat and that your cows shall have good fodder and shall give thick and fat milk. Do you want to have plenty of food and milk—oh, men?

**LAST BLACK MAN.** We do, we do.

**EUROPE.** Sparta in Africa!

**KALI.** And the Good Mzimu will tell the Great Spirit to send to you the wind, which will blow away from your village that sickness which changes the body into a honeycomb.

**LAST BLACK MAN.** He! Let him blow it away!

**KALI.** You have paid homage to the Good Mzimu; therefore rise, gaze and fill your eyes.

**STAŚ.** Are you not a Christian?

**KALI.** I am, oh, great master!

**STAŚ.** Listen, then! The Wahimas have black brains, but your brains ought to be white. And I am black, but O! my soul is white. You, as soon as you became their king, should enlighten them and teach them what you learned from me and from the bibi. They are like jackals and like hyenas—make men of them.

**KALI.** And I am black, but O! my soul is white.

**EUROPE.** Is that still Sienkiewicz? We're really beyond geography now.

**KALI.** Kali have white brain now!

**NELL.** And I am black, but O! my soul is white.

**KALI** (*pointing at the cross*). This is the sign of the Great Spirit! Accept it as your own.

**EUROPE** (*to Staś*). What are you doing, importing into Africa, for God's sake, this utterly alien, Gothic obsession with the ugliness and mortality of the human body? If you have to import Europe into Africa, is there not a better case for importing the Greeks? Renounce your gods. You can be like gods yourselves. Look at the Greeks.

**STAŚ.** And a thought flitted through my head whether it would not be well to return here sometime, conquer a great tract of country, civilize the Negroes, found in that locality a new Poland, or even start at the head of a drilled black host for the old. Negroes, until Mohammedanism fills their souls with cruelties and hatred against infidels, are rather timid and gentle. My children, my Greeks. Now I was to turn them into invincible legions that none could defeat. Legions that would, dry-shod, cross the sea, and stand at the gates of Poland and a warlike roar would issue from their black breasts, at the sound of which the bayonets of the nation's enemies would snap like twigs buffeted by the wind of change.

**NELL.** Stanisław Tarkowski's Legions. I named them after you.

**STAŚ.** Staś, from the King's back, kept order, issued commands—perhaps not so much because they were necessary, but because he was intoxicated by the role of a commander—and with pride viewed his little army. If I wanted to, I could remain the king of all the people of Doko, like Beniowsky in Madagascar.

## SCENE 15. THE MIRAGE

**AFRICA.** The earth was so flooded with light that everything appeared white, and not a sound, not even the buzz of insects, interrupted this deadly stillness surfeited with an ill-omened luster. The valiant legion, at the head of which Stanisław Tarkowski rode, proud as Alexander the Great, pressed on in air shimmering from the heat. Seen from an oblique perspective, it looked as if some unreal phantom giant were gliding above the desert. They were like Greeks going off into battle to make a name for themselves in some tragedy.

**NELL.** I'm like this dead rattlesnake in the desert, Staś.

**AFRICA.** Everything's burned to a crisp, Africa is turning into flammable paper. Paper can bear the ink no longer.

**EUROPE.** There will be no further adventures. The Warsaw Rising will fail yet again.

**NELL.** Fill your mouth up with water from your whole body to stop me being so thirsty.

**STAŚ.** Look, look, a whitewashed manor house on the horizon.

**OBERSCOUTMASTER.** A hospitable oasis of Polishness.

**NELL.** And parakeets, Daisy, with red-and-white feathers.

**SABA.** A veritable dog-heaven. I shall no longer be a bull-mastiff, but a sleek gray khar-khar-hound.

**HARCERZ.** A Polish-African brotherhood of nations.

**STAŚ.** The Ryszard Kapuściński Polish University of Liberia.

**OBERSCOUTMASTER.** The streets of Warsaw are full of black youth. White teeth flash flash flashing in the black crowd. The whites of their eyes flash flashing.

**NELL.** A Polish-African brotherhood of culture. And Nell's all grownup now. I can be your wife now, Staś. I have this frightful itch all over: it's as if a tsetse fly bit me here, right here, Staś.

**STAŚ.** Only 'neath this cross, only 'neath this sign will a black man be a Pole, so white and fine.

**LAST BLACK MAN.** Look: blue eyes. Look: blond hair dyed black. We are the lost white tribe.

**SCOUT 1.** What do you think about this landscape?

**SCOUT 2.** Short-term.

**SCOUT 1.** Meaning?

**SCOUT 2.** It's very beautiful for the first few days, but after a week it gets so lovely you simply can't stand it. They don't have Christmas trees here.

**SCOUT 1.** So how will we be spending this Christmas?

**SCOUT 2.** Reckon we'll have to put that there baobab in the living room.

**STAŚ.** The ecumenism of ancestors! We venerate our ancestors, and you venerate yours. We want a shared black-and-white Mass.

**CHOIR OF SCOUTS.** Dark as far as the eye can see,
What will be, what will be?

**OBERSCOUTMASTER.** Close the chapel door and shut in the night.
Here lies the casket; let us gather round.
Let there be neither lamp nor candlelight.
Cover the windows with heavy shrouds.
Not even the palest light of the moon
May come through the cracks of this darkened room.

**NELL.** As sometimes in dreams, so here I can observe myself, can note with pleasure how the full hem of my white skirt plays with the rhythms, can watch, as if in a mirror, how the smile begins with the softening of lips.

IMAGE 7.10 **Crowd scene**

Directed by Bartosz Frąckowiak. Teatr Dramatyczny im. Jerzego Szaniawskiego, Wałbrzych (2011)

*Photograph by Bartłomiej Sowa*

I realize, like a shaft of terror struck though me, that it is no longer myself whom I watch. Yet it is myself, for as that terror strikes, we two are made one again, joined by and upon the point of the left leg which is as if rooted to the earth.

Resting upon that leg I feel a strange numbness enter it from the earth itself and mount, within the very marrow of the bone. To be precise, I must say what, even to me, is pure recollection, but not otherwise conceivable: I must call it a white darkness, its whiteness a glory, and its darkness, terror.

ALL. *To the tune of a traditional Voodoo chant. The words of the Polish anthem interweave with a Creole song until the Creole supplants the Polish lyrics.*

Behind us, Victoria's sun-kissed lake—
Our ship sails into the ocean's expanse.
The white-and-red flag of Poland waves
with pride above these foreign lands.

To these dark lands the Polish barge
Bearing Civilization calls
'Mong emeralds and crocodiles
The lion of the Piasts shall roar.

An eagle soared over the bush—
Its blood baptized the savage throng.
The jungle drums began to play
And carried to their kings this song.

The Black Madonna's son shall sit
enthroned among the verdant palms
Warmed by the equatorial sun
Listening to Swahili psalms.

Coffee, cocoa, rubber, gold—
The black man awaits with precious gifts.
New schools and factories rise—behold,
as Africa's golden age begins.

The desert parts for a new Wawel's birth—
Victory songs ring through jungle trees.
Africa, we swear we'd first
see you drown in blood before we'd leave.

Coda:
Fair Africa, bountiful but coarse,
As our colony, you will thrive,
And from your lands, we will bring forth
the Polish empire, come alive.

*The End*

WOJTEK ZIEMILSKI

SMALL NARRATION

IMAGE 8.1 **Wojtek Ziemilski and, on the screen, Wojciech Dzieduszycki**

*Photograph by Krzysztof Bieliński*

**NOTE**

*Small Narration* is the text of a performance by Wojtek Ziemilski, which the author has been performing since 2010 in the form of a performative lecture extensively illustrated with video footage. Clips of performances by artists Ziemilski admires, such as Jérôme Bel or Xavier Le Roy, make up an autobiographical discourse on the author's inspirations, artistic choices and aspirations, while documentary material consisting of press clippings and archives sets the stage for the personal family drama that the piece addresses.

In *Small Narration*, Wojtek Ziemilski takes stock of his response to the disclosure, in 2006, that his grandfather, Count Wojciech Dzieduszycki—a well-known singer, actor, journalist, and writer for the cabaret—had been an informer collaborating with the communist secret police. Ziemilski's personal narration has become an important contribution to the political debate regarding the process of "lustration" that seeks to identify and hold accountable people who had collaborated with the Communist authorities. Additionally, on the level of theory, it is a meaningful attempt to join in the debate on the politics of remembrance and the status of archives.

# SMALL NARRATION

*Words in brackets or underlined appear on screen.*

[Small Narration]

[#471. It is so difficult to find the beginning. Or, better: It is difficult to begin at the beginning. And not try to go further back.]

You think: It started with the name.

[Wojciech]

You think: Wojciech is not a good name.

Michael is just Michael. Matthew is Matthew. Mark, Andrew, those are good names. Wojciech has no neutral form. He is either called Wojciech, and that sounds official and stiff, or Wojtek, and then you're a kid from the neighborhood. The name Wojciech is impossible to identify with.

You think: It began when you were 6 and you were sent to the US. For half a year you lived with a crazy aunt who decided that nobody would be able to pronounce the name Wojtek, so she switched it to your second name, Anthony. For six months you went to an American school, you spoke English, you thought in American, and your name was Tony.

[Tony]

When many years later you were living in Portugal and began doing theater, the problem with the name returned.

An artist called Wojciech would have a tough life in Portugal. They even pronounce Wojtek [Wojtek] like this [UOJ-TEK]

So you simplified.

Instead of this [Wojtek] the simplest spelling would be this [Voitek]. You allowed yourself one nostalgic addition. The result was this [Vvoitek].

This might look good in Portugal, but in Poland it's just a silly spelling. With a name spelled this way, it was clear you would not be in a rush to go back.

[#472. When a child learns language it learns at the same time what is to be investigated and what not. When it learns that there is a cupboard in the room, it isn't taught to doubt whether what it sees later on is still a cupboard or only a kind of stage set.]

It began with the last name. At some point of your childhood, someone suggested you should have a double name, both from your father and your mother's side. Wojciech Dzieduszycki-Ziemilski, the aristocratic sound of it feels nice. You would like to believe it was the Tony in you that refused to be manipulated. But probably it began with Father saying no.

It began with the blood-ring. When you were 13, grandmother convinced you to wear a family ring. You were very proud. Breaking off a bit of the stone aptly called "blood-stone" in Polish took you about a week. You lost it after three months.

It began with running away.

It began when you left to follow a girl. And when you were abroad, for the hundredth time you explained the dramatic history of your family during the war, yes, *that* war, because we in Poland say "the war" in reference to WW2.

It began while telling the story, when you realized you don't want this history. You don't want World War 2, or WW1, or Communism, or the fall of Communism, you don't want September 1, September 17, May 8, July 11, May 3, April 19, August 1, December 13, June 4. You don't want the Holocaust, you don't want the Ribentropp-Molotov treaty, you don't want Solidarność, you don't.

Neither the November uprising, or the January one, or any such thing as an uprising. You want to know nothing about how someone was rising up, someone else who you are not. A history you are not.

It started just about when Tony spoke up (by then he was called Vvoitek).

It began with the question, isn't each of us a self-made man?

Isn't each of us above all his o w n body? Doesn't he begin with it and end with it?

[#189. At some point one has to pass from explanation to mere description.]

It began when Claudia Dias [Claudia Days] stuck everyday objects with some tape to her body and used them to make a map, a guided tour of her world.

The critic wrote:

"The body of Claudia Dias is a body-object which is used as a framework, or a setting, in which she draws disenchantment—and re-enchantment—with life. It is a body which frees itself of the litter of urban life, to create an intimate map of emotions."

[*in the video*: Claudia Dias "It was at the Caparica Coast that for the first time I went to a hotel room with a boy. I was very young. So was he. And we had never been in such a situation. We felt very insecure. We went to a hotel called Sea and Sun. The receptionist looked at us disapprovingly. This made us laugh. We entered the room. I remember I felt very strange. Everything here was impersonal. The windows had heavy, green curtains. It was a bottle green. Everything smelled of dust. I remember my first gesture was opening the curtains, to open the space up a little."]

It began, when French choreographer Jerome Bel [Jeremy Beautiful] decided he wanted to get down to his own self. That if dance is the body on stage, that is where one should start.

The critic wrote:

"The absence of utopia allows the dancers to discover their specific qualities. Their bodies are not shown to provoke repulsion or empathy, but are put on stage as an essential part of their 'owners' identities. It is all the more powerful since they avoid any superficial theatricality."

[*video*]

It began when you were watching a performance by the French choreographer Xavier Le Roy [Xavier The King] called "Self Unfinished". Le Roy considers that the thing we are is not a unity, although seemingly it is one body.

The critic wrote:

". . . the loss of identity becomes the topic of discussion. Le Roy investigates the point where 'Owning' a body and 'Being' a body cross.

How can we show the loss of control? The body stops being the medium, to become a dismembered thing which keeps changing depending on the point of view. The body of Xavier Le Roy seems to have a middle, but no head. Which is of course an illusion: it is the head that moves that creature, on the stage or in the mind."

[*video*]

It all began in Autumn of 2006.

[*scans of articles:*

The popular actor and singer collaborated with the Communist Secret Police for 20 years.

IMAGE 8.2 **Wojtek Ziemilski**
*Photograph by Krzysztof Bieliński*

I do not know today if I hurt someone, or whom to ask for forgiveness.

The letter is disproportionate in relation to the scale of the collaboration. Nearly everyone was shocked by the information.

In a special letter read during the closed session of the City Council, the popular Tunio asked for forgiveness for his contacts with the communist secret services.

The Count wrote: I was recently reminded of embarrassing and painful events from my past.

In 1949 I was made to sign a paper making me a collaborator of the secret police.

I would like to believe my deeds made no serious evil to anyone, but I may be wrong.

Coincidence is excluded from the case.]

[#504. Whether I know something depends on whether the evidence backs me up or contradicts me. For to say one knows one has a pain means nothing.]

It all began when the phone rang, and Mom said it seems it's true after all, at least that Grandfather wrote things.

You were in Lisbon, sitting on the roof of a building with a friend, you were drinking, but not porto, or even normal wine, only the fairly bad Portuguese Sagres beer. It was the evening and very chilly, as winter was approaching, but the lights, there were so many tiny lights, and you were probably talking about life, or about how awful it is that the Portuguese only say bad things about themselves.

And that's when everything began.

Pedro asked what's happening, and you told him you had just learned that your grandfather was an agent of the communists. Although a week earlier Pedro had sung Happy Birthday to the melody of L'Internationale, he nodded his head.

And it all began by you saying, you know, when he signed the papers, it was the peak of Stalinism. And he was accused of sabotage. And many people were executed for sabotage then. And he was an enemy of the people because he was an aristocrat. And an engineer, and a mill director. And an opera singer. And a critic. And that's why. And because of the war, and the concentration camp. Three concentration camps. Because of being used to compromises. Because of his father who worked on the farm—although he was an aristocrat. Because of what it was like before. Because of the war. Because of Communism. Because of the stupidity of someone who left the concentration camp a few years before and believed he can get away with all this. Because of the stupidity of someone who left the concentration camp a few years before and believed he can't get away with all this. And it's impossible that he wanted evil things. It's impossible because he helped, even later, he hid illegal pamphlets, he protected dissidents, because there was opposition, illegal opposition, it wasn't always that bad, later it wasn't that bad, and later he didn't stop either, or maybe he did stop, hard to say, because what was a report, who has ever seen a report, was a report always a bad thing. Now we can say so if we are stubborn ambitious historians, but people back then, they were people living in this world, they were, I'm sorry to be boring you, but this is important, it wasn't like what you think, they were all, they all were part of the system, they made films and theater and music and they even got money for paintbrushes, it depends when, because it was the Poland they had, you know, it wasn't like Salazar who didn't allow anything, it was, it's difficult to explain, you know, history, man, history, man.

It began with the search for a title.

[Tunio: a reading about contemporary performance art. And history.]

[Tunio: a read attempt of coming to terms]

[On Certainty. An attempt at reading.]

[The Beginning. An attempt at reading about myself.]

[Tunio and Me]

[WOJTUNIO. Trying to read.]

[Tunio. A small written narration about someone else.]

[Tunio. A lecture about smaller narrations.]

[Smaller than narration]

[Smaller narrations]

[Small narration]

It began with the article by the Institute of National Memory: "A Life in Hiding. The agent-collaboration of Wojciech Dzieduszycki with the secret services of Communist Poland between 1949 and 1972."

It began with an actual Institute which was in charge of the memory of a nation. With the affirmation that a nation has a memory, that it is this memory. With assuming that that memory is working inside of every memory.

[#589. For how does a man learn to recognize his own state of knowing something?]

It began with the cases.

The cases from the Institute's article, the only available source of history.

Case No. 1

Dzieduszycki reported: "After the show by the Soviet Theater, journalist Tadeusz Lutogniewski from the 'Worker's Gazette', Mieczysława Urbańska from the District Culture Department and Mrs. Olszewska from the ZSCh were returning by tram to the Krzyki part of Wrocław. Lutogniewski was criticizing the show severely, saying it was as naive as a children's play, that it seems the Soviet artists have no idea of the high level of Polish theater art."

Possible defense:

Tadeusz Lutogniewski was a Communist. Tadeusz Lutogniewski was someone who was commonly known to have been sent by the Communist Party executives to destroy the "Odra" magazine.

Case No. 2

In his reports for the Secret Police, he did not even miss accidentally overheard conversations in the train. The precision of the informant is here astonishing. He wrote: "Going by sleeping couch from Warsaw to Wrocław on 03.18.53, at 10.37 PM I overheard a conversation between two passengers." The conversation concerned management problems in a construction company in the town of Tychy. "Unfortunately I couldn't get the passenger's name. He got off in Opole."

Possible defense:

Sense of humor. It's about sense of humor. The meaningless precision of the report gives a completely abstract image of anonymous people talking in a train. It is rather the proof of trying to fill the ever-thirsty Secret Police with meaningless reports. It is possibly the most useless report in history.

Case No. 3

In April 1963, the Secret Police received very extensive descriptions of people working in the arts, including quantities of gossip concerning their intimate lives. The Secret Informant gave his own often quite far-reaching opinions: Radio and TV—"Dir. Aleksander Mokrzyszewski. I know him little. From what I hear, a reasonable man. Hanek—the director of the music department—a very small personality. Lesław Bajer—TV—He never had anything to do with theater, radio or cinema and, without a doubt, putting him in charge of the TV station was a very risky step, which was confirmed by the embarrassment of his first programs."

Possible defense:

You don't know

Case No. 4

Possible defense: You don't know.

Case No. 5

Possible defense: You didn't check.

It began with the possibility of defense.

It began with the lack of access to the archives. It began with the refusal of access, first to the family, then to journalists, and to historians. It began with the memory being national, and so not yours. It began with an impossible defense.

It began when you made a show called "Small Narration." A show where, almost at the very beginning, you stopped reading, you got up, and, every single time, you pointed at spectators randomly, asking: What do you know? What did you learn? Where did you get to? Is it enough for you to know yourself?

It began with a show where you got mad, genuinely mad, at your own impotence. Where you told the gathered bunch of people that we are here together, we are a group, we can do something, since our views are not so different, we can go and force them to open up history. We can rewrite it, retrieve it, regain it. We can change history just as any reader does. We can learn who we are, who our grandfathers are.

But of course, not yours, you told them in this show, not yours, because it was my grandfather who w r o t e, and that is a lot, that is too much, that forces me to ask questions you do not need to ask. To get fucking furious, that's what you told them, to get fucking furious at being enclosed in non-history.

It began with you having a grandfather. And no history fitted him. But a lack of history did not fit him either.

While it fitted you just fine. You felt great watching "Spiderman 3" with a Coke and popcorn. His simple fight with his own self, his Jekyll and Hyde, his portrait of Dorian Gray, all of this so spectacular.

But it all begins with the discovery that nothing is <u>spectacular</u> here. All that is important appears as non-cinematographic, it does not explode, it does not shine, but happens modestly, what a pity, the things that happen dissolve in triviality.

You are impressed with the young historians from the Institute of National Memory. How do they manage to make it all seem so colorful? Is it through misrepresentation or ignorance?

But isn't it true that all of us, starting with Tunio, don't stop until we see a colorful version of history crystallize in our minds?

[#126. My doubts form a system.]

[#127. For how do I know that someone is in doubt? How do I know that he uses the words "I doubt it" as I do?]

It all began when Beata wanted you to write a book. It began when you told her, I don't want to bring my private history out through the artistic guts, it began when Beata said it is not your private history. It began with your answer, so where is my private history? What happened to my private history? Is it that my private history becomes public because public history remains private?

It began when you did not want to go on stage, because you do not like being on stage, but there was no one else, except for the gentlemen from the Institute of National Memory, it began when the National Memory was not being written by the nation, but by a few individuals, it began when you realized that you could talk about it publicly, more than that, on stage you can go further, you can say that the Institute historians named Iwaneczko and Kaczmarski are unfair, more, on stage you could say that they are unfair stupid motherfucking cunts, who in the name of the p u b l i c hide knowledge, manipulate, destroy a man, you could say that, or maybe it began with your grandfather, who if he really did so much evil, was an unfair stupid motherfucking cunt who in the name of the *public* hid knowledge, manipulated, destroyed people. It began with the discovery that one possibly awful deed does not exclude another. It began, it began it began with no one having access to history. It began with Tunio not leaving his house for the last two years of his life. Exactly from the publication of the article. It began with him shuffling his feet through the house. Not remembering. Being his own body. Starting in it and ending in it.

[#164. Doesn't testing come to an end?]

It began when you took memory for a given. When you decided it was nothing new, nothing special, just an institute, and an institute is the institutionalization of something already present. It began with a memory that makes up a nation, with a memory that is never plural, that says I am, I am a nation.

It began with memory.

With your memory to replace his memory. With a memory sprouting somewhere else than the source, a replacement memory.

IMAGE 8.3 **Wojtek Ziemilski and, on the screen, "It began with a memory."**
*Photograph by Krzysztof Bieliński*

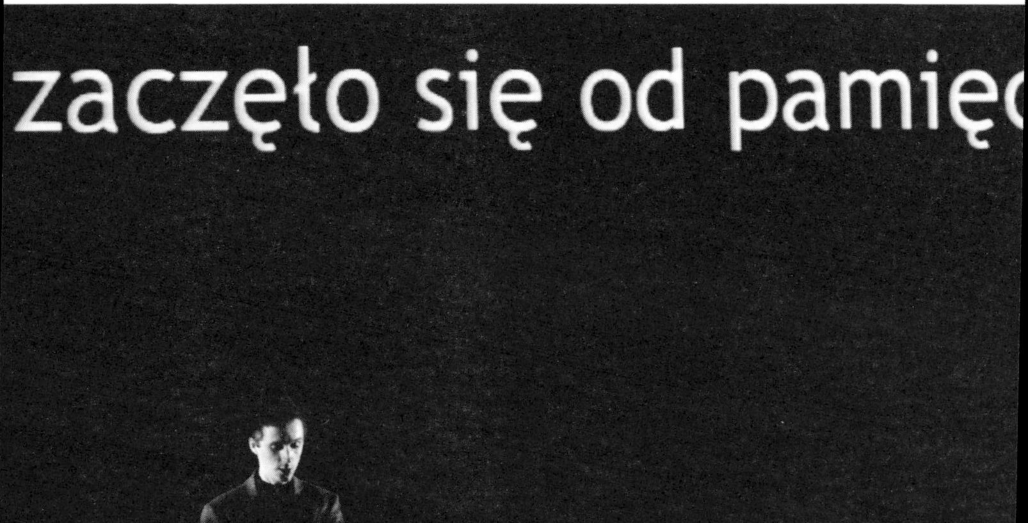

With Tunio stating he does not remember.

It began with a smile,

[*smiles*]

with a smile that's seductive, you feel it, it is seductive against your own will. Can one take courses for not seducing? It began with a smile which is too much like this foreign smile, this stranger's smile from the past, it isn't, it is not your smile, it is someone else's smile, someone else's deceit.

How is one to account for someone else's memory? How to count someone else's cases? And unexpectedly, from case to case, someone else starts appearing, someone you are, or rather: Who is also you.

It all began when, while preparing for the show, you were looking for materials about Tunio. You looked on the Net—you wrote Dzieduszycki on YouTube, and instead of films with Tunio in them, this appeared:

[*film*]

It began with hesitation. With a body that hesitates. With the enclosure in a body that hesitates.

It began with a simple declaration: I don't remember. It began with being enclosed in a house. With walks from the bedroom to the office and back. To the bedroom with the TV turned off.

It began with the body forgetting.

With it remaining contained within itself, and opaque, with it waking up to another dream, with it moving obliviously, writing itself, devouring itself, discharging itself. It began when the body suffered, or was suffered as one suffers a cost or a sacrifice. It began when the body suffered itself.

It began when, while preparing this show, you had technical problems.

[*video*]

You were trying to find publicly available material, if possible, online. And you managed to download the films, but there was a problem with the format. And something completely different appeared. But it began with the .flv format, you thought you wouldn't have any problems converting it to .avi, but you discovered none of your programs wanted to convert it, finally you managed to convert it to .mp4, and that seemed like universal enough, but then something went wrong with the codecs.

It began with the note on 2009-01-19:

Yesterday Paweł called and said someone stole the tombstone. The entire tombstone. For the last few days your aunts have been saying someone had been to the graveyard and destroyed the grave, that it was probably some extreme right-wing group. But this is a real shocker.

You will have to inform the police, go and take pictures . . . It had to be an impressively organized action! By coincidence Mom is on her way to Wrocław where the grave is, and she calls you. You hesitate, then you tell her. And she starts laughing. And while laughing, she repeats "No . . . " almost hysterically. You think, she broke down completely, but the reaction is strange, so film-like.

Through her laughter Mom tells you it's the tomb maker. He took the stone to change the letters.

Because the old letters aren't good. They keep disappearing. And one has to correct them all the time.

And one cannot spend his life constantly correcting golden letters.

It began on November 1, 2008. The day when the Poles go to the graves. When memory becomes vital.

You all go to the graves. You came to Wrocław just for that. You were going to stay longer—but that didn't work out. You managed not to come here once during the two months when you said you would "take care of everything".

IMAGE 8.2 **Wojtek Ziemilski and, on the screen, Wojciech Dzieduszycki**
*Photograph by Krzysztof Bieliński*

You discover the tablet that had Tunio's name on it was taken off by the tomb maker, because when he arrived he saw that it had graffiti on it saying "SB" ("Communist agent").

So today there is no tablet. Tunio is buried here anonymously. The mother, the son, the wife are described . . . and Tunio is passed over in silence. Better not to have anything than to have a bad description. Thought the tomb maker. And threw it out. And none of you reacted. You didn't decide anything f o r  n o w . Of course, in the future, you will change the tombstone, change the letters, the letters are impossible to see, the paint disappears, it was a bad idea, a new stone, a different color, a clearer one, but the costs, you know, let's think about it, let's talk about it, let's find the time, let's find the money find the focus find the courage let's decide, and meanwhile, and meanwhile you look at the crowds flowing through the cemetery like on a field trip. They stop, they watch, oh, the Dzieduszyckis, look, of course he died, don't you watch TV, right, that's why all the candles, and it's set.

There are eight candles. Is it worth counting?

You all lost count. One report is minus 100 articles, give or take. More? Less? What about the candle? How many articles is each? People nod, they look curiously, they watch they watch, as if waiting for something special to happen. And nothing happens, so they nod, yes yes, and they leave, discretely, somewhat embarrassed (really!), and now you have no doubts that this lack of a tablet is crucial, that it participates in your dynamics of the lost sheep. Shepherd, shepherd . . . why, there is no story of the lost shepherd.

It began when on All Saints' Day your grandfather didn't even have a tablet, because someone sprayed something on the temporary one, and it had to be thrown out, and the people came by and they hesitated, for how were they to know, and even if they knew, how were you to be sure, that's right, how, how were you to be sure, a grave with no sign, now that's a sad affair, sometimes one of you would stop, and whispered to the others, you whispered quieter than you have ever whispered in a graveyard.

[#517. But might it not be possible for something to happen that threw me entirely off the rails? Evidence that made the most certain thing unacceptable to me? Or at any rate made me throw over my most fundamental judgements?]

[(Whether rightly or wrongly is beside the point.)]

It began on <u>June 5,</u> 1912.

It began on <u>February 12,</u> 1949.

It began with the pseudonym.

Tunio chose the pseudonym <u>ONE</u>.

You remember exactly when it began. You are <u>four</u> years old, you are in Tunio's office. <u>You write</u>. You invent your <u>own</u> alphabet, because you can't stand that the grown-ups have an alphabet you don't understand, that they write something unattainable for you. So you invent your own alphabet, unattainable to anyone but you. You write, lying on the ground, and behind you, behind a massive wooden desk with lion paws, sits Tunio, typing something. The rhythm of typing is different from that of your journalist parents. Tunio first spends a long time looking through papers, magazines, programmes, then he sits staring in front of him, in silence—although he doesn't mind that his office is really just a passage from the corridor to the sleeping room, and all the time someone passes through here, and in the sleeping room the TV is always on. And then he leans over the typewriter and the letters spill out in a current, non stop, non stop, non stop. Today you would say there is something compulsive in it, but in your memory remains the pure, freely flowing sound of the fonts hitting paper. Tunio stops writing, looks at you and asks what you are doing. Writing. And wouldn't you like to learn to write? You would. You get up, go to Tunio and sit on his knees. He takes a sheet of yellowish paper and a crayon. Then some time passes, maybe a few weeks or days, you sit on Tunio's knees and write. One other thing you remember: you look at what you've been writing before, in your language, and you don't remember what you wrote, and you can't read it any more.

[#522. We say: if a child has mastered language—and hence its application—It must know the meaning of words.]

It began on some afternoon of 1981, when you were sitting in Tunio's lap. Tunio just taught you how to read. You remember the letters, you quite distinctly remember the letters, that's how it began.

[#523. And indeed no one misses doubt here; no one is surprised that we do not merely g u e s s the meaning of our words.]

Then as a reward, Tunio begins your favorite game. He throws you up in the air with his knees, reciting the poem: Riding goes the LORD, on the horse ALONE.

It began with text. With reading. With writing. With noting. With passing on. With losing grip of the language. With falling into narration. It began with the word, and then the word inscribed itself in body.

It began when Beata wanted to convince you to write a book. And you shrugged your shoulders. And said nothing, smiled enigmatically, and thought you want something exactly the opposite. You want erasing. Yet, nothing can be erased, the letters burn out slowly, and we don't know their butterfly effect, we can only hastily write over them, overwrite them with subsequent layers, while we could, we could wish to have it all be simpler. Enough already of the flesh of the forefathers in this face in this hand, why, it is its own flesh, this hand has much more of this hand than of other hands. And if so, if we can, for our own sake, accept this, than let's start with it being simpler.

It began with the show by Simon Bowes and his group Kings of England. It began with the group he created with his elderly father. It began with the show "Where We Live And What We Live For".

The critic wrote:

"In a touching meeting on stage, Bowes Junior guides his father, who is losing his memory, around his own past. He tells him of the fall, the last one, when he lost his memory, and the previous one, kept in the family archives, which was to be a beautiful jump into the sea from a rock cliff, and ended up as a fall. The distinguished elderly gentleman represents his own life, with its simple and serious choices, and no less serious consequences. At the same time, the meeting is the acceptance of everything that constructs us, and that we have no influence on."

[*picture of jump*]

It begins when Tunio teaches you to dive. You are 9 or 10 years old. Tunio teaches you to jump, first diving head first, then with a flip. A flip into the water. You don't know how to swim yet. You swim to the shore doggie-style, drinking some water. But you love it. For a long time you will only know how to swim doggie-style. But you can do some nice flips.

[*film*]

It begins when you wake up in the morning and, quite unexpectedly, nothing has changed. It begins when you can't distinguish his smile from yesterday's, how is it possible, so many things have happened, and here you have conversations by the table and I'm glad to see you, indeed, thank you, I will help, I'll see what I can do, can do, can do, and yet nothing has changed, you get up in the morning and he is sitting by the typewriter or in the armchair and looks into the same void as yesterday, no other end of the world will there be, the garden is still fading just as sadly.

It began with the article by the Institute of National Memory: "A Life in Hiding. The agent-collaboration of Wojciech Dzieduszycki with the secret services of Communist Poland between 1949 and 1972."

[*a scan of the article*]

It began with the subtitle:

["truth and freedom either exist together, or together they miserably die"]

It's a quote from John Paul II.

But it's not complete.

["When truth is taken away from a man, any attempts at freeing him are completely unreal, as truth and freedom either exist together, or together they miserably die."]

It began when you came back to Poland. And Tunio died, and here it goes again, the history again, not yours again again again again again again again again again again again again again again again again again, and you had to write a text, a text to the papers to say they couldn't write such things. A text for the funeral to remember. It began with the idea of remembering, and with the desperate search for appeasement. With visits, it began with visits to bookstores, because maybe someone somewhere knows something more, it began with the hopelessly similar, hopelessly dissimilar stories of o t h e r  p e o p l e, but really, really it began when you grabbed a small book by Ludwig Wittgenstein called "On Certainty". Not knowing it was the last thing he wrote. And the last paragraph, that last difficult paragraph he wrote two days before dying.

[#676. If something has taken away my consciousness, then I am not now really talking and thinking. I cannot seriously suppose that I am at this moment dreaming. Someone who, dreaming, says "I am dreaming," even if he speaks audibly in doing so, is no more right than if he said in his dream "it is raining," while it was in fact raining. Even if his dream were actually connected with the noise of the rain.]

It began when the Portuguese choreographer João Fiadeiro stood on the middle of the stage in his show "I Am Here".

[João Fiadeiro]

And in front of him he had a huge shadow of himself. And then the lights went out, and we heard him dance, or maybe just shake his body, and when the lights went on again, he was standing again, with his shadow. Only it was slightly blurred.

[*pictures*]

And when this situation returned several times, we realized it wasn't his shadow, but black pigment. And until the choreographer disappeared, we were wrong as to who was whose shadow.

The critic wrote:

"We look at the body, and the body suddenly ends with feet, hands. It ends there. There is nothing more, it is like a rock cliff by the sea. Suddenly, it's gone."

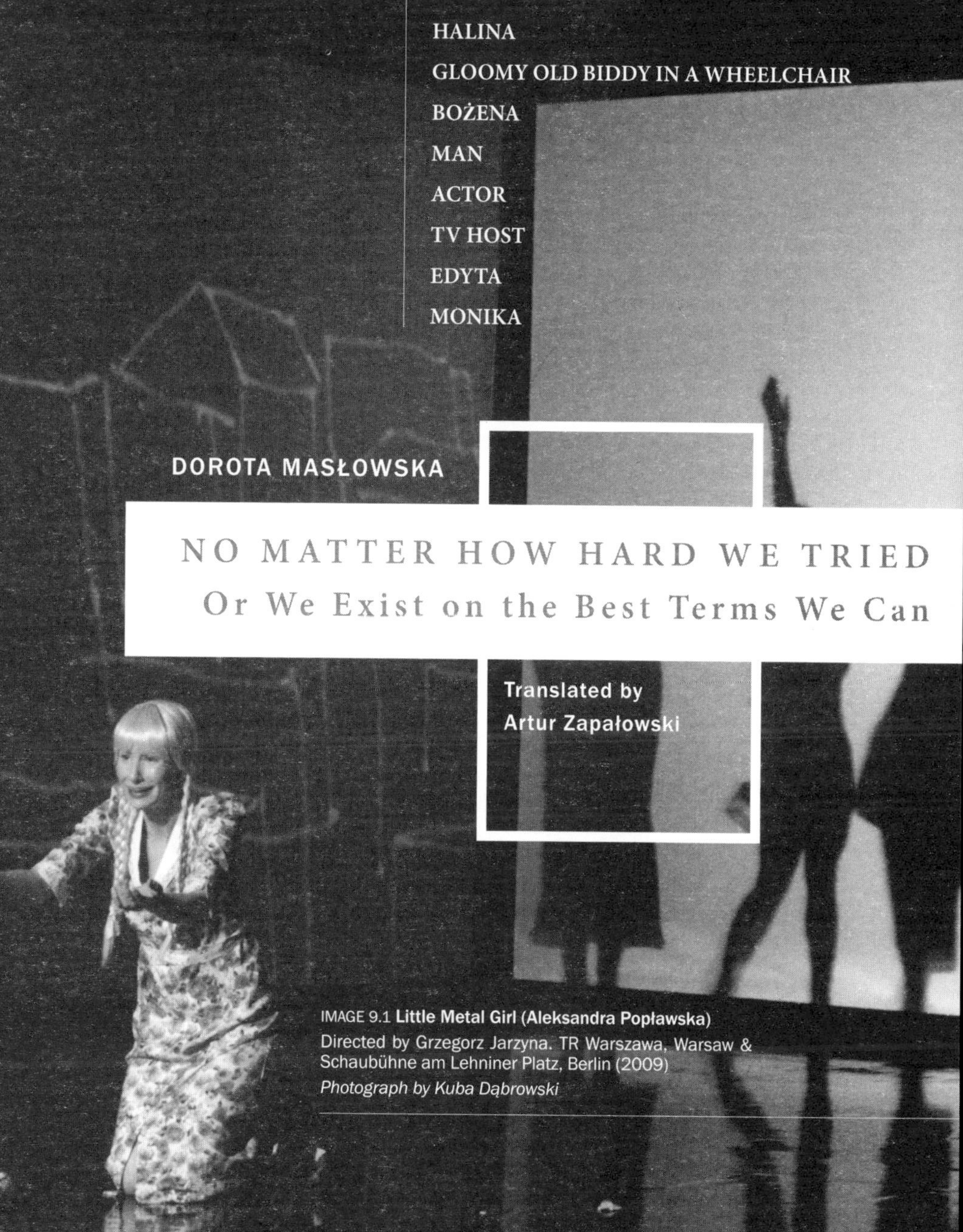

CHARACTERS

LITTLE METAL GIRL
HALINA
GLOOMY OLD BIDDY IN A WHEELCHAIR
BOŻENA
MAN
ACTOR
TV HOST
EDYTA
MONIKA

DOROTA MASŁOWSKA

# NO MATTER HOW HARD WE TRIED
## Or We Exist on the Best Terms We Can

Translated by
Artur Zapałowski

IMAGE 9.1 **Little Metal Girl (Aleksandra Popławska)**
Directed by Grzegorz Jarzyna. TR Warszawa, Warsaw & Schaubühne am Lehniner Platz, Berlin (2009)
*Photograph by Kuba Dąbrowski*

## NOTE

*No Matter How Hard We Tried* portrays a society that is divided mentally, economically and culturally, deeply rooted in history, and torn between national pride and shame. It brings together the worlds of people living on the verge of poverty, media celebrities and opportunistic artists faking a commitment to social change. The protagonists are Gloomy Old Biddy, who lives in and celebrates the past, and Little Metal Girl, who subverts Polish myths and national icons. The play's reality is made up of the tacky language of advertising brochures, the logorrhea of commercial media, the national-Catholic rhetoric of the church-run radio stations, opportunistic, exploitative art, and idealized visions of the past. Little Metal Girl's attitude to all this is one of mockery and ridicule—yet, paradoxically, in rejecting her Polish identity, which she associates with poverty, drabness and boredom, she keeps recalling, reviving, invoking and incarnating that identity.

*No Matter How Hard We Tried* premiered as a co-production of TR Warszawa and Berlin's Schaubühne am Lehniner Platz, in 2009. The staging for director Grzegorz Jarzyna's production, with projections animating the walls of the set, was light and entertaining, in contrast with the aggressive humor of the dialogue.

# NO MATTER HOW HARD WE TRIED
## Or We Exist on the Best Terms We Can

### ACT I

#### SCENE 1

*An old multistory human tenement in Warsaw. A one-room apartment. Two doors: one looks onto a courtyard with recycling bins, the other barely muffles constant toilet noises, burbling water and gurgling pipes. Spinning all the while outside the window is the wild, all-consuming merry-go-round of the big city with its trams, cars, horns and airplanes flying past across the low-hung sky and setting the bottle of stale knock-off vermouth in the drinks cabinet rattling, the elaborate pyramids of chipped and leftover-encrusted pots and pans on the kitchen counter shaking, jittering the image on the ever-flickering TV, and short-circuiting the crackling overhead bulb. The interior looks as if it were built on a fault-line or were in the process of being bulldozed: Little Metal Girl in a sailor-suit and a rampant bow in her sparse metallic hair, and her wheelchair-bound grandma, Gloomy Old Biddy, with the tangled wiring of her braids or cobwebs dragging across the carpeting behind her, are inside it like passengers on a sinking ship—teetering between panic and boredom, mindless activity and mindless torpor, claustrophobia and fear of open spaces. As is typical when dealing with people doomed to one another's company, it is hard to tell whether they are chasing or fleeing one another, or, weary of both, remaining stock-still. Between their alternating fits of inertia and hyperactivity, the girl's mother, Halina, performs her daily chores with the placidity of a mechanized beast of burden, and is currently taking out the trash.*

GLOOMY OLD BIDDY IN A WHEELCHAIR. I still remember the day the war broke out . . .

LITTLE METAL GIRL. The what broke out?

GLOOMY OLD BIDDY IN A WHEELCHAIR. The war. Back then, I was a fair young lass, my face like the spring, heart a-flutter in my youthful breast like a quail caught in a . . .

LITTLE METAL GIRL. In a pail.

GLOOMY OLD BIDDY IN A WHEELCHAIR. I could still walk on my own two feet back then. God, how I used to walk.

LITTLE METAL GIRL. You and your "how I used to walk."

GLOOMY OLD BIDDY IN A WHEELCHAIR. Of course I used to walk. I remember how . . .

LITTLE METAL GIRL. You must be all walked out, what with walking so much, Gran. Now you can finally NOT go somewhere. Jeez, if I was you, I'd sure love to not go somewhere; my English class, for one.

GLOOMY OLD BIDDY IN A WHEELCHAIR. Back and forth, back and forth. My, how we used to walk places before the war. To the cinema, for waffles and cupcakes, down to the river. Across the sand, over the ground, down to the river. On the grass, on velvety violets, down to the river on hot summer days, when its thick, clear current, etched by sunbeams like a crystal decanter . . .

LITTLE METAL GIRL. What river are you talking about?

GLOOMY OLD BIDDY IN A WHEELCHAIR. What river? The Vistula, of course.

LITTLE METAL GIRL. That shit-stream? Jeez!

GLOOMY OLD BIDDY IN A WHEELCHAIR. What shit-stream? The Vistula: right here. Clogs on your feet, a slice of bread in your hand, and off you'd go to bathe, bask and daydream, dream the sweetest, holiest dreams of youth, pure as the tears down your cheeks . . .

LITTLE METAL GIRL. What's bread? Nah, just kidding. I love swimming in the Vistula too—it's a timeless thrill. Whenever I climb out onto the bank, spluttering gasoline with gusto, I get fistula, typhoid and cadmium poisoning, and I'm dead, and I get a sick note so I don't have to go to school.

**GLOOMY OLD BIDDY IN A WHEELCHAIR.** We used to catch minnows, small and sprightly. How they'd flap about, the little rascals, smudging our hands with their oily silver scales.

**LITTLE METAL GIRL.** You don't say, Gran. We catch johnnies too sometimes—used condoms, that is. How they squirm and struggle to be free! It cracks the guys up, but I see red when I realize how many wily, opportunistic potential Polacks wriggle out of existence every day.

**GLOOMY OLD BIDDY IN A WHEELCHAIR.** They all said that Hitler, Father said that Hitler fellow . . .

**LITTLE METAL GIRL.** And how they squirm! As if they thought the Vistula veered straight off to America somewhere in mid-Poland, so that they could be born over there with a hundred-and-fifty-dollar bill in one hand, and a three-hundred-and-fifteen-dollar bill in the other, while we'd be left to toil all alone in this potato field. Born, they'll be born, all right: with a broom and a dustpan, and a gnawed Christmas turkey drumstick from the garbage. Or rather they won't be born, 'cause of us plopping them in the you-know-what...

**GLOOMY OLD BIDDY IN A WHEELCHAIR.** Nobody believed in Hitler back then. We were young, hearts thrashing about in our breasts; thrashing about like a . . .

**LITTLE METAL GIRL.** . . . condom in a pail!

**HALINA.** What pail?

*Enter Halina, with a freshly emptied dustbin dangling dejectedly at her side, carefully wiping her slippers in the threshold. Pleased with herself, she carefully wipes her slippers on the doormat, and hangs the key on a hook. She could also be bringing coal or preserves from the cellar, or a child's sled, so useful for hauling laundry from the mangle in winter, but, most importantly, under her arm she has a freshly unearthed treasure: a woman's magazine scavenged from the recycling container and read halfway to shreds.*

**HALINA.** What's that about a pail? Mind your language!

LITTLE METAL GIRL. You're in such a huff, mom. It's as if I'd been conceived by means of your straddling a filthy seat on an InterNoCity train.

*Halina bustles around in her kingdom—a kitchenette crammed to the ceiling with a veritable festival of charred, grungy pots and pans, recipes torn out of calendars, Tesco leaflets, carefully preserved flyers from language schools, canned-food labels and piles of carefully washed used yogurt pots. Behind her, drooling hungrily and peeking over her shoulder, Little Metal Girl tries to get her hands on the sugar bowl. Halina slaps her dirty mitts away.*

HALINA. Had your lunch?

LITTLE METAL GIRL. Lunch? What's for lunch?

HALINA. Dry chuffs with vinegar.

LITTLE METAL GIRL (*Lifting the -lid of a pot*). Dry chuffs, my favorite. What's that stink?

HALINA (*Grabbing the pot away from her, and slamming the refrigerator door shut*). Don't bother about that, I'll warm it up for my supper.

GLOOMY OLD BIDDY IN A WHEELCHAIR. And then the Germans entered Warsaw. Me in just my summer frock, nothing but my handbag, my handbag with only . . .

LITTLE METAL GIRL. Germans, Germans? I heard something about some kind of Germans . . . Oh yeah, they're the ones who yodel!

GLOOMY OLD BIDDY IN A WHEELCHAIR. Me with just my handbag, wearing only the frock with the roses . . .

LITTLE METAL GIRL. Wilted, I bet. Dried, that is!

GLOOMY OLD BIDDY IN A WHEELCHAIR. I was walking home from the Vistula because it was quite a hot day, my eyes still blue from gazing into the sleepy, cool, soapy, limpid . . .

LITTLE METAL GIRL. . . . filthy warm greenish foamy virulent currents of that shit-stream . . .

GLOOMY OLD BIDDY IN A WHEELCHAIR. . . . when suddenly . . .

LITTLE METAL GIRL WITH A SATCHEL ON HER SHOULDERS. When suddenly BANG!

GLOOMY OLD BIDDY IN A WHEELCHAIR. Beg pardon?

LITTLE METAL GIRL. Smoke, fire, flames. Did you see them, Gran?

GLOOMY OLD BIDDY IN A WHEELCHAIR. Did I see what?

LITTLE METAL GIRL. It burning?

GLOOMY OLD BIDDY IN A WHEELCHAIR. What's burning?

LITTLE METAL GIRL. The bicycle. The bicycle.

GLOOMY OLD BIDDY IN A WHEELCHAIR. What bicycle?

LITTLE METAL GIRL. I dunno. The burning-bicycle smell was deafening, I'd know that particular stench anywhere.

GLOOMY OLD BIDDY IN A WHEELCHAIR. No I didn't see it.

LITTLE METAL GIRL. But I did.

*Unperturbed by the family squabbles, Halina, after clanging the pot lids a while to perk herself up a bit, brushes invisible crumbs off the tabletop with her hand, which she then wipes on her cardigan, and, sighing to the heavens, settles down to read the newly acquired magazine.*

LITTLE METAL GIRL. What've you brought me-Mom-mee? The latest discount coupons?

HALINA. No, it's *Not For You* magazine. Saw it lying in a wastepaper bin. Free, so I figured, why not, I can afford it.

LITTLE METAL GIRL. Not bad.

HALINA. It's from last April. Just the thing not for me.

LITTLE METAL GIRL. They've even done the crossword for you.

HALINA. Now I know the hidden phrase without having to do it myself: "Springtime tête-à-tête."

LITTLE METAL GIRL. Show-me-Mom-mee. Springtime tête-à-tête . . . Hang on . . . Springtime snogging by the shit-stream?

HALINA. Has Grandma not had her dinner yet?

LITTLE METAL GIRL. Gran, have you not had your dinner yet?

GLOOMY OLD BIDDY IN A WHEELCHAIR. What was for dinner?

**HALINA.** Lecso.

**LITTLE METAL GIRL.** Lecso. All sorts of gunk with paprika and Hungarian space-jizz. See also: soup of the week, soup of the month, waste not want not, World War II, famine.

**GLOOMY OLD BIDDY IN A WHEELCHAIR.** Oh, that. No, I haven't.

**LITTLE METAL GIRL.** Gran hasn't eaten.

**HALINA.** Why's that?

**LITTLE METAL GIRL.** The hell should I know? The hell should . . . I KNOW! I bet she's slimming. I'm slimming, too.

**HALINA.** Has Grandma not been out anywhere today?

**LITTLE METAL GIRL.** Me! Me! Me! I didn't take Gran out anywhere.

**HALINA.** Good. Now I don't have to not take her anywhere, not that I would anyway, because I won't be home from work until 11 pm.

**LITTLE METAL GIRL.** The thing is, Gran's stuck in a building without an elevator all day long, with no one to talk to, so when I get back from school and watch TV 'till late, I don't have the time to wheel that old turnip around anywhere! Perkily did my pigtails bounce in the breeze when we were out not strolling through the autumn park. She was telling me those gripping stories of hers, like when she went off to that concentration camp. I'd say she's ripping off scenes from "The Great Escape" and " 'Allo, 'Allo," but whatever . . . We've got postmodernism after all.

**HALINA.** What are you on about? What kind of word is that?

**LITTLE METAL GIRL.** I don't know either, I just downloaded it. So there we were, not strolling to our heart's content, to and fro down lanes burnished by autumn, when all of a sudden, this nasty man starts bugging us. Come to think of it, he might have been German—all very debonair, he even bowed to us, clicked his heels and said: "Good day, Arzheimer's the name," but his name has slipped my mind. Some well-known name, starts with an A . . . Never mind. Anyway, I'd barely forgotten his name when another man showed up.

He also knocked, very debonair, with a wig on, and said: "I'm the renowned German philosopher . . . " You know, what's-his-name? The one who wrote the "Critique of Pure Reason," remember? Because I can't . . . Yes, I. KANT. That's him! How the pair of them started rambling on and muddling things . . . I felt my continued absence in Gran's lack-of-a-room was beside the point, and awkward to boot. So, not wanting to disturb them, I went to my own lack-of-a-room, and sat here watching TV with you until it got dark.

*Halina settles into the position of someone reading the paper and watching TV at the same time, a task hindered by the Old Biddy idling all over the place in her wheelchair.*

HALINA. Your old man's a glassmaker, yo momma's a pane! You keep thinking you're transparent, Mom. Why don't you have some of that gunk with paprika? Who did I not make it but kept pouring from pot to pot all week for?

LITTLE METAL GIRL. Bet she's on a diet; she doesn't want to be slim any more, just transparent.

GLOOMY OLD BIDDY IN A WHEELCHAIR. My, how we used to walk places before the war, did we ever run . . . to the cinema, for waffles and cupcakes, down to the river.

LITTLE METAL GIRL. Well, if you keep eating those waffles, eggnogs and such, then good luck. You'll never lose weight that way.

GLOOMY OLD BIDDY IN A WHEELCHAIR. Across the sand, over the ground, down to the river. A slice of bread in your hand, and off we'd go . . .

LITTLE METAL GIRL. You need to kiss the bread goodbye, especially white bread—it makes you fat. And you need to get around more. If you keep sitting in that wheelchair of yours, you'll never get any slimmer. You need to get about more, or push yourself around more at least.

Quiet, I hear knocking. Knock-knock.

GLOOMY OLD BIDDY IN A WHEELCHAIR. Who's there?

**LITTLE METAL GIRL.** I'll open it and see. No . . . I thought it was World War II coming.

**HALINA.** What are you on about this time?!

**LITTLE METAL GIRL.** I swear. Well, never mind. Must have been some model airplanes flying past.

SCENE 2

*The apartment and everything are as before. Biddy is in a stupor, the girl is bored and playing with a chicken push-toy. Eventually concluding the activity to be futile, she starts using the toy to push her granny around the apartment. Halina, half-peeved by the pushing and shoving, and half-inured to it, sinks back into her magazine, while catching, with acrobatic dexterity, various objects falling off the shelves and cabinets. People might be wandering round the courtyard throwing refuse into the relevant containers. Lurking among them might be the morbidly obese Bożena, who, commando-like, is keeping out of their line of sight behind containers incapable of concealing her offensively huge bulk. Biddy manages to break free of the hijinks and hurriedly lock herself in the toilet amidst the soothing burbling of the pipes.*

**HALINA.** "The primroses are in flower, and spring is well upon us, stirring us with its balmy breeze. You're more inclined not to go on invigorating walks; it's time not to break out that bicycle you don't own. Sunny afternoons are just made for physical activity, and seeing friends, whom you don't see because you have none, as well as for throwing picnics, and getting thrown out of restaurants, *if you know what I mean*. It's high time you spring-cleaned your wardrobe! So it's not back on the hanger with those grays, browns, bulky tights, thick sweaters, coats and jackets. Dare not to wear those breezy dresses you don't own and the fine tights you don't own either. Most likely you don't have any lighter jackets, but the one you do have certainly won't fit your fat frame. Not to worry. We have last year's tips to keep you from landing squarely on the sidelines with your finger on the sphincter of springtime trends."

**LITTLE METAL GIRL.** "Shake the moths out a little, spray on a little deodorizer, wash it a little, don't wash it a little, don't bother to wash it all a little. Don't take out of the closet and put on what you've slept in, and sleep in what you wear. Now just have nothing to wear a little and you're done! It takes absolutely no effort, and has just as much effect."

**HALINA.** "Skirt: Tesco, 28 zloty. The grease stain lends it mystique. T-shirt: out of the closet, faded at the tits. Grays, browns and urine yellows, grease stains, and threadbare patches, are all in vogue this season, just like any other season. Sweat stains, our top tip: they'll show up on their own sooner than later. Men's socks—from the Russian Market: 17 pairs for 10 zloty. Shoes—imitation leather. Everything for 5 zloty to 12 zloty. Accessories—plastic carrier bag. One-fifty, Lidl. Huge and hefty; capacity—10 kilos of potatoes, five bottles of vinegar, chicken feet, yesterday's issue of freebie "Metro" daily, with room left over for a little purse. Sink-washable.

**LITTLE METAL GIRL.** Last spring's treatments for complexions made gray by the winter, ruined by cigarettes, a bad diet and coronary heart disease.

**HALINA.** Wash your face with soap and apply Nivea cream or plain old margarine. Scouring it with a towel will also work wonders.

**LITTLE METAL GIRL WITH A SATCHEL ON HER BACK.** Our tip: If you want your Nivea cream to last longer, don't use it.

**HALINA.** Don't wash one side of your head with your regular shampoo, or the other side either, for that matter. Our top tip —the more you don't do this, the more apparent your hair loss will be, and that disturbing shoe-cabinet and sweating-lard aroma will linger longer in your locks. Last April is finally the time for the springtime sun not to glint in your dull and lifeless strands.

*After a suitable interval, Biddy ineptly wheels herself back inside the apartment to the sound of flushing water.*

**LITTLE METAL GIRL.** Don't oil your wheelchair: The shrill squeaking will be the perfect way to let others know you've just trundled in to resume your endless prattle . . .

**HALINA.** Will you look at that, Mom, I could have sworn you went there for the peace and quiet, and, gracious, was I ever right. (*Still engrossed in the magazine, she vigorously pushes Old Biddy's wheelchair so it doesn't block the view of the TV set.*)

**LITTLE METAL GIRL** (*pretending to be reading to the Biddy*). "In April last year, everything will be the way it was. You will get a mysterious letter: it might be a reminder from the gas company! Meaningful dates: the 15th. A windfall of mothballs awaits you. Meaningless dates: all the rest of them.

Your lucky colour: transparent. Your lucky stone: the gallstone."

**HALINA** (*goes back to her reading*). Phew! Right! "Now that you've got your wardrobe in order, it's time to sit back and wait for the lack of compliments, indifferent glances and a slap on the kisser from time to time. Now you can relax and wait for World War II to come again, and for those yogurt pots you've been collecting so assiduously all these years to finally come in handy."

**LITTLE METAL GIRL.** Knock-knock!

**HALINA.** Who's there?

**LITTLE METAL GIRL** (*peeking into the pots*). It's just me, World War II back again. I see that not only do you have lots of yogurt pots, but that you've whipped up some delicious biohazard, too. I'm impressed.

**HALINA.** What are you on about? Go to your lack-of-a-room!

**LITTLE METAL GIRL.** I seem to be right here, but let me double-check. Hello? Hello! Where am I?

Right here. Right here? Then go right here and stay there. Right away.

*Enter Bożena, sans knocking, with the agitation typical of someone who has nothing of import to impart, yet laboring under the delusion that they do. She is morbidly obese and mobility-impaired. Unable to shut the door behind her, she rips it off its hinges and puts it to one side. Puffing, grunting and holding her aching back, she hurriedly staggers towards the armchair, onto which she immediately plops, as if unable to stand on her own two feet. Everything in the apartment rises by 40 cm.*

**BOŻENA.** Sorry for not calling your mobile before I came, but I don't have a mobile—why should I when I'm fat as a pig? So I just dropped in.

**HALINA.** I'm not saying this just to be polite, but . . . God, you're so fat, just like a pig. You'll pant me out of house and home.

**BOŻENA.** Thank you. I can see it in your eyes. All the same, you could carry on showing contempt a bit longer, so as to spare me any doubts that I'm a fat pig, who shouldn't obnoxiously wobble around in other people's field of view. People should have the right to choose what makes them puke.

*Taking advantage of Halina's preoccupation with lighting the stove, Little Metal Girl, bustling about the place in search of something to break or rip up, intercepts the magazine and starts reading it innocent as you please.*

**LITTLE METAL GIRL.** "Star-sign: Fat Pig. Last April, Fat-Pigians can expect many wonderful surprises. Biedronka[1] will launch a new, affordable luncheon meat—*Ye Olde Poultry Loin*. Ingredients: water (97 percent), pork rinds, dishwashing liquid, window-cleaner, gelatine, spices; as well as a new brand of out-of-date cream—*A Few Days Off*. Ingredients: water, gelatine, white coloring, thickener, thinner, decalcifier, detoxifier, live salmonella cultures. Wash down what others won't eat with what they won't drink. It's time you accepted who you are and reinvented yourself. So try and get out a lot and go for walks

---

**1** A convenience-store chain in Poland.

because, like all Fat-Pigians, you ARE a fat pig, but don't go out for walks, especially in other people's field of view: they have the right to puke for better reasons than that."

*Virtually unnoticed, she puts down the magazine. Bożena glances at it with thinly veiled curiosity, but doesn't dare lay her hands on it.*

BOŻENA. Ooh, what a lovely mag—*Not For You*.

HALINA. That's right, *Not For Us*.

BOŻENA. It's very nice.

HALINA. I bought it in the waste-paper bin today. It was a bargain: For free, and the crossword was solved to boot. Such a lovely surprise, as if I had the time to do crosswords!

IMAGE 9.2 **Halina (Magdalena Kuta), Bożena (Maria Maj), and Little Metal Girl (Aleksandra Popławska)**

Directed by Grzegorz Jarzyna. TR Warszawa, Warsaw & Schaubühne am Lehniner Platz, Berlin (2009)

*Photograph by Kuba Dąbrowski*

**BOŻENA.** Now that I'm performing the duties of a filth-removal specialist in personal private premises, like I always have, I simply have no time for that sort of thing. The work's by no means demanding, but it's tiring and unsatisfying.

**HALINA.** I can relate to that, because, as a specialist in charge of shifting palettes in the tried-and-tested manual fashion in the retail sector, I have to get up before I go to bed, and I come home from work much later than I get up for it the next day.

But, in the future I don't have, I'll be up for promotion to manager in charge of electronically determining the real weight of goods in the fruit and vegetable section; so I figure, why not give it a shot?

**BOŻENA.** Sure, you've got what it takes. Language skills—Foreign. Job experience—Street-corner advertising material dispatcher; national scent ambassador via direct frottage in buses and trams for Old Bag fragrance, with its dominant note of sweat, subtly complemented by hints of musk, mothballs and old soup . . .

**HALINA** (*fussing around in the kitchen, blending impressive expertise with total futility*). I keep thinking about the holiday I won't be having. I've been reading up on it, and I've finally decided: No way, we're not going on holiday again this year.

**BOŻENA.** You don't say!

**HALINA.** That's right! We're not going again this year.

**BOŻENA.** So where is it you're not going to?

**HALINA.** Nowhere.

**BOŻENA.** Naturally, where else? We're not going to the seaside this year. God, it's just so unaffordable! We haven't got the money! Besides, I'm fat as a pig and shouldn't obnoxiously wobble around in other people's field of view.

**HALINA.** Sure thing, you bet.

**BOŻENA.** On our way, we'll not stop off in Kobyłka, where we've got a cousin, and we'll be going nowhere straight from there!

**HALINA.** I guess I'll see you there, then—call my lack-of-a-mobile, you've got the number. Nowhere, good old nowhere: All the memories it brings back! But it's getting crowded there lately. I mean: My brother-in-law, sister-in-law, brother, uncle, cousin and sister are all there already . . .

**BOŻENA.** How dark and cozy it is in here!

**HALINA** (*vigorously pushes Old Biddy's wheelchair which is blocking her view and stopping her from simultaneously talking, following the TV show, and pawing at the magazine*). Your old man's a glassmaker, yo momma's a pane! Mom, if you think you've turned transparent, better think again. And you, go to your lack-of-a-room!

**LITTLE METAL GIRL.** That's where I seem to be right now, but let me double-check. Hello? Where am I? Ah, here I am. Just where I thought I was.

*Little Metal Girl once again intercepts the magazine without anyone noticing.*

**LITTLE METAL GIRL.** "Unlike the apartments designed nowadays, in which family members fruitlessly call to one another for hours down spacious corridors, halls and separate bedrooms, trying to figure out their own whereabouts, not to mention those of their nearest and dearest, these claustrophobic, cramped quarters give an impression of smallness, and it's here that the whole extended family eat, sleep, excrete, can't sleep, toss and turn, vomit and get the shits, don't live, and die, all without ever having to look for one another, but nevertheless still find themselves there. This effect has been achieved with a simple architectural trick: The apartment has been cleverly partitioned so that Little Metal Girl's lack-of-a-room, the gloomy cripple's lack of peace and quiet, and the anxieties of Halina (51) all fit into the same room, where all day long they make no room for one another. It's hard to believe that they've also managed to fit in an entire authentic 1970s (fiberboard) furniture set. Over the years, its surfaces have been finely buffed, scratched and utterly covered in children's scribbles. Moreover, a blend of foodstuffs, hard drinks and bodily fluids has veneered this King Mieszko set with a remarkable, grime-like palimpsest. The edges of the wallpaper have been slightly moistened and torn, while the mildew on the wall, covered by a wall-hanging, isn't there at all. An old halva box, the tastefully framed lid of a Solidari-Tea tin, a plastic ribbon pinned to a potted asspidistra, the odd vegetable-peelings and chicken bones strewn here and there, quaint, fluffy dustballs, a year's worth of freebie "Metro" daily, a "casually-placed" tube of periodontal paste, yogurt pots . . . It's not that the local brats have knocked the trash over, it's just . . . "

HALINA (*irritated, snatching the magazine and putting it back in its safe place on the table*). She won't give me a moment's peace!

LITTLE METAL GIRL. But I am in my lack-of-a-room!

SCENE 4

*In the kitchen, Halina is scraping at her pots and pans, Little Metal Girl pushes the wheelchair until it gains momentum then nimbly hops on the back and scoots around the TV until the wheelchair falls over on its side. At this point, all the pills stashed in the blanket on Biddy's lap could come cascading, Pachinko-like, onto the floor. Unable to return her grandma to an upright position, the Girl leaves her lying on the carpet, mopes around in search of something to do, then starts scratching varnish off the furniture with a nail. The recumbent Old Biddy braids her hair or knits a ten-meter snood. She then puts away the needlework and starts wriggling in a desperate attempt to sit up. In her armchair, Bożena plucks up the courage to reach out for* Not For You *magazine. With trembling hands, she turns a few pages, then starts leafing through it with increasing confidence, and even hazards a comment.*

BOŻENA. This personality quiz hasn't been done yet.

HALINA. Well there you go.

BOŻENA. I'll do it so it doesn't go to waste.

"Are you a: spontaneous excursionist, a hearth-hugging stay-at-home, a sexy vamp, an overworked workaholic, an imaginative troublemaker, an inveterate globe-trotter, a fat pig, or a cut-price frozen panga from Liddull?"

HALINA (*wiping her hands on her sweater, and looking over Bożena's shoulder*). I'm an inveterate globetrotter, me.

BOŻENA. That's right, "A"—same here. "All A's—you're an inveterate globetrotter." Why don't I tick one "B" just to mess with them. There, finished!

HALINA. Do mine in a different color, so we don't mix them up. Seems like a silly game, but it's right on the nail.

BOŻENA. Isn't it just! Remember how I didn't go to France and how I'll never set foot there again? French fries and French bread—they really go for that over there, but it's just like Wrocław White, worse even. The monumental outline of the famous Eyefull Tower that's supposed to be so tall, they say, but in the paper it looked about so big, shorter than my finger.

HALINA. That's nothing, we didn't go to Italy, but I wasn't at all happy that we didn't go. What a waste of time! Food's nothing to write home about: sardines, Roman lettuce, Italian meatballs, Neapolitans, and their pizza's just cut-price Tesco deep-freeze, with mildew, no less! I had one, couldn't waste it, but the digesting part didn't go down too well, so the trip ended up in York, if you know what I mean. Besides, what's the point of going to Italy, now that the Pope's no longer the man, but a Ger-man. Good thing I didn't go there and didn't take any photos. Now I can not show them to you.

GLOOMY OLD BIDDY IN A WHEELCHAIR (*rolls up in her creaking wheelchair*). Until Warsaw was invaded by the Germans . . .

LITTLE METAL GIRL. Germans? Oh yeah, they're the ones who yodel!

HALINA (*edifyingly*). Germans are people who live in the Federal Republic. They never reuse their plastic bags, but just throw them out; and as for yogurt pots, they don't even bother with those. If they have any chicken skins left over, what'll they make their aspic in, I wonder? And when World War II comes again, they'll have to come running to us.

IMAGE 9.3 **Little Metal Girl (Aleksandra Popławska), Halina (Magdalena Kuta), Gloomy Old Biddy In a Wheelchair (Danuta Szaflarska), and Bożena (Maria Maj)**
Directed by Grzegorz Jarzyna. TR Warszawa, Warsaw & Schaubühne am Lehniner Platz, Berlin (2009)
*Photograph by Kuba Dąbrowski*

*Bożena produces, from God-knows-where, a charred and slobbery photo album.*

**HALINA.** How fat you are! How untanned! My, my! It's a wonder you fit inside the frame.

**BOŻENA.** This is where we didn't go. We didn't go here either. And that there's not us. I would have shown you if I had the album. (*Pockets the album as quickly as she had produced it.*)

**HALINA.** Some people have it good. Dead lucky they are.

**BOŻENA.** Sure. Takes luck to be dead.

*The stagnation continues. Halina and Bożena are lost in thought, their hands folded pensively on their midriffs. The creak of Biddy's wheelchair, the scratching of Little Metal Girl's nail on the cabinets, or the grating and crackling noises as she stabs at the wiring.*

HALINA. Would you like something to eat? I found a great recipe here—"LECSO: Take Ye Olde Luncheon Meat from Tesco's; don't throw it out, just scrape off the mildew; sauté it when it turns slimy, then cut it into a few slices of prosciutto. Grate some mock-cheese into Parmesan once its consistency has started to resemble chewed plasticine, otherwise it might still be good for something. Add it to a pot of old mushroom soup, which should have acquired a pearly glaze by now . . ."

BOŻENA. Where do you get the soup from?

HALINA. Cook it the week before.

BOŻENA. That IS simple. What are those bitter, rancid thingies sprinkled on top?

HALINA. Pine nuts.

BOŻENA. Pine? What kind of nuts are those?

HALINA. Never heard of them myself, but they're quite good, kind of like bargain-bin peanuts—one and the same actually. My tip is: They don't taste rancid at all if you don't eat them. You can also add bread wrappers, gristle and veins . . . Don't throw them out, fry in suet, boil in chicken-foot stock, mince, then refry, don't throw it out, just add more salt, store in yogurt pots, reheat, heat up, refry, eat. If it starts frothing—puke it up . . . (not that you really have to) and voilà! They might laugh now, but next time World War II comes around, they'll be wolfing it down like so many Hoovers.

BOŻENA. Thank you. Look at me: so fat and still gorging myself. Gobbling it up like a Hoover, I am. Dig in, piggy, dig in! It'll put hairs on your chest. I'd serve it with breadcrusts.

HALINA. I'm sorry it's all make-believe, but I ate everything before it spoiled.

BOŻENA. Right. Well, never mind. I'll be off now. Tomorrow I have to get up before I go to bed.

HALINA. When I get home much later than I'll get up, I'll still have to clean the lake with newspaper.

BOŻENA. I'm out of here.

HALINA. If anybody asks, I'm out of here too.

*Meanwhile, Little Metal Girl sneaks up again and starts reading the women's magazine.*

LITTLE METAL GIRL. "The air of apparent chaos and bric-a-brac haphazardness pervading this beautiful old, utterly devastated apartment has been achieved thanks to genuine chaos and haphazardness. The overall mess could well be mistaken for a real mess, which it actually is. Now it's over to our resident interior decorator: 'This miserable dump is actually a beautiful prewar apartment, but, despite the ongoing failure to renovate the premises since the war ended, or thereabouts, it still lacks the tidiness, dryness and spaciousness so fashionable of late. There are two possible ways out of this annoying nightmare: The first, yet rather expensive, option is to convert this hole into a wine cellar, and move into a luxury apartment. Graceful shelves and stands, if properly placed, might permit the storage of several truly tasty vintages here! Or, more affordably: The family members all kill one another to return in more fitting incarnations—or simply never get born and don't live at all, which is far better for all concerned, especially for all the others concerned. As for the building, it would be best if it were bombed (preferably during the war, as bombing might prove hard to do later on), the rubble giving way to a fairly elegant high-rise building, in which normal people could buy apartments, furnish them with RIKKA sofa-beds from IKEA, STAKKA tables from IKEA, ROSTE vases, HAMMA flowers, in LIKKE water, GRETTA ambient air, and their own SELVVES, and, while paying off their mortgage for the next 40 years, they could drop by for a snooze after work, wash their butts, and go back again."

## ACT II

### SCENE 1

*The same interior with the same two doors and window, outside of which the city leers ravenously; the same gurgling in the pipes, and sounds of soccer coverage and sexual intercourse heard through the walls, with the same environmentally friendly garbage cans outside. A Man comes into the apartment: Elegant, scrubbed, and stylish, he looks around and scowls at the moldy plaster, the peeling wallpaper, and the scuffed wheelchair-marks on the carpet. Neat Swedish workmen from IKEA come in behind him bearing cardboard boxes, which they put down in the places the man indicates with his foot. The man uses spit to stick several stylish heirloom pictures from IKEA on the walls. The pictures either immortalize the beauty of his ancestors, or depict gerberas and sunflowers in extreme close-up (oil on canvas). The man takes a laptop and a bottle of wine out of his briefcase, and starts drinking.*

MAN. They've shut up at last! I totally can't focus on my feature-film screenplay entitled "The Horse Rode Horseback" which caused quite a buzz and scooped up all the awards! It takes place in Poland, in places like Łódź or Wałbrzych, or a mining village in Lower Silesia, but it's partly shot on location in Lithuania, and partly in Katowice. The hero, whom I'm calling JASIEK for now, lives in a radioactive block of flats. One day, his drunken father, a coal-miner, staggers into a glass-fronted sideboard left behind by the Germans, breaking both his arms and legs. Jasiek's family falls on hard times. To support his cancer-stricken family, the boy is unemployed and falls in with the wrong crowd.

Violence reigns amid gloomy run-down residential housing, leaking batteries, burning bicycles and CGI slag-heaps, on one of which our hero sees the deaf and blind but still passable MONIKA, dejectedly using a stick to rummage through the shifting pixels. He befriends her. Together they pick scrap in the radioactive rubble of the run-down Gdańsk shipyard so perfectly re-created for us in Chernobyl. Monika teaches him to see the things that our hectic, weekly lifestyles prevent us normal people from noticing. Until one day, Jasiek's brother falls ill with leukaemia. Undaunted, Jasiek takes fate into his own hands.

*Not bothering to knock, the Actor enters the room making anguished gestures.*

ACTOR. I don't want to live in this apartment building anymore!

MAN. To make matters worse, there's this queer always hanging around, whom everyone treats with intolerance in this Polish den of bigotry, though he turns out to be a normal guy, who's simply well-groomed and not tolerated.

ACTOR. I want to live in some other apartment building!

MAN. The penultimate scene: Jasiek's parents' apartment. It's stuffy, typically Polish:

cramped and squalid. Jasiek's mother is washing her feet in the sink, his under-aged sister, still a baby, is playing with fish bones wrapped in a grease-stained Polish flag. The camera pans across the trembling father sprawled in delirium on the couch and drinking dirty brake-fluid through a hose coming out of a flagon, which makes him throw up blood violently onto the scruffy carpeting. Pan to window. A solitary stray sunbeam plays upon the grimy, still-not-double-glazed window. Digital zoom through the pane: In the courtyard paper-recycling bin, a sweet mongrel puppy is frolicking with a discarded magazine such as *For You*, on the cover of which is a pretty smiling young woman's face. Now let any of those two-bit critics tell me I don't leave the audience any room for hope!

## SCENE 2

*Enter the TV Host with a sheaf of papers flying every which way. She stuffs the brand-name tags dangling from her apparel up her sleeves, and, without so much as a look at her interlocutor, sits down in an armchair, twisting her legs into a graceful braid. She starts reading from a piece of paper, as if her mind were on other, more important things. The actor's replies can be spontaneous, but he can also be glancing at a magazine, or reading haltingly from a prompt sheet, or playing a cassette and lip-synching to it.*

TV HOST. You play Jasiek in the exciting and talked-about film "The Horse Rode Horseback." Why don't you let us in on your secret? How do you manage to look so great?

ACTOR. I drink a liter of regular real liquid water a day. I also eat fruit and vegetables made out of organic fruit and vegetables. I try to avoid sweets, fast food and cigarettes because they have 1,100 calories. I work out regularly; I trim my nose and ear hair. My wife even laughs at me and calls me a poof. Not that she has anything against gays, mind you. She just makes fun of that endearingly comical, distasteful effeminacy of theirs.

TV HOST. I see. (*She puts her notes in order, crosses out something, then stares at something else. She reads from her notes hastily and with some difficulty.*) Your character also goes through a life-changing experience. Set against the backdrop of a Poland that time forgot, in an age of transition and rampant capitalism, our homespun "here and now," our homespun "over there and no sooner than 2045," our homespun "the West is there already, and we're not," our homespun "how I hate the Kaczyński twins," our homespun "and off I dive into my piggy-print sheets where I . . . snore-snore." What made you go into acting? What do you have?

ACTOR. I have a car, a regular one for driving, and an off-roader for driving off the road, and I have an apartment, and a wife with whom I share my great love of me. I have a daughter, and I want to spend as much time as I can with her . . . but sadly, I drink a bit, and then I snort coke, and then I get sleepy and agitated, so I have to snort more, until I get incoherent and the only prescription is more coke, so I snort on the set, off the set, before rehearsals, before the show and after the show. Even before this interview I had to chop out a line this long in order to get that rapturous feeling of me being me and the happeningness of things happening; I don't feel a thing, I've stopped sleeping with the wife, and I don't give a shit about my daughter. I've sold both my cars and the apartment, but I'm through with that crap now, and I've started drinking to unwind a bit, and at night off I dive into my piggy-print sheets where I . . . snore-snore . . . I'm such a . . . What? A sleepyhead!

TV HOST. As a child, you were said to be short, but that changed as you got older. And now for my last question. Can you describe your average everyday day?

ACTOR. It was a very demanding part, very demanding. A lot of scenes were actually shot in Poland. We stayed in the local hotels, some didn't even have shampoo, soap or separate foot-towels. That's why I'm in need of peaceful total silence, rest, meditation and a new off-roader. I also want to go to Peru and drive a four-wheel drive through the cradle of our civilization. Then another week on vodka, a week of coke, a couple of days' detox, psychotherapy, and three days as a tampon in a Hellinger constellation. I also mean to get around to reading all the titles and the last name of the author of books by that famous Hoolybeck. And then off I dive into my piggy-print sheets where I . . . you know what. I'm such a . . . sleepyhead. I also enjoy fine wine: I like drinking it, and pissing it out. Of an evening, I like chilling to this smooth-jazz compilation that came free with Knorr soup . . . (*Saying this, the actor opens a door in the wall unit, revealing a cabinet resplendent with bottles of wine, which he proceeds to take out and place on the table.*)

TV HOST. Not familiar with it . . .

ACTOR. It's a very well-known soup. Wine, wine, wine is like a prayer. You have no idea what an arduous, complex, intricate, all-but mantra-like process goes into its making. Each and every bottle in my cellar has a vivid tale to tell, like a symphony of elaborate processes, procedures, formulae, and people's hard work, patience, knowledge of the rules, and time, time, time. Just picture this, if you have the imagination for it . . .

*The two of them abandon their armchairs and assume positions traditionally associated with weather-persons.*

ACTOR. China—little Feng-Shui stands by the production line, making grapes. His serial number in this huge European fruit factory is 1,760,182 . . . which numerologically adds up to a Six, and that means . . . He sticks pips into the pulp and wraps it in skins 32 hours a day, in peril of his life, for which he has no break, and no hope. He doesn't loaf around—there are 15 million other four-year-olds just like him, waiting to take his place. He works quickly and gives it his all, not wanting the foreman to notice his exhaustion otherwise he might get

IMAGE 9.4 **Actor (Rafał Maćkowiak), Man (Adam Woroniwicz), and TV Host (Agnieszka Podsiadlik)**

Directed by Grzegorz Jarzyna. TR Warszawa, Warsaw & Schaubühne am Lehniner Platz, Berlin (2009)

*Photograph by Kuba Dąbrowski*

transferred to a less inspiring job, such as assembling blackberries or attaching stems to blueberries. At night, he goes back to his shed made of twigs, eats Korean-flavoured Chinese pot noodles, and dives into his pile of discount Chinese bras and panties, and . . . snore-snore.

**TV HOST.** Meanwhile, an old Indian woman named Delhi is scurrying about, wearing those incense-reeking blotchy rags she got practically free down at the Oriental shop. For breakfast today, she'll make do with a little curry powder. She hurriedly lowers the branch to bar the door of her car-tire hovel, and rushes to sift grains of sand: Only the roundest and most symmetrical ones can be made into bottles.

**ACTOR.** Now it's time for the Polish economic migrants: Jan from Tłuszcz, with a PhD in social sciences, is shaping soil into lumps and painting them black. Back in Poland he was a jack-of-all-trades. Maria, a downsized weaver from Łódź, is devotedly helping him out. Into the lumps she weaves imitation earthworms, artificial beetle grubs, and roots painstakingly braided around real roots. Now it's time to go to her second job: After hours she cuts out serrations and paints tiny veins onto leaves. No wonder—she was always artistically gifted, and has a graphic arts degree from the Academy. She looks after every penny, and the hard-earned money will allow her to buy a ticket back to Poland, plus the airport taxes. Meanwhile, political prisoners from Russia are wiping the air clean of exhaust fumes. And children in Uzbekistan are selecting the prettiest sunbeams . . .

**TV HOST.** And then chop-chop, hocus-pocus, the wine goes onto the racks, into the boxes, crates and trucks. Along the way, several not particularly attractive Bulgarian women by the roadside will manage to fill their pails with foreign condoms, or maybe not. And then there's the checkout girl from Tesco who breaks a bottle and, to pay for it, takes out a loan without guarantees, endorsers, or her husband's consent. Unable to repay it, she hangs herself on her handbag strap. Her desperate deed makes the photo-feature section in many a tabloid. Exactly how the quick-witted photographer managed to capture the suicide as it happened will remain forever unremarked by the horror-struck readers, but will strengthen their reluctance to leave their houses after 4:30 pm.

*Halina and Bożena appear out of nowhere, coming back from either the basement or the toilet or somewhere else altogether, and quickly take their erstwhile places: Bożena in the armchair with her hands folded on her gut, and Halina by the cooking range with the tabloid spread out in front of her.*

HALINA (*Reading the tabloid*). "She hanged herself on her handbag strap! Before that, they killed and raped her, rolled her up in a carpet, and braided its fringes. They were ruthless!"

BOŻENA. You don't say?

HALINA. Look at the pictures! They cut off her head and used it to play ball with her legs! Me, I never go out after 4:30 pm anymore because it's dangerous, and besides I don't leave work until 11 pm.

BOŻENA. Me neither, I don't go out after 4:30 pm or any other time because I'm fat as a pig, and I shouldn't wobble around in other people's field of view. It's their field of view and they have every right to puke for better reasons than that.

*Halina and Bożena quickly walk off, or leave the stage in some less obvious way. The Actor and the TV Host sit back down in the armchairs. The changeover is very fast. The Actor sits down at the table, and starts handling the bottles and stroking their labels with undisguised pleasure. He wipes the glasses, inspects them under the light, and pours the wine.*

ACTOR. So you see, this ridiculously expensive wine is truly worth the price, and today, in the Vistula, your urine will really blow away other people's urines. Have a sip. Well?

TV HOST (*tasting, sniffing, smacking her lips, swirling the liquid in its glass*). Well . . . Nice glass.

**ACTOR.** Exactly. That's because I drank it all. And this is my cork collection: I drank this one. I drank this one. I drank this. I drank this. I drank this. I drank it! This one I didn't drink. My wife necked it out of sheer delight, when she realized whose wife she was.

**TV HOST.** Well then, you can be sure that when World War II comes back, your corks will really blow away the flames in the fire.

*Little Metal Girl appears in the doorway, gracefully swinging her pigtails.*

**LITTLE METAL GIRL.** Knock-knock!

**TV HOST.** Who's there?

**LITTLE METAL GIRL.** It's me again, World War II, I've brought some flames along. Nobody here but us flames. Wow, did you really drink all this? What splendid corks. Mind if we lick at them?

**ACTOR.** Not at all. Frankly, I do it myself sometimes.

**TV HOST.** Society has many problems. Your character comes from a dysfunctional family, his father drinks . . . Thanks for the interview. Best of luck. Goodbye.

## SCENE 3

*Edyta is pacing the apartment, unable to find a place for herself. Well-dressed, with a handbag and a face puffed up with tears, she is chain-smoking slim cigarettes, and holding a dismal pair of soggy and flaccid lace panties. Halina takes out the garbage, while Bożena crouches commando-like behind the garbage can.*

**EDYTA.** Ohmigod, how I cried watching that film, I was so moved! You could wring the discharge from my panties. I guess I'll have to throw them out and buy a new pair, because these are out of fashion anyway! It was all so moving, so cruel. I keep moaning about my problems and complexes and that my titties are as small as socks, but now I see that, with the grace of God, other people have it worse, and life is just so real! I can still see the mother rinsing her privates in the washbasin, and her father the miner drinking brake fluid through a hose coming out of a flagon and vomiting onto the carpet. I haven't been so afraid since Freddy Krueger and that rollercoaster, because we're blinded by our selfishness. After all, we could have been born as someone else, not us. It wasn't bound to be that way.

**BOŻENA.** A word of advice to the characters in the film: if your husband or boyfriend drinks brake fluid, I'd wholeheartedly recommend RUBOLEUM flooring—vomit and blood mops up easier, and it stinks less, while people with cataracts, and especially the blind, might even take it for a parquet floor. But I won't say that, because I'm fat as a pig and won't go imposing my point of view on people.

**HALINA.** I didn't like that film at all. Nothing but cursing and cigarette-smoking. I like films about pretty ladies, them dancing, them singing, them not living and not shitting. A film about horses. Horses! What do I care about horses?! Incidentally, that's just my subjective opinion, because I haven't seen the film.

**EDYTA.** Ohmigod, I was so afraid today when I saw the checkout girl at Tesco. Ohmigod, I was scared to think that someone could let herself go so much. Ohmigod, it scared me; all she needed was a few minor tweaks: a good hairdresser, a touch of makeup and at least five hours' sleep instead of two, and she'd look like a normal person. Ohmigod, I was scared that might not be enough, and she'd still need a hair graft, a face transplant, and possibly a whole new body and personality, a new set of ancestors going back four generations, plus a brand new wardrobe, and she should also change her date and, above all, her country of birth, and she might be able to look like a normal person. I haven't been so afraid since Freddy Krueger and that rollercoaster. I haven't been so afraid since "Critters." Life is just so real, injustice is just so unjust, the disadvantaged are completely disadvantaged, and social sensitivities are so sensitive. Today I swore that as soon as I found a river, from which I could save people from drowning, or a fire, from which I could save people from burning . . . Though that might not be so easy, because disasters are hard to find in peacetime, when all the wars are in other countries, and that limits your options for performing out-and-out good deeds. So at least I'll buy a kilo of nice sweets and I won't take them to an orphanage, I'll just eat them in the car myself to calm my nerves—munch munch munch. Why don't I just take all the handouts by the underpass and wait until I'm round the corner before I throw them away. Or else, instead of hanging around in underpasses after 4:30 pm, because it's dangerous, I'll sort out the junk in my handbag: plastic with plastic . . . paper with paper . . . lipstick with lipstick . . .

*Edyta fussily takes stock of the contents of her handbag. She leaves the room, and meticulously segregates all unnecessary items and throws them in the appropriate containers. Bożena makes to grab the magazine, but Halina is nimbler and more assertive.*

EDYTA. Would you believe this mess? It's last April's *For You* magazine, with the crossword puzzle done! Into the waste-paper bin with you! What a mess, everything's laying around, the environment's dying, and whenever I look for anything, all I end up with is dirty fingernails!

HALINA. Oh, it's last April's *Not for You* magazine. Lovely! It's cheap, for free, I can afford it.

*Halina leafs through the magazine. Little Metal Girl rides up on a squeaky kid's bicycle and ventures a glance at the glossy pages.*

LITTLE METAL GIRL. Not bad at all.

HALINA. It's from last April. Just the thing not for me.

LITTLE METAL GIRL. They've even done the crossword for you.

HALINA. So I know the hidden phrase without having to do it myself: "Springtime tête-à-tête."

LITTLE METAL GIRL. Show-me-Mom-mee. Springtime tête-à-tête . . . Hang on . . . Springtime snogging by the shit-stream?

SCENE 4

*All the characters are in the apartment: The Man is sitting at his table, now strewn with wine bottles, smoked cigarettes and half-snorted lines of dope, his heirloom paintings of ancestral gerberas have long since come unstuck and fallen off the walls. Halina, Bożena, Gloomy Old Biddy and Little Metal Girl are sitting in their natural positions and avidly following the action on TV.*

**MAN.** Cut! Obviously that wasn't the end, but just the beginning, a brief overview of the out-takes that didn't make it into the final cut of the film, as a goodwill gesture towards the 4 million punters who didn't come to see the film, because they wouldn't fork out 20 zloty for a ticket, not to mention the "Buy 8 Get 2 Free" nachos, M&M's, sugar-frosted nuts, Coke and seven beers, just to get a glimpse of Dumpsville and listen to fake barfing in Dolby Surround, as if they didn't get the real thing in Dolby Surround every day. So I had to agree to some minor concessions, a man's got to make a living somehow, I've got a mortgage to pay off too! Monika is tired of being blind and deaf . . .

**HALINA.** No wonder, you'd have to be blind to want to be deaf!

**LITTLE METAL GIRL.** She might not be blind or deaf, but she's too fat. She ought to lose weight.

**BOŻENA.** She ought to lose weight and change her outfit. Dressed like that, I wouldn't even go and buy vinegar from Biedronka!

**MAN.** . . . Monika decides to break with her dead-end life and give it her best shot. She sells the rotting coop with her favorite pigeons and buys a ticket to Warsaw. There, she moves into a computer-rendering in an advertising brochure for a gated community . . .

**GLOOMY OLD BIDDY.** Is that really Warsaw? Solec Street? I don't recognise it . . .

**LITTLE METAL GIRL.** Oh, Gran, it's that building, you know, the one they haven't built yet.

**GLOOMY OLD BIDDY IN A WHEELCHAIR.** I was walking down there the day the war broke out . . .

**HALINA.** Some people's noses get longer, others blow smoke, while others still can do it with a deadpan expression, but, whatever the method, it's all: Strictly Bullshit!

**LITTLE METAL GIRL.** It's not nice to keep nicking someone else's life and passing it off as your own

in stories to slobber on your pillow to! All my life, ever since I can remember, Gran never walked anywhere or went to any con-densation camp either.

**MAN.** Where she finds a job with an advertising agency as an up-and-coming copywriter, in a reputable law firm as a successful solicitor, and in a design studio as a gorgeous architect. She works a lot professionally, and has a fax machine, but after work she feels lost, because she has no kids. She goes down to the Photoshop where she sips Knorr soup . . .

**HALINA.** Monika, don't overpay! You can get the same soup, only worse, in Biedronka for half the price.

**BOŻENA.** Soup on its own won't fill you up: You'll just get hungry again! Try adding noodles, or some bones at least.

**LITTLE METAL GIRL.** Don't make her add noodles! She'll never lose weight. She'll stay fat, and obesity is an illness.

**BOŻENA.** Maybe in that backward Poland of yours. Things are completely different back home in America. That was just a thought, because I'm fat as a pig and I won't go imposing my point of view on people.

**MAN.** There, she meets Max: They touch lips naked in the toilet and then in the elevator. Nonetheless, they run into problems. Monika is fed up with the emptiness and lack of values, while Max turns out to be an irresponsible slacker who doesn't want to start a family, but keeps a cabinet full of cut-price brown flour next to his Knorr soup . . .

**HALINA.** He's overpaying. Regular's much cheaper.

MAN. . . . Hot on his heels are three heavy-set, sloppily self-tanned Colombians from the Russian mafia, a sexy policewoman, a bungling, Tramal-addicted gumshoe, and a gay hairdresser. The latter, though not tolerated, turns out to be a good guy and saves a poor child from a fire, because in fact he isn't gay at all, just a normal guy who's simply well-groomed and not tolerated.

LITTLE METAL GIRL. I hate intolerance. Seriously. I also hate those Vanilla Swirl and Malt Creme chocolates from selection boxes. Rock on!

MAN. Monika gives birth to a husband and kids, a boy or a girl, and feels very happy and fulfilled as a woman. She has frank chats with her toilet bowl about the new Domestos. Looming on the horizon are three computer-simulated skyscrapers, and they walk off laughing hand in hand. The End. That would be the last scene of the film, if I ever got round to making it.

TV HOST. Hi. Just recently she was digging through pixels on a slag heap, and today she's a big star. She sold her rotting pigeon coop, and took the one shot she had, and today she'll be openly laying bare the contents of her handbag.

MONIKA. In my bag, I normally carry the items I need most: a magnetic lasso tool plus Alt, a polygonal lasso tool, an eye dropper tool, a paintbrush, brightness/contrast, colours, gradients, masks, a Shift key, and I'm never without an eraser—it's especially handy for pubic hair, which is so easy to come by these days.

TV HOST. So the life of a star is not all as one would think—whee and coochie-coo with a polyester cat on a red carpet, but . . .

MONIKA. Honestly . . .? . . . It's hard work. There were times when after a whole day of monotonous non-eating, non-drinking, followed by non-pissing and non-shitting, and non-sweating in between, I was so squashed, stretched and weary that I'd lie down on the Photoshop couch, too weak to go to the house I was too tired to remember I didn't have, because I didn't exist, and for days and nights on end I lay there waiting for someone to come along and unsquash and unstretch me, not to mention the phantom pain I had after having my navel removed. And yet I owe a lot to not existing and not being. On the one hand I'm nobody, but then again, I'm not Polish.

**TV HOST.** If that's the case, your Polish is excellent—you speak it with hardly any accent at all.

**MONIKA.** It wasn't easy. I was born here as a little baby, entirely by chance. You see, this is where my great-great-grandparents, great-grandparents, grandparents, parents, siblings, uncles, aunts and cousins lived, blown here on the winds of fate, naturally, always longing for the West, whence they came. They say that at first I cried a lot and waved my tiny fists. Even then I wanted to go back where I came from, to the West, that is, but being a helpless infant, I wasn't able to speak a word of Polish, let alone book a ticket. They didn't even have the Internet in 1970s Poland. What could I do, I learned Polish willy-nilly and now I speak it without an accent, but still, I can never remember the meaning of certain long words, not that it stops me from saying them. I must also confess that the local water and air disagree with me, I don't like the landscape, the architecture, and I don't like the people, all so glum, unhappy with their lives, and insecure.

## SCENE 5

*Edyta with her wet panties bundled up in her hand, Halina, Bożena, Little Metal Girl.*

**EDYTA.** Ohmigod, I was so unsettled and upset, all this makes me want to go home and have a Lausanne salad, a goat-kid pâté, and a bucket of Parmesan, and if that isn't enough, I'll have a bushel of carrots, wash it all down with a liter of makeup remover, and another kilo of nice sweets, that I won't take to the poor orphans in the orphanage, but eat them in the car myself to calm my nerves, and once I've stopped by the gym along the way, to fight the flab, I won't be able to bear the fact that there were no rivers en route, from which I could save people from drowning, and no fires, from which I could save people from burning, so I couldn't . . . And the fear that the doors of existence might slam shut behind me without the same bang without which they opened, will get too intense, so I feel I should shout it out loud and clear. I'll shout it out, straight and calm. I'll say it forcefully, but not too sharply, or maybe I'll just whisper it into my own ear—pssst, or think it, poker-faced, not letting on, otherwise they'll blame me for not shaving my beaver again. The film "The Horse Rode Horseback" perpetuates and sugarcoats the stereotypical role of women in the morass of pseudo-bliss, objectifying, squashing, stretching and denying them their natural navels.

**BOŻENA.** Well, I'm no feminist. I'm a fat pig.

**HALINA.** Nobody's talking me into having an abortion! I would never let them kill the tiny wee babe sheltered in my womb! Where would I get the money?!

**BOŻENA.** How would I get the money for it?

**HALINA.** I can't afford to be a baby killer like that.

**LITTLE METAL GIRL.** I'm no lisbian either!

**HALINA.** What are you on about? What kind of word is that?

**LITTLE METAL GIRL.** I don't know either, I just downloaded it.

## ACT III

### SCENE 1

*In his apartment, the Man is furiously putting his papers and wine bottles in order, rolling up cardboard boxes, and folding the pictures of gerberas.*

**MAN.** What's all the fuss about? Tell the one in glasses to shave her beaver and buy some contact lenses, then she can give birth to a husband and kids, have all the Domestos she wants, and stop thinking about this nonsense. Because of them I totally can't write my screenplay entitled "The Horse Rode Horseback", which caused quite a buzz, scooped up all the awards and single-handedly revived Polish cinema, which is in a sorry state, not to be confused with a united state. Because of them I totally can't write my screenplay: As if it weren't bad enough that I drink and eat too much, drive four-wheel drives through the cradle of our civilization, frequent Egyptian swimming pools and New York boutiques, and when I come back wanting to make a film about present-day Poland and its disadvantage and deracination, its fraying social fabric, poverty, intolerance, unbalanced national identity, and the other dreadful problems that Hoolybeck wrote about so convincingly . . .—not that I'd know, never read him; that stuff doesn't concern me—. . . I simply can't, I don't know how. When I fly back to Warsaw, to this potato patch blighted by sick systems, sick concepts and sick relations, and the Metro going whoosh, the trams going vroom, the planes going whizz, the polluted shit-stream going glug glug glug, I want to have a life and I still have to pay the mortgage on my apartment, which, honestly, would make a much better wine cellar.

*Exit. The Biddy fiddles with the radio dial. Eventually, an announcer's voice comes out of the static and drone of the airwaves.*

RADIO. In the old days, when the world still lived by divine laws, everyone in the world was Polish. The Germans were Polish, the Swedes were Polish, the Spaniards were Polish, everybody was Polish, simply everybody. Poland was a fair country to behold back then; we had magnificent seas, islands and oceans, a fleet to sail them all and discover ever-new continents that also belonged to Poland. There was the famous Polish explorer Krzysztof Kolumbus who, predictably enough, was later renamed Christopher, Chris or Isaak or something. We were a great power, an oasis of tolerance and multiculturalism, and everyone not coming here from another country, because, as we've said, there were no other countries to come from, was welcomed with bread . . .

*Little Metal Girl rides up on her bike. She circles nervously around the radio, as if jealous that something had elbowed her out of the soundscape.*

LITTLE METAL GIRL. Bread, bread; I've heard something about inbreds once.

GLOOMY OLD BIDDY. Bread.

LITTLE METAL GIRL. Bread or bred, I don't know what it means, but if it's that white, flaky crap from Tesco's, we should have told them that it's great for drawing on asphalt. And it doesn't wash off in the acid rain. But it's very fattening.

RADIO. . . . and salt. But our nation's heyday eventually came to an end. First they took away America, Africa, Asia and Australia. Polish flags were defaced and painted with stripes, stars and other squiggles. Polish was officially replaced by fancy-pantsy foreign languages that nobody knows except for the people who speak them, so that we Poles don't understand them and feel like right snot-rags . . .

LITTLE METAL GIRL. Whatever. I download subtitles off the Net and understand everything.

RADIO. Next they took Egypt, France, Italy and Brazil away from us, and then they took Germany . . .

LITTLE METAL GIRL. Serves us right! Where else would we find work otherwise?

RADIO. . . . the Poles living there were immediately Germanized and forced to yodel. And last of all they carved off Russia, where the Polish populace was made to speak in some outlandish dialect. We were left with a sandy parcel of our beloved native soil. The Vistula sliced through the fields of blood-red mallows like a silver thread, and the golden wheat ripened, our daily bread . . .

LITTLE METAL GIRL. Then tell them to get that white flaky crap from Tesco's, they're great for writing on the asphalt, only they're lethally fattening, and Gran will never get to be transparent!

**RADIO.** Until Warsaw was invaded by the Germans who said Poland would no longer be Poland, and that Warsaw would no longer be its capital, but just a rubble-filled hole in the ground . . .

**LITTLE METAL GIRL.** That's right, a hole! A godforsaken hole. I hate this city! The Metro goes whoosh, the trams go vroom, the buses stink, and wherever you go, it's always over someone's dead body!

**RADIO.** . . . and that we would no longer be Poles . . .

**LITTLE METAL GIRL.** Damn right! Damn right! I'm no Pole either, why should I be? That's a choice I couldn't make, not even subconsciously. I'm a European.

**RADIO.** . . . we're not Poles, but Germans or Russians—or their corpses, to be exact, and those who aren't corpses yet will soon be ones anyway . . .

**LITTLE METAL GIRL.** Exactly. I fully agree with that radio. Why bother being Poles?

**GLOOMY OLD BIDDY.** O Poland, glorious land, I can still see your beauty dying.

**LITTLE METAL GIRL.** If it was dying, it should've popped a couple of aspirin! Everybody knows Poland's a stupid country: it's poor and ugly. The architecture's ugly, the weather's gloomy, the temperatures are cold, even the animals have run off to hide in the woods. The shows on TV are bad, the jokes aren't funny, the prime minister looks like a pumpkin, and the president looks like the prime minister. In France they have France, in America they've got America, Germany in Germany, and even the Czech Republic is Czech, but in Poland all you get is Poland. In France they have baguettes, England's got toast, the Germans have rolls, but in Poland it's bread, bread, bread. In France, they all speak French, they speak English in England, but in Poland, I curse, like everybody else does, in Polish, which nobody understands. I've long since made up my mind that I'm not Polish, just European, and I learned the language from records and tapes left behind by the Polish cleaning lady.

This here's not my mom, but our personal salesperson from Tesco. She brings Tesco to our house on a forklift and we just point at what we don't want and she takes it back again, and how she skids round those corners!

This is not our neighbour, but our private leaflet dispenser. She brings the underpass to our door and hands out leaflets there, she ignores them for us and throws them away 'round the next corner! She's so fat we keep her locked up at home. Won't have her wobbling around in normal people's field of view.

And this here is not my Gran, she's our cleaning lady. She's so old and transparent because she just rode in from Ukraine today in this wheelchair. And we exist on the best terms we can!

We're no Poles, just normal folks! We came to Poland from Europe to get good bio-organic potatoes grown in real soil, not like those watery ones from Tesco's, and we learned Polish from records and tapes!

*Static on the wire, a broken connection, a humming sound; the Little Metal Girl turns the dial on the radio, and big-beat music comes blasting out.*

RADIO. The horse rode horseback and hollered whoa, the fish took a ship, the fridge went brrr. The horse rode horseback, a pre-shut door, blood in the bloodstream, watch it flow . . .

GLOOMY OLD BIDDY. Knock it off! I remember the day the war broke out.

LITTLE METAL GIRL. The Cola war?

GLOOMY OLD BIDDY. Me with just my handbag, with just the floral-print dress on, walking home from the Vistula because it was quite a hot day, my eyes still blue from gazing into the sleepy, cool, soapy, limpid current . . . My leather shoes clicked jauntily along the boulevard . . .

LITTLE METAL GIRL. . . . dragging cattails, old rubbers, sanitary pads and a soggy plastic bag stuck to their heels . . .

**GLOOMY OLD BIDDY IN A WHEELCHAIR.** Then I was back in our courtyard. I'd just opened the gate, and was by the door of our building, reaching out my hand to my little brothers and sisters, when I happened to notice that, while strolling down by the river, something had got stuck to the heel of my shoe. I stopped by the rubbish bins to scrape it off, and I can still remember that . . .

## SCENE 2

*Change of lighting. By the recycling bins, Gloomy Biddy—without her wheelchair, and wearing her floral-print dress—and Little Metal Girl are painstakingly trying to remove the trash stuck to Biddy's shoe.*

**LITTLE METAL GIRL.** That it was a big old empty lunchmeat can, with a few soggy Tesco leaflets, a degradable bag, a tampon applicator, a body-bag, and a McDonald's take-out with nearly all the fries inside that, despite lying in the water for over a year or even two, retained their shape and aroma, so I scarfed a couple even though they're very fattening, and I can kiss being transparent goodbye if I don't get a grip on myself . . .

**GLOOMY OLD BIDDY.** When all of a sudden . . .

*Sirens wail, planes roar, bombs are dropped.*

**LITTLE METAL GIRL.** When all of a sudden BANG! This stench seems familiar. We'd better run, there's a bicycle burning here.

**GLOOMY OLD BIDDY IN A WHEELCHAIR.** The whole sky, the whole sky grew dark . . .

**LITTLE METAL GIRL.** That's because of the incoming model airplanes. Why don't you fall down the stairs into the cellar, Gran, and break your arm and crack your skull on the bricks lying there!

*Gloomy Old Biddy and Little Metal Girl tumble down the stairs.*

**GLOOMY OLD BIDDY IN A WHEELCHAIR.** The whole sky, the whole sky . . .

**LITTLE METAL GIRL.** They rented the whole sky for a model airplane show. Somebody must have been busy with the glue!

GLOOMY OLD BIDDY IN A WHEELCHAIR. A terrible noise, my heart was a-flutter like a quail . . .

LITTLE METAL GIRL. . . . being bashed with a pail.

GLOOMY OLD BIDDY IN A WHEELCHAIR. And then silence, a silence so cold and echoing . . .

LITTLE METAL GIRL. Let's go, it stinks of potatoes and soggy cardboard in here. I'd rather puke at the sight of Auntie Bożena.

GLOOMY OLD BIDDY IN A WHEELCHAIR. Stop, don't go!

LITTLE METAL GIRL. Oh, what a surprise. I could have sworn that our building was just where all this flying rubble, stones, glass and loosely scattered pixels are hanging in the air now weren't here just now, where I recognize these splintered drawers, but I could have sworn they were intact, in a chest of drawers. We used to have splinters exactly like the ones flying there, only they were chairs. These here teeth are the spitting image of the ones that we had in our combs back home. These shreds are just like shreds of our photos, except that ours were whole. And those Poles whizzing past used to live nearby, but the ones we knew were alive and in one piece, not some unidentified remains flying every which way. Could it be that I'm so drunk that not only do I not remember ever drinking anything, but that I can't even find my own house? The one that's collapsing now bears a striking resemblance to it, and in fact it is. How strange.

GLOOMY OLD BIDDY IN A WHEELCHAIR. It all fell down and piled up in layers. I shut my eyes even tighter, and when I opened them it was all lying there: rubble, bodies, dust, bodies, grit, bodies, rubble, bodies, like some kind of ghastly lasagne.

LITTLE METAL GIRL. Whenever Mum doesn't make lasagne, that's exactly the way she doesn't layer it. Cool slag-heap! It's great for poking through the pixels.

*They rummage in the rubble.*

GLOOMY OLD BIDDY IN A WHEELCHAIR. I don't know how long it's been: I forgot my wristwatch when I left the apartment that autumn day. Exhausted and famished, I wandered for a long time through a huge heap of rubble. Bread!

LITTLE METAL GIRL. Just as long as it's whole-grain, and not that radioactive crap. I don't want to be slim, I want to be transparent.

GLOOMY OLD BIDDY IN A WHEELCHAIR. Bread!

LITTLE METAL GIRL (*Keeps on digging*). Did you see that bicycle burning, Gran? There it is, at last! There it is, at last! I recognize the cracked peephole, it's ours . . . The door to our apartment, what a relief! Knock-knock! Knock-knock! You need to knock harder; knocking on a pile of ash doesn't make much of a sound.

GLOOMY OLD BIDDY IN A WHEELCHAIR. I suppose they must all be in their rooms. Wipe your feet. This is where the doormat used to be. And hang up your coat. I saw a hanger lying around near that broken crockery.

LITTLE METAL GIRL (*Running to meet him*). Uncle Maurice! Uncle Maurice! Uncle Maurice, I've found your leg: It was standing in the living room. Where's the rest of you, Uncle? And whose mouth is this? Who left it lying so carelessly under these burnt shelves of charred books, making that repulsive smacking sound from under the embers?

GLOOMY OLD BIDDY IN A WHEELCHAIR. Daria! I'll tell mother—if I ever find her face, still reflected in the mirror clasped in her severed hand, that is.

LITTLE METAL GIRL (*Still rummaging in the rubble*). Well, what's this? Some perfectly good arms; only one of them's broken. It must have broken when you fell into the cellar, Gran. But I'll have to pry them loose, because they're clutching on to something! Aaargh! They're clutching real hard here! What could it be? All bloody, mangled and dead. It must've smashed into those bricks! In America, they give you rubber gloves for this sort of thing. Ah, here we are. Isn't that your face, by any chance? And isn't that all the rest of you, Gran? Oh what a tangled bundle of nerves, if you can find the tooth of a comb, we'll straighten them out, because you look like a shredded parachute. (*Drags all of her grandmother from beneath the rubble.*) You really should take better care of yourself, Gran. Is this is that famous frock you've been blathering on and on about; so these are the roses? All gone to seed and broken. You are what you wear! Nettles, balding dandelions, some bloodied bandages, do you think we'll be able to get the stains out? What have they embroidered on it? Spent cartridges, lurking earwigs, barbed wire: All that's gone out of style, couldn't they have just gonc for little skulls instead? Jeez, you should have called Mom. Everybody knows you can't programme the washing machine, Gran: it's better to ask someone to do it for you than to end up breaking it again.

## SCENE 3

*The Man's apartment. The layout is exactly as it was before, only there is no more trace of mold, wall units, wall hangings, or yogurt pots under the IKEA pseudo-glitz. The only trace of their existence is a heap of pixels sifting around by the garbage cans, running around on top of which Little Metal Girl in a thoroughly mouse-eaten sailor-suit with wasps' nests in her hair, and—if possible—making dramatic gestures out of a medieval epic: Roland on a hilltop, thrusting his sword in his Adam's apple. Off in the distance, on their sun-bleached armchairs, are Halina and Bożena in couch-potato mode; moping about next to them is Edyta, not knowing where to hang her emotion-drenched lace panties and a bag full of mixed chocolate wrappers, and Monika, still in search of her missing navel.*

**MAN.** And this is where the audience realizes that Grandma died in that air-raid. But the girl still says:

**LITTLE METAL GIRL.** Gran! Gran! Get up, Gran!

**MAN.** And then she turns on the waterworks, because she realizes that not only did her beloved grandma die in the air raid, but that, consequently, her mother was probably never born either, which would not only make her an orphan, but mean that she too doesn't exist, and never has, which is far better for all concerned, especially for all the others concerned, me most of all, because now I have peace and quiet and a room all to myself.

**LITTLE METAL GIRL.** Bread! Bread!

**MAN.** Cries the girl in the last scene, as she starves to death on a heap of rubble. The audience feels moved, and ponders their life in peacetime, when all the wars and famines happen to occur in other countries.

**LITTLE METAL GIRL.** Bread!

**HALINA.** Have those mildewy crusts I put out for the birds on the windowsill. Why let them go to waste?

**BOŻENA.** I'll have them! I didn't go down to Tesco's today because I can't go wobbling around in other people's field of view. After all, they could be puking for better reasons than that.

**EDYTA.** Would you care for a sweet? They're very nice. I've got some left over in the car that I didn't eat when, after seeing that film, I got too emotional to take them to the orphanage.

**MONIKA.** Me, I don't eat anything because even nothing makes you put on weight and gives you navels.

**LITTLE METAL GIRL** (*To herself*). Bread! Gran, did you see that bicycle burning? (*Bangs on the Man's door with her fists.*)

Bread!

**MAN** (*Looks suspiciously through the peephole and opens the door*). Get out of here, you filthy brat, I don't have any bread to give you. Bread, huh! Give them bread, and they'll waste it all on vodka and drugs.

*The End*

PAWEŁ DEMIRSKI

Translated by Artur Zapałowski

# DIAMONDS ARE COAL THAT GOT DOWN TO BUSINESS

IMAGE 10.1 **Astrow (Piotr Tokarz), Sonia (Aleksandra Cybulska), and Nanny (Sabina Tumidalska)**

Directed by Monika Strzępka. Teatr Dramatyczny im. Jerzego Szaniawskiego, Wałbrzych (2011)

*Photograph by Kuba Dąbrowski*

## CHARACTERS

TIELEGIN

NANNY

UNCLE/WOJNICKI

ASTROW

SONIA

## NOTE

*Diamonds Are Coal That Got Down to Business* is a freely paraphrased adaptation of Anton Chekhov's *Uncle Vanya*, set in the present day, where Chekhov's frustrated, maladjusted characters cannot cope with the challenges of a neoliberal economy. Expecting them to "cultivate small business" and "take part in free competition" is as ridiculous as it is cruel. The play's critique of society is directed partly against the indolence of its protagonists, but is primarily a fervent accusation of free-market ideologists.

Within the context of Poland, this critique relates to the economic "shock treatment" implemented to revive the economy after 1989, with little heed to the ensuing social costs. In *Diamonds Are Coal That Got Down to Business*, Chekhov's Professor Serebryakov is the mouthpiece for the views of the father of Polish economic reform, Leszek Balcerowicz: "Those people need to suffer more if things are to get any better / We don't like it but there's nothing we can do / And nothing is what we should be doing."

The premiere of *Diamonds Are Coal That Got Down to Business* was directed by Monika Strzępka at Teatr Dramatyczny im. Szaniawskiego, in the southwestern industrial city of Wałbrzych, in 2008. The center of the stage was occupied by a huge table covered with oilcloth, at which a group of spectators were invited to sit together with the actors. The production employed grotesque and slapstick; it also created a homey atmosphere, with elements ranging from outmoded furniture to actors in provincial, small-town dress. The resulting performance was irresistibly funny, with a strong political bite.

# DIAMONDS ARE COAL THAT GOT DOWN TO BUSINESS

SONIA. The worst thing about this story is that this story here—
is already over.
At the end of the story, its protagonist will realize he won't win,
that he could not have won,
that he could not have stopped and won

TIELEGIN. Occupied!

SONIA. Gentlemen!
. . . that it's not possible simply to walk the line and win,
or do something good and win,
or do something bad and win,
or cast your vote and win,
or not cast your vote,
or believe in civil society and win,
or in universal human rights and win,
or believe in the equal opportunities and unfettered personal growth
that this new economic system—his own—has provided
and win.
Someone else will always win,
and that's why that someone is there—while he's right here.
Or something to that effect.
Astrow, warn the people about Uncle before Uncle gets here,
won't you?

ASTROW. Me?—warn people?

Good day.

About Wojnicki?

SONIA. About Wojnicki.

ASTROW. Good day, ladies and gentlemen.

It so happens that the worst thing about this story is that every story
has the protagonist it deserves, and I personally think that this story
deserves a better hero than some Wojnicki you have to warn people against,
therefore why don't I—say a little about myself?

SONIA. No.

ASTROW. And yet if I were to say something—something that could make us feel like a community—a community that will be spending this evening together—something to help us feel comfortable in our own company—among our own kind, so to speak—why don't I tell an anecdote taken from my medical practice? So—

SONIA. No.

ASTROW. Why not?

SONIA. We're waiting for Uncle? Ba-boom?

ASTROW. Ba-boom?

SONIA. I've seen Uncle running around with his gun out—hanging right down to his knees—gearing up to shoot my father straight in his professorial face, so there!

ASTROW. Speaking of faces—I had this patient . . .

SONIA. Speaking of faces—shut your pie-hole!

ASTROW. Well, anyway— they never found the scalpel.

SONIA. Astrow!

ASTROW. Present!

SONIA. The worst thing about this story is that Uncle and his gun will be here any moment, and one will have to feel sorry for Uncle and his gun.

As soon as a person—a woman—myself, that is—arrives at her family home,

she has to feel sorry for Uncle.

As soon as I step inside this house, I feel guilty, while Uncle doesn't care: Uncle's been practicing at the firing range all week.

**ASTROW.** He's been practicing all week—because it's been a week since he found out that Sieriebriakow was coming today—he's been talking about shooting all week—about shooting at the Professor.

**TIELEGIN.** Whenever Wojnicki talks about shooting at the Professor, that's when I try to avoid Wojnicki.

**NANNY.** The worst thing about this story is that we have to get to like Uncle because he is the protagonist of this story, after all.

**ASTROW.** One could have Uncle withdraw inside himself—but it's unlikely that Uncle has a self big enough to contain his frustration—which hangs right down to his knees.

**SONIA.** I don't give a damn about Uncle's frustration—I can feel sorry for him but not much—the pace of the life I lead won't let me.

**TIELEGIN.** The worst thing about this story is that it's mostly Uncle's ups and downs that we'll be following.

**ASTROW.** Downs—yes—it'll be mostly his downs we'll be following.

**NANNY.** And this evening together could have been so lovely—like the good old days—because—ladies and gentlemen—the Professor is coming today to deliver a lecture and eat potatoes with us—I peeled them myself.

**SONIA.** But Uncle, instead of stuffing his face full of potatoes—will bring up stuff nobody wants to think about.

**TIELEGIN.** Without Uncle things would be so pleasant and homely like a new year's concert at the philharmonic.

**SONIA.** Uncle is mad that the concert and the potatotes aren't for him—that even though he is the protagonist—it's the Professor that we're waiting for.

**TIELEGIN.** But we're waiting for Uncle now.

**NANNY.** Well, we're waiting for Uncle now so as to be able to wait in peace for the Professor later—and for the potatoes—I peeled them myself.

**SONIA.** Uncle has a sense of entitlement—but Uncle's done nothing to deserve today's celebration.

**NANNY.** That's right

**ASTROW.** Deserves or not—right or not . . .

Ladies and gentlemen—if we don't want to throw money for theatre tickets and potatoes down the drain, it's in your interest and ours to like Uncle.

**NANNY.** Because he is the protagonist of this story, after all.

**ASTROW.** And we really have to be together in this.

**SONIA.** That's the rule: Get to like the protagonist, so that later we can care about his fate on stage and watch that fate unfold and not be bored—much.

**TIELEGIN.** If he weren't the protagonist we really wouldn't give a shit about Uncle—social reality throws a lot of deals and ordeals our way.

**ASTROW.** But we'll face them head on—right—he'll be here any moment now—so we have to hurry up and get to like him.

**SONIA.** I'm on it.

**ASTROW.** Right—how about this? In the first scenes of a movie, we always get to like the protagonist for something—right? Right.

**ASTROW.** Like he takes care of his grandma—right?

**ASTROW.** Well, you think of something.

**SONIA.** Me? You bet I'll think of something!

**ASTROW.** Then think of something.

**TIELEGIN.** Me, me, me! I'll think of something.

**SONIA.** Tielegin!

**TIELEGIN.** Me, me, me! I'll think of something, I'll think of something, I'll think of something.

**SONIA.** Well?

**TIELEGIN.** Well, for instance, we could get to like Uncle because we don't give a shit about him.

**SONIA.** Tielegin!

**TIELEGIN.** Sorry.

**SONIA.** It's not that simple . . . Maybe we could like him because he's funny . . .

ASTROW. Ha ha ha!

TIELEGIN. I'll tell you, I'll tell you.

SONIA. . . . and because he's getting fired . . .

ASTROW. Ha ha ha!

TIELEGIN. I'll tell you, I'll tell you.

SONIA. . . . and that's funny in a way?

ASTROW. Ha ha ha!

TIELEGIN. I'll tell you, I'll tell you.

SONIA. Tell him, Nanny.

NANNY. Tielegin, shut your pie-hole!

TIELEGIN. Sorry.

ASTROW. Or because his friends beat him up for no good reason, and the people around him don't accept him . . .

TIELEGIN. Because we don't give a shit about him.

SONIA. Tielegin!

ASTROW. . . . and he has to deal with that somehow—and somebody has to treat him—so why don't I tell an anecdote taken from my medical practice?

SONIA. No!

ASTROW. Well, excuse me!

SONIA. Or because he's lost and . . .

TIELEGIN. I'll tell you, I'll tell you!

SONIA. Tielegin!

TIELEGIN. Nanny—Miss—they're not letting me say we don't give a shit about him!

ASTROW. Tielegin!

SONIA. I got it! Picture this: We see Uncle for the first time, and for the first five minutes we see him looking for a toilet because he wants to pee . . .

ASTROW. That's good.

SONIA. . . . he was on the bus a very long time, and he left his bag on the bus—and he needs to pee—he doesn't have his bag—and all the toilets are closed, so he goes up to the counter to ask about the bag, and he can't hold it in any longer—but there's a line in front of the window, and then he sees the bus riding off to the capital with his bag, and he can't hold it in any longer, so he starts running around—running like a headless chicken with a full bladder—so he runs after the bus but he can't run that good, so he starts looking for a toilet, but the bus station's closed and it's full of people who don't need to pee . . .

**ASTROW.** So he runs around, but does he find a toilet in the end—yes or no?

**SONIA.** Astrow—please—we've all peed in a public space at least once in our lives—so now why doesn't each of us imagine that he or she has peed along with Uncle—some relief, huh?

**ASTROW.** What about the bag?

**SONIA.** Yes—this does take some intellectual effort—getting to like someone who couldn't hold it in and peed in the street in front of our house—but it's worth it.

**SONIA.** Mary and Joseph, he's coming here!

**TIELEGIN.** The Professor? And me not dressed for the occasion.

**SONIA.** No, not my father—it's my uncle—alas—he's coming here and there's no stopping him.

**ASTROW.** Let's all stay calm—staying calm's our only hope—that, and a bulletproof vest.

**TIELEGIN.** Our uncle is a special kind of person.

**NANNY.** Ever since he's seen human misery . . .

**TIELEGIN.** . . . he's been talking to things about shooting.

**NANNY.** He prefers talking to parked cars.

**TIELEGIN.** He tells them he's seen human misery . . .

**NANNY.** . . . human misery in all its enormity.

**TIELEGIN.** Exactly.

**NANNY.** That misery . . . was his misery.

**TIELEGIN.** His misery—why his?

IMAGE 10.2 **Tielegin (Jerzy Gronowski) and Nanny (Sabina Tumidalska)**
Directed by Monika Strzępka. Teatr Dramatyczny im. Jerzego Szaniawskiego, Wałbrzych (2011)
*Photograph by Kuba Dąbrowski*

---

NANNY. He's been observing it ever since—and telling objects about it.

SONIA. What objects? I saw him kneeling by the toilet bowl once, and I thought he was vomiting.
Nanny, is there anything stuck to my ass?

NANNY. What?

TIELEGIN. Shit.

SONIA. Uncle, I said, if you have to get falling down drunk, you could at least eat well, and then he said: Don't talk nonsense. I never vomit, ever. I was just telling the toilet bowl about Helena.
Why does everybody keep talking about Helena?
Why does everybody keep talking about Helena on their knees?

Why doesn't anybody kneel by the toilet for me the way Uncle does for her?

**NANNY.** Helena is the Professor's new wife—Sonia was always measuring up in her shadow.

**SONIA.** Nanny dear—keep your pie-hole shut next time around.

**TIELEGIN.** Uncle spoke to my toilet bowl once.

**NANNY.** But you don't have a toilet bowl.

**TIELEGIN.** Exactly—but I'm trying to get to like him.

**ASTROW.** What is there to like? Just because he has conversations with toilet bowls?

**SONIA.** Moving right along: The point is that Uncle goes on and on without realizing he's all washed up, and that there's nothing better in store for him, alas. Nothing.

**WOJNICKI.** You know—it's actually a consolation when I think that I'm not all washed up, yet. I'm telling you—if I were—I'd have shot myself in the head with my own hands right away. The head of the Polish intelligentsia.

**ASTROW.** And missed.

**WOJNICKI.** Missed what? What do you mean - missed? How could I have not missed?

Greetings, Sonia, how good of you to come visit us. How could I have not missed? When I couldn't see straight?

My name is Wojnicki—Jan Wojnicki—and five minutes from now . . .

**SONIA.** Uncle! Lucky that the car didn't run you over after all.

**WOJNICKI.** No car ever ran me over—never.

**SONIA.** Uncle was talking to a tire, and the car started rolling.

**WOJNICKI.** But Uncle jumped away—it rolled over his shoe, is all.

**SONIA.** Uncle!

**WOJNICKI.** I'm no Uncle!

My name is Jan Wojnicki.

And five minutes from now, I'm going to shoot a man.

*Exit Uncle.*

**ASTROW.** I think that's what you call a repeat offence.

**SONIA.** Uncle's been through this before.

**ASTROW.** He missed a man at close range twice—Professor Sieriebriakow— and then he saw human misery.

**SONIA.** My father.

**NANNY.** Who'll be here soon: your father.

**TIELEGIN.** Everything that happened—that happened—that happened—that happened . . . it's all good.

**NANNY.** And your father is a remarkable man.

**ASTROW.** Entirely—that is, he still is—until Uncle hits him, that is—meaning not for another hundred years or so.

**TIELEGIN.** He was also the husband of his sister, your mother, whose dowry for him was this-ole-house, and when she died he married Helena and wanted to sell this-ol'-house—the house of an entirely remarkable woman.

**ASTROW.** So now why don't you tell the story—so people know what this is about—so the audience knows what's up with this house.

**SONIA.** I'm not telling—theatre's no place to drag out the garbage.

**NANNY.** By the ears . . .

**TIELEGIN.** But are they Uncle's ears?

**SONIA.** Year after year, in the year '90, this house was no longer able to pay for itself.

So my father did the math, and the neoliberal calculator—which was the only calculator he had—told him the house should be sold, and that was that.

And that the only therapy that would keep us alive was shock therapy, and mass layoffs, too.

**TIELEGIN.** The Professor said he wasn't a practical man and didn't know much about anything.

**SONIA.** The point is that it—the sale—paid off.

**TIELEGIN.** For whom?

SONIA. What do you mean: for whom?

TIELEGIN. For whom did it pay off? Sorry.

SONIA. It paid off for everybody in the end: Look at how your standard's gone up.

TIELEGIN. My standard?

SONIA. The thing is that the house was only partly paid off by Uncle.

Meaning he had a real stake in the, so to speak, assets, but refused to understand that it would pay off for everybody to sell the house and let free competition do its thing.

His archaic habits of all-too-obvious origin . . .

NANNY. The old Commie . . .

SONIA. . . . hindered him from understanding what was good for him.

As a result, he lost out, and there's nothing better in store for him anymore.

But there could have been. That's why he was dismissed, ridiculed and yelled at for not being able to cope. And now Uncle's moping around as one of the last victims of transformation. Because everybody else is getting by somehow.

TIELEGIN. Except for a million other uncles, that is.

SONIA. Tielegin, shut your pie-hole! What's one million compared to all the millions of others?

NANNY. So how did they all get by?

SONIA. On prosperity.

If only he could afford a new fridge at least. And the little things in life.

The thing is, we have to let you know that when the Professor comes here and starts laying it on, Uncle will try to shoot him.

But Uncle isn't very dangerous

The best he can do is a lot of noise and swearing. Uncle's hanging on to his grudge.

TIELEGIN. Grudgingly thinking about hanging himself?

SONIA. Hanging on for dear life, actually—but all he's capable of is grudges and frustration.

*A gunshot in the proverbial wings.*

WOJNICKI. Where is he? Where is that man who's got me fearing things?

TIELEGIN. He's not under the table—sorry.

NANNY. Not the samovar—just don't hit the samovar.

TIELEGIN. Hold on to him—hold on!

ASTROW. Just don't hit the samovar.

*A gunshot.*

WOJNICKI. Bang! Ba-boom! Lust for life!
What?
Well what?
Well what?

NANNY. Better not look.

SONIA. Otherwise you'll be kneeling by the toilet bowl again, Uncle.

SONIA. Uncle, the soup!

ASTROW. That won't be the only soup that's gone—flown—to waste.

WOJNICKI. I never throw up soup, ever. That's why I want to see the man who's ruined my existence, which was miserable enough to begin with.

WOJNICKI. What?
Well, fuck me!
The human misery!
I missed!
A man can't step twice in the same shit he's already stepped in.

NANNY. Stepped in, seen human misery, and got sick as a dog—c'mere, pooch!

ASTROW. And that's more or less the way it was back then—

SONIA. And since then Uncle's been shooting at least once a month, if not once a week.

ASTROW. Naturally, we were slightly concerned at the time.

**SONIA.** We found it no laughing matter at the time—after all he did try to shoot my father—but we basically ignored it—Uncle's a minority.

**ASTROW.** Exactly—that would have been around '90?

**NANNY.** So it would—so it would.

**ASTROW.** Sonia's father told Uncle he was no longer needed and he'd best leave this-ol'-house. That's when the first shot was fired. And it missed.

**WOJNICKI.** How the fuck could it have not missed? Seeing as Chekhov's play . . .

**TIELEGIN.** That's this Russkie.

**WOJNICKI.** "Uncle Vanya," whose protagonist I am after all, has been staged some 10 million times with a run of 50 nights each—I wonder in whose interest it was to back all those productions?

Anyway, how am I supposed to not be upset when I missed 500 million times—times two? And I don't even know for whose money. For whose money do I keep missing? Night after night?

**SONIA.** For Uncle, the moment when he shoots and misses . . .

**WOJNICKI.** Did I miss?

**SONIA.** . . . lasts forever.

Happily, I left home a long time ago, and I manage to miss these moments,

usually. And I was this close to staying with Uncle—in the guerrilla movement. Then I would have been firing two shots blindly any number of times, too.

We shall live Uncle. We shall live through the long procession of days before us, and through the long evenings. And we shall work for others without rest, both now and when we are old; and when our last hour comes we shall meet it humbly, and there, beyond the grave, we shall say that we have suffered and wept, that our life was bitter, and God will have pity on us. Ah, then dear, dear Uncle, we shall see that bright and beautiful life; we shall rejoice and look back upon our sorrow here; a tender smile—and—we shall rest.

Mary and Joseph! Good thing I didn't say that to Uncle back then.

TIELEGIN. You said it!

SONIA. Uncle, I'd be glad to look after you. But what am I, the welfare state?

Well I'm not. Solidarity with the working man, sure. But, for the love of God, not with all the unemployed Uncles who've missed their shots, and who complain instead of making a killing.

TIELEGIN. Killing themselves off—the Professor would say.

ASTROW. Uncle's shooting his gun like that, on economic grounds, has a long tradition: It started out somewhere around the French Revolution, maybe.

SONIA. But there were an awful lot of French Uncles—while our Uncle is in the minority.

TIELEGIN. Good thing, too.

WOJNICKI. How am I supposed to be in the majority? There can only be one protagonist after all—how am I supposed to take part in free competition when I keep missing my shot all the time?

ASTROW. Where there's a will there's a way, isn't there, Sonia?

WOJNICKI. What do you mean—a will and a way? I know the way to the lottery stand and that's about it.

SONIA. Stop waiting for a miracle, Uncle, and get down to business. As if you didn't have enough coal in the shed.

TIELEGIN. The only thing left in the shed are potatoes.

WOJNICKI. Once, when the lottery jackpot was 12 million, I could have spent it all and still have been some 25 thousand short.

ASTROW. Take a hike, Unc. We need to pick up the Professor now—to move the action forward some.

WOJNICKI. Action—action. Nobody gives a thought to me and my shopping basket when I'm pushing it down the aisle. Nobody cares that action leads me further afield—into a field of potatoes, at that, and into social passivity.

And how am I supposed to say that I don't have . . . That I don't have . . .

That I haven't ruined it, my life—your father ruined it—everything that happened—was all good—it's only that I wound up badly badly badly—and that's why now I'll –

ASTROW. Now Uncle will go see a psychiatrist.

WOJNICKI. Your father ruined it, the founding father of the condition I find myself in—a condition of injured self-respect—injured self-respect.

Injured when it turned out that working—years of working for Father—your father—didn't result in anything tangible. On the contrary—verce-visa, even.

SONIA. Everything that happened was all good, and my father is a remarkable man.

WOJNICKI. Especially when I told him I didn't agree to being treated this way, and he said history has proven me wrong and that I'm a millstone around the neck of social transformation and I should keep my opportunities to myself.

So, what now? Out on the street? On the street? Of history? The street?

NANNY. Why the street? Just be a laughing-stock, is all.

SONIA. Everything that happened was all good, and my father is a remarkable man.

ASTROW. Sonia, you will now go with Uncle to the psychiatrist—because Uncle, so to speak, won't get there—on his own. Sonia?

SONIA. But Uncle has his psychiatrist's appointment in three months or so.

NANNY. Exactly, that's why it's worth setting off now and taking your place in the bulletproof line.

**ASTROW.** Human misery—this ol' human misery—Uncle's human misery is something I can tell an anecdote taken from my medical practice about—so . . .

**NANNY.** Astrow, I believe your meeting has started already?

**ASTROW.** It has—exactly—so why don't I tell another anecdote taken from my medical practice?

**NANNY.** But you can still make it.

**NANNY.** Yes, this is a solution—having a psychiatrist see you for lack of social opportunities.

**TIELEGIN.** It was Sonia who sent Uncle to have his social opportunities seen to by a psychiatrist.

**NANNY.** Right after Uncle started brandishing the gun—waving it around—right after Sonia's father went back to the capital and never returned. But today there's a chance, a big chance, that the Professor will come, if his train's not late, accompanied by his wife.

**TIELEGIN.** Exactly, ladies and gentlemen, that's right! Right after the Professor's departure, we received the Professor's letter. It went like this . . .

**NANNY.** Excuse me, could you hand me that letter?

So we can read it out?

Thank you very much.

**TIELEGIN.** Uhh . . .

"Dear friends,

Be so good as to fucking convince Wojnicki somehow, or else . . ."

Actually, no—sorry, this must be a draft.

"I was greatly saddened to learn of your refusal regarding the sale of the house.

Bearing in mind Hele . . . Sonia's future, and mindful of Hele . . . Sonia's fate . . ."

**NANNY.** What is this Hele . . . Sonia?

**TIELEGIN.** It's French.

"... and the future of future generations, maybe you'll manage to convince Wojnicki—that egoist—that the house needs to be sold and he needs to be requalified. Uncle's demanding welfare from us Sieriebriakows will no longer stand. Besides, maybe Wojnicki did pay a large part of the installments, but the only thing we want to have coming from him is his coming to grips with the fact that I'm right."

Ha ha ha. Not bad not bad.

**NANNY.** Uncle replied to that letter . . .

**TIELEGIN.** But he was very boring.

**NANNY.** And I don't know whether he mailed it or not.

**TIELEGIN.** Besides, he didn't have anything to offer the Professor.

**NANNY.** No reply—because he couldn't get his head around it, and it started sticking out.

**TIELEGIN.** That is, I was supposed to mail that reply, but I said—no way, God forbid—I'm staying out of this.

**NANNY.** Me too.

**TIELEGIN.** Exactly.

**NANNY.** Astrow why don't you tell us a story, my dear? Instead of listening to Uncle and not giving a shit—let's talk about man for a change—talk about the human condition.

**TIELEGIN.** Exactly—let's stop here and march off to the philharmonic! Sorry.

**ASTROW.** Me? But what?

**NANNY.** So, Astrow, our beloved family doctor, how did the meeting go?

**ASTROW.** Hello—my name is Michał, and I've been sober for eighteen years.

**TIELEGIN.** That means he doesn't drink as much as he used to—he no longer gets falling-down drunk.

**ASTROW.** Eighteen years ago, my friend decided to change his life and kill a man—I've been in love with that man's wife for eighteen years, and I'm sorry my friend missed—so much for being able to count on your friends—but the main thing is that Helena is—well, she's not for everyone, but that's because we can freely compete—and I decided to join the competition today —so why don't I tell an anecdote taken from my medical practice . . .

NANNY. The real reason he stopped drinking was that he would see mice in the forest.

TIELEGIN. A forest of mice.

NANNY. Coming against him.

ASTROW. That woman made an inedible impression on me—I arranged to meet her in the forest, but she never came.

TIELEGIN. Helena felt harassed by the place to which she had come. She hadn't known such places existed. And that they had doctors. Because why should you bother treating those people if they're going to die out like Uncle anyway?

SONIA. What have you got to tell me?

ASTROW. But Sonia—I don't find Helena attractive at all. Her world is corrupt and her spiritual life empty.
Empty as an empty bottle, and—speaking of bottles—back when I still drank . . .

SONIA. Can it.

*Astrow takes Sonia's book.*

ASTROW. How goes it with the economy, Sonia? Are the taxes holding up?

SONIA. Astrow, please—don't you use words.

ASTROW. But I'm not . . .

SONIA. Don't use words at all—not in my presence.

ASTROW. Sonia, don't you think . . .

(*Reads from the book.*)

I don't like Uncle one bit—the nature of poverty is spiritual, its cause should rather be sought in metaphysics. And the proper field in which to cultivate such spirituality is a deregulated market. That is why one ought . . .

*Sonia sees her book and takes it back.*

SONIA. To leave?

ASTROW. No, no—one ought—well, I agree with your father—the point is that one owed—want to see my cell phone?—I know what one is owed—one is owed nothing.

SONIA. I'll teach you to dig in my handbag.

ASTROW. Sonia.

SONIA. What?

ASTROW. Why can't you play Helena—huh?

SONIA. Astrow!

ASTROW. Go on, play her.

SONIA. No!

ASTROW. It's such a lovely feminine part for feminine women—so they can be femininely—something . . .

TIELEGIN. The words you want to say here have no place in a respectable household—unless there's vodka on the table because it's your birthday.

NANNY. Alright, alright—if Polish Rail schedules are anything to go by, the Professor will be here in an hour or so.

TIELEGIN. The Professor is traveling on a comfortable first-class train.

NANNY. He's traveling and not noticing how this country has changed, because he's the one who changed it.

TIELEGIN. And he prefers not to look.

But, ladies and gentlemen—the Professor will enter through here, and then, after he takes a few professorial footsteps, I'll ask you for a round of applause.

But not like that—Like this—

Sieriebriakow will come in here and say: How good to see you, Tielegin—my good old friend from the provinces—are you keeping up your monthly, if no longer weekly, visits to the philharmonic?

And I'll say: Yes, come what may—I can still afford tickets to the philharmonic. Or maybe not, because he'll be sorry to hear me talking about poverty and expensive concert tickets. Because I can't take care of everything—everything in its time—and the philharmonic finally has to start breaking even.

NANNY. The Professor can't be bothered with nonsense—the Professor will come in and say: Nanny, Nanny—if it weren't for you, Nanny, and your teas, Nanny, I wouldn't be who I am today, Nanny. How's your health, Nanny? Have you followed my advice and started growing blueberries or diamonds on the coal you have left over in the cellar? Your small business?

And I'll be touched and serve something he likes for lunch because nobody down there can cook like me, certainly not Helena who can only cook noodles.

And he'll eat, and we'll listen how best to grow diamonds, and how everyone has to be the captain and grocery store of his fate.

ASTROW. So what's for lunch? Because I'll be a bit late because of working my butt off at the hospital, but I'll sew that butt back on after 24 hours.

"Astrow! You're just the kind of people we need—quiet, hard-working people who know that work and further education is the way to go—and how good to see you—I respect people like you—regular people, quiet as a mouse—who are making this country great—doctors, working stiffs and psychiatrists—and are the salt of the earth—a leavening salt—who believe in living decently—but only after death—exactly—how good it is that the provinces have put their trust in our neoliberal lady of the economy and never ask her whether things couldn't have been better by any chance."

SONIA (*as Helena*). But things are better.

God, Doctor, you've aged something awful.

These provincial sights are so beautiful. My husband says it would be worth leaving towns like these just the way they are, untouched by hand or shovel.

So where is that brute Wojnicki, with whom, as with every poor person, I cannot come—to an understanding?

WOJNICKI. How did this letter get here? Am I supposed to shoot at the Polish post office too?

TIELEGIN. It wasn't me—this man brought it here—these people, actually—the nation.

ASTROW. We sent Uncle to see a psychiatrist so the psychiatrist would stop him from shooting at your husband today—pharmacologically.

NANNY. Sonia convinced him there's nothing shameful about going to see a psychiatrist—they're the fringe benefit of the new order he keeps complaining about—psychiatrists, that is.

TIELEGIN. This will be a scene about how the last victim of transformation goes to seek professional help when prayer and the lottery have failed him.

WOJNICKI. I finally concluded there was nothing shameful about seeing a psychiatrist about my condition.

TIELEGIN/PSYCHIATRIST. That's just great—that's okay—vere is ze point?

WOJNICKI. Ja.

TIELEGIN/PSYCHIATRIST. How may I help you?

WOJNICKI. Exactly—but do you really want to know?

TIELEGIN/PSYCHIATRIST. Yes—I really do.

WOJNICKI. I don't believe you.

TIELEGIN/PSYCHIATRIST. There's no challenge I wouldn't undertake to treat pharmacologically—sir.

WOJNICKI. Would you swear to that?

TIELEGIN. With one hand behind my back.

WOJNICKI. Mister—I want to shoot a man.

TIELEGIN/PSYCHIATRIST. A man?

WOJNICKI. I want to shoot the man who'd like to shut down the town I live in because that town is unprofitable.

TIELEGIN/PSYCHIATRIST. A whole town?

WOJNICKI. Several towns, actually—in the name of universal prosperity and the rise of the middle class and its global capital.

TIELEGIN/PSYCHIATRIST. Does that capital come back to haunt you at night?

WOJNICKI. It haunts me all the time, mister—I think it would like to get rid of people like me—people living on the edge—the edge of the living wage—but that's not true—the truth is it wants to exploit me—that's what I hear.

TIELEGIN/PSYCHIATRIST. You're hearing things?

WOJNICKI. I keep hearing it said it's because of people like me that capitalism can't fully develop, because the public health service should finally be dissolved.

TIELEGIN/PSYCHIATRIST. No shit—really?

WOJNICKI. That's right—and because strong interest groups pose a threat to democracy, and when someone earns low wages he only has himself, and not global capital, to blame.

TIELEGIN/PSYCHIATRIST. And all this is because of one man—right?

WOJNICKI. That's just it—one man—my situation is all the more miserable for being caused by one man and not by history as they say . . .

TIELEGIN/PSYCHIATRIST. You want to shoot the man you're blaming for your failure in life—right?

WOJNICKI. Right—shoot him, that's right.

TIELEGIN/PSYCHIATRIST. You have suicidal thoughts—right?

WOJNICKI. Right.

TIELEGIN/PSYCHIATRIST. Often?

WOJNICKI. I often think that, once I've killed him—I won't let them arrest me—they won't take me alive—but I hope it won't come to that—that I'll manage to run, to make a break for it.

TIELEGIN/PSYCHIATRIST. What is it you're running away from?

WOJNICKI. I don't know, but I think it has to do with Margaret Thatcher—and her stooge, Professor Balcerowicz.

ASTROW. What did he prescribe? Big Pharma won't give you a break—why don't I prescribe a cheaper generic?

**SONIA.** Hang on a fucking moment—maybe the patient could keep his thoughts about my father, to whom he doesn't measure up, to himself and his unemployed human misery?

**NANNY.** Whoa!

**SONIA.** Why don't I finally say who my father is? Using an example.

**NANNY.** Oh!

**SONIA.** Example: There was this time, sometime in the late '90s, when my father . . .

**TIELEGIN.** And everything that happened—was all good.

**SONIA.** Exactly.

**NANNY.** Oh!

**SONIA.** . . . invited me for breakfast to his favorite café. This would have been around 1 pm.

**ASTROW.** Right—breakfast at one. What do you mean—one?

**SONIA.** It was a big-city brunch, actually!

**NANNY.** Right!

**SONIA.** My father works late. We had coffee in these bowls.

**ASTROW.** What do you mean—coffee in bowls?

**SONIA.** My father was telling me how diamonds are polished, if you know what I mean.

**ASTROW.** No, I don't.

**SONIA.** Exactly. So, when Father went for a pee I felt like they knew I wasn't from here. From over there, that is. I was waiting and hoping my father would be back soon . . .

**NANNY.** And then the waiter brought the prawns. "No, these prawns can't be for us—who would have ordered prawns?" says Helena—because Sonia forgot to mention that Helena was there, too—but the waiter says: "That lady ordered them," meaning Sonia. And Sonia ordered the prawns and couldn't wait for them to be served even though she was scared she wouldn't know how to eat them—and Helena laughed at Sonia: "Dahling please—prawns? Who orders prawns? Prawns are pointless and in such bad taste." Sonia had found the prawns tasty and felt terribly ashamed.

**SONIA.** Nanny dear, next time around shut your pie-hole.

**ASTROW.** I wouldn't be caught dead eating a prawn.

**SONIA.** Do you mind?

**NANNY.** Go ahead.

**SONIA.** There were people demonstrating outside the window, with crowbars, clubs and bolts in their hands, making a terrible racket. Thank God the police were there, otherwise Helena would have cowered under the table in fright—wouldn't she?

**ASTROW.** Yeah, Helena—under the table—right.

IMAGE 10.3 **Astrow (Piotr Tokarz), Sonia (Aleksandra Cybulska), and Nanny (Sabina Tumidalska)**

Directed by Monika Strzępka. Teatr Dramatyczny im. Jerzego Szaniawskiego, Wałbrzych (2011)

*Photograph by Kuba Dąbrowski*

**SONIA.** Astrow, shut your pie-hole.

**NANNY.** Oh.

**SONIA.** "Oh, there go the Wojnickis," Helena said. But everybody knows Uncle's too shy to ever go to a demonstration like that.

**WOJNICKI.** When they was closing down our mine . . .

**SONIA.** Uncle!

**WOJNICKI.** . . . I didn't know what the deal was. And when they done shut it down for good, they left the door closed, and there was me left down that defunct mine, down in the shaft without a voice. Until now.

**NANNY.** What do you mean—down?

**WOJNICKI.** Well, I was down.

**TIELEGIN.** But you didn't even work in the mine.

**WOJNICKI.** Why do you people always have to go and spoil everything?

**SONIA.** Stop moping around here! I don't want to be some element of your narrative! I'm superstitious!

**NANNY.** Knock on wood.

**ASTROW.** Who's there?

**TIELEGIN.** It's occupied.

**SONIA.** Moving right along: One of the demonstrators is standing in the window of the café, my father comes back from peeing, sees the demonstrator, and backs away. The guy stands there a while, looks around, and walks off.

**ASTROW.** Jeez—the guy rode all night to get to the demonstration—he had a hangover and wanted a beer. He saw the prices above the bar: A pint of beer cost as much as his shoes. His head was buzzing the rest of the day, and he was pissed at his buddies for yelling so loud.

**SONIA.** Are you done?

**ASTROW.** I am.

**SONIA.** In that case . . .

**ASTROW.** He never even had a beer because he got arrested.

**SONIA.** Anyway, my father came back and said:

**WOJNICKI/SIERIEBRIAKOW.** So that's exactly what I'm talking about. About those who aren't—who won't be polishing diamonds anymore. Those people—we have nothing to offer them.

**SONIA.** Exactly!

**WOJNICKI/SIERIEBRIAKOW.** Those people need to suffer more if things are to get any better. I don't like it either, but there's nothing we can do. And nothing is what we *should* be doing. Doing something only stops things from getting better. Honesty is the name of the game here. Our job is to tell them what things are like. We're not pretending things won't get worse for them, and that's the long and short of it.

**SONIA.** Anyway, my father came back and said that the guy from the demonstration . . .

**WOJNICKI/SIERIEBRIAKOW.** I wish I could dissolve this society. And make myself another one: One that knows its place in line. I don't mean a picket line either, but a line of consuming consumers.

**SONIA.** Not true—that's not what he said.

**WOJNICKI.** He did so, he did so.

**SONIA.** Meaning he had a far more exclusive solution in mind.

**WOJNICKI.** He also said that every nation has the intelligentsia it deserves.

**ASTROW.** Though I'd say that our nation has a better intelligentsia than it deserves.

**WOJNICKI.** Exactly, and it's not a question of the quotient—of that intelligentsia.

**SONIA.** My father later admitted that the guy from the demonstration reminded him of Uncle, whom he didn't want to run into. So he preferred to take no chances. He didn't have his glasses, so he couldn't tell whether Uncle was carrying a crowbar or a bolt or not.

**TIELEGIN.** Which he wouldn't have hesitated to use.

WOJNICKI. Your father would rather be peeing than face a victim of transformation like myself.

SONIA. He said he didn't want to see you because you'd nag him to death—instead of getting down to business like he did.

NANNY. Or getting down at all—from here, from there.

WOJNICKI. I'll get—I'll get around—all my life I've been getting around to working for your father, and where did it get me?

NANNY. Should of changed your job, so there!

TIELEGIN. He tried.

ASTROW. But it didn't quite work out.

WOJNICKI. What?

ASTROW. Right.

TIELEGIN. Uncle doesn't like talking about the time he went for a job interview.

NANNY. Uncle doesn't want to but he has to.

SONIA. Don't be a schmuck, Uncle—go for it.

WOJNICKI. Alright—but this is the last time—I wasn't prepared back then.

SONIA. But I gave you a handbook, Uncle.

WOJNICKI. So?—I read it—and that's why I got upset.

TIELEGIN. This will be a scene about why Uncle didn't get a job because he couldn't live up to the new standards—and about why he blew it.

ASTROW/EMPLOYER. Get out of my office—that's right—that's it—so there's this senior-citizen employment program—and I've got one right here now—how old?

(*Looking at Uncle*)

I don't fucking know how old—looks about seventy—yeah—later, dude.

(*Switches off his phone*)

Right, let's get down to business—an accountant—right?

WOJNICKI. Right.

**EMPLOYER.** You're applying for an accountant's position—right?

**WOJNICKI.** Right—accountant's, that's exactly right—but actually I'm more interested in interpersonal relations than in crunching numbers—no to boredom—yes to creativity.

**EMPLOYER.** Creativity?

**WOJNICKI.** Creativity.

(*The phone rings*
*the employer looks around but it's not his phone*
*Wojnicki realizes it's his*
*it looks like he doesn't want to answer it*
*but he sees who's calling and answers.*)

No no no—I can't talk right now.
Oh yeah?—Really?—Fuck, man—go on—no—it can wait.

(*Wojnicki looks reproachfully at the employer*)

Well, I can't just tell him to leave because this is a private conversation—

No shit! Well then you tell him that next time he's gonna have me to you know what—but I'll ask, maybe he'll give me a lift—no no, I can't eat anything fatty if we're drinking vodka—just let it chill.

Right, so where were we?

**EMPLOYER.** Creativity.

**WOJNICKI.** Creativity—right—I can't handle boredom—besides—I won't be working long anyway, you know.

**EMPLOYER.** Oh?

**WOJNICKI.** Because I have this niece—and she told me she'd put me in her will—to tell you the truth she doesn't look too good lately—all this talk about cervical cancer these days—broads don't get themselves examined at all, no sir!

**EMPLOYER.** Do you have any letters of reference from your previous employer?

**WOJNICKI.** Exactly—the fucker wouldn't—give me one.

**EMPLOYER.** You don't?

WOJNICKI. Well no—because after I tried to shoot him he left town and now he's not speaking to me.

*(Pause*
*Wojnicki gives Sonia a look—'What?'*
*He realizes what he's done.*
*He takes a comb out of his pocket and runs it nervously through his hair.)*

Yes yes yes—very funny—I think I'll roll the fuck over laughing—if only you could talk to them—about literature for instance—or about childhood—I'd get him to see things my way somehow over a vodka.

ASTROW. Meaning that the employer would have hired him. Especially for the creative accounting. And he also liked talking about literature, and even more about his childhood.

TIELEGIN. And he had got his job over a vodka or whisky, too.

SONIA. But Uncle was too old—for the position, that is.

NANNY. Uncle's scared of getting old.

TIELEGIN. I really don't know what is there to be scared of.

NANNY. Maybe there's your reason?

ASTROW. What he's most scared of is growing old in a small town around here somewhere. He's eighty already. Cancer didn't get him.

SONIA. Alas.

ASTROW. He's friends with a doctor.

SONIA. Astrow!

ASTROW. Whom he buried. He's walking with a plastic bag, hunched over, through the town to his apartment, which he'd sold cheap to some people on the condition that he can live there, in his room, until he dies, and use the toilet.

NANNY. And the Professor sends him postcards from Cuba.

TIELEGIN. And offensive images of naked women.

SONIA. That's what Uncle was telling the fridge yesterday.

WOJNICKI. And the fridge started humming.

NANNY. Uncle's looking for a way to make things better for himself.

TIELEGIN. He could look in highbrow literature, like I do . . .

SONIA. But Uncle's chosen a different tack.

WOJNICKI. I have it!

My son! He has tremendous talent. But he doesn't have money. I'm going on strike, because no Professor can stop me from going on strike. But, for my son, I'd break that strike—to bet it all on him—my son—so my son can have a career in show business and I could be his agent.

But I don't have a son, and the mine's closed down.

ASTROW. Uncle wanted to rob a bank, but the bank was closed down, too.

WOJNICKI. Nothing works the way it should in this country!

NANNY. Uncle plays the lottery every week.

WOJNICKI. Well, fuck me, oh the human misery—I didn't hit the numbers.

SONIA. Uncle likes to grumble.

WOJNICKI. Yes, and your father would like to stop me from doing that as well but he can't.

SONIA. If Uncle had listened and grown diamonds, Uncle wouldn't be grumbling now.

WOJNICKI. I'm not growing any diamonds

TIELEGIN. Not true—Uncle wanted to grow one on the windowsill, but the wind blew the window open and broke the pot.

NANNY. Gone with the wind.

SONIA. Exactly—I look after my windowsill in the capital.

ASTROW. Exactly—that's why I said today, and yesterday at the rehearsal, that every story has the protagonist it deserves. Now, I think that this story deserves a better protagonist than Wojnicki, and so why don't I say a few words about myself . . .

SONIA. So what is it you have to say exactly?

**ASTROW.** Me?

**SONIA.** Yeah.

**ASTROW.** I wanted to say . . .

**SONIA.** Yeah?

**ASTROW.** I want to say how much I appreciate you—

**SONIA.** Yeah?

**ASTROW.** I want to say how much I admire you—

**SONIA.** Yeah?

**ASTROW.** And now that you've reached the age when biology starts taking its leave of you . . .

**SONIA.** Give me one good reason I should fall in love with you.

**ASTROW.** One?

**SONIA.** Can you come up with more?

**ASTROW.** So maybe—a story taken from my medical practice?

**TIELEGIN.** Say what you told Helena in the forest.

**NANNY.** Good gracious! We'll be late—Tielegin, pass the bread and the salt.

**SONIA.** My father never uses salt.

**TIELEGIN.** What about bread?

**SONIA.** As long as it's whole grain. Where's your gun Uncle?

**WOJNICKI.** What?

**TIELEGIN.** The Professor, arriving in a first-class compartment, is almost here.

**NANNY.** There's no time to lose.

**SONIA.** Astrow, have Uncle hand over his gun—or he's not coming with us.

**WOJNICKI.** I'm not going with you—I'll assume a strategic position.

**SONIA.** Uncle!

**WOJNICKI.** No, no one's stopping me—nothing—don't ask me—the banner with the red ribbon above the gate is there for a reason– and besides I still have some potatoes to peel.

SONIA. Aha.

TIELEGIN. And me not dressed for the occasion.

NANNY. Astrow, are you coming?

*Exit Sonia, Tielegin and Nanny.*

ASTROW. No, no—not yet.

WOJNICKI. And then you left, my lovely son,
with your black gun at midnight . . .

ASTROW. Give me the gun.

WOJNICKI. No.

ASTROW. Listen—there were two of us—right?

WOJNICKI. Right.

IMAGE 10.4 **Uncle/Wojnicki (Włodzimierz Dyła) and Astrow (Piotr Tokarz)**
Directed by Monika Strzępka. Teatr Dramatyczny im. Jerzego Szaniawskiego, Wałbrzych (2011)
*Photograph by Kuba Dąbrowski*

IMAGE 10.5 **Astrow (Piotr Tokarz)**

Directed by Monika Strzępka. Teatr Dramatyczny im. Jerzego Szaniawskiego, Wałbrzych (2011)

*Photograph by Kuba Dąbrowski*

ASTROW. Two of the most up-and-coming guys in town—yeah?

WOJNICKI. Yeah.

ASTROW. And now there's only one left—right?

WOJNICKI. Right.

ASTROW. And that's because—one of us is a loser—right?

WOJNICKI. Right—thanks.

ASTROW. Somebody had to tell you.

WOJNICKI. Right, the rest of them aren't up to it.

ASTROW. Exactly.

WOJNICKI. Man—when I finally hit the Professor—you'll be able to take Helena, make a fresh start and be up-and-coming again—time to get going.

**ASTROW.** What do you mean make a fresh start—you want me to up-and-come again? Hey, I was the one left up-and-coming. Besides—don't try to distract me—hand it over.

**WOJNICKI.** What?

**ASTROW.** The gun.

**WOJNICKI.** The gun?—I didn't take the gun, or the Prozac from the cabinet.

**ASTROW.** Hand it over.

**WOJNICKI.** What?

**ASTROW.** The Prozac from the cabinet.

**WOJNICKI.** Why don't you make up your mind what it is you want from me?

*Wojnicki hands over the Prozac—exit.*

**ASTROW.** Well well well—interesting, interesting—what are you going to do with those blanks?

**WOJNICKI.** Well I sure as hell won't be drawing them anymore.

**ASTROW.** Did you ever see anyone in the theater shoot anything but blanks?

**WOJNICKI.** You want me to run around the stage with a fucking cap pistol?

**ASTROW.** The Professor's safe in the theater, just like our economic system is safe outside it.

**WOJNICKI.** That's why I'm leaving.

**ASTROW.** Where do you think you're going? I, for one, am fine—with the way things are. What's it all for—what are you trying to prove here? Like you could be someone for instance—well, who? Even if you did manage to shoot him somehow? Generation X?

**WOJNICKI.** We'll see—you coming?

**ASTROW.** Me? Coming? No no no—I'm staying right here.

**WOJNICKI.** In five minutes—this time for real I hope—in five minutes it'll all be over.

*Exeunt.*

*A while later, Astrow returns.*

**ASTROW.** What do you mean five minutes? Man, I studied medicine for eight—well maybe six—years.

*Astrow tries to tell his medical anecdote.*
*Nanny, Sonia and Tielegin return.*
*Sonia to Astrow.*

**SONIA.** I really don't want to listen to this anymore—and, besides, your time is up.

**NANNY.** It's damn cold outside.

**ASTROW.** Just because no one's listening to me doesn't mean I won't keep talking. I'll talk more and louder until it gets me somewhere. I'll say all the things I have to say—and I do have things to say.

**NANNY.** Why don't you have a nice vodka instead?

**TIELEGIN.** Sure.

**NANNY.** We still have a moment before Uncle gets here—he's usually back within the hour. So we'll go out and then come back again to make as if—as if we're coming back from the station.

**TIELEGIN.** I don't even want to think what would happen if Uncle were to catch on.

**ASTROW.** Vodka! Why don't we take a break now?

(*Pause.*
*Uncle comes running in.*)

**WOJNICKI.** Bang! Ba-boom! Where is he? Where and in what hole is he hiding? Oh, sorry. I know you shouldn't speak badly of the dead—but this time I won't let this situation slide. He's as good as dead, and that's why the Professor, God rest his soul—you're not stopping me, Sonia—won't be spoken of badly by me.

**WOJNICKI.** Bang! Ba-boom! I have a lust for life!

**WOJNICKI.** Where is he? I'm not sitting here on the john waiting until the honorable Professor bothers to come to the toilet.

**NANNY.** Alright.

TIELEGIN. I don't know anything—but why get so upset?

NANNY. Relax.

SONIA. Because, well, he's not coming today.

WOJNICKI. He's not coming?

ASTROW. He's not coming—why don't you give it a rest already?

WOJNICKI. Well, fuck me, oh the human misery—I missed.

ASTROW. And the thing is that you'll always keep missing out.

WOJNICKI. What do you mean—I'll keep missing? I'll keep missing out? Me?

ASTROW. Well, because he's, you know—he's, you know . . .

WOJNICKI. What?

NANNY. Done and died, God rest his soul.

WOJNICKI. Died? How? When? What are you sitting around here for?

TIELEGIN. Give me your hands if we be friends—and we shall restore amends.

SONIA. Well, because he died some ten years ago and that's that, now let's finish this story once and for all.

WOJNICKI. This story's not over yet!

NANNY. Not ten—better yet—it'll be fifteen by now.

WOJNICKI. Fifteen? Yeah, right. So why did you go down to the station?

Huh? The station? You went there?

ASTROW. Well—it's just that—you have to keep up the suspense somehow—so there's this, well—what's it called—drama . . .

SONIA. Dramaturgy—where the hero isn't aware of what's going on and that's what makes him the protagonist—and now we're thinking: Well, what do you know? He wasn't aware of what's going on. If he'd known the Professor was dead, he might have shot himself in the head and there wouldn't have been anything to see—because a play about me wouldn't be interesting because I have everything and I'm doing fine.

WOJNICKI. Badly.

**SONIA.** Don't give me that "badly," Uncle—you've already spoken badly of the deceased.

**TIELEGIN.** But Uncle had no idea.

**WOJNICKI.** But why didn't you . . .

**NANNY.** Beats me—you must have been out for a walk.

**TIELEGIN.** I was at the philharmonic—how was I supposed to tell you?

**NANNY.** We cried and shouted he was dead—but you didn't hear—so we figured: Why waste our breath—how long can you keep that up?

**ASTROW.** Well, because we have to make this watchable—in Chekhov your character is interesting because he's at a loss spiritually—everybody would give their eyeteeth to play Uncle—well, fuck me, oh the human misery, I missed—so there.

**WOJNICKI.** So what was I shooting at, then?

**ASTROW.** No no—a character who's not aware of what's going on—you need one in every play—just like in every society there's also—you know—this sap at whose expense the whole thing is watchable and moves right along somehow.

**WOJNICKI.** What moves right along? I read all sorts of newspapers—I really like to read.

**SONIA.** Exactly—this play is about a hundred years old, Uncle—for a hundred years now, there've been uncles like you, and there's nothing anyone can do about it—just like there's nothing anyone can do about poverty and social exclusion, which is the cost you have to pay for transformation and our neoliberal economy; and your character, Uncle, has precisely this educational tenor.

**ASTROW.** A tenor gritting his teeth.

**SONIA.** His cavity-ridden teeth.

**TIELEGIN.** Through which he sings about the unchanging nature of human fate.

**SONIA.** Which shows that there've always been people whose teeth fall out and you have to deal with it.

ASTROW. There's nothing you can do that ain't been done.

NANNY. And that's why you're fucked—end of story.

TIELEGIN. My, doesn't Uncle have a lovely gun, though? A gun of national liberation you could say—it's lovely.

SONIA. Yes, but that particular weapon doesn't help him anymore—it won't help him—because he's got other jobs to do, actually.

ASTROW. See? I told you—now you can think about what you'd have done if you'd shot him.

SONIA. Because no one's responsible anymore for the policies that are oppressing Uncle.

ASTROW. Maybe no one ever was—maybe the plot structure was responsible.

WOJNICKI. So what am I supposed to do now?

NANNY. Exactly—why don't you think about what you're supposed to be doing?

WOJNICKI. I want to shoot a man five minutes from now.

TIELEGIN. As long as you doesn't see human misery again.

WOJNICKI. I want to shoot a man five minutes from now.

NANNY. Five minutes?

WOJNICKI. I want to shoot five minutes from now.

ASTROW. But who do you want to shoot now?

WOJNICKI. I want to shoot a man five minutes from now.

NANNY. Well then—maybe—maybe you could shoot Tielegin—what do we need him for anyway?

TIELEGIN. Sorry.

WOJNICKI. I want to shoot a man five minutes from now.

NANNY. Exactly.

TIELEGIN. Sorry.

ASTROW. It's true, come to think about it.

TIELEGIN. Sorry.

NANNY. Tielegin, my dear friend—how much are you actually costing us?

TIELEGIN. But I—but I . . .

WOJNICKI. I don't want to shoot Tielegin—I could just as well shoot myself in the head with my own hand.

TIELEGIN. And miss? Sorry.

WOJNICKI. So what am I supposed to do now?
What am I supposed to do now?
What am I supposed to do now?

WOJNICKI. Maybe he just didn't come?
Maybe he got scared, right?
And got off along the way?
Please!

TIELEGIN. Sorry.

WOJNICKI. Theater's all about the imagination, isn't it?

SONIA. Can't you imagine something else?

WOJNICKI. Imagine what? This is the only text I have—so what am I supposed to do? Read a book out loud? An economics handbook?

NANNY. Maybe some educational classic—it wouldn't hurt.

*Uncle's Dance.*
*The door slams.*
*Reprise.*

NANNY. Good gracious! We'll be late—Tielegin, pass the bread and the salt.

SONIA. My father never uses salt.

TIELEGIN. What about bread?

SONIA. As long as it's whole grain. Astrow, are you coming?

ASTROW. Sure.

NANNY. It's damn cold outside.

SONIA. So he hasn't come.

WOJNICKI. Hah—oh, the human misery—he got scared!

IMAGE 10.6 **Tielegin (Jerzy Gronowski) and Nanny (Sabina Tumidalska)**
Directed by Monika Strzępka. Teatr Dramatyczny im. Jerzego Szaniawskiego, Wałbrzych (2011)
*Photograph by Kuba Dąbrowski*

NANNY. And where exactly was he supposed to come here?

TIELEGIN. The train stopped—but there's no sight of the Professor in first or second class.

WOJNICKI. Hah—he's scared—right? He's scared.

ASTROW. He hasn't come? And I had this anecdote prepared—so . . .

NANNY. Now who's going to eat all this food?

TIELEGIN. He felt bad as soon as he got in that first-class compartment . . .

NANNY. . . . and he got off at the nearest stop.

ASTROW. I'll eat it.

IMAGE 10.7 **Sonia (Aleksandra Cybulska) and Nanny (Sabina Tumidalska)**
Directed by Monika Strzępka. Teatr Dramatyczny im. Jerzego Szaniawskiego, Wałbrzych (2011)
*Photograph by Kuba Dąbrowski*

WOJNICKI. He doubled back.

TIELEGIN. And took a taxi home—right.

SONIA. But he's better now—he's fine.

WOJNICKI. I told you so—he was so scared he nearly pissed himself, or worse.

SONIA. Uncle!

WOJNICKI. Well what? What? He's not afraid when he's on television, but face-time? No sirree! I saw him on television once and I wouldn't say he had all that much to say.

SONIA. Uncle—you're being jealous again.

**WOJNICKI.** What am I supposed to be jealous of—well? That he wears suits? I don't think so—whenever I get a pair of pants—I tell them pants: I know you could have ended up better but there's no sense complaining.
And you know what? Never—and I mean never—have those pants complained yet.

**WOJNICKI.** But on the other hand—well, fuck me, oh the human misery—once again, my only chance—to express myself as a citizen—has been taken away from me.

**SONIA.** Nobody's taken anything away from you—it's just that my father felt weak because he was worn out from working for universal prosperity. Moving right along . . .

**WOJNICKI.** Are you going to move something along with your fairy tales here?

**NANNY.** I can read you a fairy tale—that's what I'm here for, purposewise.

**WOJNICKI.** I don't wanna fairy tale!

**NANNY.** Wojnicki! Go stand in the corner.
And now, ladies and gentlemen—dear friends, yadda-yadda-yadda.
This is an important scene.
It's important for this show,
for this country,
and for the Chinese Olympic Games, too.
So I'd like to ask for your active impartial, yadda-yadda-yadda.
And ask you to move these tables a bit.
Because we can't have a scene of national importance not be seen.

**NANNY.** The whole nation reads to its children—that is, it used to.

**SONIA.** We always had reading in our house—always a lot and always the same thing.

**NANNY.** Have you brushed your teeth?

**TIELEGIN.** Nanny nanny, Miss! Astrow didn't brush his teeth.

**ASTROW.** Yeah, well you didn't floss your ass.

NANNY. Tielegin, Astrow! What about you, Sonia?

SONIA. Forgot.

NANNY. You're in your family home—your father's house—you have to take care of your teeth and your customs—not many of which have survived anyway—and neither have well-read people—like us.

All right:

"Once upon a time there lived two brothers . . ."

TIELEGIN. Nanny nanny, Miss! Astrow's in love with Sonia.

NANNY. Astrow, why do you do these things?

ASTROW. Because I can't afford anything else.

TIELEGIN. Because he doesn't make enough, and he can't afford Helena.

NANNY. Anyway:

"Over the seas and far away
there lived two brothers.
One of them died in the hospital
because the heating coal ran out.
He was shaking in the hospital bed,
shaking and crying himself silly,
while the second brother, who was quite verce-visa,
set off on a journey inside the mountain
and into private education.
As is well-known,
the distribution of diamonds among the classes is uneven.
That's why some prefer to lie in the hospital
eating their way through the heating,
while others prefer the opposite."
Sonia, so what did the other brother do?

SONIA. "Both had the same prospects and talents,
but only one had enough resolve to roll up his sleeves,
roll out a rented crane, and,
with the help of a hundred Negroes . . ."

**NANNY.** Now where did he get the Negroes from?

**SONIA.** From Africa of course.

**ASTROW.** I never had a Negro.

**SONIA.** Shut your pie-hole, Astrow!
"With the help of a hundred Negroes
tap into calc-alkaline igneous rock
at a great depth.
And, in temperatures of over 1,000 degrees centigrade,
and under enormous economic pressure,
to hit on a violent igneous upsurge
thanks to which he grew diamonds for himself
and had a lot of cash generally
and bought himself a jewelry store."

**NANNY.** And that's why he should be an model to us all. And a model student. Because in brothers like that the wisdom of the nation lies, just like it does in proverbs. What proverbs are those? Astrow?

**ASTROW.** Forgot.

**TIELEGIN.** As you make your bed, so shall you sleep in it.

**SONIA.** So is it comfortable?

**TIELEGIN.** I didn't make my bed because I was just coming home from the philharmonic.

**NANNY.** Sonia, what struck you most about this fairy tale?

**SONIA.** Pass . . .

**NANNY.** Pass?

**SONIA.** Passivity. I was struck by the passive attitude of the first brother, who dropped out of the race and spent his youth bedridden.

**NANNY.** Bedridden?

**SONIA.** While the second brother drilled patiently until he hit paydirt. And so did his Negroes. I'm saving up for a Negro myself, so that later I can polish diamonds instead of varnishing potatoes like Uncle.

And may prosperity eternal shine forever upon us, amen.

WOJNICKI. As soon as the Professor gets here, I'll shove a varnished potato down his throat—but naturally he's not here

ASTROW. Hmm—well if the guest isn't here—why not an anecdote taken from my practice as a physician . . .

SONIA. No!

ASTROW. Then I guess I'll be going.

SONIA. Go ahead.

ASTROW. An awkward pause—nobody's asked me to stay—so, listen, if you ever—if you ever need anything, then you know you can count on me, as the saying goes—you can bank on it—call me if there's anything . . .

*Uncle calls.*

*Astrow turns around.*

What?

WOJNICKI. I have a ticket to the capital waiting in that bank you mentioned.

ASTROW. But you went there once and you didn't like it.

WOJNICKI. I lied.

Nanny, pack the trunks please!

Tielegin, find me a fucking fast train to the capital, please!

NANNY. Yes, well, Uncle often imagines it—his trip to the capital.

TIELEGIN. Those are wise-guy dreams—dreams you have in the shower.

UNCLE. I never have any dreams when I'm in the shower.

TIELEGIN. At least I have dreams based on universal classical literature.

NANNY. At least mine are based on cookbooks.

TIELEGIN. You couldn't have these dreams without literature—the Germans wouldn't have come up with anything great if they didn't have Goethe.

ASTROW. And me—I have this dream that Sonia and Helena . . .

SONIA. Stop!

NANNY. Uncle hits the capital and stumbles upon a boxing match . . .

ASTROW. How did he know where to stumble when he doesn't even have a plan of the city?

WOJNICKI. I don't need a plan—not at all—a taxi will take me out into the world.

ASTROW. Uh-huh—a taxi!

WOJNICKI. I have money for the taxi and for the ticket, too.

ASTROW. Wonder where you got that from? Sonia must have left you something.

SONIA. Leave me alone.

WOJNICKI. I earned it.

But anyway: I enter the room. The house is full of people.

NANNY. Uncle feels a little insecure.

TIELEGIN. What with so many people there, and all.

WOJNICKI. I see him from afar—standing there, in the ring. Oh, he's standing there and he's just won a fight. The Professor.

ASTROW. At his age?

WOJNICKI. This is long ago—this is one of those dreams in flashback. He wins fight after fight—a cigar in his teeth and one hand behind his back.

Helena's squealing in the front row. I climb the ropes and get into the ring.

ASTROW. As if they'd let you in with a musket in your pocket.

WOJNICKI. Yeah, but that's not the point: He's taking on challengers, you know, and you can sign up. But not a lot of people want to. Because he's whupping all comers. You know: politicians, economists, guys like that. So I get in the ring, and it's on!

ASTROW. But you don't even know how to fight, and all. I'm not exactly saying you miss, but you didn't do that well at the hitting part.

WOJNICKI. Exactly. So I charge, and Bang—I'm down.

Helena's laughing and blowing kisses to the Professor, fuck her.
So I get up. And one, and two, and three, and—what the fuck—make it four: a surprise upset. He's swaying on his feet, swaying, swaying, and Pow!
He's down for the count. Silence—everyone's astounded.
Silence.
Silence.
Ovations—ovations, applause. They come up and congratulate me. They carry me to the locker room.

**ASTROW.** Who's carrying you?

**WOJNICKI.** Just bottle up.
There's a bottle of champagne. And this serious guy—all business—comes up and goes: I've read the stuff you write, it's great. We want to publish it. We've been looking for someone who has an idea how to finally get this country out of the dumps—someone like you.
I say: Okay call me later, man. I need to take care of my busted brow ridge.
And when Helena comes to the locker room and says: Well, Wojnicki, who would have thought? Why don't I give you a massage?
I say: No.

**ASTROW.** No?

**WOJNICKI.** I say: No—go back to your husband, woman, I wouldn't touch you with a ten-foot pole.

**ASTROW.** Hey, don't overdo it. You should have told her that I box a little, too.

**WOJNICKI.** Like I had the time for that. Then some woman in a red dress smiles at me in that locker room. She shows me she'll call.

And then he comes in, face all battered, man, battered like the human dignity of the excluded, and says: Congratulations—hell of a fight! Why don't we go have a vodka somewhere? And talk about what you've written?

And I say: I'd love to, but see that girl in red? She's waiting for me, I can't let her down!

ASTROW. So? So? Did anything go down with the girl in red? Did it?

WOJNICKI. What do you think? You think we fucking read Chekhov? Line by line? Man . . .

TIELEGIN. I don't get it.

SONIA. Uncle, where exactly is it you want to go?

WOJNICKI. To the capital for a boxing match—to shoot the Professor and finally hit him.

SONIA. But how, Uncle—what for?

WOJNICKI. What for? Hasn't enough been said already? What for? What for? For the exclusion, that's what!

SONIA. And the money.

WOJNICKI. Exactly—for the money, too—for lack of it.

SONIA. But you don't lack money for the ticket, do you?

WOJNICKI. What? You want to lend me some?

SONIA. Uncle!

WOJNICKI. Astrow's got some—you can bank on it.

ASTROW. I do—and I'll lend it—see if I don't.

WOJNICKI. See me off to the station and wave goodbye.

SONIA. Do all of you have to fucking scatter like that?

TIELEGIN. Sorry.

ASTROW. Sorry, man, but it looks like Sonia's made up her mind—I think we'll read a bit, you know—heh.

SONIA. No no no—I need you here, Uncle.

WOJNICKI. But . . .

SONIA. Sit down, Uncle—where do you have to go and why?
It's not your place to be showing yourself in society.

Let me tell you a story: I was sitting this one time in a bar downtown, having lunch. In a regular bar, having lunch to fill my stomach. Of course I'd never tell Helena I ate there. And that I ate potatoes—having potatoes for lunch is bad.

TIELEGIN. Sorry.

SONIA. Never mind.

Anyway: this well-dressed woman walks into the bar—must have been around fifty, but she looked really good. Good clothes, expensive hairdo, purse, and all. So she's looking at the prices above the counter, and a girl comes in after her—a teenager. Sneakers; socks stretched up high; an ugly, knee-length dress with this '80s look, baggy. She comes in all hunched over—her hair is a bit greasy and badly cut. What do you want, the woman asks, kind of like the girl wasn't there. Over her head, you know? A hamburger, the girl replies and

IMAGE 10.8 **Sonia (Aleksandra Cybulska), Uncle/Wojnicki (Włodzimierz Dyła), and Astrow (Piotr Tokarz)**

Directed by Monika Strzępka. Teatr Dramatyczny im. Jerzego Szaniawskiego, Wałbrzych (2011)

*Photograph by Kuba Dąbrowski*

only now do I see that she's sort of slow: probably a little retarded, is all. The woman sighs and orders a hamburger. She sees me looking, and I see that she wants to let me know she's ashamed of that retarded daughter and that hamburger. I look down at my lunch, then the girl reaches out for the hamburger her mother's holding out to her. The mother is nervous as she pays and harshly tells her to hurry up, and I see the retarded girl's ashamed of wanting that hamburger, that she'd rather not have come in there at all, and that she's ashamed of even eating it and, most of all, she's ashamed of liking that hamburger. She likes it very much.

So that's my story about how I felt back there.

But any day now. Any day now, everything will be different. And good. And Helena won't be laughing at me for ordering prawns.

WOJNICKI. Child, why didn't you say anything before?

SONIA. Astrow, get your paws off me or I'll clock you!

ASTROW. You promise?

WOJNICKI. Yes.

ASTROW. Not you.

WOJNICKI. I wasn't listening—I'm just minding my own business but, you know, I've been busy lately—I'm telling you, it's been one big rush, but I can arrange it for you, no sweat.

SONIA. What? Arrange what?

WOJNICKI. Arrange things, generally

ASTROW. I'll go down to the store then, huh? Get some prawns? No? I mean I don't know if they have prawns.

SONIA. Astrow!

ASTROW. Prawns . . .

WOJNICKI. You should have told me. Listen, I have all sorts of contacts.

Here and there. I have contacts in my phone, for instance. Look, I can arrange to make a call.

Prawns, huh!

Like I wouldn't arrange things for my all-but daughter? I know the prawn guys, I'll arrange a connection with them. Fishermen, chefs. I also know a lot of sailors—this one sailor specifically—was married to a woman I know, knew actually—by sight. And I can arrange for you to be the agent of my son the star who made a career.

**SONIA.** But you don't have a son.

**WOJNICKI.** Exactly—but I can arrange for you to be his agent.

**SONIA.** Fuck! Uncle, the one thing you could arrange is to fucking get packed
but you're packed already—so now I just need you to listen to me.

**WOJNICKI.** Yes, I'm listening—I'm all ears—I'm listening—what?—but, you know, if there's anything—I have contacts in telecoms—Okay? Okay?

**SONIA.** Just give me a moment to focus—okay?

**WOJNICKI.** So do I call them?

**SONIA.** No! I have a phone, too.

**WOJNICKI.** Oh, a phone—you have a phone—you have—a phone.

**ASTROW.** There was this time—when the Professor . . .

**WOJNICKI.** I know—well, fuck me, oh the human misery, I missed—I know, I remember.

**ASTROW.** The Professor wanted to sell his house—his estate—or privaterize it as it's called or something.

**WOJNICKI.** No!

**ASTROW.** Yep!

**WOJNICKI.** No, no—this is about something else.

**ASTROW.** What?

**WOJNICKI.** Cervical cancer—I'm telling you, she doesn't look so good—she's signed the house over to me.

**ASTROW.** That's because she doesn't go get tested. I told her—more than once—that she could come see me.

**WOJNICKI.** Someone should finally look after the house, you know—she never really had the time somehow. The poor child. My God: so young, so young.

**TIELEGIN.** I've already seen this once, and I tell you it was beautifully done but with this kind of theater here, I wouldn't be so sure.

**NANNY.** Now, who's going to eat all this?

**TIELEGIN.** No no—no sweat—I'll eat it—and then we'll go to the philharmonic.

**NANNY.** Been there, done it.

**SONIA.** So then, ladies and gentlemen, my dears, I have called you together to tell you an unpleasant piece of news—hang—so to speak—your ears on the peg of attention—it's time we finally went to Moscow—to Moscow.

**TIELEGIN.** To Moscow—maaan—but they have Russians there—a whole lot of them, so I heard.

**SONIA.** Just kidding.

**TIELEGIN.** Well, I should hope so.

**SONIA.** Exactly—but as I was saying when Uncle offered to arrange those prawns for me—there are things stopping me from enjoying equal opportunities—and, wanting to have a shot at those equal opportunities—I've decided to be the captain and real estate developer of my fate.

**TIELEGIN.** Bravo—so are you going to sell fish now?

**NANNY.** I had some here somewhere . . .

**SONIA.** Nanny—stay put a bit longer, please. What's the rush? The chickens have been fed.

**WOJNICKI.** Chickens?

**SONIA.** Whatever—the horses or something—I know it might sound strange—but for the sake of progress and the well-being of future generations and restructuring, and seeing as I'm the one building this country because somebody has to make the GDP grow—I'll keep building, and, so as not to have time for myself, I'll work hard and go on exotic business trips to Siberia and have no time for myself and call from airports and taxis—so I've decided.

WOJNICKI. How much time do you have left?

SONIA. I just need a bit more.

WOJNICKI. I understand.

SONIA. Thank you.

WOJNICKI. Yes, you'll have peace and quiet, and everyone will pussy-foot around so as not to disturb you.

SONIA. Uncle—I really need this—so that I can fully enjoy everything without the loan killing me—I need that money.

WOJNICKI. What money?

SONIA. You know, the house—I've decided to sell the house—this-ol'-house and the land lying fallow here.

ASTROW. Wojnicki, sit.

WOJNICKI. I beg your pardon?

SONIA. Uncle—

WOJNICKI. Uncle what—Uncle what? Hold on, did I get this right?

ASTROW. She wants to have no time for herself and to only make calls from airports and taxis.

WOJNICKI. No no no, the next bit—the one that came later.

SONIA. Uncle—please.

WOJNICKI. The gun—the gun.

SONIA. Uncle, you're not proud at all.

WOJNICKI. The gun—the gun.

SONIA. You have no pride at all, Uncle. No pride at being a victim of that fate and history thanks to which all of us are doing better now.

WOJNICKI. The gun—the gun.

TIELEGIN. Grab him—stop him.

ASTROW. Don't shoot at the samovar.

WOJNICKI. Well, fuck me, oh the human misery—I missed.

IMAGE 10.9 **Sonia (Aleksandra Cybulska), Tielegin (Jerzy Gronowski), Uncle/Wojnicki (Włodzimierz Dyła), Astrow (Piotr Tokarz), and Nanny (Sabina Tumidalska)**

Directed by Monika Strzępka. Teatr Dramatyczny im. Jerzego Szaniawskiego, Wałbrzych (2011)

*Photograph by Kuba Dąbrowski*

---

SONIA. Uncle, just because you missed out doesn't mean that I should as well. I'm missing out on being able—to enjoy all the achievements, and it's only natural that some make it and others don't—besides, I need a nest egg for my equal opportunities and opportunities to compete—so that's why you can shoot all you want, Uncle—but I don't have to watch—which doesn't mean I'm not sorry—but I'd rather feel sorry for you than be sorry I neglected the path of my own growth, so there!

SONIA. Now, Nanny, I'd like to get the formalities done. Where are the documents I need?

NANNY. Documents?

SONIA. You know, all the papers.

**NANNY.** Papers?

**SONIA.** Papers.

**NANNY.** Beats me, they must be someplace here. Will this do?

**SONIA.** What is this?

**NANNY.** You know, papers.

**SONIA.** Papers?

**NANNY.** Papers.

**SONIA.** Nanny—I meant the deed to the house and the land that's lying fallow.

**NANNY.** Right—fallow.

**SONIA.** Fallow.

**NANNY.** Fallow—right. Will this do?

**SONIA.** Nanny—stop messing around.

**NANNY.** Ah—I know—what about this?

**SONIA.** No—not that.

**NANNY.** Then I don't know what you mean.

**SONIA.** Nanny, I can find it myself, just tell me where to look instead of giving me this garbage.

**NANNY.** Garbage?

(*Nanny looks at the piece of paper she'd written on.*)

It all looks fine on paper. Papers are papers.

Tielegin, come on, get the papers.

**TIELEGIN.** Papers? I know—I have a ticket to the philharmonic—will that do?

**SONIA.** No.

**TIELEGIN.** Then maybe—maybe—I have an opera ticket, too—but I've only just booked it . . .

**NANNY.** What's the show?

**TIELEGIN.** . . . so I don't know if it'll do.

**NANNY.** Sure it'll do—right?

**SONIA.** Nanny! The fuck?

NANNY. Sure—sure—they think yelling's the answer—but who'll be left to appreciate high culture, then? Well? No respect, I tell you.

SONIA. I'll find them myself, then.

NANNY. Well, I don't think so.

SONIA. Obviously! There's no order at all in this fallow country of yours.

NANNY. The thing is you won't find them—because the thing is it's good to have the hope that you can sell something—it's just that hope is lack of information, and the information you don't have is that your father . . .

TIELEGIN. Your father turned out to be a remarkable man.

SONIA. Flatulence will get you nowhere, Tielegin.

NANNY. Exactly—he went and sold the house sometime before dying so Uncle wouldn't know.

TIELEGIN. Exactly—he sold that child's house—meaning yours—but it was all fair and square—along with the chattels and dependencies.

NANNY. But in a market economy it would have been a waste not to sell it—and you weren't supposed to lose out, really.

TIELEGIN. Exactly.

SONIA. How's that?

TIELEGIN. Exactly.

SONIA. So how come nobody told me?

NANNY. I couldn't get you on the phone.

TIELEGIN. I was busy then—I was busy going to the philharmonic.

SONIA. Shut your pie-hole, Tielegin.

TIELEGIN. And anyway, you people are such horrible materialists—there was so much more spirituality back in the day.

SONIA. Whose spirituality?

TIELEGIN. Ours?

SONIA. How come nobody told me?

**NANNY.** I didn't know anything.

**TIELEGIN.** Neither did I—besides, they let us live—down here, in the cellar.

**NANNY.** I wonder if you'd have let us do that, missy.

**SONIA.** But . . .

**TIELEGIN.** Exactly—I'm sure you wouldn't have—I didn't have a duty to talk—but your duty is to respect my gray head.

**NANNY.** And not give vent to these offensive grievances now.

**TIELEGIN.** You've gone to the dogs, my child, regarding—

**NANNY.** Oh—the garden's been sold as well.

**TIELEGIN.** And besides—what would grow in that garden of yours?

**NANNY.** That's right—counting on Daddy to send you pennies from heaven.

**TIELEGIN.** Instead of getting down to business and working in the garden.

**SONIA.** But there's no garden here!

**NANNY.** I'm sorry to say, Sonia, that your morals have gone downhill.

**TIELEGIN.** And now they're fooling around—at the bottom of the garden!

**NANNY.** Nobody will let me have their seat on the bus.

**TIELEGIN.** Nobody—there's nothing you can count on.

**SONIA.** Here, have a seat.

**NANNY.** No thanks—I'm getting off at this stop.

**TIELEGIN.** What else is there to do? On a bus like this, full of people with no respect for tradition at all—who brought them up like that, Nanny?

**NANNY.** Tielegin, take me to the philharmonic right now.

**TIELEGIN.** But I have a seat booked for the opera.

**NANNY.** What's the show?

**TIELEGIN.** "Giselle." You should have not voted for your father.

**SONIA.** So who was I supposed to vote for—Uncle?

NANNY. Exactly—so what's your beef with us?

TIELEGIN. Ladies and gentlemen, this here Sonia's totally fucked up.

NANNY. Nothing has any value—not a whit.

TIELEGIN. Why did you leave? In Chekhov, Sonia stays with Uncle and doesn't grumble—but you knew better—now deal with it.

ASTROW. But if this house was hit by all these financial swindles, how come you don't know anything? Maybe you didn't read the contract carefully?

WOJNICKI. What contract?

ASTROW. The one where it says in fine print.

WOJNICKI. But I know the house has been sold—it's not that.

ASTROW. What do you mean—sold?

WOJNICKI. You know—sold, all legit—that's not what I mean—I mean—there has to be some setting for the action—what would you have otherwise? With no setting?

ASTROW. I prefer not to imagine anything—I imagine something and then I'm sorry it's not real.

WOJNICKI. Exactly—I only wanted not to be told: Shoot if you must—meaning I wanted to be able to shoot that old gray head.

ASTROW. But I never imagined this.

WOJNICKI. You know what?

ASTROW. What?

WOJNICKI. You know what I hate the most?

ASTROW. I hate it when my dreams frustrate me.

WOJNICKI. I hate it that every night I make an idiot of myself as if I didn't know how this play ended—but I do know—I've known it for how long now?

ASTROW. Yeah—but the night will be over any moment now.

WOJNICKI. I hate it that I'm going to say—I have lost—and that I have to live with it because I have no choice.

ASTROW. And it's the same thing tomorrow—that's the way the cookie crumbles, as they say.

**WOJNICKI.** Why couldn't I have been born in another time? So as not to have to do the same thing over and over—why can't I go back and play another part?

**ASTROW.** So what are you going to do now? Any ideas?

**WOJNICKI.** Beats me. I still have some things left to talk to.

**SONIA.** Well, fuck me, oh the human misery, I missed!

**WOJNICKI.** The little boy can't fall asleep.
He will be taking First Communion tomorrow.
The bedsheets his mother changed
smell of detergent and are scratchy in a funny sort of way.
We can't eat anything on Sunday morning because you can't eat anything before your First Communion.
There's lettuce and ham and glass bottles of sparkling mineral water in the fridge.
The boy is eight and believes in Christ very much.
He believes so much he can't sleep.
He knows he'll be getting a bicycle tomorrow, and he promises Christ
he'll ride that bicycle for Christ
tomorrow, in his navy-blue suit.
He looks in the mirror and likes what he sees a lot.
He prays.
The sermon is about talents that cannot be hidden in the ground.
The boy resolves never to hide his talents.
After lunch, he gets on his bicycle.
He rides the bicycle wearing his suit.
After a few meters, when the wind is blowing in his hair,
and he's a little scared he might be going too fast,
he falls.
The inner tube bursts.
An old man sitting on a bench sees it and tells him it's a very bad omen.
He says he'll never make it in life.
That it's already been written

that nothing good is in store for him.
That the best thing that happened was that wind and sun in his hair
when I was eight and riding a bicycle.
The boy cries as he drags the broken bicycle,
saying: Don't say that.
Go away.
I hate you.
The bicycle is heavy
and it's too much for the boy.
He falls and nothing is any fun anymore:
neither the bicycle,
nor the suit,
nor Christ the Lord, our Savior.
He cries.

Well, was it moving?
Little boys,
uncles
are way fucking moving, man.
But it's not some man on a bench,
nor is it fate,
nor is it Christ the Lord, our Savior.
The worst thing about this story is not that I've lost.
The worst thing about this story is that
I'm no good.
That I was told I was no good.
And I know that I'm no good.
That I'm not up to
dealing with all of this somehow.
That I couldn't find myself.
And I know that, but it doesn't change a thing for me, knowing
that there are people who are up to it.

*The End*

PRZEMYSŁAW WOJCIESZEK

# I LOVE YOU NO MATTER WHAT

Translated by Artur Zapałowski

CHARACTERS

MAGDA, 18, dishwasher at a fried-chicken restaurant

SUGAR, 20, Magda's friend

SŁAWEK, 20, actor

TADEK, 45, owner of a fried-chicken restaurant chain

HENIEK, 25, Tadek's son-in-law

JAN, 50, Magda's father

TERESA, 45, Sugar's mother

PIOTR, 25, Sugar's brother, a soldier

MIKOŁAJ, 25, slam poet, a construction-site watchman

LESZEK, 20, slam poet, bartender

WRESTLER, around 30

IMAGE 11.1 **Sugar (Roma Gąsiorowska) and Magda (Agnieszka Podsiadlik)**

Directed by Przemysław Wojcieszek. TR Warszawa, Warsaw (2005)

*Photograph by Stefan Okołowicz*

## NOTE

*I Love You No Matter What* is a play about love; it is also a trenchant portrait of patriarchal society. In a world of capitalist exploitation and the cult of masculinity, a lesbian relationship becomes a vehicle for social critique, shattering stereotypes and challenging cultural preconceptions. The play's positive potential is realized not just in its sentimental happy ending, but also through its emancipatory power—nearly all the characters are driven to change their outlook on life.

*I Love You No Matter What*, directed by the playwright, premiered in Warsaw's TR Warszawa in 2005. The production, set in a confined space that drew the audience into the events onstage, featured a live performance by the rock band Pustki and slam poetry by theatrical newcomer Marcin Cecko.

All poems, except the last, were written by Marcin Cecko

# I LOVE YOU NO MATTER WHAT

## IN A WAREHOUSE. NIGHT.

*A deserted warehouse. The whole space is lit by one strong lamp. Mikołaj, Leszek and Sugar are circling inside the illuminated space. Two chairs with clothes flung on them make up the only other furnishings. Next to them is a bottle of mineral water, a thermos and so on.*

MIKOŁAJ. pick up the phone
come on
pick up my call
pick up my clothes
all of them now
pick my clothes off me
all of them all the way

I must tell you something to your mouth
I must tell you something to your mouth

I could lose on this
I'm ready
I will do it, you see

I've left my fridge open
remnants of old light seeping out
and the cold

I've grown my moustache so long
that you can climb it up to me
on the third floor

I've waxed my legs and arms
to make things clean between us

I've knocked my front teeth out
to clarify the message

my cleanly shaved head perfectly matches
your rough unshapely thighs

wine's boiling
beer's boiling
tobacco's boiling
vodka's boiling
joint's boiling

pick up pick up pick up pick up pick up pick up

LESZEK. I know what's on the tip of your tongue
that's why I want to touch it
I know this dye
I know this process
I know the color of your illness

sodium glutamate keeps me wide awake
sodium glutamate keeps me wide awake

the highest values are hidden in our food
in our stomach in our throats and pipes
I know this process
the meeting season continues
the heating season continues
because
the heat hits you the hits heat you
the hit heats you the heats hit you

sodium glutamate keeps me wide awake
sodium glutamate keeps me wide awake

let's take an invisibility test
let's take a detectability test
let's take an inedibility test
let's take a test test test

all data is gathered
all words have spoken themselves

hey man! don't scratch my sofa
leave my carpet alone
sit in an armchair

because when there's silence
thoughts just make it
they just need to be enhanced
so pass the sodium glutamate please

sodium glutamate keeps me wide awake
sodium glutamate keeps me wide awake

SUGAR. awaiting enlightenment in the kitchen
awaiting enlightenment in the kitchen

it's good
slowly the first animals are coming out
ants
it's good
the flood
the water spilled
it's good
the sign
my pen stopped writing

someone has their birthday
someone walked in on the truth
someone would kill himself while reading my book

I
am awaiting enlightenment in the kitchen
am awaiting enlightenment in the kitchen

free not to eat free not to look to listen not free
free to wait wait to be free

better leave it's hot in here
I am connecting
you've got a car then back off

take my poster touch and sign

there's an inbox somewhere here
am connecting now

am awaiting enlightenment in the kitchen
am awaiting enlightenment in the kitchen

*She finishes her poem. Everybody pauses. Silence.*

SUGAR. Well? No praise? Not one kind word?

LESZEK. You didn't blow us away.

SUGAR. I don't have to blow you away.

LESZEK. You have to expose yourself before us. All the way. That's how you win. (*To Mikołaj*) I told you we shouldn't have let a girl in. She'll screw everything up for us.

SUGAR. Fuck off, okay?

MIKOŁAJ (*to Sugar*). Who are you voting for?

SUGAR (*to Mikołaj*). You.

LESZEK. Mikołaj?

MIKOŁAJ. Sugar. I liked her. What about you, Leszek?

LESZEK. Congratulations, Maestro. You win again.

*Mikołaj is clearly pleased.*

LESZEK. Hold on, I'll give you the money . . .

*Leszek and Mikołaj go up to the chairs on which their clothes are hanging. They get dressed. Leszek reaches into his pants pocket and hands Mikołaj a roll of bills.*

SUGAR. That wasn't fair.

LESZEK. What?

SUGAR. I was better than Mikołaj.

LESZEK. You weren't. I'm very sorry.

MIKOŁAJ. You didn't win. Tough. It happens. Better luck next time.

SUGAR. That's not the point. I lost again, even though I was better. I'm sick of this. I want to bring in someone new.

MIKOŁAJ. No.

**LESZEK.** Out of the question.

**SUGAR.** I want to level the playing field.

**MIKOŁAJ.** It is level. You win when you're the best.

**SUGAR.** I never win.

*Leszek shrugs.*

**SUGAR.** I'm backing out of this then.

**LESZEK.** Go ahead, back out.

*Mikołaj is silent. Sugar goes up to a chair, takes her jacket, puts it on, and leaves the room without saying a word.*

## BACK OF THE FRIED-CHICKEN RESTAURANT. DAY.

*In the back of a fried-chicken restaurant. This is where Magda works. She is doing the dishes. There is a small stack of clean plates and a large stack of dirty ones in front of her. She is alone. Enter Sławek.*

**MAGDA.** You're late.

**SŁAWEK.** Yeah.

**MAGDA.** Don't just stand there. Get your apron on and help me out. I'm not grinding here on my own all day.

**SŁAWEK.** No way. You're on your own. I quit. (*Beat*) I got into acting school. I appealed, and bang, I'm one of the chosen.

**MAGDA.** Congratulations.

**SŁAWEK.** I'm throwing a little keg party today. My place. Why don't you drop by? A lot of cool dudes will be there.

**MAGDA.** I'm too tired.

**SŁAWEK.** Too tired? You're only eighteen! Girl, you can't be too tired. You have to give us all a load of kids! Come over, maybe you'll find a man for yourself . . .

*Magda shakes her head.*

**SŁAWEK.** Got someone already?

*No reply.*

SŁAWEK. No offence, but when I become an actor, I'll be getting so much pussy . . . Jeez, the stuff that'll go down! Acting . . . It could be something for you. You ought to give it a shot.

MAGDA. Me?

SŁAWEK. You won't be doing dishes all your life, will you? When did you move to the city?

MAGDA. About a month ago . . .

SŁAWEK. And you've been sweating at that sink all month. This job will be the death of you. You're too young for that. You're beautiful, you should be an actress. You could do something really amazing.

MAGDA. You're joking, right?

SŁAWEK. I am dead serious.

MAGDA. I never actually thought about it.

SŁAWEK. Did Joanna Brodzik[1] ever think about it? I don't think so. You're eighteen, you're beautiful and you should be doing beautiful and amazing things. When you're a 27-year-old wreck, you can sweat over the dishes all you like because you won't have anything better coming your way. But right now you're too young.

MAGDA. Well, I don't know . . .

SŁAWEK. You know how simple the entrance exams are? You pass them, and whee . . .! Sex, 24/7, for the rest of your life.

*Magda does not reply, Sławek gives her a pat on the back.*

SŁAWEK. I'm off. Need to pick up my paycheck. (*Exit.*)

*After a while, Heniek enters the room, goes over to Magda, and gazes in Sławek's direction.*

HENIEK. He tell you he was quitting?

*Magda nods.*

1 Joanna Brodzik is a popular Polish actress starring in TV series and sitcoms.

**HENIEK.** Son of a bitch. Wonder how he'll make the child support he's paying. You be careful, she used to work here, too. He'll be back in a week or so. We'll see if my dad's gonna take him back . . . (*Faces Magda. Pregnant pause*) So what are you doing tonight?

**MAGDA.** Sleeping.

**HENIEK.** Alone?

**MAGDA.** With this African guy. Black all over. Dick this big. (*Holds her hands apart to demonstrate.*) Seriously. He's from the Congo. Studying to be a dentist.

**HENIEK** (*stretching*). You're slow today. I'm not washing those dishes for you. (*Takes the stack of clean plates and walks off.*)

*Magda says nothing. After a while, she turns off the tap, throws down the dishcloth and heads down a narrow hallway to the back office. She stops by the door of Tadek's office, a cramped room at the back of the restaurant. Tadek is sitting at his desk. He looks up from his papers and waves her in.*

**TADEK.** Well what do you know? He quit!

**MAGDA.** Tadek, that son-in-law of yours is harassing me again.

**TADEK.** Heniek?

*Magda confirms.*

**TADEK.** I'll go chew his ass out . . . Get back to the dishes.

**MAGDA.** I can't do this on my own. Get me some help.

**TADEK.** I'll see what I can do. There's always someone hanging around. Wait it out a while longer.

**MAGDA.** Now that I'm doing the dishes alone, I want to be able to go out for a smoke whenever I feel like.

**TADEK** (*shrugs*). Fine.

*Magda heads for the door.*

**TADEK.** Your father called. He's in town. He wants to see you.

**MAGDA** (*stops in her tracks and turns around*). Did you tell him I was out?

*Tadek does not reply, just looks at her as if he hadn't.*

MAGDA. Don't let him come over here, please.

TADEK. Damn, girl. He is your father.

MAGDA. Please don't. (*Goes back to the sink.*)

*After a while, Heniek is heard shouting outside the door leading to the lot behind the restaurant.*

HENIEK'S VOICE. Magda! Magda!

*Magda steps out into the dusty lot behind the fast-food bar. Heniek is out there smoking. He offers Magda a cigarette.*

HENIEK. Did you snitch on me?

MAGDA. Yeah.

HENIEK. I married into the best family in town. You have no right to ruin that for me.

MAGDA. Then stop harassing me.

HENIEK. You know I'm just playing. But seriously, what kind of guys are you into?

MAGDA. Dead ones.

*After a while, Tadek starts yelling inside the bar.*

TADEK'S VOICE. Magda, Magda, your help's here! Get back to work!

MAGDA (*flicking her cigarette away*). My help? The fuck . . . ?

*Magda and Heniek go back inside the bar. Sugar is standing by the sink. She is doing the dishes quickly and efficiently. Magda and Heniek go up to the sink. Sugar flashes them a big smile; without saying a word, Magda gets to work.*

SUGAR. Hi.

*Heniek lifts a hand in greeting. Sugar stretches out her hand in Magda's direction.*

MAGDA. Magda.

SUGAR. Sugar.

HENIEK. Sugar?

SUGAR. Sugar.

HENIEK. Is that your real name?

*Sugar nods.*

HENIEK. Fascinating. I gotta say, Sugar, you couldn't have done better for yourself.

SUGAR. Seriously?

HENIEK (*pompously*). You see, this is no ordinary fried-chicken joint. This is the best fried-chicken joint in town. Frying fowl for fifteen years: That's our motto. Even KFC's jealous. I'd like you to know, and mark my words please, that, working with us, you're working with the best. (*Adjusts his jacket*) I'm off to stock up at the farm. See you tomorrow. (*Exit.*)

SUGAR. Who is that jerk?

MAGDA. Owner's son-in-law. Perfectly harmless.

*The girls do dishes in silence for a while.*

SUGAR. You from around here?

MAGDA (*shakes her head*). From Rawicz.

SUGAR. Jeez, where is that?

MAGDA. I don't know. I've managed to forget.

SUGAR. I can't say I've been there but . . . You're very nice, so I guess it's nice there, too.

*Magda smiles as she scrubs a plate.*

SUGAR. Been working here long?

MAGDA. A month.

SUGAR. That's long. I never held a job longer than two weeks. I'll be out of here any day I guess.

MAGDA. But you just started . . .

SUGAR. It's a rule I have. Besides, I never look for work, work always looks for me. I came in just now because there was a want ad in the window. And now here I am in this lovely apron, doing these lovely dishes, in the best fried-chicken joint in town—man, even the guys over at KFC are shit-scared of this place! And at the end of the month, I get paid for it. Isn't that beautiful?

*A moment's silence, broken only by the clatter of tableware.*

**SUGAR.** You go to college or something?

**MAGDA.** You sure ask a lot of questions.

**SUGAR.** Okay, we don't have to talk. (*Looks away and goes back to the dishes.*)

*A moment's silence.*

**MAGDA.** I came here . . . to be an actress.

**SUGAR.** An actress?

**MAGDA.** Somebody told me I looked like Joanna Brodzik and that I should give it a shot.

**SUGAR** (*bursts out laughing*). What if that someone said you looked like Valentina Tereshkova: Would you be flying off into space now? You're some character! But I like you. I like freaks.

**MAGDA.** I'm not a freak.

**SUGAR.** I just like people whose time is cheap and who have plenty of it. That means they can share it with other people. I'm like that myself. (*Shuts off the tap*) Do you go to bars, Valentina?

**MAGDA.** I even work in one.

**SUGAR.** That's not what I meant. Do you party?

*Magda shakes her head.*

**SUGAR.** You've been living here a month and you don't go to parties? What are you doing tonight?

*Magda shrugs. Sugar raises her hands, fingers spread so Magda can see them.*

**SUGAR.** Fifteen minutes and my skin's peeling already. Been a long time since I washed dishes. (*Shuts off the other tap and goes up to Magda*) Let's call it a day and go hang out together. There's a couple of parties we can go to. This city isn't so bad, you'll see.

**MAGDA.** No thanks.

**SUGAR.** Then I'll give you a lift home in my snow-white carriage.

**MAGDA** (*shakes her head*). I'll be fine.

**SUGAR.** Jeez, what a bore. And you want to be an actress? In silent movies, I bet! (*Puts on her jacket*) I'm out of here anyway.

There's a sea of booze to be drunk tonight, and I'm not passing that up. (*Stops next to Magda*) Don't worry. You're not going back to Rawicz. I'll rescue you. (*Exit.*)

*Magda is left alone, doing the dishes in silence. After a while, Tadek comes into the room.*

TADEK. Did she split already . . .? Didn't even get fifteen minutes in! Just let her try and come back tomorrow. (*Leans against the sink*) Those crooks are at it again. Did you hear the news?

MAGDA. No.

TADEK. Guy got hold of government guarantees worth tens of millions. Obviously, the whole project was a scam, so that means us taxpayers can kiss the money goodbye. Now they're looking for the guy in . . . Ecuador or somewhere. (*Snorts indignantly*) The Mafia's running this country! It breaks your heart, the times we're living in, girl!

*Magda keeps doing the dishes and does not reply. Tadek leans over in her direction.*

TADEK. You have a guest. He's in my office.

MAGDA (*looks at Tadek*). No . . .

*Tadek nods.*

MAGDA. But I asked you . . .

TADEK. Go see him.

*Magda makes no move.*

TADEK. He's your father! How could I refuse?!

*Magda dries her hands.*

TADEK. Well go, go on!

*Magda steps into the narrow hallway and walks to Tadek's office. Jan is sitting in a chair. Seeing Magda, he gets up. Magda shuts the door behind her. Silence.*

JAN. I was looking for you. Your roommate told me . . .

MAGDA. Go home.

JAN. Come back with me.

*Magda shakes her head.*

**JAN.** Your mother's sick.

**MAGDA.** She's been sick a long time. My going there won't change anything.

**JAN.** A family should stay together.

**MAGDA.** Should have thought of that before you kicked me out of the house.

**JAN.** I made a terrible mistake. I'm sorry. But you know how people were talking . . .

**MAGDA.** So what?! Who are these people to you? Neighbors who think you're nuts anyway? Your old army buddies? Most of them shipped out a long time ago. Only the guys too old to move are left!

*Awkward silence.*

**JAN.** You could have told us you were . . .

**MAGDA.** What?

*Silence.*

**MAGDA.** Well?

*No reply.*

**MAGDA.** Dad, will you finally say it?!

*Silence.*

**MAGDA.** I'll stay here a month or two then move out.

**JAN.** Where to?

**MAGDA.** Where there's a lot of sick little girls like me. I'm sure I'll fit in just fine.

**JAN.** What about school?

**MAGDA.** Whatever.

**JAN.** Whatever?! You flunked your finals. If you don't come back to Rawicz and retake them, you have no chance of going to college!

**MAGDA.** You shouldn't have kicked me out! This conversation's over. Go back to Rawicz! Say hi to Mom. Tell her I hope she gets better.

*Jan waits a while for her to say something more. Silence. Jan walks out. Magda is left alone. Fade-out.*

MIKOŁAJ'S APARTMENT. DAY.

*Mikołaj and Sugar rush into an empty kitchen. Mikołaj draws Sugar up against him. A kiss.*

SUGAR. I like doing it with you. You're good. You're really good at it. It's so nice.

MIKOŁAJ. Who says we have to stop?

SUGAR. I do.

MIKOŁAJ. Come back tomorrow.

SUGAR (*shakes her head*). I won't. Not tomorrow, not ever again.

*Mikołaj laughs and resumes his caresses. Sugar stiffens up.*

SUGAR. I told you I'm not coming to see you again.

MIKOŁAJ. You always do. Waiting on the doormat, wet as a bitch.

*Sugar slaps Mikołaj in the face. Hard. After a while Mikołaj starts laughing again.*

MIKOŁAJ. Take your clothes off. I'm so fucking horny.

SUGAR. I don't love you.

MIKOŁAJ (*laughing*). I don't love you either.

SUGAR. You mean nothing to me.

MIKOŁAJ. You mean nothing to me either. Start with your shirt. Slowly . . . (*Goes up to Sugar*) And then all the rest.

*Sugar slaps Mikołaj in the face again. Silence. No grounds for caresses this time.*

SUGAR. When I say you mean nothing to me, I mean nothing. Zip. Zero. There's nothing left between us. Nothing to hold on to.

*Mikołaj stares at Sugar for a while. He tries to make her smile, but the girl shows icy indifference. Mikołaj turns his back and walks away.*

MIKOŁAJ. I'll be out of the shower in five minutes. I want you out of here by then, got it?

*Sugar is left on her own.*

## AT THE BACK OF THE FRIED-CHICKEN RESTAURANT. DAY.

*Dishwashing sink. Late afternoon. Magda and Sugar are doing the dishes. Dirty dishes piled on both sides of the sink. Sławek walks in.*

**SŁAWEK.** Yo! (*Notices Sugar*) Oh, you have a friend! I'm a great fan of friends. (*Shakes Sugar's hand*) Sławek.

**SUGAR.** Sugar.

**SŁAWEK.** That's what they christened you?

*Sugar nods.*

**SŁAWEK.** Fucking sweet. I'd love to meet your mom. (*Gives Sugar the once over*)

**SUGAR.** What?

**SŁAWEK.** Just checking to see if you'll fall in love with me at first sight.

**SUGAR.** Not a chance.

**MAGDA.** You coming back to work?

**SŁAWEK.** Me? Doing dishes? In a fried-chicken joint?! Did I tell you how much I'm gonna score once I become an actor? It's all true. I got more groupies than Enrique Iglesias. I can do you girls too, if you want.

**MAGDA.** No thanks.

**SŁAWEK.** Memorize this number, in case you ever change your mind. Sexual healing: six-oh-three-six-eight-four-two-six-eight. I do housecalls.

**SUGAR.** I'll pass it on to my grandma. She's been fidgety ever since Gramps died.

*Magda laughs and stops working.*

**SUGAR.** I could do with a party tonight, what about you?

**SŁAWEK.** I know about a couple of parties these actors are throwing.

**SUGAR.** I hate actors more than I hate dead chickens.

**SŁAWEK.** There is this one other thing, but I don't know if it's your style.

**SUGAR.** Go on?

**SŁAWEK.** It's in some crib by the Market Square. A couple of friends from school will be performing. It's all being paid for by this wrestler, I forgot his name, the one who won two silver medals at the last Olympics. The President himself shook his hand. The wrestler retired and decided to try something new, so he's recording an album of sung poetry. He wants to get in with the local bohemians.

**SUGAR.** Fuck that. You want us to go there?

**SŁAWEK.** Free food and booze . . .

**SUGAR.** What happened to all the young people in this town? Are all the parties being thrown by wrestlers with silver medals? What's with these times?

*Meanwhile, Heniek has entered the room.*

**HENIEK.** What are you doing here?

**SŁAWEK.** Checking up on my harem, yo!

**HENIEK.** You don't work here anymore. You can't be here.

**SŁAWEK.** Why? So it's your chicken-coop and your hens now? (*Laughs out loud*) Oops, sorry, I forgot you prefer your meat fried and greasy.

**HENIEK.** Get out!

**SŁAWEK.** How's things on the pimped-out VW Golf scene? What's hot these days? Flashing rims?

*Heniek fumes in silence. Sławek doubles over laughing. A fight is in the air.*

**SŁAWEK.** Later, girls. (*To Heniek*) Vroom, vroom . . . (*Exit.*)

**HENIEK** (*restrains himself*). Now there's an example of bad recruiting policy. (*Watches Sławek walk off, then turns to look at the girls*) Going to a party?

**SUGAR.** Yeah.

**HENIEK.** Why don't we go together? I could take you there in my Golf . . .

**SUGAR.** If my friends saw me in that Golf of yours, I'd have to kill myself for shame.

**HENIEK.** Why don't you look at your rust-bucket! When was the last time you washed that piece of shit?

*Sugar does not reply. Heniek sidles up to Sugar.*

**HENIEK.** What's the matter . . . Don't you like the way I roll?

**SUGAR.** Not one bit. You hick.

**HENIEK.** Yeah, sure. Bet you prefer two-bit actors.

**SUGAR.** Bad call. I personally can't stand actors.

**HENIEK.** I might be simple, but I have the soul of an artist. I don't just play dance in my ride, I listen to the classics, too. (*Beat*) Ever heard of Tchaikovsky?

**SUGAR.** What, does he sell spare parts or something?

**HENIEK.** Fuck, man, we rolling or not?

**SUGAR.** No.

**HENIEK.** I read a lot . . .

**SUGAR** (*smiles*). You're married.

**HENIEK.** Now, why did you have to go and remind me . . . (*Straightens his back, adjusts his jacket*) I'm going down to the chicken farm to stock up. Carry on. (*Exit.*)

**SUGAR.** Are they all like that in this joint?

*Magda nods. Sugar reaches under the sink. She takes out a bottle of brown liquor, opens it and takes a swig. Magda notices.*

**SUGAR.** This isn't a job you can do sober. Want some?

*Magda shakes her head. Sugar hides the bottle under the sink.*

**SUGAR.** I hate actors. What a bunch of jerks. You really want to be one?

**MAGDA.** Got a better idea?

**SUGAR.** I don't know, but you're too good for that shit, I can tell. Actors are morons, they're the dumbest people in the world. Why do you think all movies are so stupid? It's because of actors.

**MAGDA.** I love the movies.

**SUGAR.** I hate them!

**MAGDA.** You must be a very unhappy person.

**SUGAR.** Bullshit! I'm the happiest person in the world! It's just that movies are crap, I hate that shit. They're all the same. Five minutes into any movie, and I already know the ending. The hell do I need that kind of entertainment for?

*Enter Tadek. He watches the girls work for a while.*

**TADEK** (*to Sugar*). I give you a piece of my mind and you start working. Maybe you'll make something of yourself after all. (*Exit.*)

**SUGAR** (*watches him leave*). Screw you.

**MAGDA.** Did he chew you out?

**SUGAR.** In his dreams. (*Shuts the tap, reaches for the cloth. She goes up, drying her hands, to Magda*) Forget about acting. Such a cheap career. It's not for you, sweetie.

*Magda does not reply.*

**SUGAR** (*leaning toward her*). So, are we going to that party?

**MAGDA.** To the wrestler's?

**SUGAR** (*nods*). I have a feeling it's going to be great.

**MAGDA.** No way, I'm beat.

**SUGAR.** Come on, don't act like some fucking pussy actress! You're not one yet, and you never will be, not if I can help it.

## WRESTLER'S APARTMENT. EVENING.

*A large, elegant apartment. House music is blaring in the room next door. Magda and Sugar are in a room with a full buffet table. The Wrestler is sitting on a sofa in the middle of the room. He is very drunk and plucking randomly at a guitar.*

**WRESTLER.** My friends, let me play you a serenade . . . (*Arranges his fingers on the neck and strikes a chord.*)

My soul, fly to heaven
My heart, be soft and sensitive for once
Yes, I have softened many male bones and throats

But a change is coming over me now
I'll swap the mat for a stage
The referee will be my director
The coach will become my agent
I'll lay off my doctor
I am the fighter
I am the crusher
I am the winner
I have a Polish heart and might in both hands
And if I have to show what my Polish heart can do
I shall do it
I'll become Chopin
I'll become Kieślowski
I'll become Szymborska
The greatest son of this nation is yet to rise
And shall present his great acting face
I am the fighter
I am the crusher
I am the winner

*Meanwhile, Magda and Sugar are going through the drinks on the table and helping themselves to the hors d'oeuvres.*

**SUGAR.** Awesome grub. (*After a while, she reaches for the napkins and starts wrapping the food in them*) Let's take as much as we can.

*Magda starts packing the food and stuffing it in her pockets.*

**SUGAR.** And then let's get the fuck out of here. This is the shittiest party I've ever been to. (*Points at a salad*) Take the salmon.

**MAGDA** (*puts a slice of salmon on a napkin. She notices a stain on her T-shirt*). That salmon's all over me. (*Tries to rub the stain off. To no avail.*)

**SUGAR.** Keep packing while no one's looking!

**MAGDA.** Wait. (*Heads for the bathroom. She tands by the sink, turns on the tap, and tries to clean her soiled T-shirt.*)

*After a while, the bathroom door opens, and the Wrestler stumbles in, still holding his guitar. He is very drunk. He drops the guitar on the floor and makes for the sink. There, he stops and, breathing heavily, looks at himself in the mirror. He scoops cold water on his fat face. He sees Magda in the mirror and raises his sweating head.*

WRESTLER. I'm out of caviar canapés . . . Those cocksuckers ate all the canapés.

*Magda does not reply; she shuts off the tap. The Wrestler gives her a long look.*

WRESTLER. Are you a hostess?

*Magda inches toward the door.*

WRESTLER. Or a hooker?

*Magda retreats without a word. She is almost by the door.*

WRESTLER. Talk.

*Magda has her hand on the doorknob. In a split second, the Wrestler cuts her off and brutally pushes her back inside the bathroom. Silence, broken only by the Wrestler's heavy breathing.*

WRESTLER. What are you afraid of?

*Magda trembles in silence. The Wrestler presses in on Magda, who retreats until her back hits the wall. The Wrestler reaches out and puts a hand on Magda's hip. His fingers brush against her bulging pocket. He tightens his grip.*

WRESTLER. What you got there? (*Feels inside Magda's pocket, and fishes out the wrapped food*) My hors d'oeuvres!

*Magda tries to wriggle out of his clutches, but the big man won't let up. Soon, he has her crushed up against the wall, with his hand on her breasts.*

WRESTLER. You thieving bitch.

*Magda gasps for air. Meanwhile, Sugar has come into the bathroom. Without hesitating, she picks up the guitar and brings it down with all her strength on the Wrestler's neck. The strings ring out as the instrument breaks on the big man's back. The Wrestler turns swaying on his feet, and, with a dull expression, searches for his assailant. Sugar starts circling the Wrestler.*

SUGAR. You wanted to rape her? (*Lands a hard punch on the Wrestler's face.*)

*The fat man can barely stand. Magda moves in terror to the middle of the bathroom.*

SUGAR. Still got the hots for her? She's all yours. Go for it.

*The Wrestler is reeling woozily, trying to get a grip on reality.*

SUGAR. What? Don't feel up to it any more? Why don't you do me instead?

*The Wrestler has very little to say as Sugar spins and delivers a roundhouse kick in his gut. Three hundred pounds of flesh topple with a crash to the floor. Sugar spits at the motionless man.*

SUGAR. Fucking scumbag. (*Turns to look at Magda*) Are you okay? No bones broken?

*Magda shakes her head.*

SUGAR. You need to stand up for yourself. You have to start fighting back. Force is the only thing they understand! Otherwise you're forever fucked, get it? Guys like him will beat on you all the time!

MAGDA. Sugar.

SUGAR. What?

MAGDA. I'm scared.

SUGAR (*Bends over the motionless Wrestler*). He'll live.

MAGDA. He's alive?

SUGAR (*Nods*). But he ain't winning no more Olympic medals. (*Starts laughing.*)

*Magda goes over to the collapsed man. Magda and Sugar stand on either side of him. Soon, Magda is laughing, too. She lifts her hand and touches Sugar's cheek. Sugar responds by drawing Magda to her. The girls start kissing. Long and hard, over the prone body of the Wrestler.*

*Fadeout.*

*Sugar and Magda run into the back room. Sugar turns on the light and faces Magda.*

**SUGAR.** I think you're hot.

**MAGDA.** How hot?

**SUGAR.** Fucking totally. You kill me.

*Magda does not reply; Sugar is out of breath.*

**SUGAR.** I'll make you mine. If you're not cool with that, fine, I'll quit tomorrow and we'll never see each other again.

**MAGDA.** I don't want that.

**SUGAR.** I promise not to make out with you until you ask me to.

**MAGDA.** This is all happening too fast.

*Moment's silence.*

**MAGDA.** You still have that vodka?

*Sugar smiles, reaches under the sink, grabs the bottle and hands it to Magda.*

**MAGDA.** No juice?

**SUGAR.** Only wimps drink it with juice. Pansies and lipstick lesbos.

*Magda hesitates. Sugar laughs out loud.*

**SUGAR.** Well, what are you waiting for? A written invitation?!

*Magda puts the bottle to her mouth. She takes a sip.*

**MAGDA** (*Choking*). Fuck . . . !

*She screws up her face at the taste. Sugar takes the bottle and takes a swig. The alcohol doesn't seem to affect her.*

**MAGDA.** What now? What next? What's going to happen with my life?

**SUGAR.** Let's get shit-faced.

*Magda looks up at Sugar.*

**SUGAR.** Here, now. As soon as possible. And then we can move on to the heavy philosophical questions. (*Hands Magda the bottle*) Drink!

MAGDA. I can't.

SUGAR (*Laughing*). Don't give me that shit.

*Magda takes a drink and starts coughing. Sugar takes the bottle from her and drinks. She passes the alcohol back to Magda.*

SUGAR. Have some more.

*Magda takes a swig. She claps a hand to her mouth.*

SUGAR (*Takes the bottle and looks at her friend*). Are you drunk?

MAGDA (*Leaning against the sink*). I'll need to think about that.

SUGAR. I asked you a simple fucking question!

MAGDA. I don't know, I've never been . . .

SUGAR. You've never been drunk before? What is it with you people from Rawicz?! (*Gives Magda a look*) You're pretty wasted, far as I can tell. (*Goes up to Magda and looks her in the eye*) So, what's your problem?

MAGDA. I thought I'd forget who I am. That this wouldn't happen to me again.

SUGAR. What?

MAGDA. Falling in love.

*Moment's silence.*

MAGDA. But I won't let you fuck me. Not a chance. You have to earn it first.

SUGAR (*Laughing*). Shame I didn't know that earlier. I would have beat that asshole to death.

MAGDA. You were very professional.

SUGAR. My brother's a soldier. (*Hands Magda the bottle*)

MAGDA (*Turns it down*). I'm gonna throw up.

SUGAR. Anyway, things can only get better from here.

*Magda raises her head, breathes deep and calms down.*

SUGAR. You never had vodka before?

*Magda shakes her head.*

SUGAR. Fuck, Rawicz! I forgot! (*Looks at Magda, stifling a giggle*) Are you still afraid?

MAGDA (*Nods*). Of change. It comes too fast.

SUGAR. Change is good. It reminds you that you're still alive. That's why I change jobs every two weeks. I have a week left to go here.

*Magda does not reply.*

SUGAR. Don't be scared. When I was a kid I used to light sparklers: It's the best way. I'd sneak them from my mom's drawer. I'd go through two or three packs a night. (*Reaches into her pocket, takes out a pack of sparklers, and lights one*) Everything will be just fine, you'll see. (*Hands the sparkler to Magda and lights another for herself*) Now those fuckers can kiss your ass.

*Magda raises her head, and looks at the shooting sparks.*

SUGAR. I felt it for the first time when I was fifteen. I felt it and I got scared because I realized what it meant. It's like your love is sinful, and always has been. When you love someone, you hurt them and yourself. Soon, you're scared of loving anyone, and the emotion just swells inside you until it rots. And you feel guilty, so fucking guilty. And you're sick. And bad to the bone. Everybody hammers it in: your teacher, your friends, the priest. Almost everybody: I mean, there's Mom, I love her, but I know it would kill her if she found out. Shit, if I had known this would be so much hassle, I would have fucking killed myself. Meanwhile, a couple of years go by. Mom finally finds out, and lives it down somehow. Today, I'm an ordinary 20-year-old dyke: a bit resigned, a bit cynical. I don't go to school. I take odd jobs serving food or doing dishes. I used to go to high school, but things got hairy when they found out who I was. I couldn't stand that stupid shit. When people give you shit all the time, you start feeling inferior, you start thinking that they just might be right. If you want to survive, you have to lash out, you have to answer humiliation with violence. An eye for an eye, no point fucking around, or else they'll tear you to pieces. I beat up a couple of assholes, so they finally expelled me. But I don't regret it. As soon as I find a good job, I'll go to a private school, where all they'll care about is my money. For the time being, I'm reading a lot, and that's all the education I'm getting. And I go to poetry slams. Whenever I can. When you're saying your poem out loud, it doesn't matter who you are: dyke, shmyke, whatever—nobody cares. There's only you and God speaking through you. You become an instrument in the hands of God, a servant of the Lord in a state of grace. (*Laughing*) Fuck, I'm still pissed. (*Looks at Magda and turns serious*) You have to take part in a slam. It's the only good thing in this shitty town.

MAGDA. I've never written a poem in my life.

SUGAR. It's simple. I'll show you. All you need is paper and a pencil.

MAGDA (*Looks at her watch*). I need to be going . . .

SUGAR. You can sleep over at my place. I live close by.

*Magda hesitates.*

SUGAR. I'll introduce you to my mother. We'll have cake and coffee. You're my new girl after all, aren't you?

*Magda does not reply. She is very drunk. Sugar turns off the light in the back room. The girls leave.*

## KITCHEN IN SUGAR'S HOUSE. MORNING.

*Teresa walks into the empty kitchen. She is carrying a small portable TV set. She plugs it in and fiddles with the antenna. After a while, the breakfast show for housewives starts babbling from the set. Sugar and Magda stand in the doorway.*

SUGAR. Good morning, Mom.

*The girls come into the kitchen.*

SUGAR. Magda. My new girl.

TERESA (*Shakes Magda's hand*). Teresa. Her old lady.

*Sugar and Magda sit down at the table.*

SUGAR. You fell asleep in front of the TV again last night.

TERESA. Thanks for putting that blanket around me. One of these days, I'll die in front of that set, and you'll have to bury me with the armchair.

SUGAR. What are you talking about, Mom?

TERESA. On the other hand, life would be unbearable if it wasn't for television.

SUGAR (*Pointing at Magda*). Magda here's from Rawicz. We met washing dishes. I want her to stay with us.

TERESA. For long?

SUGAR. Forever, if possible.

TERESA. Are sure about this?

SUGAR (*Nods*). We'll start a little lesbian family. A tiny, subversive cell that will blow this fucked-up society to smithereens.

TERESA. What do you say, Magda?

MAGDA. Sounds great.

TERESA. You've known each other long?

SUGAR (*Nods*). A week.

TERESA. Isn't that a little early to be making a commitment?

SUGAR. Mom, would you be asking me that if I showed up here with a boy?

TERESA. You know I want you to be happy. But I can't support four people on one salary. Piotrek's coming back any day now . . .

SUGAR. He's coming back from the war. He'll be totally loaded!

TERESA. We don't know how things will work out for him . . .

SUGAR (*To Magda*). That's my brother, he's a bit of a meathead. On a six-month tour in Iraq now. Mom's real proud of him.

TERESA. Because he's a good kid.

SUGAR. Sure. Always wears his Virgin Mary medallion. He went off to war as soon as he found out I was queer. Decided to redeem my sins by fighting for the fatherland.

TERESA. He's fighting for all of us. You could show a little respect.

SUGAR. Fighting? He spent half a year sitting on his ass in that camp. Now he's sitting at some airport waiting for an army plane to take his ass back to Poland. Mom, I really don't understand how you could have brought up someone like him.

TERESA. I brought both of you up the same way.

SUGAR (*To Magda*). Mom used to be pretty wild, but ever since her liver went bad she's been all traditional. Though her and Dad still managed to put one over on me. Isn't that right, Ma? Why don't I tell her?

TERESA. Okay, you can live here. As long as you chip in with the bills.

SUGAR. We're working.

MAGDA. I have some money saved up.

SUGAR. Magda's in love with Warsaw. She's even writing poems about it.

MAGDA. That's not true.

*Fadeout.*

## BACK OF THE RESTAURANT. DAY.

*Sugar and Magda are doing dishes by the sink.*

SUGAR. Did I ever tell you how I got my fucked-up name?

(*Magda shakes her head.*)

My mom's a film buff, and my last name's Kowalczyk. It's my father's name, but I barely knew him—Mom kicked him out when I was a kid. Says he never took an interest in the family. He lives somewhere outside of Szczecin now— never mind. Mom's favorite flick is "Some Like it Hot"—ever see it? This American piece of shit. Two guys in drag on the run from a bunch of gangsters. And they keep breaking into song. My old lady named me Sugar Kane after that fucking masterpiece's

IMAGE 11.2 **Sugar (Roma Gąsiorowska)**
Directed by Przemysław Wojcieszek. TR Warszawa, Warsaw (2005)
*Photograph by Stefan Okołowicz*

female lead who—get this—is also named Kowalczyk. She's played by this blonde . . . what's her name? I didn't get it for eighteen years. Finally, I made the effort of watching that fucking flick all the way through. What a load of crap. I really don't know why my mother got so excited over it. "Some Like it Hot" is the worst trash I ever saw, and that chick is a boring stuck-up cow. My folks must have been totally stoned when they decided to name me the way they did! So now you see what films can do to people. That's why I hate them. I hate actors most of all. What a bunch of fucking jerks!

*Magda smiles. They do the dishes in silence for a while.*

MAGDA. Do you ever think about your father?

SUGAR (*shakes her head*). No, never. Fathers are a pain in the ass. What do I need more worries for? Do you?

MAGDA. I keep thinking about him. My old man was in the military. They downsized the unit and he had to go on early retirement. I see how hard it is on him. He can't live without that job. Every morning he goes out of the house. He spends two hours having breakfast in a bar by the main street, then reads all the day's papers in the library, which takes him another few hours. Then he spends another two hours eating lunch and comes home. Rain or shine. Anything not to be a couch potato.

*Moment's silence.*

MAGDA. I love him even though he kicked me out of the house.

(*Sugar looks up at Magda.*)

They caught me in the locker room with this stupid little cunt. My fault, of course. The shit really hit the fan . . .

SUGAR. Good thing they didn't burn you at the stake.

MAGDA. They were too late. I jumped a train and came to Warsaw.

*Sugar laughs, shuts off the tap and dries her hands.*

SUGAR. I'm starving. Let's take a break.

MAGDA (*Keeps working*). We keep taking breaks. They'll catch us, put our names in some computer register, and we'll never work in this town again!

SUGAR. Stick with me, and the work will start looking for you.

MAGDA (*Keeps working*). Get yourself some chicken from the bar.

SUGAR (*Shakes her head*). No fucking way I'm eating that shit. (*Takes a cell phone out of her pocket*) What was that number? Six-oh-three-six-eight-four-two-six-eight. I'll text him, maybe he'll bring us takeout. (*Writes a text message, then puts down her phone. She sits down on the floor by the sink. She takes a tiny notepad and a pencil from her pocket*) I have an idea for a poem. A great idea! (*Starts writing down a poem in her notebook. After a while, she turns to Magda*) Write your first poem. This is a good as a time as any. (*Tears out a sheet and hands it to Magda.*)

*Magda keeps working.*

SUGAR. Take it, my arm's getting sore!

*Magda abruptly shuts off the tap and dries her hands. She takes the piece of paper from Sugar, who also hands her a small gray pencil.*

SUGAR. I always have a couple of these on me. I get them from IKEA.

*Magda stares helplessly at the paper and pencil.*

SUGAR. I even have the first line for you. Arise, you workers, from your slumber and trash all fried-chicken joints. (*Laughing*) Well, what do you say?

*Magda does not reply, she is at a loss.*

SUGAR. Go on, write. I said I'd get that Rawicz out of your head, and I will!

*Magda hesitates, then starts writing.*

SUGAR. There's a slam tomorrow. I'll take you. You'll see another world, a better one.

*Meanwhile, Sławek has entered the room. He is holding a KFC takeout bag.*

SŁAWEK. Hi girls! What's up?

SUGAR (*Notices the logo on the paper bag*). What the fuck is that?! I asked for toast!

SŁAWEK. They're closed. It's Sunday.

SUGAR. I've been scraping dried chicken fat for eight hours, and you bring me chicken for lunch? The smell alone makes me sick.

SŁAWEK (*Hides the bag*). Have it your way.

SUGAR. Hang on, let me have that.

*Sławek places the bag on the sink. Sugar greedily rips it open and starts eating.*

SUGAR. These dead chickens will be the death of me. I'm an emotional wreck.

*Magda starts eating as well.*

**SUGAR.** This is the most fucked-up job ever. Lucky my two weeks are through on Thursday.

*Heniek enters the room. Sławek grins at him.*

**SŁAWEK.** Yo, Cluckmeister! How's it hanging?

*Heniek notices the KFC bag. He walks up and puts it in the sink.*

**HENIEK.** Nice try.

*Sławek grins.*

**HENIEK.** You know that anywhere we open a restaurant, KFSick's profits go down 30 percent?

*Sławek does not reply, just grins ironically.*

**HENIEK.** You don't give a damn, do you? Get out of my chicken bar!

**SŁAWEK.** "Get out of my chicken bar?" Man, you've got better lines than Clint Eastwood. Ooh, I'm scared!

**HENIEK.** You'll forgive me for not busting your face. There's ladies present. (*Turns his back on Sławek, leans against the sink, and looks at the girls*) So, what are you doing tonight?

**MAGDA.** What's your wife doing?

**HENIEK.** Sitting at home. Eight months pregnant.

**SŁAWEK** (*To Heniek*). You know, there's one thing that worries me . . .

**HENIEK.** Yeah?

**SŁAWEK.** You married the daughter of the owner of a chain of fast-food bars. You got it made in the shade. On top of that, your father-in-law does all the dirty work. But that's not good enough for you. You keep looking for trouble. You cruise the town in that Golf of yours and pick up girls . . .

**HENIEK.** Look who's talking. You're a hound dog yourself, shithead. Why don't you tell her about your child-support payments?

**SŁAWEK.** My brief period of sexual hyperactivity is a thing of the past. I am now seeking happiness in a permanent relationship, cemented by love, and a partner with whom I can spend the rest of my life. That's why I don't get you. You're cheating on a wife who's about to give birth. And you're risking your father-in-law kicking you out into the street. To my mind, you are a total fucked-up low-life.

HENIEK. You want to take this outside? Just you and me.

SŁAWEK. If I win, you'll be skulking around and avoiding me. Even in here.

HENIEK. That's it. You're dead.

SŁAWEK. Girls, I'll drop by with flowers tomorrow.

*Heniek and Sławek go out into the yard. Sugar finishes doing the dishes.*

MAGDA. Want to go outside and watch?

SUGAR. Sure.

*The girls go outside. Fade-out.*

## WAREHOUSE. NIGHT.

*A dark, deserted interior with a circle of light from a single lamp. Sugar and Magda step inside. Mikołaj and Leszek are standing in the light. They eye the girls. Sugar greets the guys. They do not respond.*

LESZEK. Who's she?

SUGAR. Magda. A newbie.

LESZEK. We said—no newbs.

SUGAR. She's just going to watch . . .

LESZEK. No fucking newbs I said!

*Sugar looks at Mikołaj, Leszek catches her eye.*

SUGAR. Magda's my girlfriend.

MIKOŁAJ (*Smiles. To Leszek*). Let her in.

LESZEK. Are you nuts? We don't let anybody new in. Especially girls. You know what they're like. Weak, man, fucking weak. They'll spoil everything, you'll see.

*Mikołaj gives it a thought.*

**SUGAR.** Today, she watches. Next time, she's in. You always wanted to have someone in reserve.

**MIKOŁAJ.** Okay.

**LESZEK.** No, it's not fucking okay! I don't agree. I never will!

**SUGAR.** Why do you hate me so much?

**LESZEK.** Because you're stupid. You think this is all fun and games? That I come here to relax? That every idiot off the street can fit in here?

**SUGAR.** She's not an idiot. You don't know her. No need to be nasty.

*Moment's silence.*

**LESZEK.** Fine, today she just watches. If one of you doesn't win the next slam, you're both out.

**SUGAR** (*Without a moment's hesitation*). Fine.

**LESZEK** (*To Sugar*). Chip in the pot. You and your bitch. Watching doesn't come free.

**SUGAR** (*Goes up to Magda*). Give me a fifty.

*Magda reaches into her pocket, takes out a fifty-zloty bill and hands it to Sugar, who adds a fifty of her own and hands the money to Leszek. After a while, Mikołaj throws in his share.*

**LESZEK** (*To Sugar*). You go first.

**SUGAR** (*Softly*).

Come on kiss me
lick lick lick lick lick lick lick lick lick lick lick
I come over because I never know if it's you
I watch because I never know if it's you
what brand you smell of darling
what brand can you take off
have any boys left a mark here

from eleven yards away you look like just the one
at six yards I close my eyes and hear blood
(and this is the blood that connects us with its fiber-optic cable

from hand to hand and from mouth to mouth out of sight and
into the heart and from thigh to thigh)

though I never know if it's you
you
you you
I touch
to check
whose side you're on

who's buying today?
where's this planet heading?
what time is everyone waking today?

so I touch one more time one more time
I undress because I never know if it's you

take it off take it off take it off

I lie down because I still don't know

is it you
is it you

who will walk
me home today
who will get
me home today

lick lick lick lick lick lick lick lick lick lick lick lick. (*Ends, bends over coughing.*)
I'm exhausted.

**LESZEK.** inside route
gated community one-way artery vein burst vessel
door cracked open scrubbed floor
you let me in distract my attention
as you take off your rings
panties pulled down then removed

all lingerie erased
fresh sheets with unlimited access

all the world's husbands are away on business today
all the world's fathers are on leave, sunning the kids
at the beach
and me
I only clean here

no parking
order to assault
order to speed
order to have right of way

when you moan like that
with the hand brake on
I wonder if there's a place for me in your family album
so we're done
with this

I am in a gated community
I love the gated community
I drive into the protected mystery

route to the inside

the route is inside

one-way
(*Finishes.*)
And now, the maestro.

MIKOŁAJ. the fact is I've already told her everything
gave all the facts, waiting for the effects
maybe she needs an adjustment
or requires a better offer
is it wet yet is it wet yet is it hot yet?

(hey

pass me another skin
I swirl here and roll
r o l l
I turn pack
turn hunt
roll roll)

action
we go out
en route in a taxi—action
taxi driver gets a boner—action
taxi driver stops
we rush out
action

her:
everything's all right
just add some charm
just add the clicking of a heel
just add anthropology major

me:
gave generous tips today
two cans two bottles two joints
and her curls

only a true master
won't get hard today
though my friend is doing her best
barely anything will play

LESZEK. Let's vote. Sugar?

SUGAR. Mikołaj.

LESZEK. Then he wins. I'd say he was definitely the best, too. (*To Mikołaj*) We'll settle up now.

MAGDA. Sugar said the best poem. I'm voting for her.

LESZEK. Your vote doesn't count . . .

MAGDA. My money's as good as anybody's.

LESZEK. But you didn't take part. You can vote next week. If you lose, both of you are out of here. For good.

SUGAR. You are such an asshole. I wonder where you get your talent from.

*Leszek does not reply, just smiles. He leaves the warehouse with Mikołaj. Magda and Sugar are left alone. Sugar is getting dressed.*

MAGDA. Who are those guys?

SUGAR. Radical Warsaw poets. One's a night watchman at a construction site, the other's a bartender.

MAGDA. How am I supposed to win with them? I've never written anything in my life!

SUGAR. You will. Don't worry. I'll be with you, no matter what.

MAGDA. You were really great. Your poem was the best. That . . . Mikołaj puts on a good show, but his stuff was lame.

SUGAR. I'll never get any respect around guys. I'll never be as tough as they are. They get really turned on by that. I wish I could move out of this dump.

MAGDA. Where to?

SUGAR. Prague? Berlin? But nobody cares about Polish poems there. (*Goes up to Magda and puts her arm around her*) This slam tired me out. We have a whole day scrubbing chicken fat ahead of us. Let's get some sleep.

*Sugar and Magda head for the door. Fade-out.*

## FIRST FLOOR IN SUGAR'S HOUSE. MORNING.

*The first floor is all in colorful ribbons and little white-and-red flags. Teresa, in her Sunday best, runs in and shouts up the stairs.*

TERESA. Get up girls. Piotrek's here. I just brought him from the airport!

*After a while, Magda and Sugar come downstairs. Piotr stands in the front door. He is wearing a uniform and clutching a bag with his things. Piotr notices the girls, who are now holding hands. Piotr drops the bag on the floor. A strained silence.*

SUGAR. What gives? Aren't you going to say hi to your kid sister?

*Piotr says nothing. He gapes dully at the girls' entwined hands.*

TERESA. Sit down. You too. I made lunch. I cooked all the things you must have missed over there . . .

*Piotr does not respond.*

SUGAR. Your mother whipped up half the fucking cookbook. Why do you have to piss all over your own parade?

*Piotr says nothing. Magda and Sugar sit down at the table. Piotr stays put.*

PIOTR (*pointing at Magda*). Who's that?

SUGAR. Magda, my fiancée.

PIOTR. Dykes don't have fiancées. (*To Teresa*) What are they doing here?

TERESA. They live here. It's their home.

PIOTR. Don't you remember our deal, Mom? That I'd come back, we'd all live together and I'd start a family!

TERESA. Your sister has just as much right to live here as you do—with whoever she wants! It's a big house, there's plenty of room for all of us.

PIOTR. But this is sick, Mom! I can't live with this!

TERESA (*silent for a while*). You're hurting me . . .

PIOTR. How? By wanting things to be normal?!

MAGDA (*gets up*). I'll be going then.

SUGAR. Sit!

PIOTR. Get out!

*Magda gets up from the chair again.*

SUGAR. Sit when I tell you to!

*Magda sits down.*

PIOTR (*turns to face Sugar*). I thought you'd get over it, that you'd be a normal girl. Because you're not bent, I know it! You're just like me!

SUGAR (*laughing*). You wish!

PIOTR. But you haven't changed at all. I want to have a normal, extended family in this house. And you're messing up my plan, you're turning it into a some kind of joke!

TERESA. Don't be silly! You thought if you went off to war you'd make Sugar like boys?

PIOTR. Did she bother to even try?! She's too lazy for that!

SUGAR. Maybe I don't have the time for those knucklehead buddies of yours?!

PIOTR (*points at Magda and Sugar, and starts laughing*). Look, Mom! This is bullshit, some kind of total bullshit! (*Sputtering in rage*) Grandfather's sister wasn't no lesbian when he laid down his life at Monte Cassino![2] (*Faces Sugar*) I could have been killed, and you . . . You're doing this to spite me! If you only had the decency to keep it to yourself. But you're flaunting it!

SUGAR. Look, the food's getting cold, and I haven't had my breakfast . . . (*Starts eating*)

PIOTR (*loses his temper, goes up to the table, takes a knife and starts popping the balloons. Noise*). What is this—a celebration? Nothing to celebrate here!

TERESA (*Starts pulling Piotr away*). What are you doing . . . ?

PIOTR (*calms down and puts away the knife. He pulls himself together and turns to Teresa*). Mom, I started writing letters to Father when I was over there . . .

TERESA. I can't believe this . . .

PIOTR. I want him to move back in with us.

TERESA. You didn't even ask me what I thought . . .

---

2 Site of a protracted battle in Italy in World War II, where Polish forces were crucial in the Allied victory.

**PIOTR.** He's a good man. He doesn't deserve to be out in the cold.

**TERESA.** What if I don't agree?

**PIOTR.** Mom, it's what I want more than anything!

*Teresa does not reply, she is tense and reaches for a cigarette.*

**PIOTR.** What will Dad see when he comes here? What will he think about us?

**TERESA.** Don't tell me you invited him?

*Piotr does not reply, just bows his head. Teresa goes up to Piotr.*

**TERESA.** Have you lost your mind? Don't you remember how poor we were when he lived with us? You were ashamed of going to school in rags, that's how poor we were.

**PIOTR.** Mom . . . It's just one visit . . .

**TERESA.** How many years we suffered before I finally kicked him out of the house, remember that?

**PIOTR.** People change . . .

**TERESA.** Not as far as I'm concerned. I don't want to see him here.

**PIOTR.** Mom, Father's coming here tomorrow. Whose side are you on anyway?!

*Teresa does not reply. Piotr grabs his bag.*

**PIOTR.** I'm moving out.

**TERESA.** Where to?

**PIOTR.** To die in the street for all you care. (*Storms out of the kitchen*)

*The front door slams. Teresa starts crying. Sugar goes up to Teresa and hugs her.*

## IN THE BACK OF THE RESTAURANT. DAY.

*Magda is doing the dishes. She is alone. After a while, Sławek enters the room. He has a bouquet in his hand.*

**SŁAWEK.** Hi. (*Gives Magda the flowers*) This is for you.

**MAGDA.** For me?

**SŁAWEK** (*nods*). Where's your friend?

**MAGDA.** She wasn't in the mood.

**SŁAWEK.** Pity. (*Leers at Magda*)

**MAGDA.** What's this about?

**SŁAWEK.** I was talking about you with Joanna Brodzik. She wanted to know when you'd be taking her place.

**MAGDA.** Nail anyone lately?

**SŁAWEK.** I'm not into nailing anymore. I've totally got my sights set on a long-term relationship.

**MAGDA.** Talk it over with Brodzik.

**SŁAWEK.** She's not my type. Enough fooling around. I want to have a serious conversation.

**MAGDA.** You come here, you play games. I don't know what you're all about. How am I supposed to have a serious conversation with you?

**SŁAWEK.** I like you. We're on the same wavelength. You're pretty, sensitive and smart. You'll make a great actress.

**MAGDA.** I don't want to be an actress.

**SŁAWEK.** You will. I can see it's still bothering you.

**MAGDA.** My ass. (*Beat*) I'd rather be a poet.

**SŁAWEK.** Anybody can be a poet. Anybody can write. It's no big deal. What is a big deal is when you can bring a dead text to life, and make people laugh and cry. Remind them that they're alive.

*Heniek appears in the door to the back room. Sławek casually turns his way.*

**SŁAWEK.** Fuck off.

*Heniek walks off without a word. Sławek turns his attention back to Magda.*

**SŁAWEK.** Will you be my girlfriend?

*Magda does not reply.*

**SŁAWEK.** We can do without sex for the first six months. You'll jump in the sack once I've stirred up true passion within you.

MAGDA. Sorry. I'm afraid that's not going to happen.

SŁAWEK. Why not?

MAGDA. I'm a . . . Damn, I can't say it either. It's just that I like girls.

SŁAWEK. More than boys?

*Magda nods.*

SŁAWEK. But that means you still like boys some.

MAGDA. Very little. It's not even worth trying.

SŁAWEK. Ah.

*Silence.*

MAGDA. We can be friends if you want.

SŁAWEK. Friends? This is awkward . . .

MAGDA. You could give the flowers to Sugar, but she likes girls, too.

SŁAWEK. There's no hope for me. I'll end up like all the great actors in this country. I'm off to fuck. I'm off to screw. I'm off to nail all the women in the world! (*walks out slamming the door*)

*After a while, Heniek comes back into the room. He walks up smiling to the sink and leans over Magda.*

HENIEK. So you're a lesbian?

MAGDA. I'm gonna throw up . . .

HENIEK. I know everything about lesbians.

MAGDA. Please, don't . . . Or else I'll call your father-in-law.

HENIEK. I've watched more lesbian porn than Tarantino did B-movies.

MAGDA. Meaning you have the theory down . . .

HENIEK. What if I combined my theory with your practice . . . I lick pussy like a boss.

MAGDA (*Grabs Heniek by the wrist and shouts in the direction of Tadek's office*). Tadek, Tadek, come here!

*A few seconds later, Tadek comes running into the room. He sees Magda struggling with Heniek.*

TADEK. Not again?

*Magda nods.*

**TADEK.** Your wife's due in a month, and you're . . . ! (*He runs up to Heniek, grabs him by the collar, and twists his arm behind his back*) I'll have that Golf of yours repossessed!

*Tadek and Heniek disappear down the hall. Magda is left alone. She shuts off the tap and finishes up.*

## A ROOM IN SUGAR'S HOUSE. NIGHT.

*Sugar and Magda are in bed. Sugar is smoking. Magda is writing in her notebook.*

**MAGDA.** What have you been up to?

**SUGAR.** I was sick. Mother spent all day looking for Piotrek. But she didn't find him. Bet he's shacked up with one of his army buddies. (*Notices Magda's notebook*) What's that you're writing?

**MAGDA.** A poem. For the slam.

**SUGAR.** Is it ballsy? It won't win if it isn't. You need to give them a taste of their own medicine. I can't write like them, unfortunately. What is it about?

**MAGDA.** Us.

**SUGAR.** Let me see.

**MAGDA.** I'm embarrassed.

**SUGAR.** You're going to have to perform it in public anyway.

**MAGDA.** I know, but I'm still ashamed.

**SUGAR.** I'm often ashamed to read my poems, too. When I read Halina Poświatowska, I think: God, what's the point. I won't ever be that good no matter what. I'll never be able to take what's inside me and around me and put it in two or three sentences that make you open your eyes this wide. But then I always think that, if I know how weak I am, and that I'm doing my best, maybe there's still hope for me.

**MAGDA.** It's been two weeks. Are you staying in the bar?

IMAGE 11.3 **Magda (Agnieszka Podsiadlik) and Sugar (Roma Gąsiorowska)**
Directed by Przemysław Wojcieszek. TR Warszawa, Warsaw (2005)
*Photograph by Stefan Okołowicz*

**SUGAR** (*shakes her head*). Time for a change. They're hiring down at the pizza place. I'm going for an interview. If they take me, I'll get you in as well. I need to go back to writing poetry. I have to win that next slam.

## A PUB. NIGHT.

*Inside an empty pub. Leszek is behind the bar, washing beer glasses. Piotr is siting alone at the bar. There is a Polish flag draped around his shoulders. He is very drunk.*

**PIOTR** (*mumbling*). What sort of an army . . .!

(*Leszek looks up at Piotr.*)

What sort of an army . . . ! (*Piotr straightens up. He gears himself for a rant*) What sort of an army goes around drunk all the time . . .? What sort of an army . . .? Sometimes I was the only sober guy in camp. It pissed me off so much . . . But I told myself—no, I won't drink, I'll have a drink in Poland. Half a year behind razor wire, half a year . . . (*Looks up at Leszek*) Lemme have another one.

**LESZEK.** What are you having?

**PIOTR.** Absolwent. (*Leans back from the bar. Launches into another speech*) The order came to repair the waterworks in the village. We go there. Nobody understands what those hicks are barking at us. We're just looking to make sure none of them pulls an AK on us. Who the fuck am I running with here—the army or some utility company!? Am I supposed to get myself killed because their towel-head pals blew their sewers up?!

**LESZEK.** Why didn't you tell that to your buddies? You were here with them all night . . .

**PIOTR.** What was I supposed to tell them? That I wasted half a year?! (*Shrugs the white-and-red flag off his shoulders*) They gave me a flag. The fuck I need a flag for? (*Walks away from the bar and stands in the middle of the room. He struggles to keep his balance for a while*) I need to get a life. I need a fresh start. To piece it all together . . . (*Falls down on the floor. After a while, he tries to get back to his feet.*)

**LESZEK.** Want me to call you a cab?

**PIOTR.** Where to? The shelter?! I don't fucking have anywhere to go!

**LESZEK.** You can sleep in the back.

**PIOTR.** No thanks . . . (*Goes up to Leszek, takes a bunch of crumpled bills out of his pocket, and pays.*)

*Leszek gives him the change.*

**PIOTR.** Keep the change; what do I need it for? When the money runs out, I'll go off to war again.

**LESZEK.** It might be over by then.

**PIOTR.** Turn on the TV. This shit will never be over. (*Turns his back and walks out of the pub*)

**LESZEK.** Want me to call you that cab?

**PIOTR** (*shakes his head*). It's close. No point. (*Goes out the door.*)

*Fade-out.*

## OUTSIDE SUGAR'S HOUSE. NIGHT.

*Middle of the night. It's cold. Piotr, his jacket open, is standing outside Sugar's house and shouting.*

**PIOTR.** Mom, Mommy, open up! It's me, your son!

(*No reply.*)

Mom, I walked all the way across town.

**SUGAR** (*leaning out the window*). Get the fuck out of here!

**PIOTR.** Open up!

**SUGAR.** Shut up! You'll wake the neighbors! (*Shuts the window*)

*Piotr sits down on the wet sidewalk. After a while, the front door opens. Magda is standing in the door. Piotr, seeming not to notice her, walks into the hall.*

**PIOTR.** Thanks. Ma . . . Maa . . . What was your name again?

**MAGDA.** Magda.

**PIOTR.** Thanks. Maggie. (*Heads for the kitchen*)

*Sugar is in the kitchen, smoking on the windowsill.*

**SUGAR.** You really called Father?

(*Piotr nods.*)

I'm sorry they didn't waste your ass over in Iraq.

PIOTR. So am I.

*Sugar walks up to Piotr. She punches him in the shoulder a couple of times. Piotr reels drunkenly.*

SUGAR. You think I'm scared of you? You think I'm scared of you, huh?

(*Piotr does not reply.*)

You are seriously fucked up. I'm going back to bed. (*Exit.*)

PIOTR (*Wags a finger at Magda, who is standing in the hall*). Maggie, get me something to drink, will you?

*Magda goes up to the fridge and opens it.*

PIOTR. Juice would be nice, dear.

MAGDA (*Takes a carton of juice from the fridge and hands it to Piotr*). I might be queer but I'm not stupid. You don't have to talk to me that way.

PIOTR (*Smiling as he drinks straight from the carton*). You love each other, don't you? True love, straight out of the soaps, huh?

*Magda does not reply. Piotr puts away the carton.*

PIOTR. This is bullshit. This isn't for real. (*Goes up to Magda*) Who are you to her? Who do you want to be? Where is this all going?

*Magda is silent.*

PIOTR. Are you her man? (*Laughs at his own joke.*)

MAGDA. You could call it that if you want . . .

PIOTR. Not "If you want . . ." What the fuck is it?!

*Magda does not reply.*

PIOTR. Do you love her?

MAGDA. None of your goddamn business.

PIOTR. Would you die for her?

*Magda does not reply.*

PIOTR. Come on, men die for their girlfriends.

MAGDA. None of your goddamn business.

**PIOTR.** You know, I spent the last six months of my life in a place where things were for real. Death was for real and life was for real. And now I come home and everything's make-believe! Two chicks planning a wedding and a wonderful life together. It's ridiculous, man! (*Closing in on Magda*) Would you die for her?

**MAGDA** (*looks Piotr in the eye*). Yes.

**PIOTR.** Without whining? Like a man?

**MAGDA.** Always.

*Piotr crouches and punches Magda hard in the belly. Magda doubles over in pain and gasps for air.*

**PIOTR.** Are you positive? Sure you won't change your mind?

*Magda straightens her back, making a supreme effort to hide the pain. She shakes her head—no, she won't change her mind. Piotr hits Magda again. Fast and lethal. Magda crumples, she is not breathing.*

**PIOTR** (*Bends over her*). If I hit you again you'd really be dead. But you need to live, you need to breathe, you need to feel all the pain yourself. (*Grabs Magda's head and pries her mouth open*) Breathe. Go on, breathe!

*Magda starts struggling for air.*

**PIOTR.** You love each other, huh? You think she's faithful to you? That she'll look after you when something fucks up? That you'll be all mom-and-pop? She doesn't even know who she is. I get home and she still doesn't know it. God, the humiliation of it all! I know all her lovers, they call me to laugh and tell me how they banged her at some party. What a load of shit.

**MAGDA.** That's not true . . .

**PIOTR.** What?

**MAGDA** (*less slurred*). That's not true.

**PIOTR.** You want to meet one of them? Maybe you'll fall in love? I doubt it, though. Let me tell you about them. (*Puts his mouth by Magda's ear and whispers something for a while.*)

*Meanwhile, Teresa has appeared in the kitchen door. She sees Magda propped up on the floor and Piotr leaning over her.*

**TERESA.** What are you doing?

*Piotr releases his hold. Magda slumps to the ground. Teresa rushes up to her and helps her get up.*

**PIOTR.** She'll be fine. I know where to punch.

*Magda chokes and gets up with Teresa's help. Very slowly.*

**PIOTR.** Good thing you're here. We need to talk.

*Magda takes a chair. Teresa walks over to Piotr.*

**PIOTR.** I've been gone half a year, and this house is still messed up. I'm moving in. Time for me to make the rules here. As soon as Dad gets here . . .

**TERESA.** If that fucker shows up at my house, I'm calling the police.

**PIOTR.** You wouldn't do that.

**TERESA.** This is my house, and things will be the way I want them to.

**PIOTR.** And how does this house look? Take a look. (*Pointing at Magda*) What's she doing here? Is she renting a room or is she your daughter's fuck-toy?! You call this normal? Is this how you brought us up? This isn't normal. Not for me it isn't!

**TERESA.** Did you ever lack for anything here? Don't you have enough room for yourself?

**PIOTR.** I don't want anything for myself. I never did. I want us to be happy.

**TERESA.** You can take that happiness. I don't need it.

**PIOTR** (*backs away*). I'll bringing Father over tomorrow. Ribbons, cake. Make sure it's all prepared. (*Goes out of the kitchen.*)

*Teresa and Magda are left alone.*

*Magda is doing dishes by the sink. Sugar's workstation is empty again. After a while, Tadek enters the room.*

TADEK. You know, they caught that guy who lit out for Ecuador. Now if they put him in jail I'll believe I'm living in a normal country.

MAGDA. Where's your son-in-law?

TADEK. This place is off-limits to him until my daughter gives birth. (*Leans against the sink. It is obvious that he wants to have a serious conversation*) I don't know what to do; I don't want my kid to be a single mother. Though that beats living with a jerk like him. (*Grows pensive*) The government ought to ban discos. (*Turns to face Magda*) Magda . . . There's someone here to see you.

MAGDA. No . . .

*Tadek nods. Magda shuts off the tap and goes into the hall. She opens the door to Tadek's office. Jan is alone in the room. He gives Magda a look as she comes in. They say nothing for a while.*

JAN. Good to see you. You're looking prettier.

(*No reply.*)

Your mother's very ill.

(*Magda lowers her head in silence.*)

The doctors say she has six, maybe eight months left. You ought to be with us.

MAGDA. But I haven't changed, so . . .

JAN. Nobody's going to make a big deal about that. (*The conversation is very hard for him*) If you don't flaunt it.

MAGDA. But I can't live like that anymore. I can't "not flaunt it"!

(*Jan's bemused silence.*)

Do you still think I'm sick, Dad?

JAN. I'd rather not talk about that.

MAGDA. I want to know what you feel.

(*Jan does not reply.*)

You still haven't accepted me for who I am. I'm not going to apologize for being me. I'm not coming to Rawicz with you, I'm staying in Warsaw!

JAN. Come home.

MAGDA. That's not my home! There's nothing for me to go home to.

JAN. Mom would like you to be there when she dies at least.

*Magda breaks down crying. Jan looks on helplessly.*

MAGDA. Go now, Dad . . . Go.

*Exit Jan. Magda is left alone. She undoes the strings of her apron and throws it across the counter, trying to keep back the tears.*

## LIVING ROOM IN MIKOŁAJ'S APARTMENT. DAY.

*The living room in Mikołaj's apartment. Magda is standing by a table laid for breakfast. Mikołaj enters the room half-dressed.*

MIKOŁAJ. Want something to eat?

MAGDA. Where is she?

MIKOŁAJ. In the bathroom. She's been there for an hour.

*Silence.*

MIKOŁAJ (*walks up to Magda*). She keeps talking about you. I hope she says good things like that about me one day. (*Touches Magda's cheek*) You're . . . Very . . . Beautiful . . . (*Moves away with a jolt. Laughs*) But you smell of tuna a mile off. You'd be no use to me. How did you find her here?

MAGDA. Her brother gave me the address. (*Moment's pause*) Has she been cheating on me for a long time?

MIKOŁAJ. She's not cheating on you. (*Laughs*) She only comes here on business. I turn the shit she brings into poetry. I can turn your shit into poetry too, if you want. Do you?

*Silence.*

MIKOŁAJ. Sugar! (*No reply*) Sugar! (*Silence*) Sugar!

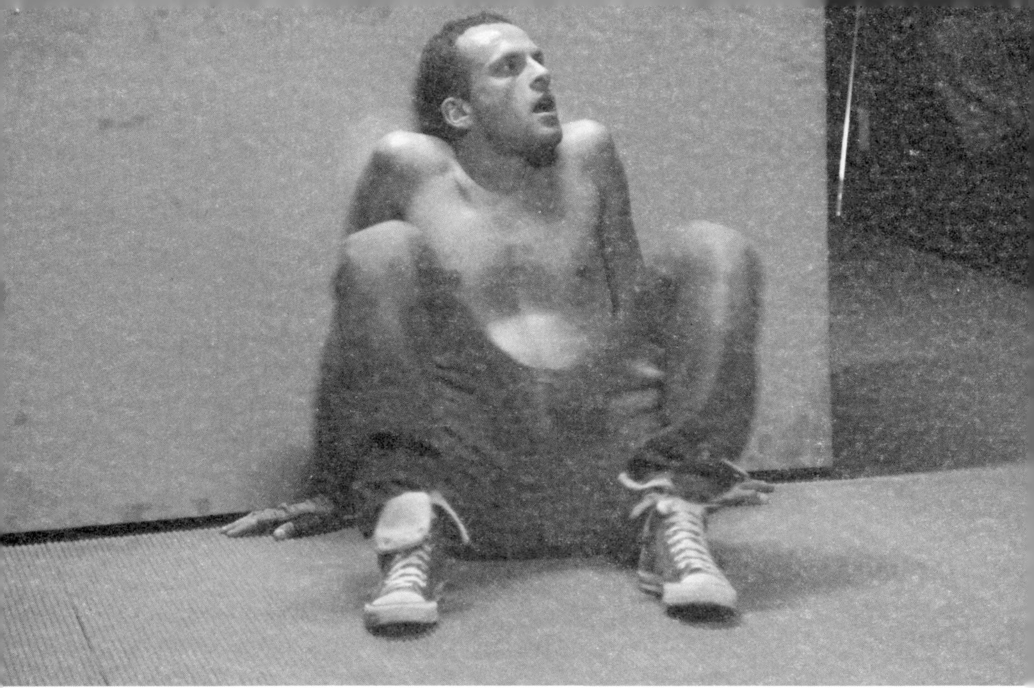

IMAGE 11.4 **Mikołaj (Tomasz Tyndyk)**
Directed by Przemysław Wojcieszek. TR Warszawa, Warsaw (2005)
*Photograph by Stefan Okołowicz*

*Sugar doesn't show. Mikołaj smiles. Magda hesitates a while. She leaves.*

**MIKOŁAJ**. Sugar, baby, don't come out. I'm coming in!

**BACK OF THE RESTAURANT. DAY.**

*Magda is working by the sink. She's alone. After a while, Sugar walks in.*

**SUGAR**. (*goes up to the sink and opens the tap*) Hi.

(*Magda ignores her.*)

Hello. I'm here. Want to talk?

(*No reply*.)

Are you going to talk to me or not?

*Magda spins and hits Sugar in the face.*

*Silence.*

MAGDA. I love you and I want to be with you, but only when you're faithful to me. I'm faithful to you. Want to know why? Because you're the most important person in my life. I was dead inside when I came here. And the only literature I knew was Radiohead lyrics. Now I want to live, my head's full of ideas and you can't hurt me.

SUGAR. I'm not hurting you.

MAGDA. You are.

SUGAR. I'm sorry. He means nothing to me. Nothing. I've been feeling down lately. I see you making progress while I'm stuck where I am. I can't find anything that would get me out of this rut.

*Silence.*

SUGAR. We've stayed in this fucking corpse-factory long enough as it is. Let's get out of here.

MAGDA. I don't need changes. Not now.

SUGAR. Any time is good.

MAGDA (*shakes her head*). I'm going back home.

SUGAR. To Rawicz?

MAGDA (*nods*). I want to go back to school.

SUGAR (*laughing*). Where'd you get that idea?

MAGDA. You'll get mad when I tell you.

*Sugar says nothing, waiting for an answer.*

MAGDA. Next year, after I pass my finals, I could apply to college. I need a degree if I want the job of my dreams.

SUGAR. Meaning?

MAGDA. I want to be an actress.

SUGAR. What?!

**MAGDA.** You heard me.

**SUGAR.** You're hopeless. So fucking hopeless! And I thought . . . (*Leaves the sentence hanging. She is indignant*) It doesn't make any sense! Actors are . . . They're . . . They're not even human. They're some kind of fucking puppets! Who do you want to be, did you ever think about that? Do you want to have the kind of awareness Poświatowska did, or do you want to be . . . Whom exactly? Nobody!

*Magda does not reply.*

**SUGAR.** You want to give up poetry.

**MAGDA.** I don't want to give up poetry.

**SUGAR.** But that's where you're fucking heading! You'll be a vegetable, some fucking vegetable on TV. Actors are vegetables, that's all they are!

*A moment's silence.*

**SUGAR.** It's so pathetic. I showed you that you can be somebody, live differently, not be like that bunch of idiots. But . . . I see it was all for nothing. You let them brainwash you. You betrayed me. Yeah, that's betrayal, the worst kind of cheating!

**MAGDA.** Stop the bullshit.

**SUGAR.** It's not bullshit. I'm seriously hurt. I'm fucking bleeding right here!

**MAGDA.** It's my life. I know I need to give it a shot.

**SUGAR.** You call that life? It's vegetating if you ask me!

*Magda turns her back. Silence. Sugar stifles her anger for a while. Eventually, she calms down and looks at Magda.*

**SUGAR.** I'll never leave you. I'll be with every step of the way. I love you—no matter what. I'll be true to you until my dying day.

**MAGDA.** Fuck you. You have no respect for my choices. On top of that, you cheat on me. I've had it with you.

**SUGAR.** I'll do anything for you. For you I'll . . . Shit . . . Yeah, I'll do it! I'll stay in the bar. Forever. I'll get to love chickens. I'll become a real chicken queen . . . Look, I've never held a job for so long. My skin reeks of dead chickens. I'll never get rid of the stench.

MAGDA (*smiling*). Serves you right.

SUGAR. Anything for you. Anything. I'll be all yours (*Extends a hand in Magda's direction*) So, what's it gonna be—peace?

MAGDA. No, Sugar. I don't need this relationship. I'll get over breaking up with you somehow.

SUGAR. Don't lie. You'd never get over it. You're crazy about me. You told me yourself that I was the most important person in your life.

MAGDA. I lied. You're a filthy promiscuous dyke.

SUGAR. Don't say that!

MAGDA. You're right, I shouldn't say that. You're no dyke, because you fuck guys. You're a common slut.

SUGAR. Don't say that, I'm warning you.

MAGDA. Why's that, are you going to hit me?

SUGAR. You know I never forgive an insult. Anyone who doesn't show me respect gets their ass kicked.

MAGDA. Blah, blah, blah . . . Bring it on, bitch!

*Sugar sprays a jet of water from the hose at Magda. Magda retaliates. They exchange "blows" for a while. Magda and Sugar are soaking wet. Sugar shuts off the tap, sits down by the sink and reaches into her pocket.*

SUGAR. Wonder if they'll light . . . (*Takes a packet of sparklers out of her pocket and lights one. Magda sits down next to her*) I think the idea with acting school is a total mistake. Another moth flying into the flame.. But I'm not stopping you . . . (*Hands the sparkler to Magda and lights another*) Come have lunch at my place tomorrow.

*Magda shakes her head.*

SUGAR. I don't want to be alone when the shit hits the fan.

MAGDA. You'll manage. Maybe he won't come . . .

**SUGAR.** Nobody called it off. And it's a little late to be sending letters. (*Pensively*) He can stand outside the door for all I care. Along with my fucked-up brother who's not allowed inside the house.

## GROUND FLOOR OF SUGAR'S HOUSE. DAY.

*Streamers and white-and-red flags are still hanging from the ceiling. Magda, Sugar and Teresa are in the living room, sitting by a table covered with a white tablecloth. The doorbell rings. Teresa gets up and opens the door. Piotr is standing in the doorway.*

**PIOTR.** I'm sorry.

*Teresa says nothing, the pause drags on. After a while Teresa gestures in the direction of the living room.*

**TERESA.** Join us.

**PIOTR.** Thank you. (*Crosses the hall, enters the living room, and sees Sugar sitting at the table.*)

*Silence.*

**TERESA.** Want something to eat?

*Piotr nods and takes his place at the table. Teresa reaches for the tureen and ladles soup into a bowl. She puts it in front of Piotr.*

**SUGAR.** Where's your daddy?

**PIOTR.** He didn't come . . .

*Moment's silence.*

**PIOTR.** And he's not coming.

**SUGAR.** Where were you these last few days? Staying with friends?

**PIOTR.** None of them give a shit about me.

*Silence.*

**TERESA.** Are you moving in with us now?

**PIOTR.** I am.

*Fade-out.*

*Sugar steps into the circle of light. Mikołaj and Leszek are already there. After a while, Magda joins them.*

MIKOŁAJ. Greetings. Can we begin?

SUGAR. I'm out. I'll just be watching today.

LESZEK. Is anything wrong?

SUGAR. I can't say other people's stuff anymore. I'll be an observer until I write something of my own.

LESZEK. You were saying someone else's lines at slams? Since when?! You know that's against all the rules?!

SUGAR (*Smiles*). I just said the ones Mikołaj wrote.

MIKOŁAJ. Edited, actually . . .

LESZEK (*To Mikołaj*). You wrote her lines for the slam?!

MIKOŁAJ. Don't get all touchy. I was just revising them.

*Moment's silence. Leszek is furious.*

LESZEK. You should be disqualified. Both of you. (*Makes up his mind*) Cough up. All of you.

*The four of them throw money in the pot.*

LESZEK (*To Mikołaj*). You go first.

MIKOŁAJ. Let the new kid go first.

LESZEK. No, you go first. It's my call. How come I ever called you Maestro?

LESZEK. attention attention
the soap bubble burst
we've had enough
reality has spilt
reality lies looks at me with its black eye
and tells me you're a very sensitive man
so fuck off to your hole little mouse
but I look at reality see the whole world
and say wound you have a small wound pus is oozing from it
from your wound tar is flooding your whole body

so I say to this world (imagine that: it actually listens)
I say:
leave fuck off rot die perish I don't want you don't care about you
disappear go go away
and imagine that—reality obeys
crosses the street passes the crossroads it's already out of town
beyond the horizon outside the country crosses over the continent goes around an island flies over the ocean
vanishes beyond the horizon
what day is it
this is the prettiest day
this is the brightest day

sun, give me the rhythm
sun, give me the rhythm
I want to disintegrate and be someone's breath
I want to be part of the wind a cloud
sun, give me the rhythm
sun, give me the rhythm

**MIKOŁAJ.** there's no lake in the area
which could take us into its depths

there's no great river in this area
which could grab our hand leg brain

there's no forest in this area
to run away from here once in a hundred years

look me eye in the eye
tooth in tooth eyebrow in eyebrow
now go

go take a bath
go do shopping
go to work at last
wash the pots get yourself together

get hold of yourself
keep up keep up

have a drink with me
buy me a round
suck my cock
lick my ass
and give me the change

you must break this mirror once every seven fat years
you must break this mirror once every seven lean years
you must break this mirror once every seven fat years
you must break this mirror once every seven lean years

fu
ck
it

LESZEK. Hey, new kid, what's your name?

MAGDA. Magda.

LESZEK. Got a poem of your own, Magda?

MAGDA. Are you trying to insult me? Sure I do.

LESZEK. Let's have it.

MAGDA. Here's my poem, though I'm not a poet, and don't know if I'll ever be, and whether I need that at all,
all I know is that you're near and that everything I do—I do it for you, like in that Bryan Adams song,
so if things are good the way they are let's try not to screw them up.
And now it's your turn now listen up to what I want to tell you
I touch you
in my sleep and in the daytime
but in my sleep you're more human, in my sleep you don't smell
of the dead chickens we flush down the drain together,
four-fifty an hour, the stink of fat and detergent, that's

the microclimate in which our love grows, in my sleep you're complete
and perfect as a Greek goddess, I touch you, I watch you I'm scared
to come up, I know you'll hurt me one day, even though
you might not want to, that's the way those Greeks roll,
they do the most damage when they don't want to, for now you're not
hurting me or maybe I don't notice, and that ignorance helps me grow,
like you, I'm striving for perfection, like you, I'm becoming a Greek
goddess, you and me—two pieces from different puzzles that by a strange twist of fate
fit together, you just have to try hard to figure out, to understand
what they represent, but that's what love and your whole life are for—
to understand, so since we're a good fit, since we're alive
and well and lack for nothing, let's try to enjoy it –
for god's sake—every second counts otherwise we'll turn
into mummies like the ones peopling this city, this city full of
palaces cathedrals this city full of solemn gravity, this city in which even
bird shit eventually turns to marble, this city which is practically
begging for a decent fuck, to be banged in every
crack of its shitty solemnity so come to me, we are
lovers
let's do it on the tombs of kings, of commanders of uprisings lost the day they began
let's do it on monuments to patriotic youth
who without hesitation laid down their lives at the command of a bunch of old men
while you and me were kissing in some corner

and we're alive and well today while they're dead, and our conscience
is clear because we came to know the taste of love instead of waving the flag,
because we were fucking all night and today our heads hurt from the booze,
you know, I need to take a leak, let me leave the house and stand in the middle of this city and take a leak where people can see me, and then I'll pull up my pants
and spread my arms out wide
I feel the blood flow from my heart to my fingertips and back again
I know that our love is the only justification for this place
and the frogs don't rain down here because of the thousand sacred paintings
but because you and me love each other and that's infinitely pure
and our lust our passion and our sex deliver you from annihilation,
so when we get the fuck out of here and get the fuck out we shall
traveling toward life and the bright lights traveling towards berlin and prague
all you'll have left is the apocalypse
but there won't be locusts or frogs or anything like that
at most a rain of even more stinking winos
yes stench filth and even more fucked-up winos
that is an end of the world that becomes this place, meanwhile we're flushing
dead chickens down the drain, the sound of the drain is the soundtrack of our youth,
the anthem of a nation made up of a pair of lovers, as
far as I'm concerned such a nation will do just fine, I don't intend to
let anyone in on our secret language, I wake up and see
you lying next to me, a wage slave morphing

into a god, you're so perfect that even if you hurt me I'll treat is as a reward, happy that things are good now.

**LESZEK.** Let's take a vote. Magda?

**MAGDA.** Leszek.

**LESZEK.** Mikołaj?

**MIKOŁAJ.** Magda. Impressive . . .

*A moment's silence. Leszek makes up his mind.*

**LESZEK.** Magda.

**MIKOŁAJ** (*To Leszek*). I don't believe it.

**LESZEK.** Her poem was the best. It was about something, not like your stuff.

*Leszek goes up to Magda and hands her the prize. After a while, Mikołaj also goes up to Magda with his hand outstretched.*

**MIKOŁAJ.** Congratulations.

**MAGDA** (*Does not shake his hand. She turns to Sugar*). I love you.

*Magda and Sugar walk out of the warehouse.*

*The End*

*7th of August 2005*